BEAT

WRITERS AT WORK

BEAT
WRITERS AT WORK

THE PARIS REVIEW

Edited by George Plimpton

 The Modern Library New York

LIBRARY OF CONGRESS CATALOGING-IN-PUBLICATION DATA
Beat writers at work/The Paris review.—Modern Library paperback ed.
    p.   cm.
    ISBN 0-375-75215-3
    1. Beat generation.   2. Authors, American—20th century—Interviews.   3. American literature—20th century—History and criticism—Theory, etc.   4. Black Mountain School (Group of poets)   I. Paris review.
PS228.B6B46   1998
810.9'11—dc21   98-7985

Modern Library website address: www.modernlibrary.com

Printed in the United States of America

LSI 001

Book design by Mercedes Everett

Acknowledgments

The editor thanks the interviewers and the following staff members of *The Paris Review* for their help in preparing this volume: Fiona Maazel, Molly McGrann, and Nina Gielen.

Contents

Photo Credits

Introduction

by Rick Moody

What a different time, the time in which you read this. By 1961, when I was born, the Beats, that never-quite-assembled assemblage of writers in and around Columbia University—Kerouac, Ginsberg, Burroughs, and Huncke, Orlovsky, Corso—and others further afield, Kesey, Creeley, Ferlinghetti, Snyder, Baraka, Olson, Bowles—had mainly disaffiliated, retired to rural or exotic landscapes. Poetry mattered then, which is not to say that poetry does *not* matter now, though the culture seems to have arrayed itself by this date against specialized meanings, by ghettoizing, by granting poetry a month on the calendar so that it can neglect poetry during the other eleven months. Could a major poet such as Charles Olson now seriously articulate his aesthetics by saying in an interview setting, "Where was I? I was going to create this diamond we were going to run. The suitor diamond, the sutra diamond. The sutra diamond for the superstar. Superstar. You know that's kind of an impressive thing." In this way making hash out of a perfectly straightforward question by Gerard Malanga. Poetry mattered and jazz mattered and the conjunction of poetry and jazz, and the *behatted tenorman* mattered, of whom Kerouac wrote at some length in *On the Road*. The novel was a reasonable form, even a diamond of its own on occasion, but the pure utterance (using the Creeley word), the first utterance, was poetry, and this could be just about anything, could be an attitude, a way of presenting the facts—the only requirement being that this poetry *was not to be rewritten*. First thought, best thought. Here's Olson: "I mean, I never have rewritten almost anything. . . . (long pause)." Or Robert Creeley, responding to a question about how long the writing of a poem takes: "For me, it's literally the time it takes to type or otherwise write it—because I *do* work in this fashion of simply sitting down and writing, usually without any process of revision. So that if it goes—or, rather, comes—in an opening way, it continues until it closes, and that's usually when I stop." Or Jack Kerouac: "By not revising what you've already written you simply give the reader the actual workings of your mind during the writing itself: you confess your thoughts about events in your own unchangeable way. . . ." Myself, I'm a writer of the nineties, no choice, and I'm a writer who beats a sentence to death, ten or twenty or thirty or even forty times on occasion, and then maybe cuts the sentence just the same, chews that sentence entirely, makes a fine paste of it, and then spits it out, so that when Creeley suggests that the breath is the thing that will determine a line or the length of a poem and that when the breath is done the line is done and you don't go back, well, this is not a nineties thing. To set down that *this snow falls vituperatively* and then to leave the thought unchanged and not come back to it—*snow makes me want to drive up to Montreal and feign Catholicism,* e.g.—seems quaint in these desperate times, when such a sentiment may not, right at the outset, merit inclusion on the shelves of the chain stores. But this quaint spontaneity nonetheless gives a contemporary writer the fiercest envy for the poetry and prose of the fifties and early sixties, for the attitude, for the style. Can it be that Beatitude, whatever it once was (Kerouac, in his later drunken incarnation, defines it thus: "Oh the Beat generation was just a phrase I used in the 1951 written manuscript of *On the Road* to describe guys like Moriarty who run around the country in cars looking for odd jobs, girlfriends, kicks. It was thereafter picked up by West Coast Leftist groups and turned into a meaning like 'Beat mutiny' and 'Beat insurrection' and all that nonsense; they wanted some youth movement to grab on to for their own political and social purposes")—can it be that Beatitude, the movement, lasted only five or six years, really, from the publication of *On the Road* (1957) into the early sixties, all but dissipated by Kesey and the Pranksters and the Summer of Love, and yet still exerting its influence, its correct attention to practice, forty years later, on people like myself who weren't even born until it had played itself out?

Mr. Plimpton and his able cohorts at *The Paris Review* have cannily chosen this historical moment for the retrieval of this archive, viz., the fortieth anniversary of Kerouac's masterpiece, and also the recent departures of Ginsberg and Burroughs to celestial addresses, and thus we have a real warts-and-all retrospective, *ex post facto,* Kerouac in the late sixties, Ginsberg (in one of two pieces here) in the late seventies, Bowles in the eighties, Snyder in the nineties, so that the high period of Beat style is well past at the time of these conversations; Plimpton's wisdom here amounts to permitting the language and form of these interviews to persist over the years and thereby to accrue historical context, in which we are enabled to see how this Beat praxis (or Black Mountain praxis) is reactive when faced with such forces as Vietnam, hippie culture, eighties consumerism, neglect by literary history, and so forth. How can one rationalize, for example, the silence that has largely greeted Burroughs's death—though without his work the novel of the late twentieth century would be unrecognizable? We can see here how a movement, how a community (though Snyder quibbles with the word), can manage what individuals cannot, how an identity is visited upon a group, though constraining, and can bring out a kind of scuffling (Robert Creeley: "People seemed very belligerent during the forties and fifties. We used to get into these ridiculous fights") that inspires ambition and accomplishment. When I read these writers looking back on what they've done, there are important convergences. There is the devotion to *spontaneity*, so unlike the miserly deployment of ideas now, and there is the devotion to *affect* (Creeley, quoting Pound: "If one respects Pound's measure of 'Only emotion endures,' and 'Nothing counts save the quality of the emotion,' then having no feelings about something seems to prohibit the possibility of [poetry] from entering"; or Kerouac: "I spent my entire youth writing slowly with revisions and endless re-hashing speculation and deleting and got so I was writing one sentence a day and the sentence had no FEELING. Goddamn it, FEELING is what I like in art, not CRAFTINESS and the hiding of feelings"; or Ginsberg: "Usually during the composition, step by step, word by word and adjective by adjective, if it's at all spontaneous, I don't know whether it even makes sense sometimes. Sometimes I do know it makes complete sense, and I start crying. Because I realize I'm hitting some area which is absolutely true. And in that sense applicable universally, or understandable universally"). How antiquated the interest in emotion amid the low-cal irony of the late nineties, an era in which exuberance is in short supply, an era in which writers have boasted of having *no adjectives* in entire book-length manuscripts, an era in which our cultural lions are more likely to be heroin-addicted suicides or nouveau-riche gangsters or professional athletes than poets.

And there is also here the matter of *politics*, of course, as Gary Snyder observes: "[West Coast Beats] were openly political and, in terms of the cold war, it was a kind of a pox-on-both-your-houses position. Clearly our politics were set against the totalitarianism of the Soviet Union and China, and at the same time would have no truck with corporate capitalism." Or Barney Rosset's politics of publishing ("We published a poem by Julian Beck that ended with the line, 'Fuck the USA.' [The printers] wanted us to take the line out. We said, would it be all right if it read, 'Fuck the Soviet Union'? They said sure—a very good example of what we were up against at the time"). Or Ginsberg's conspiracy-theory politics ("Our conversation that week included some detailed accounts of the history of the attack and near-destruction of the American underground press by the FBI"), or Burroughs's politics of power: "The Soviet Union and the United States will eventually consist of interchangeable social parts and neither nation is morally 'right.' . . . Regardless of how it's done, the same kind of people will be in charge." What are our politics now but the politics of the domestic, the domestic enlarged, made emblematic for larger national purposes (*"family values"*); there's no unanimity of opposition, no gleeful opposition (as in these remarks), even if we were reared on televised images of convention riots and university occupations. Our guilty silence is our politics.

Next, there is among Beats and fellow travelers the matter of *deformation of the senses*, which permeates these reflections, as when Kerouac demands a few of the *candies* that Ted Berrigan and Aram Saroyan (the interviewers) are taking, which turn out to be something called Obetrol. "Neal is the one that told me about them," says Berrigan, of which Kerouac observes, "Give me one of those," though there have already been multiple rounds of drinks, all recorded on the primitive tape recorder that is so integral to this dissemination of Beat as was; likewise, Charles Olson, interrupting the interview to ask Gerard Malanga, "Would you call Mrs. Tobin. I tried to. I forgot to get the liquor—Get her to send over the usual." When they aren't actually consuming lubricants of various descriptions, these Beats are theorizing on the subject—Burroughs, e.g.: "A long time ago I suggested there were similarities in terminal addiction and terminal schizophrenia. That was why I made the suggestion that they addict these people to heroin, then withdraw it and see if they could be motivated; in other words, find out whether they'd walk across the room and pick up a syringe"; or Kesey, who participates in this refracted debate of Beat aesthetics like a cranky younger sibling—charming, of course, but a little used to getting more attention: "I did write the first several pages of *Cuckoo's Nest* on peyote, and I changed very little of it. . . . There were also some sections of *Sometimes a Great Notion* written when I was taking mushrooms. Again, the effect is more on mood and voice than on vision. But for the most part, I don't write under the influence of LSD or other drugs"; or Creeley, responding to a question about the effect of hallucinogens on the creative process: "Terrific! Terrific! That's at least what I'd like to say. Things had been so uptight, almost for a year. . . . The LSD just wiped that out—the fears and the tentativeness and sense of getting lost or of being endlessly separated from the world." A jaundiced view holds sway among my contemporaries as to the value of these intoxicators. Their novelty has worn off. They don't deliver on their early promise, they are addicting, etc.

Drugs are not an area for profitable inquiry, mostly, though *deformation of the senses* does lead, in these pages, to the most radical theme addressed by the Beats, a theme adhered to rigorously by them (with the possible exception of Kesey and Rosset and Paul Bowles, who are mainly adjacent here in any case), which is *spiritual investigation.* It emerges repeatedly, in, for example, Allen Ginsberg's lengthy account of a frankly theological revelation while at Columbia: "I suddenly realized that *this* existence was *it!* And that I was born in order to experience up to this very moment, that I was having this experience, to realize what this was all about—in other words that this was the moment that I was born for. This initiation. Or this vision or this consciousness, of being alive unto myself, alive myself unto the Creator—who loved me, I realized, or who responded to my desire"; in the expostulations of the politically conservative later Kerouac: "What's really influenced my work is the Mahayana Buddhism, the original Buddhism of Gautama Śàkyamuni, the Buddha himself, of the India of old"; or in Gary Snyder's remarks on the practice of Zen: "*Zazen* becomes a part of your life, a very useful and beautiful part of your life—a wonderful way to start the day by sitting for at least twenty, twenty-five minutes every morning with a little bit of devotional spirit." Is literature inherently spiritual? How are art and spirituality related? Do art and literature slake the same thirst that gives us spiritual ambition? It's a debate that has lapsed. Better to describe, at length, *further snowfall,* for this has been a day of much snowfall, feet of it have accumulated, better with the labored and burnished prose of multiple rewrites, capture that perfect wintery discontent of the nineties. The Whitmanesque paganism of Beat writing is gone, daddy, gone. However, the *Writers at Work* series, in its excellent long view, never advocates nostalgia; rather, it observes, and in this volume we have a particularly rich sampling, a unitary system of intentions to compare with our own degraded moment (though the Beats also considered their era degraded) and the wonderful distraction of hortatory language to entertain us. "There was a time," Ginsberg says, "that I was absolutely astounded because Kerouac told me that in the future literature would consist of what people actually wrote rather than what they tried to deceive other people into thinking they wrote, when they revised it later on. And I saw opening up this whole universe where people wouldn't be able to lie anymore! They wouldn't be able to *correct* themselves any longer. They wouldn't be able to hide what they said." Forty years later, we don't have any such thing—a literature of immediacy, a language of praise, a system of divine names—though perhaps these wise, enthusiastic pages point us again in that direction.

William Seward Burroughs II

was born on February 5, 1914, in St. Louis, Missouri, to a southern bourgeois family. He graduated from Harvard in 1936, traveled widely, and then moved to New York City where he first began to toy with the fantastic and derelict lifestyle that would later inform his work. During his stay in New York, he met Jack Kerouac and Allen Ginsberg, both of whom took a serious interest in his experiments with morphine and cocaine. Ginsberg helped to promote Burroughs's first literary and semiautobiographical endeavor, *Junky* (1953), one in a series of novels recounting the perils and ecstasies of drug addiction.

In the mid-fifties, Burroughs, his wife, Joan Vollmer, and Beat hero Herbert Huncke all relocated to East Texas. On a large farm, they grew oranges, cotton, and marijuana. Pursued by the law for their drug activities, Burroughs and Vollmer fled to Mexico. There, in what Burroughs has always denied was a bravado William Tell impersonation, he accidentally shot and killed his wife.

Bereft of companionship, Burroughs resumed his travels throughout the world, settling in Tangier in the late fifties. Joined by Kerouac and Ginsberg in 1959, he completed the manuscript for *Naked Lunch*, followed by *The Soft Machine* (1961), *The Ticket That Exploded* (1962), and *Nova Express* (1964); the four novels together make up the Nova Mob quartet, detailing Burroughs's account of addiction in a post-apocalyptic world. Abandoning traditional narrative forms to experiment with dadaesque "cut-ups," the quartet experiments with "collage-writing" to generate the galvanizing sense of entropy that has contributed to the tetralogy's success. Other works include *Exterminator!* (1973), *Cities of the Red Night* (1980), *Queer* (1980), and *Mind Wars* (1980).

Marshall McLuhan once noted that Burroughs attempted "to reproduce in prose what we accommodate every day as a commonplace aspect of life in the electric age." Teeming up with pop-culture icon Kurt Cobain to release a spoken-word CD (*The Priest Thay Called Him*) in 1996, Burroughs joined the "electric age," reminding his fans that even in the years before his death in August 1997, he remained in the forefront of contemporary counterculture.

*F*irecrackers *and whistles sounded the advent of the New Year of 1965 in St. Louis. Stripteasers ran from the bars in Gaslight Square to dance in the street when midnight came. Burroughs, who had watched television alone that night, was asleep in his room at the Chase–Park Plaza Hotel, St. Louis's most elegant.*

At noon the next day he was ready for the interview. He wore a gray lightweight Brooks Brothers suit with a vest, a blue-striped shirt from Gibraltar cut in the English style, and a deep blue tie with small white polka dots. His manner was not so much pedagogic as didactic or forensic. He might have been a senior partner in a private bank, charting the course of huge but anonymous fortunes. A friend of the interviewer, spotting him across the lobby, thought he was a British diplomat. At the age of fifty, he is trim; he performs a complex abdominal exercise daily and walks a good deal. His face carries no excess flesh. His expression is taut, and his features are intense and chiseled. He did not smile during the interview and laughed only once, but he gives the impression of being capable of much dry laughter under other circumstances. His voice is sonorous, its tone reasonable and patient; his accent is mid-Atlantic, the kind of regionless inflection Americans acquire after many years abroad. He speaks elliptically, in short, clear bursts.

On the dresser of his room sat a European transistor radio; several science fiction paperbacks; Romance, *by Joseph Conrad and Ford Madox Ford;* The Day Lincoln Was Shot, *by Jim Bishop; and* Ghosts in American Houses, *by James Reynolds. A Zeiss Ikon camera in a scuffed leather case lay on one of the twin beds beside a copy of* Field & Stream. *On the other bed were a pair of long shears, clippings from newspaper society pages, photographs, and a scrapbook. A Facit portable typewriter sat on the desk and gradually one became aware that the room, although neat, contained a great deal of paper.*

Burroughs smoked incessantly, alternating between a box of English Ovals and a box of Benson & Hedges. As the interview progressed, the room filled with smoke. He opened the window. The temperature outside was seventy degrees, the warmest New Year's Day in St. Louis's history; a yellow jacket flew in and settled on the pane. The bright afternoon deepened. The faint cries of children rose up from the broad brick alleys in which Burroughs had played as a boy.

· · ·

INTERVIEWER: You grew up here?

BURROUGHS: Yes. I went to John Burroughs School and the Taylor School, and was out West for a bit, and then went to Harvard.

INTERVIEWER: Any relation to the adding machine firm?

BURROUGHS: My grandfather. You see, he didn't exactly invent the adding machine, but he invented the gimmick that made it work, namely, a cylinder full of oil and a perforated piston that will always move up and down at the same rate of speed. Very simple principle, like most inventions. And it gave me a little money, not much, but a little.

INTERVIEWER: What did you do at Harvard?

BURROUGHS: Studied English lit. John Livingston Lowes. Whiting. I sat in on Kittredge's course. Those are the main people I recall. I lived in Adams House and then I got fed up with the food and I moved to Claverly Hall, where I lived the last two years. I didn't do any writing in college.

INTERVIEWER: When and why did you start to write?

BURROUGHS: I started to write in about 1950; I was thirty-five at the time; there didn't seem to be any strong motivation. I simply was endeavoring to put down in a more or less straightforward journalistic style something about my experiences with addiction and addicts.

INTERVIEWER: Why did you feel compelled to record these experiences?

BURROUGHS: I didn't feel compelled. I had nothing else to do. Writing gave me something to do every day. I don't feel the results were at all spectacular. *Junky* is not much of a book, actually. I knew very little about writing at that time.

INTERVIEWER: Where was this?

BURROUGHS: In Mexico City. I was living near Sears, Roebuck, right around the corner from the University of Mexico. I had been in the army four or five months and I was there on the G.I. Bill, studying native dialects. I went to Mexico partly because things were becoming so difficult with the drug situation in America. Getting drugs in Mexico was quite easy, so I didn't have to rush around, and there wasn't any pressure from the law.

INTERVIEWER: Why did you start taking drugs?

BURROUGHS: Well, I was just bored. I didn't seem to have much interest in becoming a successful advertising executive or whatever, or living the kind of life Harvard designs for you. After I became addicted in New York in 1944, things began to happen. I got in some trouble with the law, got married, moved to New Orleans, and then went to Mexico.

INTERVIEWER: There seems to be a great deal of middle-class voyeurism in this country concerning addiction, and in the literary world, downright reverence for the addict. You apparently don't share these points of view.

BURROUGHS: No, most of it is nonsense. I think drugs are interesting principally as chemical means of altering metabolism and thereby altering what we call reality, which I would define as a more or less constant scanning pattern.

INTERVIEWER: What do you think of the hallucinogens and the new psychedelic drugs—LSD-25?

BURROUGHS: I think they're extremely dangerous, much more dangerous than heroin. They can produce overwhelming anxiety states. I've seen people try to throw themselves out of windows; whereas the heroin addict is mainly interested in staring at his own toe. Other than deprivation of the drug, the main threat to him is an overdose. I've tried most of the hallucinogens, without an anxiety reaction, fortunately. LSD-25 produced results for me similar to mescaline. Like all hallucinogens, LSD gave me an increased awareness, more a hallucinated viewpoint than any actual hallucination. You might look at a door knob and it will appear to revolve, although you are conscious that this is the result of the drug. Also, Van Goghish colors, with all those swirls, and the crackle of the universe.

INTERVIEWER: Have you read Henri Michaux's book on mescaline?

BURROUGHS: His idea was to go into his room and close the door and hold in the experiences. I had my most interesting experiences with mescaline when I got outdoors and walked around—colors, sunsets, gardens. It produces a terrible hangover, though, nasty stuff. It makes one ill and interferes with coordination. I've had all the interesting effects I need, and I don't want any repetition of those extremely unpleasant physical reactions.

INTERVIEWER: The visions of drugs and the visions of art don't mix?

BURROUGHS: Never. The hallucinogens produce visionary states, sort of, but morphine and its derivatives decrease awareness of inner processes, thoughts, and feelings. They are pain killers, pure and simple. They are absolutely contraindicated for creative work, and I include in the lot alcohol, morphine, barbiturates, tranquilizers—the whole spectrum of sedative drugs. As for visions and heroin, I had a hallucinatory period at the very beginning of addiction, for instance, a sense of moving at high speed through space, but as soon as addiction was established, I had no visions—vision—at all and very few dreams.

INTERVIEWER: Why did you stop taking drugs?

BURROUGHS: I was living in Tangier in 1957, and I had spent a month in a tiny room in the Casbah staring at the toe of my foot. The room had filled up with empty Eukodol cartons; I suddenly realized I was not doing anything. I was dying. I was just apt to be finished. So I flew to London and turned myself over to Dr. John Yerbury Dent for treatment. I'd heard of his success with the apomorphine treatment. Apomorphine is simply morphine boiled in hydrochloric acid; it's nonaddicting. What the apomorphine did was to regulate my metabolism. It's a metabolic regulator. It cured me physiologically. I'd already taken the cure once at Lexington, and although I was off drugs when I got out, there was a physiological residue. Apomorphine eliminated that. I've been trying to get people in this country interested in it, but without much luck. The vast majority—social workers, doctors—have the cop's mentality toward addiction. A probation officer in California wrote me recently to inquire about the apomorphine treatment. I'll answer him at length. I always answer letters like that.

INTERVIEWER: Have you had any relapses?

BURROUGHS: Yes, a couple. Short. Both were straightened out with apomorphine and now heroin is no temptation for me. I'm just not interested. I've seen a lot of it around. I know people who are addicts. I don't have to use any willpower. Dr. Dent always said there is no such thing as willpower. You've got to reach a state of mind in which you don't want it or need it.

INTERVIEWER: You regard addiction as an illness, but also a central human fact, a drama?

BURROUGHS: Both, absolutely. It's as simple as the way in which anyone happens to become an alcoholic. They start drinking, that's all. They like it, and they drink, and then they become alcoholic. I was exposed to heroin in New York—that is, I was going around with people who were using it; I took it; the effects were pleasant. I went on using it and became addicted. Remember that if it can be readily obtained, you will have any number of addicts.

The idea that addiction is somehow a psychological illness is, I think, totally ridiculous. It's as psychological as malaria. It's a matter of exposure. People, generally speaking, will take any intoxicant or any drug that gives them a pleasant effect if it is available to them. In Iran, for instance, opium was sold in shops until quite recently, and they had 3 million addicts in a population of 20 million. There are also all forms of spiritual addiction. Anything that can be done chemically can be done in other ways, that is, if we have sufficient knowledge of the processes involved. Many policemen and narcotics agents are precisely addicted to power, to exercising a certain nasty kind of power over people who are helpless. The nasty sort of power: white junk I call it—rightness; they're right, right, right—and if they lost that power, they would suffer excruciating withdrawal symptoms. The picture we get of the whole Russian bureaucracy, people who are exclusively preoccupied with power and advantage, this must be an addiction. Suppose they lose it? Well, it's been their whole life.

INTERVIEWER: Can you amplify your idea of junk as image?

BURROUGHS: It's only a theory and, I feel, an inadequate one. I don't think anyone really understands what a narcotic is or how it

William Burroughs taking aim at the New York City skyline from the Brooklyn Bridge, 1978.

© GERARD MALANGA

works, how it kills pain. My idea is sort of a stab in the dark. As I see it, what has been damaged in pain is, of course, the image, and morphine must in some sense replace this. We know it blankets the cells and that addicts are practically immune to certain viruses, to influenza and respiratory complaints. This is simple, because the influenza virus has to make a hole in the cell receptors. When those are covered, as they are in morphine addiction, the virus can't get in. As soon as morphine is withdrawn, addicts will immediately come down with colds and often with influenza.

INTERVIEWER: Certain schizophrenics also resist respiratory disease.

BURROUGHS: A long time ago I suggested there were similarities in terminal addiction and terminal schizophrenia. That was why I made the suggestion that they addict these people to heroin, then withdraw it and see if they could be motivated; in other words, find out whether they'd walk across the room and pick up a syringe. Needless to say, I didn't get very far, but I think it would be interesting.

INTERVIEWER: Narcotics, then, disturb normal perception—

BURROUGHS: And set up instead a random craving for images. If drugs weren't forbidden in America, they would be the perfect middle-class vice. Addicts would do their work and come home to consume the huge dose of images awaiting them in the mass media. Junkies love to look at television. Billie Holiday said she knew she was going off drugs when she didn't like to watch TV. Or they'll sit and read a newspaper or magazine, and by God, read it all. I knew this old junkie in New York, and he'd go out and get a lot of newspapers and magazines and some candy bars and several packages of cigarettes and then he'd sit in his room and he'd read those newspapers and magazines right straight through. Indiscriminately. Every word.

INTERVIEWER: You seem primarily interested in bypassing the conscious rational apparatus to which most writers direct their efforts.

BURROUGHS: I don't know about where fiction ordinarily directs itself, but I am quite deliberately addressing myself to the whole area of what we call dreams. Precisely what is a dream? A certain juxtaposition of word and image. I've recently done a lot of experiments with scrapbooks. I'll read in the newspaper something that reminds me of or has relation to something I've written. I'll cut out the picture or article and paste it in a scrapbook beside the words from my book. Or, I'll be walking down the street and I'll suddenly see a scene from my book and I'll photograph it and put it in a scrapbook. I'll show you some of those. I've found that when preparing a page, I'll almost invariably dream that night something relating to this juxtaposition of word and image. In other words, I've been interested in precisely how word and image get around on very, very complex association lines. I do a lot of exercises in what I call time travel, in taking coordinates, such as what I photographed on the train, what I was thinking about at the time, what I was reading, and what I wrote; all of this to see how completely I can project myself back to that one point in time.

INTERVIEWER: In *Nova Express,* you indicate that silence is a desirable state.

BURROUGHS: The *most* desirable state. In one sense a special use of words and pictures can conduce silence. The scrapbooks and time travel are exercises to expand consciousness, to teach me to think in association blocks rather than words. I've recently spent a little time studying hieroglyph systems, both the Egyptian and the Mayan. A whole block of associations—*boonf!*—like that! Words, at least the way we use them, can stand in the way of what I call nonbody experience. It's time we thought about leaving the body behind.

INTERVIEWER: Marshall McLuhan said that you believed heroin was needed to turn the human body into an environment that includes the universe. But from what you've told me, you're not at all interested in turning the body into an environment.

BURROUGHS: No, junk narrows consciousness. The only benefit to me as a writer (aside from putting me into contact with the whole carny world) came to me after I went off it. What I want to do is to learn to see more of what's out there, to look outside, to achieve as far as possible a complete awareness of surroundings. Beckett wants to go inward. First he was in a bottle and now he is in the mud. I am aimed in the other direction—outward.

INTERVIEWER: Have you been able to think for any length of time in images, with the inner voice silent?

BURROUGHS: I'm becoming more proficient at it, partly through my work with scrapbooks and translating the connections between words and images. Try this. Carefully memorize the meaning of a passage, then read it; you'll find you can actually read it without the words making any sound whatever in the mind's ear. Extraordinary experience, and one that will carry over into dreams. When you start thinking in images, without words, you're well on the way.

INTERVIEWER: Why is the wordless state so desirable?

BURROUGHS: I think it's the evolutionary trend. I think that words are an around-the-world, oxcart way of doing things, awkward instruments, and they will be laid aside eventually, probably sooner than we think. This is something that will happen in the space age. Most serious writers refuse to make themselves available to the things that technology is doing. I've never been able to understand this sort of fear. Many of them are afraid of tape recorders and the idea of using any mechanical means for literary purposes seems to them some sort of a sacrilege. This is one objection to the cut-ups. There's been a lot of that, a sort of a superstitious reverence for the word. My God, they say, you can't cut up these words. Why *can't* I? I find it much easier to get interest in the cut-ups from people who are not writers—doctors, lawyers, or engineers, any open-minded, fairly intelligent person—than from those who are.

INTERVIEWER: How did you become interested in the cut-up technique?

BURROUGHS: A friend, Brion Gysin, an American poet and painter, who has lived in Europe for thirty years, was, as far as I know, the first to create cut-ups. His cut-up poem, "Minutes to Go," was broadcast by the BBC and later published in a pamphlet. I was in Paris in the summer of 1960; this was after the publication there of *Naked Lunch*. I became interested in the possibilities of this technique, and I began experimenting myself. Of course, when you think of it, *The Waste Land* was the first great cut-up collage, and Tristan Tzara had done a bit along the same lines. Dos Passos used the same idea in "The Camera Eye" sequences in *U.S.A.* I felt I had been working toward the same goal; thus it was a major revelation to me when I actually saw it being done.

ST.LOUIS RETURN   1.

('ticket to St.Louis and return in a first-class room for two people
who is the third that walks beside you?) After a parenthesis of more
than 40 years I met my old neighbor,Rives Skinker Mathews,in Tangier.
I was born 4664 Berlin Avenue changed it to Pershing during the war.
The Mathews family lived next door at 4660--red brick three-story houses
separated by a gangway large back ok yard where I could generally see a
rat one time or another from my bedroom window on the top floor.Well
we get to talking St.Louis and 'what happened to so and so' sets in
and Rives Mathews really knows what happened to any so and so in.St.Louis
His mother had been to dancing school with 'Tommy Eliot'--(His socks
wouldn't stay up.His hands were clammy.I will show you fear in
dancing school)--Allow me to open a parenthesis you see Rives Mathews
had kept a scrap book of St.Louis years and his mother left a
collection of visiting cards from the capitals of Europe.I was on my
way back to St.Louis as I looked through Rive's scrap book dim flickering
pieces of T.S.Eliot rising from the pages--(But what have I my friend
to give you put aside on another tray?Those cards were burned in my
winter house fire,October 27,1961--Comte Wladmir Sollohub Bashir Ali
Khan Bremond d'ars Marquis de Migre St.John's College 21 Quai Malaquais
Principe de la Tour--Gentilhomo di Palazzo--you're a long way from
St.Louis and visa versa.)
'I want to reserve a drawing-room for St.Louis.'
'A drawing room? Where have you been?'
'I have been abroad.'
'I can give you a bed-room or a roomette as in smaller.'
'I will take the bed-room.'
6.40 P.M. Loyal Socks Rapids out of New York for St.Louis--
Settled in my bed room surrounded by the luggage of ten years abroad
I wondered how small a roomette could be.A space capsule is where you
find it.December 23,1964,enlisting the aid of my porter, a discret
Oriental personage and a far cry indeed from old 'Yassah Boss George'
of my day, a table was installed in this bed-room where I could set up
my Facit portable and type as I looked out the train window.Snapping an
occasional picture with my Zeis Ikon,I could not but lament the old brass
spittoons,the smell of worn leather,stale cigar smoke,steam iron and soot.
Looking out the train window--click click clack--back back back--
Pennsylvania Railroad en route four people in a drawing room::::One leafs
through an old joke magazine called LIFE:--('What we want to know is
who put the sand in the spinach?')--A thin boy in prep school clothes
thinks this is funny.Ash gathers on his father's Havana held in
a delicate gray cone the way it holds on a really expensive cigar.
Father is reading The Wall Street Journal .. Mother is puting on the
old pan cake,The Green Hat folded on her knee,Brother 'Al' they call
him is looking out the train window.The time is 3 P.M. The train is one
hour out of St.Louis Missouri.Sad toy train ith a long way to go see on
back each time place what I mean dim jerky far away./take/ look out the
window of the train.Look. Postulate an observer Mr.B. from Pitman's
Common Sense Arithmetic at Point X one light hour away from the train.
Postulate further that Mr.B. is able to observe and
photograph the family with a telescopic camera.Since the family image
moving at the speed of light will take an hour to reach Mr.B.,when he
takes the 3 P.M. set the train is pulling into St.Louis Union Station
at 4 P.M. St.Louis time George the porter there waiting for his tip.
(Are you a member of the Union? Film Union 4 P.M.?). The family will
be met at the station by plain Mr.Jones or Mr.J. if you prefer.
(It was called Lost Flight.Newspapers from vacant lots in a back alley
print a shop lifted bodily cut of a movie set the Editor Rives Mathews,

A manuscript page from William S. Burroughs's "St. Louis Return."

INTERVIEWER: What do cut-ups offer the reader that conventional narrative doesn't?

BURROUGHS: Any narrative passage or any passage, say, of poetic images is subject to any number of variations, all of which may be interesting and valid in their own right. A page of Rimbaud cut up and rearranged will give you quite new images. Rimbaud images—real Rimbaud images—but new ones.

INTERVIEWER: You deplore the accumulation of images and at the same time you seem to be looking for new ones.

BURROUGHS: Yes, it's part of the paradox of anyone who is working with word and image, and after all, that is what a writer is still doing. Painter too. Cut-ups establish new connections between images, and one's range of vision consequently expands.

INTERVIEWER: Instead of going to the trouble of working with scissors and all those pieces of paper, couldn't you obtain the same effect by simply free-associating at the typewriter?

BURROUGHS: One's mind can't cover it that way. Now, for example, if I wanted to make a cut-up of this [picking up a copy of The Nation], there are many ways I could do it. I could read cross-column; I could say, "Today's men's nerves surround us. Each technological extension gone outside is electrical involves an act of collective environment. The human nervous environment system itself can be reprogrammed with all its private and social values because it is content. He programs logically as readily as any radio net is swallowed by the new environment. The sensory order." You find it often makes quite as much sense as the original. You learn to leave out words and to make connections. [Gesturing] Suppose I should cut this down the middle here, and put this up here. Your mind simply could not manage it. It's like trying to keep so many chess moves in mind, you just couldn't do it. The mental mechanisms of repression and selection are also operating against you.

INTERVIEWER: You believe that an audience can be eventually trained to respond to cut-ups?

BURROUGHS: Of course, because cut-ups make explicit a psycho-sensory process that is going on all the time anyway. Somebody is reading a newspaper, and his eye follows the column in the proper Aristotelian manner, one idea and sentence at a time. But subliminally he is reading the columns on either side and is aware of the person sitting next to him. That's a cut-up. I was sitting in a lunchroom in New York having my doughnuts and coffee. I was thinking that one *does* feel a little boxed in New York, like living in a series of boxes. I looked out the window and there was a great big Yale truck. That's cut-up—a juxtaposition of what's happening outside and what you're thinking of. I make this a practice when I walk down the street. I'll say, when I got to here I saw that sign; I was thinking this, and when I return to the house I'll type these up. Some of this material I use and some I don't. I have literally thousands of pages of notes here, raw, and I keep a diary as well. In a sense it's traveling in time.

Most people don't see what's going on around them. That's my principal message to writers: for God's sake, keep your *eyes* open. Notice what's going on around you. I mean, I walk down the street with friends. I ask, "Did you see him, that person who just walked by?" No, they didn't notice him. I had a very pleasant time on the train coming out here. I haven't traveled on trains in years. I found there were no drawing rooms. I got a bedroom so I could set up my typewriter and look out the window. I was taking photos, too. I also noticed all the signs and what I was thinking at the time, you see. And I got some extraordinary juxtapositions. For example, a friend of mine has a loft apartment in New York. He said, "Every time we go out of the house and come back, if we leave the bathroom door open, there's a rat in the house." I look out the window, there's Able Pest Control.

INTERVIEWER: The one flaw in the cut-up argument seems to lie in the linguistic base on which we operate, the straight declarative sentence. It's going to take a great deal to change that.

BURROUGHS: Yes, it is unfortunately one of the great errors of Western thought, the whole either/or proposition. You remember Korzybski and his idea of non-Aristotelian logic. Either/or thinking just is not accurate thinking. That's not the way things occur, and I feel the Aristotelian construct is one of the great shackles of Western civilization. Cut-ups are a movement toward breaking this down. I should imagine it would be much easier to find acceptance of the cut-ups from, possibly, the Chinese, because you see already there are many ways that they can read any given ideograph. It's already cut up.

INTERVIEWER: What will happen to the straight plot in fiction?

BURROUGHS: Plot has always had the definite function of stage direction, of getting the characters from here to there, and that will continue, but the new techniques such as cut-up will involve much more of the total capacity of the observer. It enriches the whole aesthetic experience, extends it.

INTERVIEWER: *Nova Express* is a cut-up of many writers?

BURROUGHS: Joyce is in there. Shakespeare, Rimbaud, some writers that people haven't heard about, someone named Jack Stern. There's Kerouac. I don't know, when you start making these fold-ins and cut-ups you lose track. Genet, of course, is someone I admire very much. But what he's doing is classical French prose. He's not a verbal innovator. Also Kafka, Eliot, and one of my favorites is Joseph Conrad. My story, "They Just Fade Away," is a fold-in (instead of cutting, you fold) from *Lord Jim*. In fact, it's almost a retelling of the *Lord Jim* story. My Stein is the same Stein as in *Lord Jim*. Richard Hughes is another favorite of mine. And Graham Greene. For exercise, when I make a trip, such as from Tangier to Gibraltar, I will record this in three columns in a notebook I always take with me. One column will contain simply an account of the trip, what happened. I arrived at the air terminal, what was said by the clerks, what I overheard on the plane, what hotel I checked into. The next column presents my memories; that is, what I was thinking of at the time, the memories that were activated by my encounters; and the third column, which I call my reading column, gives quotations from any book that I take with me. I have practically a whole novel alone on my trips to Gibraltar. Besides Graham Greene, I've used other books. I used *The Wonderful Country* by Tom Lea on one trip. Let's see, and Eliot's *The Cocktail Party; In Hazard* by Richard Hughes. For example, I'm reading *The Wonderful Country* and the hero is just crossing the frontier into Mexico. Well, just at this point I come to the Spanish frontier, so I note that down in the margin. Or I'm on a boat or a train, and I'm reading *The Quiet American*. I look around and see if there's a quiet American aboard. Sure enough, there's a quiet sort of young American with a crew cut drinking a bottle of beer. It's extraordinary, if you really keep your eyes open. I was reading Raymond Chandler, and one of his characters was an albino gunman. My God, if there wasn't an albino in the room. He wasn't a gunman.

Who else? Wait a minute, I'll just check my coordinate books to see if there's anyone I've forgotten—Conrad, Richard Hughes, science fiction, quite a bit of science fiction. Eric Frank Russell has written some very, very interesting books. Here's one, *The Star Virus;* I doubt if you've heard of it. He develops a concept here of what he calls "Deadliners" who have this strange sort of seedy look. I read this when I was in Gibraltar, and I began to find Deadliners all over the place. The story has a fish pond in it, and quite a flower garden. My father was always very interested in gardening.

INTERVIEWER: In view of all this, what will happen to fiction in the next twenty-five years?

BURROUGHS: In the first place, I think there's going to be more and more merging of art and science. Scientists are already studying the creative process, and I think the whole line between art and science will break down and that scientists, I hope, will become more creative and writers more scientific. And I see no reason why the artistic world can't absolutely merge with Madison Avenue. Pop art is a move in that direction. Why can't we have advertisements with beautiful words and beautiful images? Already some of the very beautiful color photography appears in whiskey ads, I notice. Science will also discover for us how association blocks actually form.

INTERVIEWER: Do you think this will destroy the magic?

BURROUGHS: Not at all. I would say it would enhance it.

INTERVIEWER: Have you done anything with computers?

BURROUGHS: I've not done anything, but I've seen some of the computer poetry. I can take one of those computer poems and then try to find correlatives of it, that is, pictures to go with it; it's quite possible.

INTERVIEWER: Does the fact that it comes from a machine diminish its value to you?

BURROUGHS: I think that any artistic product must stand or fall on what's there.

INTERVIEWER: Therefore, you're not upset by the fact that a chimpanzee can do an abstract painting?

BURROUGHS: If he does a good one, no. People say to me, "Oh, this is all very good, but you got it by cutting up." I say that has nothing to do with it, how I got it. What is any writing but a cut-up? Somebody has to program the machine; somebody has to *do* the cutting up. Remember that I first made selections. Out of hundreds of possible sentences that I might have used, I chose one.

INTERVIEWER: Incidentally, one image in *Nova Express* keeps coming back to me and I don't quite understand it: the gray room, "breaking through to the gray room."

BURROUGHS: I see that as very much like the photographic dark-room where the reality photographs are actually produced. Implicit in *Nova Express* is a theory that what we call reality is actually a movie. It's a film, what I call a biologic film. What has happened is that the underground and also the nova police have made a break-through past the guards and gotten into the darkroom where the films are processed, where they're in a position to expose negatives and prevent events from occurring. They're like police anywhere. All right, you've got a bad situation here in which the nova mob is about to blow up the planet. So The Heavy Metal Kid calls in the nova police. Once you get them in there, by God, they begin acting like any police. They're always an ambivalent agency. I recall once in South America that I complained to the police that a camera had been stolen and they ended up arresting me. I hadn't registered or something. In other words, once you get them on the scene they really start nosing around. Once the law starts asking questions, there's no end to it. For nova police, read technology, if you wish.

INTERVIEWER: Mary McCarthy has commented on the carnival origins of your characters in *Naked Lunch*. What are their other derivations?

BURROUGHS: The carny world was the one I exactly intended to create—a kind of midwestern, small-town, cracker-barrel, pratfall type of folklore, very much my own background. That world was an integral part of America and existed nowhere else, at least not in the same form. My family was southern on my mother's side. My grandfather was a circuit-riding Methodist minister with thirteen children. Most of them went up to New York and became quite successful in advertising and public relations. One of them, an uncle, was a master imagemaker, Ivy Lee, Rockefeller's publicity manager.

INTERVIEWER: Is it true that you did a great deal of acting out to create your characters when you were finishing *Naked Lunch*?

BURROUGHS: Excuse me, there is no accurate description of the creation of a book, or an event. Read Durrell's Alexandria novels for four different ways of looking at the same thing. Gysin saw me pasting pictures on the wall of a Paris hotel room and using a tape recorder to act out several voices. Actually, it was written mainly in Tangier, after I had taken the cure with Dr. Dent in London in 1957. I came back to Tangier and I started working on a lot of notes that I had made over a period of years. Most of the book was written at that time. I went to Paris about 1959, and I had a great pile of manuscripts. Girodias was interested and he asked if I could get the book ready in two weeks. This is the period that Brion is referring to when, from manuscripts collected over a period of years, I assembled what became the book from some thousand pages, something like that.

INTERVIEWER: But did you actually leap up and act out, say, Dr. Benway?

BURROUGHS: Yes, I have. Dr. Benway dates back to a story I wrote in 1938 with a friend of mine, Kells Elvins, who is now dead. That's about the only piece of writing I did prior to *Junky*. And we did definitely act the thing out. We decided that was the way to write. Now here's this guy, what does he say, what does he do? Dr. Benway sort of emerged quite spontaneously while we were composing this piece. Something I've been meaning to do with my scrapbooks is to have files on every character, almost like police files: habits, idiosyncrasies, where born, pictures. That is, if I ever see anyone in a magazine or newspaper who looks like Dr. Benway (and several people have played Dr. Benway, sort of amateur actors), I take their photographs. Many of my characters first come through strongly to me as voices. That's why I use a tape recorder. They also carry over from one book to another.

INTERVIEWER: Do any have their origins in actual persons?

BURROUGHS: Hamburger Mary is one. There was a place in New York called Hamburger Mary's. I was in Hamburger Mary's when a friend gave me a batch of morphine syrettes. That was my first experience with morphine and then I built up a whole picture of Hamburger Mary. She is also an actual person. I don't like to give her name for fear of being sued for libel, but she was a Scientologist who started out in a hamburger joint in Portland, Oregon, and now has eleven million dollars.

INTERVIEWER: What about The Heavy Metal Kid?

BURROUGHS: There again, quite complicated origins, partly based on my own experience. I felt that heavy metal was sort of the ultimate expression of addiction, that there's something actually metallic in addiction, that the final stage reached is not so much vegetable as mineral. It's increasingly inanimate, in any case. You see, as Dr. Benway said, I've now decided that junk is not green, but blue. Some of my characters come to me in dreams, Daddy Long Legs, for instance. Once, in a clinic, I had a dream in which I saw a man in this rundown clinic and his name in the dream was Daddy Long Legs. Many characters have come to me like that in a dream, and then I'll elaborate from there. I always write down all my dreams. That's why I've got that notebook beside the bed there.

INTERVIEWER: Earlier you mentioned that if junk had done nothing else, it at least put you in contact with the carny world.

BURROUGHS: Yes, the underworld, the old-time thieves, pickpockets, and people like that. They're a dying race; very few of those old-timers left. Yeah, well, they were show business.

INTERVIEWER: What's the difference between the modern junkie versus the 1944 junkie?

BURROUGHS: For one thing, all these young addicts; that was quite unknown in 1944. Most of the ones I knew were middle-aged men or old. I knew some of the old-time pickpockets and sneak thieves and short-change artists. They had something called The Bill, a shortchange deal. I've never been able to figure out how it works. One man I knew beat all the cashiers in Grand Central with this thing. It starts with a twenty-dollar bill. You give them a twenty-dollar bill and then when you get the change you say, "Well, wait a minute, I must have been dreaming, I've got the change after all." First thing you know, the cashier's short ten dollars. One day this shortchange artist went to Grand Central, even though he knew it was burned down, but he wanted to change twenty dollars. Well, a guy got on the buzzer and they arrested him. When they got up in court and tried to explain what had happened, none of them could do it. I keep stories like this in my files.

INTERVIEWER: In your apartment in Tangier?

BURROUGHS: No, all of it is right here in this room.

INTERVIEWER: In case Tangier is blown up, it's all safe?

BURROUGHS: Well, more than that. *I need it all.* I brought everything. That's why I have to travel by boat and by train, because, well, just to give you an idea, that's a photographic file [*thud*]. Those are all photographs and photographs. When I sit down to write, I may suddenly think of something I wrote three years ago which should be in this file over here. It may not be. I'm always looking through these files. That's why I need a place where I can really spread them out, to see what's what. I'm looking for one particular paper, it often takes me a long time and sometimes I don't find it. Those dresser drawers are full of files. All those drawers in the closets are full of files. It's pretty well organized. Here's a file, "The 1920 Movie," which partly contains some motion picture ideas. Here's "All the Sad Old Showmen"; has some business about bank robbers in it. Here's "The Nova Police Gazette." This is "Analog," which contains science fiction material. This is "The Captain's Logbook." I've been interested in sea stories, but I know so little about the sea, I hesitate to do much. I collect sea disasters such as the *Mary Celeste*. Here's a file on Mr. Luce.

INTERVIEWER: Do you admire Mr. Luce?

BURROUGHS: I don't admire him at all. He has set up one of the greatest word and image banks in the world. I mean, there are thousands of photos, thousands of words about anything and everything, all in his files. All the best pictures go into the files. Of course, they're reduced to microphotos now. I've been interested in the Mayan system, which was a control calendar. You see, their calendar postulated really how everyone should feel at a given time, with lucky days, unlucky days, et cetera. And I feel that Luce's system is comparable to that. It is a control system. It has nothing to do with reporting. *Time, Life, Fortune* is some sort of a police organization.

INTERVIEWER: You've said your next book will be about the American West and a gunfighter.

BURROUGHS: Yes, I've thought about this for years and I have hundreds of pages of notes on the whole concept of the gunfighter. The gun duel was a sort of Zen contest, a real spiritual contest like Zen swordsmanship.

INTERVIEWER: Would this be cut-up, or more a conventional narrative?

BURROUGHS: I'd use cut-ups extensively in the preparation, because they would give me all sorts of facets of character and place, but the final version would be straight narrative. I wouldn't want to get bogged down in too much factual detail, but I'd like to do research in New Mexico or Arizona, even though the actual towns out there have become synthetic tourist attractions. Occasionally I have the sensation that I'm repeating myself in my work, and I would like to do something different—almost a deliberate change of style. I'm not sure if it's possible, but I want to try. I've been thinking about the Western for years. As a boy I was sent to school in New Mexico, and during the war I was stationed in Coldspring, Texas, near Conroe. That's genuine backwoods country, and I picked up some real characters there. For instance, a fellow who actually lived in East Texas. He was always having trouble with his neighbors, who suspected him of rustling their cattle, I think with good reason. But he was competent with a gun and there wasn't anyone who would go up against him. He finally was killed. He got drunk and went to sleep under a tree by a campfire. The fire set fire to the tree, and it fell on him. I'm interested in extending newspaper and magazine formats to so-called literary materials. Here, this is one of my attempts. This is going to be published in a little magazine, *The Sparrow*.

INTERVIEWER: [*Reading*] "The Coldspring News, All the News That Fits We Print, Sunday, September 17, 1899, William Burroughs, Editor." Here's Bradly Martin again.

BURROUGHS: Yes, he's the gunfighter. I'm not sure yet what's going to happen after Clem accuses him of rustling cattle. I guess Clem goes into Coldspring and there's gunplay between him and the gunfighter. He's going to kill Clem, obviously. Clem is practically a dead man. Clem is going to get likkered up and think he can tangle with Bradly Martin, and Bradly Martin is going to kill him, that's for sure.

INTERVIEWER: Will your other characters reappear? Dr. Benway?

BURROUGHS: He'd be the local doctor. That's what I'd like to do, you see, use all these characters in a straight Western story. There would be Mr. Bradly, Mr. Martin, whose name is Bradly Martin; there would be Dr. Benway; and we'd have the various traveling carny and medicine shows that come through with The Subliminal Kid and all of the con men. That was the heyday for those old joes.

INTERVIEWER: Do you think of the artist at all as being a con man?

BURROUGHS: In a sense. You see, a real con man is a creator. He creates a set. No, a con man is more a movie director than a writer. The Yellow Kid created a whole set, a whole cast of characters, a whole brokerage house, a whole bank. It was just like a movie studio.

INTERVIEWER: What about addicts?

BURROUGHS: Well, there will be a lot of morphine addiction. Remember that there were a great many addicts at that time. Jesse James was an addict. He started using morphine for a wound in his lung, and I don't know whether he was permanently addicted, but he tried to kill himself. He took sixteen grains of morphine and it didn't kill him, which indicates a terrific tolerance. So he must have been fairly heavily addicted. A dumb, brutal hick; that's what he was, like Dillinger. And there were so many genteel old ladies who didn't feel right unless they had their Dr. Jones mixture every day.

INTERVIEWER: What about The Green Boy, Izzy The Push, Green Tony, Sammy The Butcher, and Willy The Fink?

BURROUGHS: See, all of them could be Western characters except Izzy The Push. The buildings weren't high enough in those days. Defenestration, incidentally, is a very interesting phenomenon. Some people who are prone to it will not live in high buildings. They get near a window, someone in the next room hears a cry, and they're gone. "Fell or jumped" is the phrase. I would add, "or was pushed."

INTERVIEWER: What other character types interest you?

BURROUGHS: Not the people in advertising and television, nor the American postman or middle-class housewife; not the young man setting forth. The whole world of high finance interests me, the men such as Rockefeller who were specialized types of organisms that could exist in a certain environment. He was really a money-making machine, but I doubt that he could have made a dime today because he required the old laissez-faire capitalism. He was a specialized monopolistic organism. My uncle Ivy created images for him. I fail to understand why people like J. Paul Getty have to come on with such a stuffy, uninteresting image. He decides to write his life history. I've never read anything so dull, so absolutely devoid of any spark. Well, after all, he was quite a playboy in his youth. There must have been something going on. None of it's in the book. Here he is, the only man of enormous wealth who operates alone, but there's nobody to present the image. Well, yes, I wouldn't mind doing that sort of job myself. I'd like to take somebody like Getty and try to find an image for him that would be of some interest. If Getty wants to build an image, why doesn't he hire a first-class writer to write his story? For that matter, advertising has a long way to go. I'd like to see a story by Norman Mailer or John O'Hara which just makes some mention of a product, say, Southern Comfort. I can see the O'Hara story. It would be about someone who went into a bar and asked for Southern Comfort; they didn't have it, and he gets into a long, stupid argument with the bartender. It shouldn't be obtrusive; the story must be interesting in itself so that people read this just as they read any story in *Playboy*, and Southern Comfort would be guaranteed that people will look at that advertisement for a certain number of minutes. You see what I mean? They'll read the story. Now, there are many other ideas; you could have serialized comic strips, serial stories. Well, all we have to do is have James Bond smoking a certain brand of cigarettes.

INTERVIEWER: Didn't you once work for an advertising agency?

BURROUGHS: Yes, after I got out of Harvard in 1936. I had done some graduate work in anthropology. I got a glimpse of academic life and I didn't like it at all. It looked like there was too much faculty intrigue, faculty teas, cultivating the head of the department, so on and so forth. Then I spent a year as a copywriter in this small advertising agency, since defunct, in New York. We had a lot of rather weird accounts. There was some device called the Cascade for giving high colonics, and something called Endocreme. It was supposed to make women look younger, because it contained some female sex hormones. The Interstate Commerce Commission was never far behind. As you can see, I've recently thought a great deal about advertising. After all, they're doing the same sort of thing. They are concerned with the precise manipulation of word and image. Anyway, after the ad game I was in the army for a bit. Honorably discharged and then the usual strange wartime jobs—bartender, exterminator, reporter, and factory and office jobs. Then Mexico, a sinister place.

INTERVIEWER: Why sinister?

BURROUGHS: I was there during the Alemán regime. If you walked into a bar, there would be at least fifteen people in there who were carrying guns. Everybody was carrying guns. They got drunk and they were a menace to any living creature. I mean, sitting in a cocktail lounge, you always had to be ready to hit the deck. I had a friend who was shot, killed. But he asked for it. He was waving his little .25 automatic around in a bar and some Mexican blasted him with a .45. They listed the death as natural causes, because the killer was a political big shot. There was no scandal, but it was really as much as your life was worth to go into a cocktail lounge. And I had that terrible accident with Joan Vollmer, my wife. I had a revolver that I was planning to sell to a friend. I was checking it over and it went off—killed her. A rumor started that I was trying to shoot a glass of champagne from her head William Tell–style. Absurd and false. Then they had a big depistolization. Mexico City had one of the highest per capita homicide rates in the world. Another thing, every time you turned around there was some Mexican cop with his hand out, finding some fault with your papers, or something, just anything he could latch on to. "Papers very bad, señor." It really was a bit much, the Alemán regime.

INTERVIEWER: From Mexico?

BURROUGHS: I went to Colombia, Peru, and Ecuador, just looking around. I was particularly interested in the Amazon region of Peru, where I took a drug called *yage, Bannisteria caapi*, an hallucinogen as powerful as mescaline, I believe. The whole trip gave me an awful lot of copy. A lot of these experiences went into *The Ticket That Exploded*, which is sort of midway between *Naked Lunch* and *The Soft Machine*. It's not a book I'm satisfied with in its present form. If it's published in the United States, I would have to rewrite it. *The Soft Machine*, which will come out here in due time, is an expansion of my South American experiences, with surreal extensions. When I rewrote it recently, I included about sixty-five pages of straight narrative concerning Dr. Benway, and The Sailor, and various characters from *Naked Lunch*. These people pop up everywhere.

INTERVIEWER: Then from South America you went to Europe. Is the geographic switch as important as it once was to American writing?

BURROUGHS: Well, if I hadn't covered a lot of ground, I wouldn't have encountered the extra dimensions of character and extremity that make the difference. But I think the day of the expatriate is definitely over. It's becoming more and more uncomfortable, more and more expensive, and less and less rewarding to live abroad, as far as I'm concerned. Now I'm particularly concerned with quiet writing conditions—being able to concentrate—and not so much interested in the place where I am. To me, Paris is now one of the most disagreeable cities in the world. I just hate it. The food is uneatable. It's either very expensive, or you just can't eat it. In order to get a good sandwich at three o'clock in the afternoon, I have to get into a taxi and go all the way over to the Right Bank. Here all I have to do is pick up the phone. They send me up a club sandwich and a glass of buttermilk, which is all I want for lunch anyway. The French have gotten so nasty and they're getting nastier and nastier. The Algerian war and then all those millions of people dumped back into France and all of them thoroughly dissatisfied. I don't know, I think the atmosphere there is unpleasant and not conducive to anything. You can't get an apartment. You can't get a quiet place to work. Best you can do is a dinky hotel room somewhere. If I want to get something like this, it costs me thirty dollars a day. The main thing I've found after twenty years away from St. Louis is that the standard of service is much better than New York. These are Claridge's or Ritz accommodations. If I could afford it, keep it, this would be an ideal place for me. There's not a sound in here. It's been very conducive to work. I've got a lot of room here to spread out all my papers in all these drawers and shelves. It's quiet. When I want something to eat, I pick up the phone. I can work right straight through. Get up in the morning, pick up the phone about two o'clock and have a sandwich, and work through till dinnertime. Also, it's interesting to turn on the TV set every now and then.

INTERVIEWER: What do you find on it?

BURROUGHS: That's a *real* cut-up. It flickers, just like the old movies used to. When talkies came in and they perfected the image, the movies became as dull as looking out the window. A bunch of Italians in Rabat have a television station and we could get the signal in Tangier. I just sat there open mouthed looking at it. What with blurring and contractions and visual static, some of their Westerns became very, very odd. Gysin has been experimenting with the flicker principle in a gadget he calls a "Dream Machine." There used to be one in the window of The English Bookshop on the Rue de Seine. Helena Rubenstein was so fascinated she bought a couple, and Harold Matson, the agent, thinks it's a million-dollar idea.

INTERVIEWER: Describe a typical day's work.

BURROUGHS: I get up about nine o'clock and order breakfast; I hate to go out for breakfast. I work usually until about two o'clock or two-thirty, when I like to have a sandwich and a glass of milk, which takes about ten minutes. I'll work through until six or seven o'clock. Then if I'm seeing people or going out, I'll go out, have a few drinks, come back and maybe do a little reading and go to bed. I go to bed pretty early. I don't make myself work. It's just the thing I want to do. To be completely alone in a room, to know that there'll be no interruptions and I've got eight hours is just exactly what I want—yeah, just paradise.

INTERVIEWER: Do you compose on the typewriter?

BURROUGHS: I use the typewriter and I use scissors. I can sit down with scissors and old manuscripts and paste in photographs for hours; I have hundreds of photographs. I usually take a walk every day. Here in St. Louis I've been trying to take 1920s photographs, alleys and whatnot. This [*pointing*] is a ghostly photograph of the house in which I grew up, seen back through forty-five years. Here's a photo of an old ash pit. It was great fun for children to get out there in the alley after Christmas and build a fire in the ash pit with all the excelsior and wrappings. Here, these are stories and pictures from the society columns. I've been doing a cut-up of society coverage. I had a lot of fun piling up these names; you get some improbable names in the society columns.

INTERVIEWER: You recently said you would like to settle in the Ozarks. Were you serious?

BURROUGHS: I would like to have a place there. It's a very beautiful area in the fall, and I'd like to spend periods of time, say every month or every two months, in complete solitude, just working, which requires an isolated situation. Of course, I'd have to buy a car, for one thing, and you run into considerable expense. I just have to think in terms of an apartment. I thought possibly an apartment here, but most likely I'll get one in New York. I'm not returning to Tangier. I just don't like it anymore. It's become just a small town. There's no life there, and the place has no novelty for me at all. I was sitting there, and I thought, my God, I might as well be in Columbus, Ohio, as here, for all the interest that the town has for me. I was just sitting in my apartment working. I could have a better apartment and better working conditions somewhere else. After ten o'clock at night, there's no one on the streets. The old settlers like Paul Bowles and those people who have been there for years and years are sort of hanging on desperately asking, "Where could we go if we left Tangier?" I don't know, it just depresses me now. It's not even cheap there. If I travel anywhere, it will be to the Far East, but only for a visit. I've never been east of Athens.

INTERVIEWER: That reminds me, I meant to ask you what's behind your interest in the more exotic systems such as Zen, or Dr. Reich's orgone theories?

BURROUGHS: Well, these nonconventional theories frequently touch on something going on that Harvard and MIT can't explain. I don't mean that I endorse them wholeheartedly, but I am interested in any attempt along those lines. I've used these orgone accumulators and I'm convinced that something occurs there, I don't know quite what. Of course, Reich himself went around the bend, no question of that.

INTERVIEWER: You mentioned Scientology earlier. Do you have a system for getting on, or are you looking for one?

BURROUGHS: I'm not very interested in such a crudely three-dimensional manipulative schema as L. Ron Hubbard's, although it's got its points. I've studied it and I've seen how it works. It's a series of manipulative gimmicks. They tell you to look around and see what you would have. The results are much more subtle and more successful than Dale Carnegie's. But as far as my living by a system, no. At the same time, I don't think anything happens in this universe except by some power—or individual—making it happen. Nothing happens of itself. I believe all events are produced by will.

INTERVIEWER: Then do you believe in the existence of God?

BURROUGHS: God? I wouldn't say. I think there are innumerable gods. What we on Earth call God is a little tribal god who has made an awful mess. Certainly forces operating through human consciousness control events. A Luce writer may be an agent of God knows what power, a force with an insatiable appetite for word and image. What does this force propose to do with such a tremendous mound of image garbage? They've got a regular casting office. To interview Mary McCarthy, they'll send a shy Vassar girl who's just trying to get along. They had several carny people for me. "Shucks, Bill, you got a reefer?" *Reefer,* my God! "Certainly not," I told them. "I don't know what you're talking about." Then they go back and write a nasty article for the files.

INTERVIEWER: In some respects, *Nova Express* seems to be a prescription for social ailments. Do you see the need, for instance, of biologic courts in the future?

BURROUGHS: Certainly. Science eventually will be forced to establish courts of biologic mediation, because life-forms are going to become more incompatible with the conditions of existence as man penetrates further into space. Mankind will have to undergo biologic alterations ultimately, if we are to survive at all. This will require biologic law to decide what changes to make. We will simply have to use our intelligence to plan mutations, rather than letting them occur at random. Because many such mutations—look at the saber-toothed tiger—are bound to be very poor engineering designs. The future, decidedly, yes. I think there are innumerable possibilities, literally innumerable. The hope lies in the development of nonbody experience and eventually getting away from the body itself, away from three-dimensional coordinates and concomitant animal reactions of fear and flight, which lead inevitably to tribal feuds and dissension.

INTERVIEWER: Why did you choose an interplanetary war as the conflict in *Nova Express*, rather than discord between nations? You seem fascinated with the idea that a superterrestrial power is exercising an apparatus of control, such as the death dwarfs—

BURROUGHS: They're parasitic organisms occupying a human host, rather like a radio transmitter, which direct and control it. The people who work with encephalograms and brain waves point out that technically it will someday be possible to install at birth a radio antenna in the brain which will control thought, feeling, and sensory perceptions, actually not only control thought, but make certain thoughts impossible. The death dwarfs are weapons of the nova mob, which in turn is calling the shots in the cold war. The nova mob is using that conflict in an attempt to blow up the planet, because when you get right down to it, what are America and Russia really arguing about? The Soviet Union and the United States will eventually consist of interchangeable social parts and neither nation is morally "right." The idea that anyone can run his own factory in America is ridiculous. The government and the unions—which both amount to the same thing: control systems—tell him who he can hire, how much he can pay them, and how he can sell his goods. What difference does it make if the state owns the plant and retains him as manager? Regardless of how it's done, the same kind of people will be in charge. One's ally today is an enemy tomorrow. I have postulated this power—the nova mob—which forces us to play musical chairs.

INTERVIEWER: You see hope for the human race, but at the same time you are alarmed as the instruments of control become more sophisticated.

BURROUGHS: Well, whereas they become more sophisticated they also become more vulnerable. *Time, Life, Fortune* applies a more complex, effective control system than the Mayan calendar, but it also is much more vulnerable because it is so vast and mechanized. Not even Henry Luce understands what's going on in the system now. Well, a machine can be redirected. One technical sergeant can fuck up the whole works. Nobody can control the whole operation. It's too complex. The captain comes in and says, "All right, boys, we're moving up." Now, who knows what buttons to push? Who knows how to get the cases of Spam up to where they're going, and how to fill out the forms? The sergeant does. The captain doesn't know. As long as there're sergeants around, the machine can be dismantled, and we may get out of all this alive yet.

INTERVIEWER: Sex seems equated with death frequently in your work.

BURROUGHS: That is an extension of the idea of sex as a biologic weapon. I feel that sex, like practically every other human manifestation, has been degraded for control purposes, or really for antihuman purposes. This whole puritanism. How are we ever going to find out anything about sex scientifically, when a priori the subject cannot even be investigated? It can't even be thought about or written about. That was one of the interesting things about Reich. He was one of the few people who ever tried to investigate sex—sexual phenomena, from a scientific point of view. There's this prurience and this fear of sex. We know nothing about sex. What is it? Why is it pleasurable? What is pleasure? Relief from tension? Well, possibly.

INTERVIEWER: Are you irreconcilably hostile to the twentieth century?

BURROUGHS: Not at all, although I can imagine myself as having been born under many different circumstances. For example, I had a dream recently in which I returned to the family home and I found a different father and a different house from any I'd ever seen before. Yet in a dream sense, the father and the house were quite familiar.

INTERVIEWER: Mary McCarthy has characterized you as a soured utopian. Is that accurate?

BURROUGHS: I do definitely mean what I say to be taken literally, yes, to make people aware of the true criminality of our times, to wise up the marks. All of my work is directed against those who are bent, through stupidity or design, on blowing up the planet or rendering it uninhabitable. Like the advertising people we talked about, I'm concerned with the precise manipulation of word and image to create an action, not to go out and buy a Coca-Cola, but to create an alteration in the reader's consciousness. You know, they ask me if I were on a desert island and knew nobody would ever see what I wrote, would I go on writing. My answer is most emphatically yes. I would go on writing for company. Because I'm creating an imaginary—it's always imaginary—world in which I would like to live.

—CONRAD KNICKERBOCKER
1965

Allen Ginsberg

was born in Newark, New Jersey, on June 3, 1926. He attended Columbia University in New York City, where he befriended Jack Kerouac, William Burroughs, Neal Cassady, and Herbert Huncke. Together, they initiated Ginsberg into a culture of drugs and petty crime. Following a high-speed car chase involving a stolen vehicle, stolen goods, and an innocent right on red, Ginsberg was arrested. In order to escape imprisonment, he pleaded insanity, resulting in an eight-month stay at Columbia Presbyterian Psychiatric Institute.

Put off by his own delinquent forays, Ginsberg briefly toyed with a conservative lifestyle: after his release, he pronounced himself heterosexual and joined an advertising company. Dissatisfied, he became a dishwasher, a night porter, and a spot-welder before finally rejoining his peers in San Francisco. With a letter of introduction from William Carlos Williams, he was quickly adopted by the West Coast poets and encouraged to publish his work.

In October 1955, he unofficially inaugurated the Beat movement with his thunderous performance of "Howl" at the now-legendary Six Gallery poetry reading. An obscenity trial publicized the poem, making Ginsberg a national symbol of illicit sexuality and political defiance. Over the years, he was repeatedly arrested for participating in various antiwar, drug legalization, and nuclear disarmament marches.

In 1974, Ginsberg won the National Book Award for *The Fall of America*. Later that year, he and poet Anne Waldman founded the Jack Kerouac School of Disembodied Poetics at the Naropa Institute in Boulder, Colorado.

With over fifteen volumes of poetry including *Howl* (1956), *Kaddish* (1961), *Reality Sandwiches* (1963), *The Fall of America* (1973), and *Plutonian Ode* (1982) and ten books of prose, including *The Yage Letters* (1963), *Allen Verbatim* (1974), *Chicago Trial Testimony* (1975), and *Straight Hearts' Delight* (1980), Ginsberg was the most prolific of the Beat writers. Until his death in April 1997, he remained the acknowledged ringleader of the Beats, appearing at poetry readings and multicultural events across the country.

© GERARD MALANGA

Allen Ginsberg during a poetry reading at New York University, 1971.

Allen Ginsberg was elected King of the May by Czech students in Prague on May Day, 1965. Soon afterward, he was expelled by the Czech government. He had been traveling for several months—in Cuba, Russia, and Poland—and from Prague he flew to London to negotiate the English publication of his poems. I didn't know he was in the country, but one night in Bristol before a poetry reading I saw him in a bar. He read that night; I hadn't heard him read before and was struck that evening by the way he seemed to enter each of his poems emotionally while reading them, the performance as much a discovery for him as for his audience.

Ginsberg and I left Bristol that day after the reading and hitchhiked to Wells Cathedral and then to Glastonbury, where he picked a flower from King Arthur's grave to send, he said, to his lifelong companion, Peter Orlovsky. He carefully studied the exhibit of tools and weapons *under the huge canonical chimney of the ancient king's kitchen, as later in Cambridge he was to study the Fitzwilliam Museum's store of Blake manuscripts; Ginsberg's idea of a Jerusalemic Britain occurring now in the day of long hair and new music meant equally the fulfillment of Blake's predictions of Albion. As we came out of a tea shop in Glaston-bury (where customers had glanced cautiously at the bearded, pro-phetic—and unfazed—stranger), Allen spoke of Life's simulacrum of a report of his Oxford encounter with Dame Edith Sitwell. ("Dope makes me come out all over in spots," she's supposed to have said.)*

Leaving the town, we were caught in a rainstorm and took a bus to Bath. Then, hitchhiking toward London, we were unsuccessful until Ginsberg tried using Buddhist hand signals instead of thumbing; half a minute later a car stopped. Riding through Somerset he talked about no-tation, the mode he says he learned from Kerouac and has used in com-posing his enormous journals; he read from an account he'd made of a recent meeting with the poets Yevtushenko and Voznesensky in Moscow, and then, looking up at a knot in a withered oak by the road, said, "The tree has cancer of the breast . . . that's what I mean. . . ."

Two weeks later he was in Cambridge for a reading and I asked him to submit to this interview. He was still busy with Blake, roaming and musing around the university and countryside in his spare moments; it took two days to get him to sit still long enough to turn on the tape recorder. He spoke slowly and thoughtfully, tiring after two hours. We stopped for a meal when guests came—when Ginsberg learned one of them was a biochemist he questioned him about viruses and DNA for an hour—then we returned to record the other half of the tape.

· · ·

INTERVIEWER: I think Diana Trilling, speaking about your reading at Columbia, remarked that your poetry, like all poetry in English when dealing with a serious subject, naturally takes on the iambic pentameter rhythm. Do you agree?

GINSBERG: Well, it really isn't an accurate thing, I don't think. I've never actually sat down and made a technical analysis of the rhythms that I write. They're probably more near choriambic— Greek meters, dithyrambic meters—and tending toward de DA de de DA de de . . . what is that? Tending toward dactylic, probably. Williams once remarked that American speech tends toward dactylic. But it's more complicated than dactyl because dactyl is a three, three units, a foot consisting of three parts, whereas the actual rhythm is probably a rhythm which consists of five, six, or seven, like DA de de DA de de DA de de DA DA. Which is more toward the line of Greek dance rhythms—that's why they call them choriambic. So actually, probably it's not really technically correct, what she said. But—and that applies to certain poems, like certain passages of "Howl" and certain passages of "Kaddish"—there are definite rhythms which could be analyzed as corresponding to classical rhythms, though not necessarily *English* classical rhythms; they might correspond to Greek classical rhythms, or Sanskrit prosody. But probably most of the other poetry, like "Aether" or "Laughing Gas" or a lot of those poems, they simply don't fit into that. I think she felt very comfy, to think that that would be so. I really felt quite hurt about that, because it seemed to me that she ignored the main prosodic technical achievements that I had proffered forth to the academy, and they didn't even recognize it. I mean, not that I want to stick her with being the academy.

INTERVIEWER: And in "Howl" and "Kaddish" you were working with a kind of classical unit? Is that an accurate description?

GINSBERG: Yeah, but it doesn't do very much good, because I wasn't really working with a classical unit, I was working with my own neural impulses and writing impulses. See, the difference is between someone sitting down to write a poem *in* a definite preconceived metrical pattern and filling in that pattern, and someone working with his physiological movements and *arriving* at a pattern, and perhaps even arriving at a pattern which might even have a name, or might even have a classical usage, but arriving at it organically rather than synthetically. Nobody's got any objection to even iambic pentameter if it comes from a source deeper than the mind, that is to say if it comes from the breathing and the belly and the lungs.

INTERVIEWER: American poets have been able to break away from a kind of English specified rhythm earlier than English poets have been able to do. Do you think this has anything to do with a peculiarity in English spoken tradition?

GINSBERG: No, I don't really think so, because the English don't speak in iambic pentameter either; they don't speak in the recognizable pattern that they write in. The dimness of their speech and the lack of emotional variation is parallel to the kind of dim diction and literary usage in the poetry now. But you can hear all sorts of Liverpudlian or Gordian—that's Newcastle—you can hear all sorts of variants aside from an upper tone accent, a high-class accent, that don't fit into the tone of poetry being written right now. It's not being used like in America—I think it's just that British poets are more cowardly.

INTERVIEWER: Do you find any exception to this?

GINSBERG: It's pretty general, even the supposedly avant-garde poets. They write, you know, in a very toned-down manner.

INTERVIEWER: How about a poet like Basil Bunting?

GINSBERG: Well, he was working with a whole bunch of wild men from an earlier era, who were all breaking through, I guess. And so he had that experience—also he knew Persian, he knew Persian prosody. He was better educated than most English poets.

INTERVIEWER: The kind of organization you use in "Howl," a recurrent kind of syntax—you don't think this is relevant any longer to what you want to do?

GINSBERG: No, but it was relevant to what I wanted to do then; it wasn't even a conscious decision.

INTERVIEWER: Was this related in any way to a kind of music or jazz that you were interested in at the time?

GINSBERG: Mmm . . . the myth of Lester Young as described by Kerouac, blowing eighty-nine choruses of "Lady, Be Good," say, in one night, or my own hearing of Illinois Jacquet's *Jazz at the Philharmonic*, Volume 2; I think "I Can't Get Started" was the title.

INTERVIEWER: And you've also mentioned poets like Christopher Smart, for instance, as providing an analogy—is this something you discovered later on?

GINSBERG: When I looked into it, yeah. Actually, I keep reading, or earlier I kept reading, that I was influenced by Kenneth Fearing and Carl Sandburg, whereas actually I was more conscious of Christopher Smart, and Blake's Prophetic Books, and Whitman and some aspects of biblical rhetoric. And a lot of specific prose things like Genet, Genet's *Our Lady of the Flowers* and the rhetoric in that, and Céline; Kerouac, most of all, was the biggest influence I think—Kerouac's prose.

INTERVIEWER: When did you come onto Burroughs's work?

GINSBERG: Let's see . . . Well, first thing of Burroughs I ever read was 1946 . . . which was a skit later published and integrated in some other work of his, called "Twilight's Last Gleaming," describing the sinking of the *Titanic* and an orchestra playing, a spade orchestra playing "The Star-Spangled Banner" while everybody rushed out to the lifeboats and the captain got up in woman's dress and rushed into the purser's office and shot the purser and stole all the money, and a spastic paretic jumped into a lifeboat with a machete and began chopping off people's fingers that were trying to climb into the boat, saying, "Out of the way, you foolth . . . Dirty thunthufbithes." That was a thing he had written up at Harvard with a friend named Kells Elvins. Which is really the whole key of all his work, like the sinking of America, and everybody like frightened rats trying to get out, or that was his vision of the time.

Then he and Kerouac later in 1945, 1945 or 1946, wrote a big detective book together, alternating chapters. I don't know where that book is now—Kerouac has his chapters and Burroughs's are somewhere in his papers. So I think in a sense it was Kerouac that encouraged Burroughs to write really, because Kerouac was so enthusiastic about prose, about writing, about lyricism, about the honor of writing . . . the Thomas Wolfe–ian delights of it. So anyway he turned Burroughs on in a *sense*, because Burroughs found a companion who could write really interestingly, and Burroughs admired Kerouac's perceptions. Kerouac could imitate Dashiell Hammett as well as Bill, which was Bill's natural style: dry, bony, factual. At that time Burroughs was reading John O'Hara, simply for facts, not for any sublime stylistic thing, just because he was a hard-nosed reporter.

Then in Mexico around 1951 he started writing *Junky*. I've forgotten what relation I had to that—I think I wound up as the agent for it, taking it around New York trying to get it published. I think

William Burroughs and Jack Kerouac, 1953.

he sent me portions of it at the time—I've forgotten how it worked out now. This was around 1949 or 1950. He was going through a personal crisis, his wife had died. It was in Mexico or South America . . . but it was a very generous thing of him to do, to start writing all of a sudden. Burroughs was always a very *tender* sort of person, but very dignified and shy and withdrawn, and for him to *commit* himself to a big autobiographical thing like that was . . . at the time struck me as like a piece of eternity is in love with the . . . what is it, *Eternity is in love with the productions of Time?* So he was making a production of Time then.

Then I started taking that around. I've forgot who I took that to but I think maybe to Louis Simpson, who was then working at Bobbs-Merrill. I'm not sure whether I took it to him—I remember taking it to Jason Epstein, who was then working at Doubleday, I think. Epstein at the time was not as experienced as he is now. And his reaction to it, I remember when I went back to his office to pick it up, was, Well this is all very interesting, but it isn't really interesting, on account of if it were an autobiography of a junkie written by Winston *Churchill* then it'd be interesting, but written by somebody he'd never heard of, well then it's *not* interesting. And anyway I said what about the *prose*, the prose is interesting, and he says, Oh, a difference of opinion on that. Fi-

nally I wound up taking it to Carl Solomon who was then a
reader for A. A. Wyn (Ace Books), who was his uncle, and they
finally got it through there. But it was finally published as a
cheap paperback. With a whole bunch of frightened footnotes;
like Burroughs said that marijuana was non-habit-forming
which is now accepted as a fact, there'd be a footnote by the editor, "Reliable, er, responsible medical opinion does not confirm
this." Then they also had a little introduction . . . literally they
were afraid of the book being censored or *seized* at the time, is
what they said. I've forgotten what the terms of censorship or
seizure were that they were worried about. This was about 1952.
They *said* that they were afraid to publish it straight for fear there
would be a congressional investigation or something, I don't
know what. I think there was some noise about narcotics at the
time. Newspaper noise . . . I've forgotten exactly what the arguments were. But anyway they had to write a preface which
hedged on the book a lot.

INTERVIEWER: Has there been a time when fear of censorship or
similar trouble has made your own expression difficult?

GINSBERG: This is so complicated a matter. The beginning of the
fear with me was, you know, what would my father say to something that I would write. At the time, writing "Howl"—for instance like I assumed when writing it that it was something that
could not be published because I wouldn't want my daddy to see
what was in there. About my sex life, being fucked in the ass, imagine your father reading a thing like that, was what I thought.
Though that disappeared as soon as the thing was real, or as soon
as I manifested my . . . you know, it didn't make that much importance finally. That was sort of a help for writing, because I assumed
that it wouldn't be published, therefore I could say anything that I
wanted. So literally just for myself or anybody that I knew personally well, writers who would be willing to appreciate it with a
breadth of tolerance—in a piece of work like "Howl." Who
wouldn't be judging from a moralistic viewpoint but looking for
evidences of humanity or secret thought or just actual truthfulness.
    Then there's later the problem of publication—we had a lot.
The English printer refused at first I think, we were afraid of cus-
toms; the first edition we had to print with asterisks on some of the
dirty words, and then the *Evergreen Review* in reprinting it used asterisks, and various people reprinting it later always wanted to use
the *Evergreen* version rather than the corrected legal City Lights

version—like I think there's an anthology of Jewish writers, I forgot who edited that, but a couple of the high-class intellectuals
from Columbia. I had written asking them specifically to use the
later City Lights version, but they went ahead and printed an as-
terisked version. I forget what was the name of that—something
like *New Generation of Jewish Writing*, Philip Roth, etc.

INTERVIEWER: Do you take difficulties like these as social problems, problems of communication simply, or do you feel they also
block your own ability to express yourself for yourself?

GINSBERG: The problem is, where it gets to literature, is this. We all
talk among ourselves and we have common understandings, and
we say anything we want to say, and we talk about our assholes,
and we talk about our cocks, and we talk about who we fucked last
night, or who we're gonna fuck tomorrow, or what kinda love affair
we have, or when we got drunk, or when we stuck a broom in our
ass in the Hotel Ambassador in Prague—anybody tells one's
friends about that. So then—what happens if you make a distinction between what you tell your friends and what you tell your
Muse? The problem is to break down that distinction: when you ap-
proach the Muse to talk as frankly as you would talk with yourself
or with your friends. So I began finding, in conversations with Burroughs and Kerouac and Gregory Corso, in conversations with people whom I knew well, whose souls I respected, that the things we
were telling each other for real were totally different from what was
already in literature. And that was Kerouac's great discovery in *On
the Road*. The kinds of things that he and Neal Cassady were talking
about, he finally discovered were *the* subject matter for what he
wanted to write down. That meant, at that minute, a complete revision of what literature was supposed to be, in *his* mind, and actually
in the minds of the people that first read the book. Certainly in the
minds of the critics, who had at first attacked it as not being . . .
proper structure, or something. In other words, a gang of friends
running around in an automobile. Which obviously is like a great
picaresque literary device, and a classical one. And was *not* recognized, at the time, as suitable literary subject matter.

INTERVIEWER: So it's not just a matter of themes—sex, or any other
one . . .

GINSBERG: It's the ability to commit to writing, to *write*, the same
way that you . . . are! Anyway! You have many writers who have

preconceived ideas about what literature is supposed to be, and their ideas seem to exclude that which makes them most charming in private conversation. Their faggishness, or their campiness, or their neurasthenia, or their solitude, or their goofiness, or their—even—masculinity, at times. Because they think that they're gonna write something that sounds like something else that they've read before, instead of sounds like them. Or comes from their own life. In other words, there's no distinction, there should be no distinction between what we write down, and what we really know, to begin with. As we know it every day, with each other. And the hypocrisy of literature has been—you know like there's supposed to be formal literature, which is supposed to be different from . . . in subject, in diction and even in organization, from our quotidian inspired lives.

It's also like in Whitman, "I find no fat sweeter than that which sticks to my own bones," that is to say the self-confidence of someone who knows that he's really alive, and that his existence is just as good as any other subject matter.

INTERVIEWER: Is physiology a part of this too—like the difference between your long breath line, and William Carlos Williams's shorter unit?

GINSBERG: Analytically, ex post facto, it all begins with fucking around and intuition and without any idea of *what* you're doing, I think. Later, I have a tendency to explain it, "Well, I got a longer breath than Williams, or I'm Jewish, or I study yoga, or I sing long lines. . . ." But anyway, what it boils down to is this, it's my *movement,* my feeling is for a big long clanky statement—partly that's something that I share, or maybe that I even got from Kerouac's long prose line; which is really, like he once remarked, an extended poem. Like one long sentence page of his in *Doctor Sax* or "The Railroad Earth" or occasionally *On the Road*—if you examine them phrase by phrase they usually have the density of poetry, and the beauty of poetry, but most of all the single elastic rhythm running from beginning to end of the line and ending "mop"!

INTERVIEWER: Have you ever wanted to extend this rhythmic feeling as far as say Artaud or now Michael McClure have taken it—to a line that is actually animal noise?

GINSBERG: The rhythm of the long line is also an animal cry.

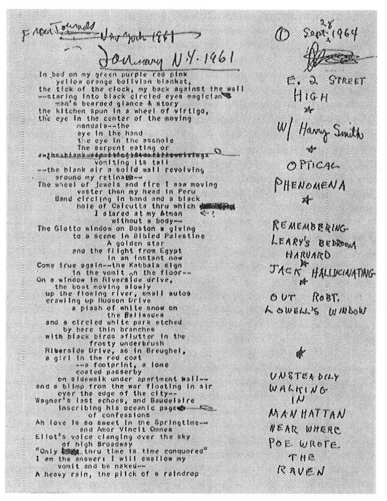

A manuscript page of an unpublished Ginsberg poem.

INTERVIEWER: So you're following that feeling and not a thought or a visual image?

GINSBERG: It's simultaneous. The poetry generally is like a rhythmic articulation of feeling. The feeling is like an impulse that rises within—just like sexual impulses, say; it's almost as definite as that. It's a feeling that begins somewhere in the pit of the stomach and rises up forward in the breast and then comes out through the mouth and ears, and comes forth a croon or a groan or a sigh. Which, if you put words to it by looking around and seeing and trying to describe what's making you sigh—and sigh in words—you simply articulate what you're feeling. As simple as that. Or actually what happens is, at best what happens, is there's a definite body rhythm that has no definite words, or may have one or two words attached to it, one or two key words attached to it. And then, in writing it down, it's simply by a process of association that I find what the rest of the statement is—what can be collected around that word, what that word is connected to. Partly by simple association, the first thing that comes to my mind like "Moloch is" or "Moloch who," and then whatever comes out. But that also goes along with a definite rhythmic impulse, like DA de de DA de de DA de de DA DA. "*Moloch* whose *eyes* are a *thous*and blind *windows.*" And before I wrote "Moloch whose eyes are a thousand blind windows," I had the word, "Moloch, Moloch, Moloch," and I also had the feeling DA de de DA de de DA de de DA DA. So it was just a question of looking up and seeing a lot of windows, and saying, oh, windows, of course, but what kind of windows? But not even that—"Moloch whose eyes." "Moloch whose *eyes*"—which is beautiful in itself—but what about it, Moloch whose eyes are *what*? So Moloch whose eyes—then probably the next thing I thought was "thousands." OK, and then thousands *what*? "Thousands blind." And I had to finish it somehow. So I hadda say "windows." It looked good *afterward*.

Usually during the composition, step by step, word by word and adjective by adjective, if it's at all spontaneous, I don't know whether it even makes sense sometimes. Sometimes I do know it makes complete sense, and I start crying. Because I realize I'm hitting some area which is absolutely true. And in that sense applicable universally, or understandable universally. In that sense able to survive through time—in that sense to be read by somebody and wept to, maybe, centuries later. In that sense prophecy, because it touches a common key . . . What prophecy actually is is not that you actually know that the bomb will fall in 1942. It's that you know and feel something which somebody knows and feels in a hundred years. And maybe articulate it in a hint—concrete way that they can pick up on in a hundred years.

INTERVIEWER: You once mentioned something you had found in Cézanne—a remark about the reconstitution of the *petites sensations* of experience, in his own painting—and you compared this with the method of your poetry.

GINSBERG: I got all hung up on Cézanne around 1949 in my last year at Columbia, studying with Meyer Schapiro. I don't know how it led into it—I think it was about the same time that I was having these Blake visions. So. The thing I understood from Blake was that it was possible to transmit a message through time which could reach the enlightened, that poetry had a definite effect, it wasn't just pretty, or just beautiful, as I had understood pretty beauty before—it was something basic to human existence, or it reached something, it reached the bottom of human existence. But anyway the impression I got was that it was like a kind of time machine through which he could transmit, Blake could transmit, his basic consciousness and communicate it to somebody else after he was dead, in other words build a time machine.

Now just about that time I was looking at Cézanne and I suddenly got a strange shuddering impression looking at his canvases, partly the effect when someone pulls a venetian blind, reverses the venetian—there's a sudden shift, a flashing that you see in Cézanne canvases. Partly it's when the canvas opens up into three dimensions and looks like wooden objects, like solid space objects, in three dimensions rather than flat. Partly it's the enormous spaces which open up in Cézanne's landscapes. And it's partly that mysterious quality around his figures, like of his wife or the card players or the postman or whoever, the local Aix characters. They look like great huge 3-D wooden dolls, sometimes. Very *uncanny* thing, like a very mysterious thing, in other words there's a strange sensation that one gets, looking at his canvases, which I began to associate with the extraordinary sensation—cosmic sensation, in fact—that I had experienced catalyzed by Blake's "Ah! Sun-flower" and "The Sick Rose" and a few other poems. So I began studiously investigating Cézanne's intentions and method, and looking at all the canvases of his that I could find in New York, and all the reproductions I could find, and I was writing at the time a paper on him, for Schapiro at Columbia in the fine arts course.

And the whole thing opened up, two ways: first, I read a book on Cézanne's composition by Erle Loran, who showed photographs, analyses and photographs of the original motifs, side by side with the actual canvases—and years later I actually went to Aix, with all the postcards, and stood in the spots, and tried to find the places where he painted Mont Sainte-Victoire from, and got in his studio and saw some of the motifs he used like his big black hat and his cloak. Well, first of all I began to see that Cézanne had all sorts of literary symbolism in him, on and off. I was preoccu-

pied with Plotinian terminology, of time and eternity, and I saw it
in Cézanne paintings, an early painting of a clock on a shelf which
I associated with time and eternity, and I began to think he was a
big secret mystic. And I saw a photograph of his studio in Loran's
book and it was like an alchemist's studio, because he had a skull,
and he had a long black coat, and he had this big black hat. So I
began thinking of him as, you know, like a magic character. Like
the original version I had thought of him was like this austere
dullard from Aix. So I began getting really interested in him as a
hermetic type, and then I symbolically read into his canvases
things that probably weren't there, like there's a painting of a
winding road which turns off, and I saw that as the mystical path:
it turns off into a village and the end of the path is hidden. Something he painted I guess when he went out painting with Bernard.
Then there was an account of a very fantastic conversation that he
had had. It's quoted in Loran's book: there's a long, long, long
paragraph where he says, "By means of squares, cubes, triangles,
I try to reconstitute the impression that I have from nature: the
means that I use to reconstitute the impression of solidity that I
think-feel-see when I am looking at a motif like Victoire, is to reduce it to some kind of pictorial language, so I use these squares,
cubes and triangles, but I try to build them together so interknit"
[Ginsberg interlocks his fingers] "so that *no light gets through.*" And I
was mystified by that, but it seemed to make sense in terms of the
grid of paint strokes that he had on his canvas, so that he produced a solid two-dimensional surface which when you looked
into it, maybe from a slight distance with your eyes either unfo-
cused or your eyelids lowered slightly, you could see a great three-
dimensional opening, mysterious, stereoscopic, like going into a
stereopticon. And I began discovering in *The Card Players* all sorts
of sinister symbols, like there's one guy leaning against the wall
with a stolid expression on his face, that he doesn't want to get involved; and then there's two guys who are peasants, who are
looking as if they've just been dealt *Death* cards; and then the
dealer you look at and he turns out to be a city slicker with a big
blue cloak and almost rouge doll-like cheeks and a fat-faced
Kafkian-agent impression about him, like he's a cardsharp, he's a
cosmic cardsharp dealing out Fate to all these people. This looks
like a great big hermetic Rembrandtian portrait in Aix! That's why
it has that funny monumentality—aside from the quote plastic
values unquote.

　　Then, I smoked a lot of marijuana and went to the basement
of the Museum of Modern Art in New York and looked at his wa-

tercolors and that's where I began really turning on to space in Cézanne and the way he built it up. Particularly there's one of rocks, I guess *Rocks at Garonne,* and you look at them for a while, and after a while they seem like they're rocks, just the rock parts, you don't know where they are, whether they're on the ground or in the air or on top of a cliff, but then they seem to be floating in space like clouds, and then they seem to be also a bit like they're amorphous, like kneecaps or cockheads or faces without eyes. And it has a very mysterious impression. Well, that may have been the result of the pot. But it's a definite thing that I got from that. Then he did some very odd studies after classical statues, Renaissance statues, and they're great gigantesque herculean figures with little tiny pinheads . . . so that apparently was his comment on them!

And then . . . the things were endless to find in Cézanne. Finally I was reading his letters and I discovered this phrase again, *mes petites sensations*—"I'm an old man and my passions are not, my senses are not coarsened by passions like some *other* old men I know, and I have worked for years trying to," I guess it was the phrase, "*reconstitute* the *petites sensations* that I get from nature, and I could stand on a hill and merely by moving my head half an inch the composition of the landscape was totally changed." So apparently he'd refined his optical perception to such a point where it's a real contemplation of optical phenomena in an almost yogic way, where he's standing there, from a specific point studying the optical field, the depth in the optical field, looking, actually looking at his own eyeballs in a sense. The attempting to reconstitute the sensation in his own eyeballs. And what does he say finally—in a very weird statement which one would not expect of the austere old workman, he said, "And this *petite sensation* is nothing other than *pater omnipotens aeterna deus.*"

So that was, I felt, the key to Cézanne's hermetic method. . . . Everybody knows his workmanlike, artisanlike, prettified-like painting method which is so great, but the really *romant*icistic motif behind it is absolutely marvelous, so you realize that he's really a saint! Working on his form of yoga, all that time, in obvious saintly circumstances of retirement in a small village, leading a relatively nonsociable life, going through the motions of going to church or not, but really containing in his skull these supernatural phenomena, and observations. . . . You know, and it's very humble actually, because he didn't know if he was crazy or not—that is a flash of the physical, miracle dimensions of existence, trying to reduce that to canvas in two dimensions, and then trying to do it in such a way as it would look if the observer looked at it long enough it would look like as much three dimension as the actual *world* of optical phenomena when one looks through one's eyes. Actually he's *re*constituted the whole fucking universe in his canvases—it's like a fantastic thing!—or at least the appearance of the universe.

So. I used a lot of this material in the references in the last part of the first section of "Howl": "sensation of Pater Omnipotens Aeterna Deus." The last part of "Howl" was really an homage to art but also in specific terms an homage to Cézanne's method, in a sense I adapted what I could to writing; but that's a very complicated matter to explain. Except, putting it very simply, that just as Cézanne doesn't use perspective lines to create space, but it's a juxtaposition of one color against another color (that's one element of his space), so, I had the idea, perhaps overrefined, that by the unexplainable, unexplained nonperspective line, that is, juxtaposition of one *word* against another, a *gap* between the two words—like the space gap in the canvas—there'd be a gap between the two words which the mind would fill in with the sensation of existence. In other words when I say, oh . . . when Shakespeare says, *In the dread vast and middle of the night,* something happens between "dread vast" and "middle." That creates like a whole space of, spaciness of black night. How it gets that is very odd, those words put together. Or in the haiku, you have two distinct images, set side by side without drawing a connection, without drawing a logical connection between them: the *mind* fills in this . . . this space. Like

> *O ant*
> *crawl up Mount Fujiyama,*
> *but slowly, slowly.*

Now you have the small ant and you have Mount Fujiyama and you have the slowly, slowly, and what happens is that you feel almost like . . . a cock in your mouth! You feel this enormous space-universe, it's almost a tactile thing. Well anyway, it's a phenomenon-sensation, phenomenon hyphen sensation, that's created by this little haiku of Issa, for instance.

So, I was trying to do similar things with juxtapositions like "hydrogen jukebox." Or . . . "winter midnight smalltown streetlight rain." Instead of cubes and squares and triangles. Cézanne is reconstituting by means of triangles, cubes, and colors—I have to reconstitute by means of words, rhythms of course, and all that—

but say it's words, phrasings. So. The problem is then to reach the different parts of the mind, which are existing simultaneously, the different associations which are going on simultaneously, choosing elements from both, like: jazz, jukebox, and all that, and we have the jukebox from that; politics, hydrogen bomb, and we have the hydrogen of that, you see "hydrogen jukebox." And that actually compresses in one instant like a whole series of things. Or the end of "Ah! Sun-flower" with "cunts of wheelbarrows," whatever that all meant, or "rubber dollar bills"—"skin of machinery"; see, and actually in the moment of composition I don't necessarily *know* what it means, but it comes to mean something later, after a year or two, I realize that it meant something clear, unconsciously. Which takes on meaning in time, like a photograph developing slowly. Because we're not really always conscious of the entire depth of our minds, in other words we just know a lot more than we're able to be aware of, normally—though at moments we're completely aware, I guess.

There's some other element of Cézanne that was interesting . . . oh, his patience, of course. In recording the optical phenomena. Has something to do with Blake: *with* not *through* the eye—*You're led to believe a lie when you see with not through the eye.* He's seeing through his eye. One can see *through* his canvas to God, really, is the way it boils down. Or to Pater Omnipotens Aeterna Deus. I could imagine someone not prepared, in a peculiar chemical physiological state, peculiar mental state, psychic state, someone not prepared who had no experience of eternal ecstasy, passing in front of a Cézanne canvas, distracted and without noticing it his eye traveling in, to, through the canvas into the space and suddenly stopping with his hair standing on end, dead in his tracks *see*ing a whole universe. And I think that's what Cézanne really does, to a lot of people.

Where were we now? Yeah, the idea that I had was that gaps in space and time through images juxtaposed, just as in the haiku you get two images which the mind connects in a flash, and so that *flash* is the *petite sensation;* or the satori, perhaps, that the Zen haikuists would speak of—if they speak of it like that. So, the poetic experience that Housman talks about, the hair standing on end or the hackles rising whatever it is, visceral thing. The interesting thing would be to know if certain combinations of words and rhythms actually had an electrochemical reaction on the body, which could catalyze specific states of consciousness. I think that's what probably happened to me with Blake. I'm *sure* it's what happens on a perhaps lower level with Poe's "The Bells" or "The

Raven," or even Vachel Lindsay's "The Congo": that there is a hypnotic rhythm there, which when you introduce it into your nervous system, causes all sorts of electronic changes—permanently alters it. There's a statement by Artaud on that subject, that certain music when introduced into the nervous system changes the molecular composition of the nerve cells or something like that, it permanently alters the being that has experience of this. Well, anyway, this is certainly true. In other words any experience we have is recorded in the brain and goes through neural patterns and whatnot: so I suppose brain recordings are done by means of shifting around of little electrons—so there is actually an electrochemical effect caused by art.

So . . . the problem is what is the maximum electrochemical effect in the desired direction. That is what I was taking Blake as having done to me. And what I take as one of the optimal possibilities of art. But this is all putting it in a kind of bullshit abstract way. But it's an interesting—toy. To play with. That idea.

INTERVIEWER: In the last five or six months you've been in Cuba, Czechoslovakia, Russia, and Poland. Has this helped to clarify your sense of the current world situation?

GINSBERG: Yeah, I no longer feel—I didn't ever feel that there was any answer in dogmatic Leninism-Marxism—but I feel very definitely now that there's no answer to my desires there. Nor do most of the people in those countries—in Russia or Poland or Cuba—really feel that either. It's sort of like a religious theory imposed from above and usually used to beat people on the head with. Nobody takes it seriously because it doesn't mean anything, it means different things in different countries anyway. The general idea of revolution against American idiocy is good, it's still sympathetic, and I guess it's a good thing like in Cuba, and obviously Vietnam. But what's gonna follow—the dogmatism that follows is a big drag. And everybody apologizes for the dogmatism by saying, well, it's an inevitable consequence of the struggle against American repression. And that may be true too.

But there's one thing I feel certain of, and that's that there's no human answer in communism or capitalism as it's practiced outside of the U.S. in any case. In other words, by hindsight the interior of America is not bad, at least for me, though it might be bad for a spade, but not too bad, creepy, but it's not impossible. But traveling in countries like Cuba and Vietnam I realize that the people that get the real evil side effects of America are there, in other words it really is like imperialism, in that sense. People in the United States all got money, they got cars, and everybody else *starves* on account of American foreign policy. Or is being bombed out, torn apart, and bleeding on the street, they get all their teeth bashed in, tear-gassed, or hot pokers up their ass, things that would be, you know, considered terrible in the United States. Except for Negroes.

So I don't know. I don't see any particular answer, and *this* month it seemed to me like actually an atomic war was inevitable on account of both sides were so dogmatic and frightened and had nowhere to go and didn't know what to do with themselves anymore except fight. Everybody too intransigent. Everybody too mean. I don't suppose it'll take place, but . . . Somebody has got to sit in the British Museum again like Marx and figure out a new system, a new blueprint. Another century has gone, technology has changed everything completely, so it's time for a new utopian system. Burroughs is almost working on it.

But one thing that's impressive is Blake's idea of Jerusalem, Jerusalemic Britain, which I think is *now* more and more valid. He, I guess, defined it. I'm still confused about Blake, I still haven't read him all through enough to understand what direction he was really pointing to. It seems to be the *naked human form divine,* seems to be Energy, it seems to be sexualization, or sexual liberation, which are the directions we all believe in. He also seems, however, to have some idea of imagination which I don't fully understand yet. That is it's something outside of the body, with a rejection of the body, and I don't quite understand that. A life after death even. Which I still haven't comprehended. There's a letter in the Fitzwilliam Museum, written several months before he died. He says, "My body is in turmoil and stress and decaying, *but* my ideas, my power of ideas and my imagination, are stronger than ever." And I find it hard to conceive of that. I think if I were lying in bed dying, with my body pained, I would just give up. I mean you know, because I don't think I could *exist* outside my body. But he apparently was able to. Williams didn't seem to be able to. In other words Williams's universe was tied up with his body. Blake's universe didn't seem to be tied up with his body. Real mysterious, like far other worlds and other seas, so to speak. Been puzzling over that today.

The Jerusalemic world of Blake seems to be Mercy-Pity-Peace. Which has human form. Mercy has a human face. So that's all clear.

INTERVIEWER: How about Blake's statement about the senses being the chief inlets of the soul in this age—I don't know what "this age" means; is there another one?

GINSBERG: What he says is interesting because there's the same thing in Hindu mythology, they speak of This Age as the Kali Yuga, the age of destruction, or an age so sunk in materialism. You'd find a similar formulation in Vico, like what is it, the Age of Gold running on to the Iron and then Stone, again. Well, the Hindus say that *this* is the Kali Age or Kali Yuga or Kali Cycle, and we are also so sunk in matter, the five senses are matter, sense, that they say there is absolutely no way out by intellect, by thought, by discipline, by practice, by sadhana, by jñāna-yoga, nor karma-yoga, that is doing good works, no way out through our own will or our own effort. The *only* way out that they generally now prescribe, generally in India at the moment, is through bhakti-yoga, which is Faith-Hope-Adoration-Worship, or like probably the equivalent of the Christian Sacred Heart, which I find a very lovely doctrine—that is to say, pure delight, the only way you can be saved is to sing. In other words, the only way to drag up, from the depths of this depression, to drag up your soul to its proper bliss, and understanding, is to give yourself, completely, to your heart's desire. The image will be determined by the heart's compass, by the compass of what the heart moves toward and desires. And then you get on your knees or on your lap or on your head and you sing and chant prayers and mantras, till you reach a state of ecstasy and understanding, and the bliss overflows out of your body. They say intellect, like Saint Thomas Aquinas, will never do it, because it's just like me getting all hung up on whether I could remember what happened before I was born—I mean you could get lost there very easily, and it has no relevance *anyway*, to the existent flower. Blake says something similar, like Energy, and Excess . . . leads to the palace of wisdom. The Hindu bhakti is like excess of devotion; you just, you know, give yourself all out to devotion.

Very oddly a lady saint Shri Matakrishnaji in Brindaban, whom I consulted about my spiritual problems, told me to take Blake for my guru. There's all kinds of different gurus, there can be living and nonliving gurus—apparently whoever initiates you, and I apparently was initiated by Blake in terms of at least having an ecstatic experience from him. So that when I got here to Cambridge I had to rush over to the Fitzwilliam Museum to find his misspellings in *Songs of Innocence.*

INTERVIEWER: What was the Blake experience you speak of?

GINSBERG: About 1945 I got interested in Supreme Reality with a capital S and R, and I wrote big long poems about a last voyage looking for Supreme Reality. Which was like a Dostoevskian or Thomas Wolfe–ian idealization or like Rimbaud—what was Rimbaud's term, new vision, was that it? Or Kerouac was talking about a new vision, verbally, and intuitively out of longing, but also out of a funny kind of tolerance of this universe. In 1948 in East Harlem in the summer I was living—this is like the Ancient Mariner, I've said this so many times: "stoppeth one of three. / 'By thy long grey beard . . .' " Hang an albatross around your neck . . . The one thing I felt at the time was that it would be a terrible horror, that in one or two decades I would be trying to explain to people that one day something like this happened to me! I even wrote a long poem saying, "I will grow old, a grey and groaning man, / and with each hour the same thought, and with each thought the same denial. / Will I spend my life in praise of the *idea* of God? / Time leaves no hope. We creep and wait. We wait and go alone." Psalm II—which I never published. So anyway—there I was in my bed in Harlem . . . jacking off. With my pants open, lying around on a bed by the windowsill, looking out into the cornices of Harlem and the sky above. And I had just come. And had perhaps hardly even wiped the come off my thighs, my trousers or whatever it was. As I often do, I had been jacking off while reading—I think it's probably a common phenomenon to be noticed among adolescents. Though I was a little older than an adolescent at the time. About twenty-two. There's a kind of interesting thing about, you know, distracting your attention while you jack off, that is, you know, reading a book or looking out of a window, or doing something else with the conscious mind which kind of makes it sexier.

So anyway, what I had been doing that week—I'd been in a very lonely solitary state, dark night of the soul sort of, reading St. John of the Cross, maybe on account of that everybody'd gone away that I knew, Burroughs was in Mexico, Jack was out in Long Island and relatively isolated, we didn't see each other, and I had been very close with them for several years. Huncke I think was in jail, or something. Anyway, there was nobody I knew. Mainly the thing was that I'd been making it with N.C., and finally I think I got a letter from him saying it was all off, no more, we shouldn't consider ourselves lovers any more on account of it just wouldn't work out. But previously we'd had an understanding that we—

Neal Cassady, I said N.C. but I suppose you can use his name—
we'd had a big tender lovers' understanding. But I guess it got too
much for him, partly because he was three thousand miles away
and he had six thousand girlfriends on the other side of the continent, who were keeping him busy, and then here was my lone cry
of despair from New York. So. I got a letter from him saying, Now,
Allen, we gotta move on to *new* territory. So I felt this is like a great
mortal blow to all of my tenderest hopes. And I figured I'd never
find any sort of psycho-spiritual sexo-cock jewel fulfillment in my
existence! So, I went into . . . like I felt cut off from what I'd ideal-
ized romantically. And I was also graduating from school and had
nowhere to go and the difficulty of getting a job. So finally there
was nothing for me to do except to eat vegetables and live in
Harlem. In an apartment I'd rented from someone. Sublet.

So, in that state therefore, of hopelessness, or dead end,
change of phase you know—growing up—and in an equilibrium
in any case, a psychic, a mental equilibrium of a kind, like of having no New Vision and no Supreme Reality and nothing but the
world in front of me, and of not knowing what to do with
that . . . there was a funny balance of tension, in every direction.
And just after I came, on this occasion, with a Blake book on my
lap—I wasn't even reading, my eye was idling over the page of

Neal Cassady shaving at Ginsberg's apartment, San Francisco, 1965.

© LARRY KEENAN

"Ah! Sun-flower," and it suddenly appeared—the poem I'd read a lot of times before, overfamiliar to the point where it didn't make any particular meaning except some sweet thing about flowers— and suddenly I realized that the poem was talking about *me*. "Ah, Sun-flower! weary of time, / Who countest the steps of the Sun, / Seeking after that sweet golden clime / Where the traveller's jour-ney is done: . . ." Now, I began understanding it, the poem while looking at it, and suddenly, simultaneously with understanding it, heard a very deep earthen grave voice in the room, which I imme-diately assumed, I didn't think twice, was Blake's voice; it wasn't any voice that I knew, though I had previously had a conception of a voice of rock, in a poem, some image like that—or maybe that came after this experience.

And my eye on the page, simultaneously the auditory hallu-cination, or whatever terminology here used, the apparitional voice, in the room, woke me further deep in my understanding of the poem, because the voice was so completely tender and beauti-fully . . . ancient. Like the voice of the Ancient of Days. But the pe-culiar quality of the voice was something unforgettable because it was like God had a human voice, with all the infinite tenderness and anciency and mortal gravity of a living Creator speaking to his son. "Where the Youth pined away with desire, / And the pale Virgin shrouded in snow / Arise from their graves, and aspire / Where my Sun-flower wishes to go." Meaning that there *was* a *place*, there was a sweet golden clime, and the *sweet golden*, what was that . . . and simultaneous to the voice there was also an emo-tion, risen in my soul in response to the voice, and a sudden *visual* realization of the same awesome phenomena. That is to say, look-ing out at the window, through the window at the sky, suddenly it seemed that I saw into the depths of the universe, by looking sim-ply into the ancient sky. The sky suddenly seemed very *ancient*. And this was the very ancient place that he was talking about, the sweet golden clime, I suddenly realized that *this* existence was *it!* And that I was born in order to experience up to this very moment that I was having this experience, to realize what this was all about—in other words that this was the moment that I was born for. This initiation. Or this vision or this consciousness, of being alive unto myself, alive myself unto the Creator. As the son of the Creator—who loved me, I realized, or who responded to my de-sire, say. It was the same desire both ways.

Anyway my first thought was this was what I was born for, and second thought, never forget—never forget, never renege, never deny. Never deny the voice—no, never *forget* it, don't get lost mentally wandering in other spirit worlds or American or job worlds or advertising worlds or war worlds or earth worlds. But the spirit of the universe was what I was born to realize. What I was speaking about visually was, immediately, that the cornices in the old tenement building in Harlem across the backyard court had been carved very finely in 1890 or 1910. And were like the solidification of a great deal of intelligence and care and love also. So that I began noticing in every corner where I looked evidences of a living hand, even in the bricks, in the arrangement of each brick. Some hand placed them there—that some hand had placed the whole universe in front of me. That some hand had placed the sky. No, that's exaggerating—not that some hand had placed the sky but that the sky was the living blue hand itself. Or that God was in front of my eyes—existence itself was God. Well, the formulations are like that—I didn't formulate it in exactly those terms, what I was seeing was a visionary thing, it was a lightness in my body . . . my body suddenly felt *light*, and a sense of cosmic consciousness, vibrations, understanding, awe, and wonder and surprise. And it was a sudden awakening into a totally deeper real universe than I'd been existing in. So, I'm trying to avoid generalizations about that sudden deeper real universe and keep it strictly to observations of phenomenal data, or a voice with a certain sound, the appearance of cornices, the appearance of the sky say, of the great blue hand, the living hand—to keep to images.

But anyway—the same . . . *petite sensation* recurred several minutes later, with the same voice, while reading the poem "The Sick Rose." This time it was a slightly different sense-depth-mystic impression. Because "The Sick Rose"—you know I can't interpret the poem now, but it had a meaning—I mean I can interpret it on a verbal level, the sick rose is myself, or self, or the living body, sick because the mind, which is the worm "That flies in the night, / In the howling storm," or Urizen, reason; Blake's character might be the one that's entered the body and is destroying it, or let us say death, the worm as being death, the natural process of death, some kind of mystical being of its own trying to come in and devour the body, the rose. Blake's drawing for it is complicated, it's a big drooping rose, drooping because it's dying, and there's a worm in it, and the worm is wrapped around a little sprite that's trying to get out of the mouth of the rose.

But anyway, I experienced "The Sick Rose," with the voice of Blake reading it, as something that applied to the whole universe, like hearing the doom of the whole universe, and at the same time the inevitable beauty of doom. I can't remember now, except it was very beautiful and very awesome. But a little of it slightly scary, having to do with the knowledge of death—my death and also the death of being itself, and that was the great pain. So, like a prophecy, not only in human terms but a prophecy as if Blake had penetrated the very secret core of the *entire* universe and had come forth with some little magic formula statement in rhyme and rhythm that, if properly heard in the inner inner ear, would deliver you beyond the universe.

So then, the other poem that brought this on in the same day was "The Little Girl Lost," where there was a repeated refrain,

> *Do father, mother weep,*
> *Where can Lyca sleep?*
>
> . . . . .
>
> *How can Lyca sleep*
> *If her mother weep?*
>
> *"If her heart does ache*
> *Then let Lyca wake;*
> *If my mother sleep,*
> *Lyca shall not weep."*

It's that hypnotic thing—and I suddenly realized that Lyca was me, or Lyca was the self; father, mother seeking Lyca, was God seeking, Father, the Creator; and "If her heart does ache / Then let Lyca wake"—wake to what? *Wake* meaning wake to the same awakeness I was just talking about—of existence in the entire universe. The total consciousness then, of the complete universe. Which is what Blake was talking about. In other words a breakthrough from ordinary habitual quotidian consciousness into consciousness that was really seeing all of heaven in a flower. Or what was it, eternity in a flower . . . heaven in a grain of sand. As I was seeing heaven in the cornice of the building. By heaven here I mean this imprint or concretization or living form, of an intelligent hand—the work of an intelligent hand, which still had the intelligence molded into it. The gargoyles on the Harlem cornices. What was interesting about the cornice was that there's cornices like that on every building, but I never noticed them before. And I never realized that they meant spiritual labor, to anyone— that somebody had labored to make a curve in a piece of tin—to make a cornucopia out of a piece of industrial tin. Not only that man, the workman, the artisan, but the architect had thought of it, the builder had paid for it, the smelter had *smelt* it, the miner had dug it up out of the earth, the earth had gone through eons preparing it. So the little molecules had slumbered for . . . for *kalpas*. So out of *all* of these *kalpas* it all got together in a great succession of impulses, to be frozen finally in that one form of a cornucopia cornice on the building front. And God knows how many people made the moon. Or what spirits labored . . . to set fire to the sun. As Blake says, "When I look in the sun I don't see the rising sun I see a band of angels singing holy, holy, holy." Well, his perception of the field of the sun is different from that of a man who just sees the sun sun, without any emotional relationship to it.

But then, there was a point later in the week when the intermittent flashes of the same . . . bliss—because the experience was quite blissful—came back. In a sense all this is described in "The Lion for Real" by anecdotes of different experiences—actually it was a very difficult time, which I won't go into here. Because suddenly I thought, also simultaneously, *Ooh, I'm going mad!* That's described in the line in "Howl," *who thought they were* only *mad when Baltimore gleamed in supernatural ecstasy*—"who thought they were *only* mad . . ." If it were only that easy! In other words it'd be a lot easier if you just were crazy, instead of—then you could chalk it up, "Well I'm nutty"—but on the other hand what if it's all true and you're *born* into this great cosmic universe in which you're a spirit angel—terrible fucking situation to be confronted with. It's like being woken up one morning by Joseph K's captors. Actually what I think I did was there was a couple of girls living next door and I crawled out on the fire escape and tapped on their window and said, "I've seen God!" and they *banged* the window shut. Oh, what tales I could have told them if they'd let me in! Because I was in a very exalted state of mind and the consciousness was still with me—I remember I immediately rushed to Plato and read some great image in the *Phaedrus* about horses flying through the sky, and rushed over to St. John and started reading fragments of *con un no saber sabiendo . . . que me quede balbuciendo,* and rushed to the other part of the bookshelf and picked up Plotinus about The Alone—the Plotinus I found more difficult to interpret.

But I *immediately* doubled my thinking process, quadrupled, and I was able to read almost any text and see all sorts of divine significance in it. And I think that week or that month I had to take an examination in John Stuart Mill. And instead of writing about his ideas I got completely hung up on his experience of reading— was it Wordsworth? Apparently the thing that got him back was an experience of nature that he received keyed off by reading

Wordsworth, on "sense sublime" or something. That's a very good description, that sense sublime of something far more deeply interfused, whose dwelling is the light of setting suns, and the round ocean, and the . . . the *living* air, did he say? The living air—see just that hand again—*and* in the heart of man. So I think this experience is characteristic of all high poetry. I mean that's the way I began seeing poetry as the communication of the particular experience—not just any experience but *this* experience.

INTERVIEWER: Have you had anything like this experience again?

GINSBERG: Yeah . . . I'm not finished with this period. Then, in my room, I didn't know what to do. But I wanted to bring it up, so I began experimenting with it, without Blake. And I think it was one day in my kitchen—I had an old-fashioned kitchen with a sink with a tub in it with a board over the top—I started moving around and sort of shaking with my body and dancing up and down on the floor and saying, "Dance! dance! dance! dance! spirit! spirit! spirit! dance!" and suddenly I felt like Faust, calling up the devil. And then it started coming over me, this big . . . creepy feeling, cryptozoid or monozoidal, so I got all scared and quit.

Then I was walking around Columbia and I went in the Columbia bookstore and was reading Blake again, leafing over a book of Blake, I think it was "The Human Abstract": "Pity would be no more . . ." And suddenly it came over me in the bookstore again, and I was in the eternal place *once more*, and I looked around at everybody's faces, and I saw all these wild animals! Because there was a bookstore clerk there who I hadn't paid much attention to, he was just a familiar fixture in the bookstore scene and everybody went in the bookstore every day like me, because downstairs there was a café and upstairs there were all these clerks that we were all familiar with—this guy had a very *long* face, you know some people look like giraffes. So he looked kind of giraffish. He had a kind of a long face with a long nose. I don't know what kind of sex life he had, but he must have had something. But anyway I looked in his face and I suddenly saw like a great tormented soul—and he had just been somebody whom I'd regarded as perhaps a not particularly beautiful or sexy character, or lovely face, but you know someone familiar, and perhaps a pleading cousin in the universe. But all of a sudden I realized that *he* knew also, just like I knew. And that everybody in the bookstore knew, and that they were all hiding it! They all had the consciousness, it was like a great *un*conscious that was running between all of us that everybody *was* completely conscious, but that the fixed expressions that people have, the habitual expressions, the manners, the mode of talk, are all masks hiding this consciousness. Because almost at that moment it seemed that it would be too terrible if we communicated to each other on a level of total consciousness and awareness each of the other—like it would be too terrible, it would be the end of the bookstore, it would be the end of civ—not civilization, but in other words the position that everybody was in was *ridiculous,* everybody running around peddling books to each other. Here in the universe! Passing money over the counter, wrapping books in bags and guarding the door, you know, stealing books, and the people sitting up making accountings on the upper floor there, and people worrying about their exams walking through the bookstore, and all the millions of thoughts the people had—you know, that I'm worrying about—whether they're going to get laid or whether anybody loves them, about their mothers dying of cancer or, you know, the complete death awareness that everybody has continuously with them all the time—all of a sudden revealed to me at once in the faces of the people, and they all looked like horrible grotesque masks, grotesque because *hiding* the knowledge from each other. Having a habitual conduct and forms to prescribe, forms to fulfill. Roles to play. But the main insight I had at that time was that everybody knew. Everybody knew completely everything. Knew completely everything in the terms which I was talking about.

INTERVIEWER: Do you still think they know?

GINSBERG: I'm more sure of it now. Sure. All you have to do is try and make somebody. You realize that they knew all along you were trying to make them. But until that moment you never break through to communication on the subject.

INTERVIEWER: Why not?

GINSBERG: Well, fear of rejection. The twisted faces of all those people, the faces were twisted by rejection. And hatred of self, finally. The internalization of that rejection. And finally disbelief in that shining self. Disbelief in that infinite self. Partly because the particular . . . partly because the *awareness* that we all carry is too often painful, because the experience of rejection and lacklove and cold war—I mean the whole cold war is the imposition of a vast mental barrier on everybody, a vast antinatural psyche. A hardening, a shutting off of the perception of desire and tenderness which everybody *knows* and which is the very structure of . . . the atom! Structure of the human body and organism. That desire built in. Blocked. "Where the Youth pined away with desire, / And the pale Virgin shrouded in snow." Or as Blake says, "And mark in every face I meet / Marks of weakness, marks of woe." So what I was thinking in the bookstore was the marks of weakness, marks of woe. Which you can just look around and look at anybody's face right next to you now always—you can see it in the way the mouth is pursed, you can see it in the way the eyes blink, you can see it in the way the gaze is fixed down at the matches. It's the self-consciousness which is a substitute for communication with the outside. This consciousness pushed back into the self and thinking of how it will hold its face and eyes and hands in order to make a mask to hide the flow that is going on. Which it's aware of, which everybody is aware of really! So let's say, shyness. Fear. Fear of like total feeling, really, total being, is what it is.

So the problem then was, having attained realization, how to safely manifest it and communicate it. Of course there was the old Zen thing, when the sixth patriarch handed down the little symbolic oddments and ornaments and books and bowls, stained bowls too . . . when the *fifth* patriarch handed them down to the sixth patriarch he told him to hide them and don't tell anybody you're patriarch because it's dangerous, they'll kill you. So there was that immediate danger. It's taken me all these years to manifest it and work it out in a way that's materially communicable to people. Without scaring them or me. Also movements of history and breaking down the civilization. To break down everybody's masks and roles sufficiently so that everybody has to face the universe *and* the possibility of the sick rose coming true and the atom bomb. So it was an immediate messianic thing. Which seems to be becoming more and more justified. And more and more reasonable in terms of the existence that we're living.

So. Next time it happened was about a week later walking along in the evening on a circular path around what's now, I guess, the garden or field in the middle of Columbia University, by the library. I started invoking the spirit, consciously trying to get another depth perception of cosmos. And suddenly it began occurring again, like a sort of breakthrough again, but this time— this was the last time in that period—it was the same depth of consciousness or the same cosmical awareness but suddenly it was not blissful at all but it was *frightening*. Some like real serpent-fear entering the sky. The sky was not a blue hand anymore but like a hand of death coming down on me—some really scary presence, it was almost as if I saw God again except God was the Devil. The consciousness itself was *so* vast, much more vast than any idea of it I'd had or any experience I'd had, that it was not even human anymore—and was in a sense a threat, because I was going to die into that inhuman ultimately. I don't know *what* the score was there—I was too cowardly to pursue it. To attend and experience completely the Gates of Wrath—there's a poem of Blake's that deals with that, "To find the Western Path / Right through the Gates of Wrath." But I didn't urge my way there, I shut it all off. And got scared, and thought, I've gone too far.

INTERVIEWER: Was your use of drugs an extension of this experience?

GINSBERG: Well, since I took a vow that this was the area of, that this was my existence that I was placed into, drugs were obviously a technique for experimenting with consciousness, to get different areas and different levels and different similarities and different reverberations of the same vision. Marijuana has some of it in it, that awe, the cosmic awe that you get sometimes on pot. There are certain moments under laughing gas and ether that the consciousness does intersect with something similar—for me—to my Blake visions. The gas drugs were apparently interesting too to the Lake poets, because there were a lot of experiments done with Sir Humphry Davy in his Pneumatic Institute. I think Coleridge and Southey and other people used to go, and De Quincey. But serious people. I think there hasn't been very much written about that period. *What went on* in the Humphry Davy household on Saturday midnight when Coleridge arrived by foot, through the forest, by the lakes? Then, there are certain states you get into with opium, and heroin, of almost disembodied awareness, looking down back at the Earth from a place after you're dead. Well, it's not the same, but it's an interesting state, and a useful one. It's a normal state also, I mean it's a holy state of some sort. At times. Then, mainly, of course, with the hallucinogens, you get some states of consciousness which subjectively seem to be cosmic-ecstatic, or cosmic-demonic. Our version of expanded consciousness is as much as *un*conscious information—awareness comes up to the surface. Lysergic acid, peyote, mescaline, psilocybin, ayahuasca. But I can't stand them anymore, because something happened to me with them very similar to the Blake visions. After about thirty times, thirty-five times, I began getting monster vibrations again. So I couldn't go any further. I may later on again, if I feel more reassurance.*

However I did get a lot out of them, mainly like emotional understanding, understanding the female principle in a way—women, more sense of the softness and more desire for women. Desire for children also.

INTERVIEWER: Anything interesting about the actual experience, say with hallucinogens?

GINSBERG: What I do get is, say if I was in an apartment high on mescaline, I felt as if the apartment and myself were not merely on East Fifth Street but were in the middle of all space-time. If I close my eyes on hallucinogens, I get a vision of great scaly dragons in outer space, they're winding slowly and eating their own tails. Sometimes my skin and all the room seem sparkling with scales, and it's all made out of serpent stuff. And as if the whole illusion of life were made of reptile dream.

---

* Between occasion of interview with Thomas Clark June 1965 and publication May 1966 more reassurance came. I tried small doses of LSD twice in secluded tree and ocean cliff haven at Big Sur. No monster vibration, no snake universe hallucinations. Many tiny jeweled violet flowers along the path of a living brook that looked like Blake's illustration for a canal in grassy Eden: huge Pacific watery shore, Orlovsky dancing naked like Shiva long-haired before giant green waves, titanic cliffs that Wordsworth mentioned in his own Sublime, great yellow sun veiled with mist hanging over the plant's oceanic horizon. No harm. President Johnson that day went into the Valley of Shadow operating room because of his gall bladder & Berkeley's Vietnam Day Committee was preparing anxious manifestoes for our march toward Oakland police and Hell's Angels. Realizing that more vile words from me would send out physical vibrations into the atmosphere that might curse poor Johnson's flesh and further unbalance his soul, I knelt on the sand surrounded by masses of green bulb-headed Kelp vegetable-snake undersea beings washed up by last night's tempest, and prayed for the President's tranquil health. Since there has been so much legislative miscomprehension of the LSD boon I regret that my unedited ambivalence in Thomas Clark's tape transcript interview was published wanting this footnote.

Your obedient servant
Allen Ginsberg, *aetat* 40
June 2, 1966

Mandala also. I use the mandala in an LSD poem. The associations I've had during times that I was high are usually referred to or built in some image or other to one of the other poems written on drugs. Or after drugs—like in "Magic Psalm" on lysergic acid. Or mescaline. There's a long passage about a mandala in the LSD poem. There is a good situation since I was high and I was looking at a mandala—before I got high I asked the doctor that was giving it to me at Stanford to prepare me a set of mandalas to look at, to borrow some from Professor Spiegelberg, who was an expert. So we had some Sikkimese elephant mandalas there. I simply describe those in the poem—what they look like while I was high.

So—summing up then—drugs were useful for exploring perception, sense perception, and exploring different possibilities and modes of consciousness, and exploring the different versions of *petites sensations*, and useful then for composing, sometimes, while under the influence. Part II of "Howl" was written under the influence of peyote, composed during peyote vision. In San Francisco— "Moloch," "Kaddish" was written with amphetamine injections. An injection of amphetamine plus a little bit of morphine, plus some dexedrine later on to keep me going, because it was all in one long sitting. From a Saturday morn to a Sunday night. The amphetamine gives a peculiar metaphysical tinge to things also. Space-outs. It doesn't interfere too much there because I wasn't habituated to it, I was just taking it that one weekend. It didn't interfere too much with the emotional charge that comes through.

INTERVIEWER: Was there any relation to this in your trip to Asia?

GINSBERG: Well, the Asian experience kind of got me out of the corner I painted myself in with drugs. That corner being an inhuman corner in the sense that I figured I was expanding my consciousness and I had to go through with it but at the same time I was confronting this serpent monster, so I was getting in a real terrible situation. It finally would get so if I'd take the drugs I'd start vomiting. But I felt that I was duly bound and obliged for the sake of consciousness expansion, and this insight, and breaking down my identity, and seeking more direct contact with primate sensation, nature, to continue. So when I went to India, all the way through India, I was babbling about that to all the holy men I could find. I wanted to find out if they had any suggestions. And they all did, and they were all good ones. First one I saw was Martin Buber, who was interested. In Jerusalem, Peter and I went in to see him— we called him up and made a date and had a long conversation.

He had a beautiful white beard and was friendly; his nature was slightly austere but benevolent. Peter asked him what kind of visions he'd had and he described some he'd had in bed when he was younger. But he said he was *not* any longer interested in visions like that. The kind of visions he came up with were more like spiritualistic table rappings. Ghosts coming into the room through his window, rather than big, beautiful seraphic Blake angels hitting him on the head. I was thinking like loss of identity and confrontation with nonhuman universe as the main problem, and in a sense whether or not man had to evolve and change, and perhaps become nonhuman too. Melt into the universe, let us say—to put it awkwardly and inaccurately. Buber said that he was interested in man-to-man relationships, human-to-human—that he thought it was a human universe that we were destined to inhabit. And so therefore human relationships rather than relations between the human and the nonhuman. Which was what I was thinking that I had to go into. And he said, "Mark my word, young man, in two years you will realize that I was right." He was right—in two years I marked his words. Two years is 1963—I saw him in 1961. I don't know if he said two years—but he said "in years to come." This was like a real terrific classical wise man's "Mark my words young man, in several years you will realize that what I said was true!" Exclamation point.

Then there was Swami Shivananda, in Rishikish in India. He said, "Your own heart is your guru." Which I thought was very sweet, and very reassuring. That is the sweetness of it I felt—in my heart. And suddenly realized it was the heart that I was seeking. In other words it wasn't consciousness, it wasn't *petites sensations*, sensation defined as expansion of mental consciousness to include more data—as I was pursuing that line of thought, pursuing Burroughs's cut-up thing—the area that I was seeking was heart rather than mind. In other words, in mind, through mind or imagination—this is where I get confused with Blake now—in mind one can construct all sorts of universes, one can construct model universes in dream and imagination, and with lysergic acid you can enter into alternative universes and with the speed of light; and with nitrous oxide you can experience several million universes in rapid succession. You can experience a whole gamut of possibilities of universes, including the final possibility that there is none. And then you go unconscious—which is exactly what happens with gas when you go unconscious. You see that the universe is going to disappear with your consciousness, that it was all dependent on your consciousness.

Anyway a whole series of India holy men pointed back to the body—getting *in* the body rather than getting out of the human form. But living in and inhabiting the human form. Which then goes back to Blake again, the human form divine. Is this clear? In other words the psychic problem that I had found myself in was that for various reasons it had seemed to me at one time or another that the best thing to do was to drop dead. Or not be afraid of death but go into death. Go into the nonhuman, go into the cosmic, so to speak; that God was death, and if I wanted to attain God I had to die. Which *may* still be true. So I thought that what I was put up to was to therefore break out of my body, if I wanted to attain complete consciousness.

So now the next step was that the gurus one after another said, Live in the body: this is the form that you're born for. That's too long a narration to go into. Too many holy men and too many different conversations and they all have a little *key* thing going. But it all winds up in the train in Japan, then a year later, the poem "The Change," where all of a sudden I renounce drugs, I don't renounce drugs but I suddenly didn't want to be *dominated* by that nonhuman anymore, or even be dominated by the moral obligation to enlarge my consciousness anymore. Or do anything anymore except *be* my heart—which just desired to be and be alive now. I had a very strange ecstatic experience then and there, once I had sort of gotten that burden off my back, because I was suddenly free to love myself again, and therefore love the people around me, in the form that they already were. And love myself in my own form as I am. And look around at the other people and so it was *again* the same thing like in the bookstore. Except this time I was completely in my body and had no more mysterious obligations. And nothing more to fulfill, except to be willing to die when I am dying, whenever that be. And be willing to live as a human in this form now. So I started weeping, it was such a happy moment. Fortunately I was able to write then, too, "So that I do live I will die"—rather than be cosmic consciousness, immortality, Ancient of Days, perpetual consciousness existing forever.

Then when I got to Vancouver, Olson was saying "I am one with my skin." It *seemed* to me at the time when I got back to Vancouver that everybody had been precipitated back into their bodies at the same time. It seemed that's what Creeley had *been* talking about all along. The *place*—the terminology he used, the *place* we are. Meaning this place, here. And trying to like, be real in the real place . . . to be aware of the place where he is. Because I'd always thought that that meant that he was cutting off from divine imagination. But what that meant for him was that this place would be everything that one would refer to as divine, if one were really here. So that Vancouver seems a very odd moment, at least for me—because I came back in a sense completely bankrupt. My energies of the last . . . oh, 1948 to 1963, all completely washed up. On the train in Kyoto having renounced Blake, renounced visions—renounced *Blake!*—too. There was a cycle that began with the Blake vision which ended on the train in Kyoto when I realized that to attain the depth of consciousness that I was seeking when I was talking about the Blake vision, that in order to attain it I had to cut myself off from the Blake vision and renounce it. Otherwise I'd be hung up on a memory of an experience. Which is not the actual awareness of now, now. In order to get back to now, in order to get back to the total awareness of now and contact, sense perception contact with what was going on around me, or direct vision of the moment, now I'd have to give up this continual churning thought process of yearning back to a visionary state. It's all very complicated. And idiotic.

INTERVIEWER: I think you said earlier that "Howl" being a lyric poem, and "Kaddish" basically a narrative, that you now have a sense of wanting to do an epic. . . . Do you have a plan like this?

GINSBERG: Yeah, but it's just . . . ideas that I've been carrying around for a long time. One thing which I'd like to do sooner or later is write a long poem which is a narrative and description of all the visions I've ever had, sort of like the *Vita Nuova*. And travels, now. And another idea I had was to write a big long poem about everybody I ever fucked or slept with. Like sex . . . a love poem. A long love poem, involving all the innumerable lays of a lifetime. The epic is not that, though. The epic would be a poem including history, as it's defined. So that would be one about present-day politics, using the methods of the Blake *French Revolution*. I got a lot written. Narrative was "Kaddish." Epic—there has to be totally different organization, it might be simple free association on political themes—in fact I think an epic poem including history, at this stage. I've got a lot of it written, but it would have to be Burroughs's sort of epic, in other words it would have to be *dis*sociated thought stream which includes politics and history. I don't think you could do it in narrative form, I mean what would you be narrating, the history of the Korean War or something?

INTERVIEWER: Something like Pound's epic?

GINSBERG: No, because Pound seems to me to be over a course of years fabricating out of his reading and out of the museum of literature; whereas the thing would be to take all of contemporary history, newspaper headlines and all the pop art of Stalinism and Hitler and Johnson and Kennedy and Vietnam and Congo and Lumumba and the South and Sacco and Vanzetti—whatever floated into one's personal field of consciousness and contact. And then to compose like a basket—like weave a basket, basket-weaving out of those materials. Since obviously nobody has any idea where it's all going or how it's going to end unless you have some vision to deal with. It would have to be done by a process of association, I guess.

INTERVIEWER: What's happening in poetry now?

GINSBERG: I don't know yet. Despite all confusion to the contrary, now that time's passed, I think the best poet in the United States is Kerouac still. Given twenty years to settle through. The main reason is that he's the most free and the most spontaneous. Has the greatest range of association and imagery in his poetry. Also in *Mexico City Blues* the sublime as subject matter. And in other words the greatest facility at what might be called projective verse. If you want to give it a name. I think that he's stupidly underrated by almost everybody except for a few people who are aware how beautiful his composition is—like Snyder or Creeley or people who have a taste for his tongue, for his line. But it takes one to know one.

INTERVIEWER: You don't mean Kerouac's prose?

GINSBERG: No, I'm talking about just a pure poet. The verse poetry, the *Mexico City Blues* and a lot of other manuscripts I've seen. In addition he has the one sign of being a great poet, which is he's the only one in the United States who knows how to write haiku. The only one who's written any good haiku. And everybody's been writing haiku. There are all these *dreary* haiku written by people who think for weeks trying to write a haiku, and finally come up with some dull little thing or something. Whereas Kerouac thinks in haiku, every time he writes anything—talks that way and thinks that way. So it's just natural for him. It's something Snyder noticed. Snyder has to labor for years in a Zen monastery to produce one haiku about shitting off a log! And actually does get one or two good ones. Snyder was always astounded by Kerouac's facility . . . at noticing winter flies dying of old age in his medicine chest. Medicine cabinet. "In my medicine cabinet / the winter flies / died of old age." He's never published them actually—he's published them on a record, with Zoot Sims and Al Cohn, it's a very beautiful collection of them. Those are as far as I can see the only real American haiku.

So the haiku is the most difficult test. He's the only *master* of the haiku. Aside from a longer style. Of course the distinctions between prose and poetry are broken down anyway. So much that I was saying like a long page of oceanic Kerouac is sometimes as sublime as epic line. It's there that also I think he went further into the existential thing of writing conceived of as an irreversible action or statement, that's unrevisable and unchangeable once it's made. I remember I was thinking, yesterday in fact, there was a time that I was absolutely astounded because Kerouac told me that in the future literature would consist of what people actually wrote rather than what they tried to deceive other people into thinking they wrote, when they revised it later on. And I saw opening up this whole universe where people wouldn't be able to lie anymore! They wouldn't be able to *correct* themselves any longer. They wouldn't be able to hide what they said. And he was willing to go all the way into that, the first pilgrim into that newfound land.

INTERVIEWER: What about other poets?

GINSBERG: I think Corso has a great inventive genius. And also amongst the greatest *shrewdness*—like Keats or something. I like Lamantia's nervous wildness. Almost anything he writes I find interesting—for one thing he's always registering the forward march of the soul, in exploration; spiritual exploration is always there. And also chronologically following his work is always exciting. Whalen and Snyder are both very wise and very reliable. Whalen I don't *understand* so well. I did, though, earlier—but I have to sit down and study his work, again. Sometimes he seems sloppy—but then later on it always seems right.

McClure has tremendous energy, and seems like some sort of a . . . seraph is not the word . . . not herald either but a . . . not demon either. Seraph, I guess it is. He's always moving—see when I came around to say getting in my skin, there I found McClure sitting around talking about being a mammal! So I suddenly realized he was way ahead of me. And Wieners . . . I always *weep* with him. Luminous, luminous. They're all old poets, everybody knows about those poets. Burroughs is a poet too, really. In the sense that a page of his prose is as *dense* with imagery as anything in St. Perse or Rimbaud, now. And it has also great repeated rhythms. Recurrent, recurrent rhythms, even rhyme occasionally! What else . . . Creeley's very stable, solid. I get more and more to like certain poems of his that I didn't understand at first. Like "The Door," which completely baffled me because I didn't understand that he was talking about the same heterosexual problem that I was worried about. Olson, since he said *I feel one with my skin*. First thing of Olson's that I liked was "The Death of Europe" and then some of his later Maximus material is nice. And Dorn has a kind of long, *real* spare, manly, political thing—but his great quality inside also is tenderness—*Oh the graves not yet cut*. I also like that whole line of what's happening with Ashbery and O'Hara and Koch, the area that they're going for, too. Ashbery—I was listening to him read "The Skaters," and it sounded as inventive and exquisite, in all its parts, as *The Rape of the Lock*.

INTERVIEWER: Do you feel you're in command when you're writing?

GINSBERG: Sometimes I feel in command when I'm writing. When I'm in the heat of some truthful tears, yes. Then, complete command. Other times—most of the time not. Just diddling away, woodcarving, getting a pretty shape; like most of my poetry. There's only a few times when I reach a state of complete command. Probably a piece of "Howl," a piece of "Kaddish," and a piece of "The Change." And one or two moments of other poems.

INTERVIEWER: By *command* do you mean a sense of the whole poem as it's going, rather than parts?

GINSBERG: No—a sense of being self-prophetic master of the universe.

—THOMAS CLARK
1966

Robert White Creeley

was born in Arlington, Massachusetts, in 1926. He entered Harvard University in 1943, leaving after one year to drive an ambulance in the India-Burma theater of World War II. He returned to Harvard in 1945 where he helped to edit *Wake, no. 5,* a special e. e. cummings issue in which Creeley's first published poem, "Return," appeared. After dropping out of Harvard in the last semester of his senior year, he befriended Cid Corman. Together, they launched *Origin,* a literary magazine that showcased Creeley's poetry throughout the 1950s. During those years, Creeley taught at Black Mountain College in North Carolina and was a founding editor of its innovative literary journal, the *Black Mountain Review.* With poets Charles Olson and Robert Duncan, Creeley inaugurated the Black Mountain school of poetry that heralded Creeley's mantra, "Form is never more than an extension of content." In 1958, Black Mountain College awarded him a bachelor's degree.

In 1960 he received his M.A. from the University of New Mexico and taught there from 1961 to 1969. He has been affiliated with universities ever since, including the University of British Columbia and San Francisco State College. At SUNY Buffalo, he was Professor of English from 1967 to 1978.

In 1962, Creeley's second volume of poetry, *For Love: Poems 1950–1960,* was published to wide acclaim. Since then, he has received numerous awards for his work, including two Guggenheim Fellowships, two Fulbright Fellowships, the Poetry Society of America's Shelley Memorial Award, and the Robert Frost Medal. He served as New York State Poet from 1989 to 1991 and in 1995 received The American Award for his collection of poems, *Echoes.* Other works include *Le Fou, The Immoral Proposition, The Kind of Act Of, All That Is Lovely in Men, IF You, Words, A Form of Women, The Gold Diggers,* and *The Island.*

Creeley is a member of the American Academy of Arts and Letters. He currently resides in Buffalo.

© GERARD MALANGA

This is a composite interview. It combines two separate discussions with Robert Creeley—held at different times, and conducted by two different interviewers: Linda Wagner and Lewis MacAdams, Jr. The questions specifically devoted to the poet's craft were put to Robert Creeley by Linda Wagner. She refers to the exchange as a colloquy—a term that Creeley insisted on because (as he put it) her questions were "active in their own assumptions. . . . We are talking together." She began the exchange at the 1963 Vancouver poetry sessions, continued it at Creeley's 1964 Bowling Green, Ohio, reading, and finished it in August 1965, at the poet's home in New Mexico.

MacAdams interviewed Creeley in the spring of 1968 in Eden, New York, a few miles from Buffalo where Creeley once spent the winter months teaching. "The first session was a failure," MacAdams said of the interview. "Both of us were tired, and although Creeley was polite and voluble, I asked a bunch of dumb questions. The interview ended in the

*dark, everybody drunk and slightly morose. Then we adjourned to his
driveway to shovel snow. We tried again two weeks later. The snow had
stopped, the sun was out, and the Creeley house was full of his friends,
among them the poets Allen Ginsberg, Robert Duncan, and Robin
Blaser. After breakfast the two of us went upstairs to his study, a big
sunny room looking out across a long wooded valley to Lake Erie. The
study had once been a nursery; the framed photographs of Charles Olson
and John Wieners and of Creeley's wife, Bobbie, are set off by pink wall-
paper, covered with horses and maids."*

•   •   •

INTERVIEWER: What do you think was the first impulse that set
you on the course to being a writer?

CREELEY: As a kid I used to be fascinated by people who, like they
say, "traveled light." My father died when I was very young, but
there were things of his left in the house which my mother kept as
evidences of his life: his bag, for example, his surgical instruments, even his prescription pads. These things were not only
relics of his person, but what was interesting to me was that this
instrumentation was peculiarly contained in this thing that he
could carry in his hand. The doctor's "bag." One thinks of the
idiom which is so current now, "bag," to be in this or that "bag."
The doctor's bag was an absolutely explicit instance of something
you carry with you and work out of. As a kid, growing up without
a father, I was always interested in men who came to the house
with specific instrumentation of that sort—carpenters, repair-
men—and I was fascinated by the idea that you could travel in the
world that way with all that you needed in your hands . . . a
Johnny Appleseed. All of this comes back to me when I find myself talking to people about writing. The scene is always this:
"What a great thing! To be a writer! Words are something you can
carry in your head. You can really 'travel light.' "

INTERVIEWER: You speak a great deal about the poet's locale, his
place, in your work. Is this a geographic term, or are you thinking
of an inner sense of being?

CREELEY: I'm really speaking of my own sense of place. Where
"the heart finds rest," as Robert Duncan would say. I mean that
place where one is open, where a sense of defensiveness or inse-

curity and all the other complexes of response to place can be finally dropped. Where one feels an intimate association with the ground under foot. Now that's obviously an idealization—or at least to hope for such a place may well be an idealization—but there are some places where one feels the possibility more intensely than others. I, for example, feel much more comfortable in a small town. I've always felt so, I think, because I grew up in one in New England. I like that spill of life all around, like the spring you get in New England with that crazy water, the trickles of water everyplace, the moisture, the shyness, and the particularity of things like blue jays. I like the rhythms of seasons, and I like the rhythms of a kind of relation to ground that's evident in, say, farmers; and I like time's accumulations of persons. I loved aspects of Spain in that way, and I frankly have the same sense of where I now am living in New Mexico. I can look out the window up into hills seven miles from where the Sandia Cave is located, perhaps the oldest evidence of man's occupation of this hemisphere. I think it dates back to either 15,000 or 20,000 B.C. and it's still there. And again I'm offered a scale, with mountains to the southeast, the Rio Grande coming through below us to the west, and then that wild range of mesa off to the west. This is a very basic place to live. The dimensions are of such size and of such curious eternity that they embarrass any assumption that man is the totality of all that is significant in life. The area offers a measure of persons that I find very relieving and much more securing to my nature than would be, let's say, the accumulations of men's intentions and exertions in New York City. So locale is both a geographic term and the inner sense of being.

INTERVIEWER: Do you credit any one writer—ancestor or contemporary—with a strong influence on your poetry?

CREELEY: I think Williams gave me the largest example. But equally I can't at all ignore Charles Olson's very insistent influence upon me both in early times and now. And Louis Zukofsky's. The first person who introduced me to writing as a craft, who even spoke of it as a craft, was Ezra Pound. I think it was my twentieth birthday that my brother-in-law took me down to a local bookstore in Cambridge and said, "What would you like? Would you like to get some books?" I bought *Make It New* and that book was a revelation to me. Pound spoke of writing from the point of view of what writing itself was, not what it was "about." Not what symbolism or structure had led to, but how a man might address himself to the *act* of writing. And that was the most moving and deepest understanding I think I have ever gained. So that Pound was very important to my craft, no matter how much I may have subsequently embarrassed him by my own work. So many, many people—Robert Duncan, Allen Ginsberg, Denise Levertov, Paul Blackburn, Ed Dorn. I could equally say Charlie Parker—in his uses of silence, in his rhythmic structure. His music was influential at one point. So that I can't make a hierarchy of persons.

INTERVIEWER: How about communicating with other writers when you were beginning?

CREELEY: I started writing to Ezra Pound and William Carlos Williams about a magazine I was involved in. That's how I got up courage to write them. I would have been too shy just to write them and say, "I think you are a great man." To have business with them gave me reason. Pound wrote specifically, but he tended to write injunctions—"You do this. You do that. Read this. Read that."

INTERVIEWER: Did you do everything he said?

CREELEY: I tried to. I couldn't do it all. He would send books at times which would be useful. *The History of Money* by Alexander Del Mar, which I read, and thought about. He was very helpful. It was very flattering to be taken at all seriously by him. Williams was always much more specific. At times he would do things which would . . . not *dismay* me,—but my own ego would be set back. I remember one time I wrote him a very stern letter—some description about something I was going to do, or *this* was the way things were, *blah blah*. And he returned me the sheets of the letter and he had marked on the margin of particular sections, "Fine. Your style is tightening." But I had the sense to know such comments were of more use to me than whether or not he approved of what I had to say. He would do things like that which were very good. While Pound would say, "Would you please tell me how old you are? You refer to having been involved in something for forty years. Are you twenty-three, or sixty-three?"

INTERVIEWER: At this point, were you raising pigeons in the country?

CREELEY: As a kid I'd had poultry, pigeons and chickens and what not. I'd married in 1946 and after a year on Cape Cod, we moved

A manuscript page from Robert Creeley's "The Finger."

to a farm in New Hampshire where I attempted so-called suste-
nance farming. We had no ambitions that this would make us any
income. We had a small garden that gave us produce for canning.
It made the form of a day very active and interesting, something
continuing—feed them, pluck them, take care of them in various
ways. And I met a lovely man, a crazy, decisive breeder of barred
rocks. He was quite small, almost elfin in various ways, with this

crazy, intense, and beautifully articulate imagination. He could *douse* for example, and all manner of crazy, mystical businesses that he took as comfortably as you'd take an ax in hand. No dismay, or confusion at all. A neighbor in New Hampshire would lose money in the woods. So he'd just cut a birch wand, and find it. The same way you'd turn on the lights to see what you're doing. I remember one of these neighbors of ours, Howard Ainsworth, a woodcutter, was cutting pulp in the woods on a snowy day. But he had a hole in his pocket, and by the time he had discovered it, he'd lost a pocketful of change. So Howard simply cut himself a birch stick and he found it. It was nearly total darkness in the woods. He only remarked upon it, that is, how he'd found it, as an explanation of *how* he'd found it. I mean, it never occurred to him that it was more extraordinary than that.

INTERVIEWER: How did it occur to you?

CREELEY: I was fascinated by it—because it was a kind of "mysticism" which was so extraordinarily practical and unremoved. He had this crazy, yet practical way of exemplifying what he knew as experience. He used to paint, for example. Once he showed me this picture of a dog. He said, "What do you think of this? It's one of my favorite dogs." It was this white-and-black dog standing there looking incredibly sick. And I said, "Well, it's a nice picture. But." And he said, "Yes, it died three days later. That's why it looks so sick." He delighted me, you know, and I felt much more at home with him than with the more—not sophisticated—because I don't think any man was more sophisticated in particular senses than he, but, God, he talked about things you could actually put your hand on. He would characterize patience, or how to pay attention to something.

INTERVIEWER: Do you think you work better in the isolated places you seem to frequent—in New Hampshire, Mallorca, New Mexico?

CREELEY: That seems to be my habit, although having been a teacher for some years I can make it with a number of people and find a place with them. But my dilemma, so to speak, as a younger man, was that I always came on too strong with people I casually met. I remember one time, well, several times, I tended to go for broke with particular people. As soon as I found access to someone I really was attracted by—not only sexually, but in the way they were—I just wanted to, literally, to be utterly with them. I found myself absorbing their way of speaking. I just wanted to get in them. And some people, understandably, would feel this was pretty damned exhausting—to have someone hanging on, you know, like coming at you. I didn't have any experience of how it was really affecting the other person. I mean, I think that a lot of my first wife's understandable bitterness about our relationship was the intensity that she was having to deal with. I mean everything was so intense and involved always with tension. My way to experience emotion was to tighten it up as much as possible, and not even wittingly. Just "naturally." Allen Ginsberg makes a remark that when I get to town nobody sleeps till I'm gone. I can't let anybody sleep because I don't want to miss anything. I want it all, and so I tend at times, understandably, to exhaust my friends—keep pushing, pushing, pushing. Not like social pushing to make a big noise, but you know, I don't want to miss it. I love it. I so love the intensity of people that I can't let anything stop until it's literally exhaustion.

INTERVIEWER: I've heard a lot of stories about your fighting in those earlier days.

CREELEY: That's when the confusions of how to be with people became so heightened I would just spill. It had to do with drinking, which I did a lot of in those days. And pot. We were smoking pot pretty continuously by about . . . let's see . . . I first had use of marijuana in India, where I was in the American Field Service. We were in a barracks at one point—about forty men, all ages. I think almost everyone in that barracks was turned on almost all day long. We were in Central India. There was literally nothing to do. It was an incredibly awkward climate for us. I mean it was very hot and so we'd sit there sweating—drinking was impossible— and getting very damned sick. I had a friend from Southern California who suggested one day that there was an alternative. He said, "Try this." There was nothing mystical. It was very, like, "Here, have an aspirin." So the barracks switched and everything became very delightful. The food was instantly palatable and life became much more interesting. So much so that I remember returning from England on the *Queen Elizabeth* and this friend and I continued smoking a lot of pot on ship. In fact, we used to go into the toilet. A lot of people depended on this toilet, and he and I would get in there and turn on, then sort of sit around. Outside there'd be this great mass of people standing and waiting, banging to get in there. They thought we were homosexuals—a consideration aided by the fact that one night, I remember, I staggered back into the room where there were these tiers of bunks, and trying to get into my bunk I climbed into the wrong one. We used to get up on the boat deck too, which was restricted. That North Atlantic—it was absolutely silent and isolated, seeing that whole sea in a beautiful full moon. Just beautiful.

INTERVIEWER: You were talking about fighting.

CREELEY: Well, see, with drinking I had the sense I was drinking in the frustration of social ineptness. Even to this day if I drink—I mean up to a point it's extremely pleasant and relieving and relaxing for me—there comes an inevitable point where my whole feeling turns into irritation, frustration, and that's when I fight. I mean, I don't think I ever fought anyone except in that condition—fighting out of just sheer frustration and a feeling of absolute incompetence and inability. Also people seemed very belligerent during the forties and fifties. We used to get into these ridiculous fights.

INTERVIEWER: I heard you had a fight with Jackson Pollock once.

CREELEY: Yes, a great meeting. Because he obviously was having the same problem I was, intensively, with a vengeance. I'd been in the Cedar Bar talking with Franz Kline, and another friend of Kline's, and Fielding Dawson probably was there. We were sitting over at a corner booth, and they were talking and drinking in a kind of relaxed manner. But I, again, you know, very characteristic of me, I was all keyed up with the conversation and I'd start to run to get the beer, or whatever we were drinking, and it wasn't coming fast enough. I'd go up to the bar, have a quick drink, and return to the table and pick up the drink that by then had come, and I was getting awfully lushed, and excited, and listening, and I was up at the bar getting another drink, when the door swings open and in comes this very, you know, very *solid* man, this very particular man, again, with this intensity. He comes up to the bar, and almost immediately he made some gesture that bugged me. Something like putting his glass on the bar close to mine, that kind of business where he was pushing me just by *being there*. So I was trying to reassert my place. The next thing we knew we were swinging at each other. And I remember this guy John, one of the owners, just put his hand on the bar and vaulted, literally, right over the bar, right between us, and he said, like, "Okay, you guys," and he started pushing at both of us, whereupon, without even thinking, we both zeroed in on him, and he said, like, "Come on now, cut it out." Then he said, "Do you two guys know each other?" And so then he introduced us, and—God! It was Jackson Pollock! So I was showing him pictures of my children and he was saying, "I'm their godfather." Instantly affable, you know. We were instantly very friendly. And he was very good to me. In those days, I remember, in the Cedar Bar, I had a big wooden-handled clasp knife, that in moments of frustration and rage—I mean I never stuck anybody with it, but it was, like I'd get that knife out, you know, and I don't think I tried to scare people with it, but it was like, when all else failed, that knife was . . . not simply in the sense I was going to kill somebody, like a gun, but I *loved* that knife. You could carve things with it, make things, and so on. And so, I'd apparently been flourishing it in the bar at some point, and I remember he took it away from me, John did, and he kept it and said you're not going to have this knife for two weeks. And then he finally said, "Look, you can't come in here anymore," and I said, like, "What am I gonna do? Where am I gonna go?" So he would finally let me in if I drank ginger ale only. Because I used to stand out front and look in the window. Then he would let me come in and sit, as long as I was a good boy and drank only ginger ale. And finally he let me have the knife back, because that knife was very—well, I've still got one like it.

INTERVIEWER: When you first took LSD did you have any problem?

CREELEY: I had a momentary one, when I remember at one point I did enter the dualism which is "yes—no," that binary factor. I felt it was going to be absolutely awful. I had just said something such as "this is the case" and I suddenly had an intensive experience of "this is the case—this is *not* the case—this *is* the case. . . ." It was like seeing a vast checkerboard—that kind of alternating situation. Then I just, by grace of something, stepped out of it. Just stepped out. In the second experience with it, last summer, blessedly that never occurred. All through that second LSD experience I had Donovan's "There Is a Mountain." I had a pleasant younger friend, and we'd taken it about two in the morning. We had a fire burning, and we were in a place in New England. The day broke clear and fresh and dewy, and there was all this moisture in the trees and the grass—these spider webs of moisture, and it was just idyllic. The whole tone of the house changed. The children had obviously neither concern nor interest nor knowledge that we were on LSD, but somehow the feeling went through the whole house, so that the girls walked down to a store, maybe a mile away, and bought us a chocolate cake. They also spent about an hour and a half that morning making a necklace of pine cones which they gave Bobbie, my wife. The cats and our dog were, you know, almost ravenous for us. The cats were crawling all over us. It wasn't just our hallucinating and thinking they were; they were with us every moment—intensively, rubbing up against us and purring. Then the fire in the fireplace, that light, beautiful light; then seeing the dawn come up back of us as the room began to transform into the day. . . . So that "The Finger" is directly, you know, that information. I remember the business of this beautiful, primordial experience of woman, in the guise of my wife; but equally her image floating between the moments of birth—as girl-child to the most cronelike, the most haggish. Just crazily—all the guises of woman. All that Robert Graves, for example, in rather didactic fashion tries to say is the case. I mean, he's right, certainly he's right. But it's not a hierarchy. It's an absolute manifestation throughout all realms of existence in this woman figure, and yet that woman is woman. She's unequivocally woman. It was absolutely delightful. I thus *jiggled a world before her made of my mind* and I thought, that's the delight.

INTERVIEWER: What do you think is the effect of hallucinatory drugs on the creative process?

CREELEY: Terrific! That's at least what I'd like to say. Things had been so uptight, almost for a year—writing, really our marriage as well, just a stale sense of effort and also confusions of feeling older. I think a lot, and at times I can box myself in with all the rationale of army logistics. It can get to be a hopeless log jam. So anyhow the LSD just wiped that out—and fears and tentativenesses and senses of getting lost or of being endlessly separated from the world, all that just went. I can't claim perhaps so simply that writing was thereby opened but I do know the past year has felt a very active one in consequence. The thing is, it's *information*—extraordinary and deeply *relieving* information. Just as if one were to hear that the war was over, that some imminent peril and/or bitter waste of time had *stopped*. Of course, there's no need to be told this over and over; that is, I don't myself feel much need to take the drug every day. It's a vision of a life, *all* life—and obviously that's a lot to be given by anything or anyone, and so one's not done with it, so to speak, in a day.

INTERVIEWER: When did your interest in painting start?

CREELEY: Well, through Pound's agency I'd come to know René Laubiès, who translated some of Pound's *Cantos* into French. The first published translation of them into French. And Laubiès was an active and interesting painter. In fact, I saw the first Jackson Pollock I ever really saw in Paris at his gallery, Paul Fachetti's gallery. Up to then my relationships had been primarily with other writers. But I liked Laubiès extremely. It wasn't really the painting as something done that interested me. It was the painter, or the activity of painting I was really intrigued by. About that time I began to look at things. And then, because I was an American living in Europe, having left the New Hampshire farm, I was particularly intrigued by the Americanism of certain painters, like Pollock, obviously, and other friends, like Ashley Bryan, and particularly John Altoon, who becomes very, very important to me because his energies were made so incredibly manifest in his work—images of my own reality so to speak. And then Guston was extremely good to me. I mean, he was very good to me in the sense that he was generous with his interest and time. I was fascinated by the condition of life these guys had. Not simply that they were drinking all the time, but that they were loners and peculiarly American, specifically American in their ways of experiencing activity, with energy a *process*—like Pollock's "When I am *in* my painting." Duncan in his notes on *Maximus* makes very clear the relation to painting that he'd felt in San Francisco with the group there—Clyfford Still and Diebenkorn and the whole roster of painters he had as friends. In writing, everything was still argued with traditional or inherited attitudes and forms. And then in the middle fifties, the painters, without any question, became very decisive for me personally. And not only for me. I was thinking about this when I saw John Ashbery the other day. At one point Ashbery gave his own sense of the New York School. He said, "Well, first of all, the one thing that we were all in agreement with was that there should be no program, and that the poem, as we imagined it, should be the possibility of everything we have as experience. There should be no limit of a programmatic order." And then he went on to qualify why painters were interesting to them. Simply that the articulation—the range of possibility—in painting was more viable to their sense of things. And I thought, "That's literally what I would say." That's precisely the imagination of the activity I had. All of us are now roughly in our early forties, and what's striking is that each one of us used precisely the same grid of initial experience and pro-

posal. John was obviously coming to it by way of the French surrealists, where he found, not only playfulness, but a very active ad-
mission of the world as it's felt and confronted. It came from other
places, too. I was finding it in jazz, for example. And that's why
Charlie Parker and Miles Davis and Thelonious Monk and those
people were extraordinarily interesting to me. Simply that they
seemed to have only the nature of the activity as limit. Possibly
they couldn't change water into stone. But then again, maybe they
could. That's what was intriguing.

INTERVIEWER: Well, when did you start writing about painters?

CREELEY: I wrote a note about Laubiès for the first issue of the *Black
Mountain Review*, which I think is the first note of that order I
wrote. Then through the association with Black Mountain, I became very intrigued by Guston and by the visual, what's seen in
the world and how all that can be a complex. I'd been so involved
with the economy of words, the experience of sound and rhythm,
that suddenly it was like having things open again. I wasn't in any
sense knowledgeable as to whether this scene had some continuity historically. Nor could I use the vocabulary of the usual art
critic. But I could, in Olson's sense, give testament, bear witness to
this, to extend an invitation to come. You can see the relevance. We
were making things. Not only of our own imagination, which was
after all finally the point, but we were making things in the materials particular to our own experience of things, just as John
Chamberlain was experiencing the materials in *his* world, namely
those car parts, and seeing how the imagination might articulate
that experience. I was trying to make do with the vocabulary in
terms of experience in *my* world. Neither one of us had history. I
remember Duncan, a lovely moment when we first met—he and
Jess and Harry Jacoby had come to Mallorca. I was in a rather
dense and difficult time in my marriage. Ann was away for some
reason—down in the city shopping. We lived in a little house outside of the city. You got there by a trolley and the four of us were
going back into the city to find them a *pension* where they could
stay. We were standing in this trolley with all the people banging
around us. I remember Robert—we were all standing holding
straps and he looked—turned to me at one point and says, "You're
not interested in history, are you?" I kept saying, "Well, I ought to
be. And I want to be. But I guess I'm not. You know, I'd *like* to be
but, no, that's probably true." That history, as a form of experience, is truly not something I've been able to be articulate with,

nor finally engaged by. Art may be, as Williams might say, the *fact* of something, but I did not have that alternative experience of accepting it as part of a historical progression in time.

INTERVIEWER: Would you describe something of the Black Mountain poets—Olson, Duncan, and the others—and something of those days?

CREELEY: I was first in touch with Olson by way of Vincent Ferrini. That is, Vincent was a friend of Cid Corman, and it really is Cid's magazine *Origin*, started in Boston in the early fifties, that makes the center for all the subsequent Black Mountain school. I didn't meet Olson until I went to teach at Black Mountain in 1954—which job saved my life in many ways, and certainly changed it altogether. Living in Mallorca, despite the ease and beauty of the place, I'd begun to feel I was literally good for nothing—so Olson's offer of a job, and equally his giving me the magazine to edit, changed that subject completely.

By the time I got to the college, things were pretty tight. There can't have been more than twenty or twenty-five students, and every day it seemed was a kind of last-ditch stand. I remember at one point there was the possibility of some wealthy man in some place like Charleston sending his mentally deficient son to us for the benefits of a college education in exchange for a donation—and after much soul searching, we agreed. He was to give us word of his own agreement by having a plane fly over the college, God knows why—but anyhow we spent at least three days, all of us, wandering around the place with eyes to the sky. I do remember the damn plane never showed up.

There was another fund-raising business that consisted of Stefan Wolpe, with me as secretary, writing letters to people like the Guggenheims and Doris Duke—which Stefan would begin with, "I bet you got a lot of money lying around you don't know what to do with," and I'd then try to turn it into socially appropriate English. But nothing ever came of that either—except for one of the Guggenheims, who'd apparently just inherited another bag of gold, sending Stefan a check for ten dollars with a note saying when her affairs were more in order, she'd try to do better. De Kooning one time made a lovely remark about it all, to wit, "The only trouble with Black Mountain is, if you go there, they want to give it to you."

But for me it was all a revelation, and the people were terrific. For example, it was there I met Ed Dorn, Mike Rumaker, Dan Rice, and many, many others. Jonathan Williams I'd met earlier in Mallorca, and Fee Dawson was then in the army in Stuttgart—but again the point is, the intensity and particularity of the people comprising, like they say, the Black Mountain scene, was absolute delight. I suppose the only problem was, in fact, how did one find an alternative—which obviously had to come.

INTERVIEWER: What are the common characteristics of the Black Mountain group?

CREELEY: I'd almost say—the *loner* quality each seems to have. There really isn't a common idiom, so to speak, as in the New York group, for example. I think there was a common feeling that verse was something *given* one to write, and that the form it might then take was intimate with that fact. That's what I at least meant by, "Form is never more than an extension of content."

Painter Dan Rice (left) and Robert Creeley at Black Mountain College, 1955.

INTERVIEWER: When did you meet Ginsberg?

CREELEY: In 1956—after leaving Black Mountain, it must have been in early January or so, then stopping in Albuquerque with friends to pull myself together, then going on to San Francisco where Ed Dorn and his family were. I was trying to get out of my own habits. My marriage had finally ended altogether—and I was sick of what I knew, so to speak. So anyhow I decided to go West. I got to Ed's place about four in the afternoon, and he and Helene drove me around a little. I remember we got very drunk or I at least did—and Rexroth had invited me over for dinner. I can remember vomiting all over the sidewalk, just before I went in, something like an hour or so late. Then later that same night, after Ed had taken off for a job he had as a baggage clerk at Greyhound, suddenly Allen appeared. He was working at the same place only on an earlier shift. It's so characteristic of Allen to be there like that, that is, to come so directly to what interests him. And I was God knows flattered—we talked most of the night about Olson and the scene at Black Mountain. And he told me what was happening in San Francisco. Later, I remember walking around the city with him and Phil Whalen, with Allen inevitably carrying the big black binder notebook, reading us "Howl" every time we sat down or stopped for something to eat. It was really a beautiful time—everything was so open, just poised on its own energies.

INTERVIEWER: You speak of corresponding with Williams and Pound. Did you correspond with your contemporaries? What sort of letters?

CREELEY: Insistently. I think at one point Olson and I were writing each other on the average of once every other day. *Mayan Letters* would give you some sense of it. The fact I was then so far away from everyone meant I depended on letters for a very necessary kind of conversation. Later, living in France, I had Denise Lever- tov and her husband, Mitch Goodman, to talk to—but more often than not there was really no one immediately available who shared the concerns I was having. Too, I very much needed a prac- tical "feedback" and letters served that fact. For example, in the early fifties Paul Blackburn and I wrote each other constantly, and he'd give me a very close reading of the poems I'd send him—not just about what he thought they meant, but a literal line to line, word to word, sense of how he took the verse to be moving. So let- ters were very important to me, and I remember at one point, in

Mallorca, calculating I was spending a full eight hours a day writing them. I think it was Williams who said once in a letter that they served as a kind of rehearsal of what it was we were to do.

INTERVIEWER: You have said that poetry is "the basic act of speech, of utterance." Are you implying that self-expression is the poet's motivation, or is there more to be said about his desire to communicate, his interest in possible readers?

CREELEY: I don't think that "possible readers" are really the context in which poetry is written. For myself it's never been the case. If one plays to the gallery in that way, I think it's extraordinarily distracting. The whole performance of writing then becomes some sort of odd entertainment of persons one never meets and probably would be embarrassed to meet in any case. So I'm only interested in what I can articulate with the things given me as confrontation. I can't worry about what it costs me. I don't think any man writing can worry about what the act of writing costs him, even though at times he is very aware of it.

INTERVIEWER: Communication per se, then, isn't a primary motive for the poet?

CREELEY: It is for some; for others, it isn't. It depends on what is meant by communication, of course. I would be very much cheered to realize that someone had felt what I had been feeling in writing—I would be very much reassured that someone had felt *with* me in that writing. Yet this can't be the context of my own writing. Later I may have horrible doubts indeed as to whether it will ever be read by other persons, but it can never enter importantly into my writing. So I cannot say that communication in the sense of telling someone is what I'm engaged with. In writing I'm telling something to myself, curiously, that I didn't have the knowing of previously. One time, again some years ago, Franz Kline was being questioned—not with hostility but with intensity, by another friend—and finally he said, "Well, look, if I paint what *you* know, then that will simply bore you, the repetition from me to you. If I paint what *I* know, it will be boring to myself. Therefore I paint what I don't know." Well, I believe that. I write what I don't know. Communication is a word one would have to spend much time defining. For example, can you make a blind man see? That has always been a question in my own mind. And if it is true that you cannot tell someone something he has no experience of, then the act of reading is that one is reading *with* someone. I feel when people read my poems most sympathetically, they are reading *with* me. So communication is mutual feeling with someone, not a didactic process of information.

INTERVIEWER: A side issue here, perhaps. Does an artist's "sincerity" have any influence on the quality of his work? Can a poet write good poems about a subject if he has no feeling about it?

CREELEY: I don't see how. If one respects Pound's measure of "Only emotion endures," and "Nothing counts save the quality of the emotion," then having no feelings about something seems to prohibit the possibility of that kind of quality entering. At the same time, there are many ways of feeling about things; it may be that—as in the case of poems by Ted Berrigan—one is made to feel by the fact that there is no attachment of subjective feeling to the words. It's a very subtle question. I remember one time Irving Layton wrote a very moving poem, "Elegy for Fred Smith." Later Gael Turnbull, very impressed by the poem, said to him, "You must feel very badly that your friend has died, because your poem concerning this fact is very, very moving." And Irving then explained that there was no man named Smith; he simply wanted to write this kind of poem. But you see, he wanted the feeling too; he wanted to gain the way one might feel in confronting such a possibility. There wasn't, as it happened, a real fact that provoked this poem, but there was certainly a feeling involved. And it was certainly a "subject" that Irving had "feeling" about. Of course, this issue of sincerity in itself can be a kind of refuge of fools. I am sure that Senator Goldwater was sincere in certain ways, but that shouldn't protect him from a hostile judgment. The zealot is often sincere. But I mean sincerity in the sense that goes back to Pound, that ideogram he notes: man standing by his word. *That* kind of sincerity has always been important to me—to what I'm doing.

INTERVIEWER: Undoubtedly there are pitfalls, too. Edgar Guest was probably as sincere as anyone writing today. Why wasn't Guest a Williams?

CREELEY: Again, you see, we have a simple answer. If we do believe that "Nothing counts save the quality of the emotion," then we have a clear measure for qualifying Guest—the emotion in Guest is of very poor quality. It's so generally articulated and so blurred with assumptional sentiment that it's a kind of mess. It's too general. So that would be the difference between him, I would feel, and someone like Williams who has the virtue of a much more complex and intimate and modulated quality of feeling— and is much more articulate in the area of that feeling, and not only gives evidence of it, but allows its evidence to be felt by the reader.

INTERVIEWER: This matter of the readers being allowed to feel their way through the poem, the active re-creation of experience. I'm not alone, I think, in feeling excluded from some modern poetry. I was reading the other day a poem by Gary Snyder, "How to Make Stew in the Pinacate Desert": "Now put in the strips of bacon. / In another pan have all the vegetables cleaned up and peeled and / sliced. / Cut the beef shank meat up small . . ." If technique is the rationale for Snyder's poem, have we gone too far with the present emphasis on technique?

CREELEY: The context of the poem is very relevant; perhaps I know too much about it. For example, it is addressed to two friends. What Gary's doing here is literally giving them a recipe for stew, and his *way* of speaking is evident. A tone or mode or kind of speech is occurring. Yes, you can literally take this poem as a recipe for how to make stew, but in this way of saying something there's also an emotional context, a kind of feeling. That, to my mind, is the significant part of this poem. It's the kind of address and the kind of feeling that is engendered by it; and it's the way the words go, literally, that is to me the most intimate aspect of this poem as poem. Now, what can we call it? Technique? Sure, there's technique in that the poem is articulated and held, in the way the words are placed in lines. There's a speed offered in the way the line is going there. But I don't think that he has gone too far, any more than I felt that the actual record of drilling that occurs in Williams's *Paterson* was going too far. It seemed to be very prosaic, but it gave an extraordinarily vivid sense of how far one did have to dig down to find what was intimate and vital to one's own needs. Just as the water was only to be found after having gone through all those levels, the very character of that report gave a real sense of what it is like to try to find something in an environment that is so covered, so much under the accumulation of refuse, and waste, and tedium, and misuse. So that I would rather not talk in that way of "technique" as something extensible or separate. And I would have respect for this particular poem of Gary's. Again I fall back on Pound's "Only emotion endures." This particular emotion is of an address to friends meant as a warmth which all three shall share, therefore anyone. In that possibility I find the most interest.

INTERVIEWER: Is the remarkable amount of obscenity in contemporary poetry the result of the letdown of barriers—or is it a reflection of the day's mood and temper?

CREELEY: One time Duncan was at a poetry workshop in Arizona, just after *Naked Lunch* had been published, and, as he said, the people were still writing poems about the moon and the rather indomitable onrush of the spring. That is, no one really rushed to say "fuck" just because it seemed now possible to do so in print. But then because one did want to be able to involve a total fact of persons, not just discreet edges thereof, it was a great relief I think to be able to do so. No doubt it's me, but I do think sexual mores have become much more relaxed in the last few years—and obscenity, or better, the words we so call obscene, have a very real energy. So one wants use of them as there seems occasion. I really dig, for example, Peter Orlovsky's journals that Ed Sanders has published sections of—not just for what they tell me of Peter but for what they make known to me as literal details of sexual event.

INTERVIEWER: How long does the writing of a poem take for you?

CREELEY: For me, it's literally the time it takes to type or otherwise write it—because I *do* work in this fashion of simply sitting down and writing, usually without any process of revision. So that if it goes—or, rather, comes—in an opening way, it continues until it closes, and that's usually when I stop. It's awfully hard for me to give a sense of actual time because as I said earlier, I'm not sure of time in writing. Sometimes it seems a moment and yet it could have been half an hour or a whole afternoon. And usually poems come in clusters of three at a time or perhaps six or seven. More than one at a time. I'll come into the room and sit and begin working simply because I feel like it. I'll start writing and fooling around, like they say, and something will start to cohere; I'll begin following it as it occurs. It may lead to its own conclusion, complete its own entity. Then, very possibly because of the stimulus of that, something further will begin to come. That seems to be the way I do it. Of course, I have no idea how much time it takes to write a poem in the sense of how much time it takes to accumulate the possibilities of which the poem is the articulation.

INTERVIEWER: Your surroundings during the time both of accumulating and writing—how significant are they?

CREELEY: Allen Ginsberg, for example, can write poems anywhere—trains, planes, in any public place. He isn't the least self-conscious. In fact, he seems to be stimulated by people around him. For myself, I need a very kind of secure quiet. I usually have some music playing, just because it gives me something, a kind of drone that I like, as relaxation. I remember reading that Hart Crane wrote at times to the sound of records because he liked the stimulus and this pushed him to a kind of openness that he could use. In any case, the necessary environment is that which secures the artist in the way that lets him be *in* the world in a most fruitful manner.

INTERVIEWER: What is your concept of the creative process per se? Would you agree with Williams's description of it: theoretic know-how plus "the imaginative quota, the unbridled mad-sound basis"?

CREELEY: Yes. One can learn a lot both by reading and by what you've accumulated by writing yourself. But then it's up to these occasions that come without much announcement and declare themselves quite apart from one's intentions. All the understanding of process possible doesn't ever guarantee their occurrence. And one curiously never does know just when or why or how or in what guise they will be present.

INTERVIEWER: No one can learn to write poetry, then? This total involvement of the poet—experiences, knowledge, technique, emotions—one is a poet perhaps by virtue of what he is, not by what he knows?

CREELEY: He's a poet in the sense that he's given the possibility of poetry by what seems to be a very mysterious process indeed. Naturally, all that he knows from his own writing and that of other writers helps to gain him articulation. It's rather like driving. A man who can't drive at all is obviously embarrassed to go down a road. The most "articulate" driver would be one who can follow the road with precisely the right response to each condition before him. The contexts are in some way equivalent.

INTERVIEWER: Do you have the sense of continually progressing—is there a sense in each successive poem of a new adventure?

CREELEY: A "new adventure" possibly—that is, like Melville's sense, "Be true to the dreams of thy youth," which Olson told me Melville had on the wall over his work table. I don't want to be *un-romantic* about it. But I have never felt I was going anywhere, in writing—not like, "Every day, in every way, I am getting better and better." What I've really loved is the fact that at times I can *take place* in this activity, just be there with whatever comes of that fact. I live in this house, or with my wife, in just the same way. It's not "getting somewhere" that is the point of it all.

INTERVIEWER: You have spoken of a poem being created almost "in a fit," or in a seizure. Does it ever bother you to think that these attacks may not come? It seems such an American phenomenon to believe that the force of inspiration disappears in time.

CREELEY: It bothers me very damn much—but I've never found a cure for it. I don't know another writer who hasn't faced the same dilemma. But I don't know what one can do about it except hold on. I did realize finally that at times I was perversely enjoying my discontent, that is, I was all but wallowing in the inertia I felt I was stuck with. That's quickly a bore. But it's still true, of my own experience, that no amount of wanting to do something can actually make writing possible.

INTERVIEWER: Well, do you consciously choose your subjects?

CREELEY: Never that I've been aware of. I may make too much emphasis upon that, but I can't remember ever consciously setting out to write a poem literally *about* something. Well, I can think of an exception. That would be a sequence of poems done to complement Robert Indiana's "Number" paintings—but after roughly a year of frustrated attempts to write these poems, the first five came to me, quite literally, between the hours of five and seven in the morning—a time I've never found possible for writing nor for much of anything else.

For myself, writing has always been the way of finding what I was feeling about, what so engaged me as "subject," and particularly to find the articulation of emotions in the actual writing. So, I don't choose my subjects with any consciousness whatsoever. I think once things have begun—that is, once there are three or four lines, then there begins to be a continuity of possibility engendered which I probably do follow. And I can recognize, say, looking back at what I have written, that some concerns have been persistent; the terms of marriage, relations of men and women, senses of isolation, senses of place in the intimate measure. But I have never to my own knowledge begun with any sense of "subject." I fall back on that point of Olson's—I think it's "Letter 15" in *The Maximus Poems* where it goes: "He sd, 'You go all around the subject.' And I sd, 'I didn't know it was a subject.' " You see, I don't know that poetry has "subjects" except as some sort of categorical reference for listing in library catalogs. Poetry has *themes*, that is, persistent contents which occur in poetry willy-nilly with or without the recognition of the writer. These themes are such as Olson once spoke of, war, love between man and woman, friendship, and the care of the earth. But I don't feel that these "subjects" are really the primary indication of the poem's merit or utility in the society in which it is present.

INTERVIEWER: You don't, then, have any "point" to make, to use a common term of reference?

CREELEY: The point I wish to make is that I am writing. Writing is my primary articulation. So when I write, that's what I'm at work with—an articulation of what confronts me, which I can't really realize or anticipate prior to the writing. I think I said in the introduction to *The Gold Diggers*, well over ten years ago, that if you say one thing it always will lead to more than you had thought to say. This has always been my experience.

INTERVIEWER: To look a little more closely at the "themes," then, in your work. Many seem to deal with love, hate—in short, human relationships. Is this human interaction the dominant interest from an artistic point of view?

CREELEY: Well, I've always been embarrassed for a so-called larger view. I've been given to write about that which has the most intimate presence for me, and I've always felt very, very edgy those few times when I have tried to gain a larger view. I've never felt right. I am given as a man to work with what is most intimate to me—these senses of relationship among people. I think, for myself at least, the world is most evident and most intense in those relationships. Therefore they are the materials of which my work is made.

INTERVIEWER: Then, in general, are you writing about what is personally most important to you?

CREELEY: Yes. People are the most important things in the world for me. I don't at all mean that in a humanistic sense. It's just that they are the most insistent and most demanding and most complex presences offered to me.

INTERVIEWER: In some ways, this kind of subject is different from that of many of Williams's poems, which you admittedly admire. Is there a contradiction here?

CREELEY: Again, remember what Williams does say, "The poet thinks with his poem." When he has a poem such as the "The Red Wheelbarrow," which occurs in that sequence *Spring and All*, a mixture of poetry and prose in its original version, that poem, and that whole sequence, is a way of perceiving—not decided upon but met, almost in full course, by "divine accident," as Stendhal would say. Williams says that particular sequence moves among the recognitions given him from his perceptions. That's what I am interested in, in those poems—not the literal material evident in the red wheelbarrow, but in *how* the perception occurs, how he thinks in the context of that relationship. Not simply *why* he says this, but *how* he says it, how he gives it credence, how he gives it recognition. We are both doing something quite akin: we're thinking, we're gaining an articulation for ourselves in the activity of the poem. As he says, "In our family we stammer until, half mad, we come to speech." Or he says, "the words made solely of air." This context for poetry is one very intimate and immediately recognizable to myself. So I don't think that you can say, "Well, this man talks about green bottles and this man talks about his wife; therefore, they are not interested in the same things." It's the way these things are perceived in the poem and how they are articulated that is significant, and in that respect I would feel a great debt to Williams and would feel that I had learned much from him indeed.

INTERVIEWER: Since two recent books are prose, *The Island* and the reissue of *The Gold Diggers*, could we talk for a while about the differences between poetry and prose?

CREELEY: Well, prose seems to offer more variety in ways of approaching experience. It's more leisurely. One can experiment while en route, so to speak. But still, for me, poetry gives a more immediate, a more concentrated articulation—a finer way of speaking. I don't prefer either. I don't say poetry is more useful for me in *this* sense, and prose in *that* sense, and therefore I write a story when I want *this* effect, and a poem when I want *that* effect. They come and go. When something has been on my mind for a long, long time and I've been in some sense conscious of it, then very often it will be prose that gives me the chance of articulating what is dogging me with such emotional insistence. I think, for example, of a park in England where I was sitting with a friend, and I was very new to our surroundings. I felt not alien but freshly arrived. We were sitting in this quiet park on a Sunday afternoon, a small sort of intimate family park with walks, not hidden exactly, but arranged so that people moved along through corridors of trees and plants, so that one had a constantly changing vista of persons as they came and went. And there was a kind of old statue, not particularly distinct or admirable but sort of interesting, as if a kind of old person had suddenly been immobilized or concretized. But in any case, that moment, sitting on that bench, talking in this rather random fashion and watching the people and seeing children all ages, impressed itself on my mind. I don't know what I'm going to do with it—or rather, I don't know what it's going to do with me. But that kind of insistence—it's one of the most intense things which I seem to have gained in England. I don't know what it means. I don't understand it. I don't know why—of all the kinds of experience that I had there—that moment suddenly is awfully intense. But at some moment that's probably something that's *coming* to be written. I feel it now, that it's coming, that I shall work with it. And when I do work with it, I would feel it will probably be with prose because it has such a complexity in it that I'll want to move with it tentatively. Prose may give me a way of feeling my way through such a thing. Poetry is more often a kind of absolute seizure—a demand that doesn't offer variations of this kind.

INTERVIEWER: So prose is very much in your future, as well as poetry?

CREELEY: I must say that as soon as I *plan* to do more prose, I do absolutely nothing. I had planned to do another novel, because I really enjoyed *The Island*, having learned in a sense some of the technical possibilities of such a form—that is, having written it—I gained some insight into what technically was possible in a long prose piece. I wanted not to lose it, so I very quickly committed myself to do another novel, which was unwise of me. I even gave the novel a title, and had what I thought was a good occasion (two years I spent in Guatemala had given me a crazily chaotic impression of so many things and persons and acts—such a wild variability of people in such a very curiously primal place—that I thought, this is an ideal thing to work with in prose). But as soon as I planned to do it, I all but stopped. I don't know how I am going to get past that. One day I'll simply sit down and start writing. Until that day comes, talking about it is a little absurd because I simply don't work in that fashion. By planning to do the novel, and by talking about it with my publisher, accepting a small advance and giving it this title and all, I seem—well, one moment last spring, for example, I really got almost hysterical and I called the publisher and said, "Look, I want to pay you back that money. I'm sick to death of the whole program." No, again, you see, Pound is so right. That quote he has from Remy de Gourmont, "Freely to write what one chooses is the sole pleasure of a writer." That is so true. So that as soon as it becomes programmed in any way, in the sense that it isn't momently recognized, it's a very, very problematic context in which to try anything.

INTERVIEWER: Were your short stories written usually in one movement? Like the poems?

CREELEY: Right. Again that's why I say that the kind of economy that Pollock was speaking of was very real to me . . . when he said, "When I am *in* my painting . . ." I remember one time in the fifties a conversation Guston was having with my first wife. She'd challenged him: "If you're painting this way, abstract expressionism or whatever you call it, how do you know when it's done?" She really was suggesting that he was in some way a phony, and that everything he was involved in was in some way phony. He took the question seriously, and gave her a very careful and generous statement of his own experience of painting. His resolution was that you know when it's done when you are both looking at and involved with what's happening, and you can't see any place where further activity is permitted. I mean, where everything has happened. And I knew that was precisely how I felt about writing, that when I couldn't say anything more, that was the end. You continued writing and/or speaking until no further possibility of continuing was there. And I thought this was what these particular men as Kline, or as Guston, or as De Kooning—not De Kooning so much because his formal procedure was rather different, but Pollock, absolutely—that they were not so much "experimenting," but that they were delighted and moved and engaged by an activity—*permitted* an experience of something—and that they were with it as long as it was possible to be. And at some point it ended. I mean *it* stopped, and they were thus pushed out or made to stop too, and that was it.

INTERVIEWER: There exists at the moment a large group of young poets writing what have been called by some "Creeley poems." Short, terse, poignant—at their best. You know, of course, you have tremendous influence on the generation to come. Do you think this influence is good?

CREELEY: I haven't the least idea. That's up to them to demonstrate. At a poetry conference, Robert Duncan—hearing many poems dedicated to himself—said, "My God, do I really sound like that?" There's a kind of horror in seeing what's taken from one's own acts as the significant aspect of them, played back. This kind of active feedback provides a very interesting disarrangement and what people make of my work in this way has sometimes delighted me and sometimes left me very disgruntled. But I don't think it's up to me to decide whether it's good or bad. It will demonstrate its own virtues or failures.

INTERVIEWER: Where can these young writers move in this imitative writing?

CREELEY: Again, I haven't the least sense of where they can go in their poetry. That is very much their own business—as it was mine and remains mine. We return to that sense of Olson's that each of us has his own "kin and concentration." So that for me to propose large rules for all poets would be absurd. I feel simply that all those engaged as poets can take what they will from what I may have discovered or from what those before me have discovered or what men after me will discover. Obviously, there's no end to it, but I believe it should all be handed over and that it can or cannot be used as each person learns for himself.

INTERVIEWER: What is the pattern? Will these young writers stay imitative?

CREELEY: No, they won't. Imitation is a way of gaining articulation. It is the way one learns, by having the intimate possibility of some master like Williams or Pound. Writing poems in those modes was a great instruction to me when I began to "feel" what

Williams was doing as well as "understand" it. This imitative phase is a natural thing in artists. I feel it should be encouraged. It is one way to learn, and it's the way I would respect, coming as I do from a rural background where learning how to plow is both watching someone else do it and then taking the handle of the plow and seeing if you can imitate, literally, his way of doing it, therefore gaining the use of it for yourself. But what you then plow—and whether you plow or not—is your own business. And there are, fortunately, many ways to do it.

—Linda Wagner

—Lewis MacAdams, Jr.

1968

Jack Kerouac

was born Jean Louis Kerouac on March 12, 1922, in Lowell, Massachusetts. By the early 1920s, Lowell had already begun to sink into financial depression. When Kerouac was awarded a football scholarship in 1941 to attend Columbia University in New York City, the family followed, settling in Ozone Park, Queens.

Following a leg injury, Kerouac lost his scholarship and financial stability. He left school to find work as a merchant marine. Shortly thereafter he was discharged as a "schizoid personality." Back in New York, he began writing his first novel, *The Town and the City* (1950), which received little critical acclaim. Disheartened, he began to travel cross-country with fellow Beat Neal Cassady. In a fevered, three-week writing spree, Kerouac recorded his adventures in his second novel, *On the Road* (1957). The novel was finally published following six years of rejection, launching Kerouac to sudden stardom. Recounting the anxious wanderings of thinly veiled personalities (Burroughs appears as Old Bull, Neal Cassady as Dean Moriarty), *On the Road* instantly appealed to a young generation of restless individuals intent on rediscovering the values threatened by the impending Vietnam War. Marked by what Kerouac dubbed "spontaneous prose," a derivative of "automatic writing," *On the Road* made Kerouac the most beloved of the Beat generation writers, a term he coined himself.

In the years that followed, he published several more novels, *The Dharma Bums* (1958), *The Subterraneans* (1958), *Big Sur* (1962), and *Visions of Gerard* (1963); as well as several volumes of poetry including *Mexico City Blues* (1959) and *The Scripture of the Golden Eternity* (1960). In 1965, he wrote *Desolation Angels*, a retrospective account of his early Beat years that looked forward to his withdrawal from the literary arena: "A peaceful sorrow at home is the best I'll ever be able to offer the world." Demoralized by the harsh judgments of his literary peers (Truman Capote called him a glorified "typist"), and disenchanted by the glamour of popular appeal, Kerouac began to drink heavily. He lived out the rest of his short life at home with his wife and mother, dying one year after the following interview's publication.

*T*he Kerouacs have no telephone. Ted Berrigan had contacted Kerouac
some months earlier and had persuaded him to do the interview.
When he felt the time had come for their meeting to take place, he simply
showed up at the Kerouacs' house. Two friends, poets Aram Saroyan and
Duncan McNaughton, accompanied him. Kerouac answered his ring;
Berrigan quickly told him his name and the visit's purpose. Kerouac wel-
comed the poets, but before he could show them in, his wife, a very determined woman, seized him from behind and told the group to leave at
once.

"Jack and I began talking simultaneously, saying 'Paris Review!'
'Interview!' etc.," Berrigan recalls, "while Duncan and Aram began to
slink back toward the car. All seemed lost, but I kept talking in what I
hoped was a civilized, reasonable, calming, and friendly tone of voice,
and soon Mrs. Kerouac agreed to let us in for twenty minutes, on the
condition that there be no drinking.

"Once inside, as it became evident that we actually were in pursuit of a serious purpose, Mrs. Kerouac became more friendly, and we were able to commence the interview. It seems that people still show up constantly at the Kerouacs' looking for the author of On the Road, *and stay for days, drinking all the liquor and diverting Jack from his serious occupations.*

"As the evening progressed the atmosphere changed considerably, and Mrs. Kerouac, Stella, proved a gracious and charming hostess. The most amazing thing about Jack Kerouac is his magic voice, which sounds exactly like his works. It is capable of the most astounding and disconcerting changes in no time flat. It dictates everything, including this interview.

"After the interview, Kerouac, who had been sitting throughout the interview in a President Kennedy–type rocker, moved over to a big poppa chair and said, 'So you boys are poets, hey? Well, let's hear some of your poetry.' We stayed for about an hour longer and Aram and I read some of our things. Finally, he gave each of us a signed broadside of a recent poem of his, and we left."

•   •   •

INTERVIEWER: Could we put the footstool over here to put this on?

STELLA: Yes.

KEROUAC: God, you're so inadequate there, Berrigan.

INTERVIEWER: Well, I'm no tape-recorder man, Jack. I'm just a big talker, like you. OK, we're off.

KEROUAC: OK? [*Whistles*] OK?

INTERVIEWER: Actually I'd like to start . . . the first book I ever read by you, oddly enough, since most people first read *On the Road* . . . the first one I read was *The Town and the City* . . .

KEROUAC: Gee!

INTERVIEWER: I checked it out of the library . . .

KEROUAC: Gee! Did you read *Doctor Sax*? *Tristessa*?

INTERVIEWER: You better believe it. I even read *Rimbaud.* I have a copy of *Visions of Cody* that Ron Padgett bought in Tulsa, Oklahoma.

KEROUAC: Screw Ron Padgett! You know why? He started a little magazine called *White Dove Review* in Kansas City, was it? Tulsa? Oklahoma . . . yes. He wrote, "Start our magazine off by sending us a great big poem." So I sent him "The Thrashing Doves." And then I sent him another one and he rejected the second one because his magazine was already started. That's to show you how punks try to make their way by scratching down on a man's back. Aw, he's no poet. You know who's a great poet? I know who the great poets are.

INTERVIEWER: Who?

KEROUAC: Let's see, is it . . . William Bissett of Vancouver. An Indian boy. Bill Bissett, or Bissonnette.

SAROYAN: Let's talk about Jack Kerouac.

KEROUAC: He's not better than Bill Bissett, but he's very original.

INTERVIEWER: Why don't we begin with editors. How do you . . .

KEROUAC: OK. All my editors since Malcolm Cowley have had instructions to leave my prose exactly as I wrote it. In the days of Malcolm Cowley, with *On the Road* and *The Dharma Bums,* I had no power to stand by my style for better or for worse. When Malcolm Cowley made endless revisions and inserted thousands of needless commas like, say, Cheyenne, Wyoming (why not just say Cheyenne Wyoming and let it go at that, for instance), why, I spent five hundred dollars making the complete restitution of the *Bums* manuscript and got a bill from Viking Press called "Revisions." Ha ho ho. And so you asked about how do I work with an editor . . . well nowadays I am just grateful to him for his assistance in proofreading the manuscript and in discovering logical errors, such as dates, names of places. For instance, in my last book I wrote Firth of Forth then looked it up, on the suggestion of my editor, and found that I'd really sailed off the Firth of Clyde. Things like that. Or I spelled Aleister Crowley "Alisteir," or he discovered little mistakes about the yardage in football games . . . and so forth. By not revising what you've already written you simply give the reader the actual workings of your mind during the writ-

ing itself: you confess your thoughts about events in your own unchangeable way . . . Well, look, did you ever hear a guy telling a
long wild tale to a bunch of men in a bar and all are listening and
smiling, did you ever hear that guy stop to revise himself, go back
to a previous sentence to improve it, to defray its rhythmic
thought impact. . . . If he pauses to blow his nose, isn't he planning
his next sentence? And when he lets that next sentence loose, isn't
it once and for all the way he wanted to say it? Doesn't he depart
from the thought of that sentence and, as Shakespeare says, "forever holds his tongue" on the subject, since he's passed over it like
a part of a river that flows over a rock once and for all and never
returns and can never flow any other way in time? Incidentally, as
for my bug against periods, that was for the prose in *October in the
Railroad Earth*, very experimental, intended to clack along all the
way like a steam engine pulling a one-hundred-car freight with a
talky caboose at the end, that was my way at the time and it still
can be done if the thinking during the swift writing is confessional
and pure and all excited with the life of it. And be sure of this, I
spent my entire youth writing slowly with revisions and endless
rehashing speculation and deleting and got so I was writing one
sentence a day and the sentence had no FEELING. Goddamn it,
FEELING is what I like in art, not CRAFTINESS and the hiding of
feelings.

INTERVIEWER: What encouraged you to use the "spontaneous"
style of *On the Road*?

KEROUAC: I got the idea for the spontaneous style of *On the Road*
from seeing how good old Neal Cassady wrote his letters to me,
all first person, fast, mad, confessional, completely serious, all detailed, with real names in his case, however (being letters). I remembered also Goethe's admonition, well Goethe's prophecy that
the future literature of the West would be confessional in nature;
also Dostoevsky prophesied as much and might have started in
on that if he'd lived long enough to do his projected masterwork,
"The Life of a Great Sinner." Cassady also began his early youthful writing with attempts at slow, painstaking, and all-that-crap
craft business, but got sick of it like I did, seeing it wasn't getting
out his guts and heart the way it *felt* coming out. But I got the flash
from his style. It's a cruel lie for those West Coast punks to say that
I got the idea of *On the Road* from him. All his letters to me were
about his younger days before I met him, a child with his father, et
cetera, and about his later teenage experiences. The letter he sent

The original manuscript roll of Vanity of Duluoz. *The roll is teletype paper which comes in sheets several hundred feet long.*

me is erroneously reported to be a thirteen-thousand-word letter . . . no, the thirteen-thousand-word piece was his novel *The First Third*, which he kept in his possession. The letter, the main letter I mean, was forty thousand words long, mind you, a whole short novel. It was the greatest piece of writing I ever saw, better'n anybody in America, or at least enough to make Melville, Twain, Dreiser, Wolfe, I dunno who, spin in their graves. Allen Ginsberg asked me to lend him this vast letter so he could read it. He read it, then loaned it to a guy called Gerd Stern who lived on a houseboat in Sausalito, California, in 1955, and this fellow lost the letter: overboard I presume. Neal and I called it, for convenience, the Joan Anderson Letter . . . all about a Christmas weekend in the pool halls, hotel rooms and jails of Denver, with hilarious events throughout and tragic too, even a drawing of a window, with measurements to make the reader understand, all that. Now listen: this letter would have been printed under Neal's copyright, if we could find it, but as you know, it was my property as a letter to me, so Allen shouldn't have been so careless with it, nor the guy on the houseboat. If we can unearth this entire forty-thousand-word letter Neal shall be justified. We also did so much fast talking between the two of us, on tape recorders, way back in 1952, and listened to them so much, we both got the secret of LINGO in telling a tale and figured that was the only way to express the speed and tension and ecstatic tomfoolery of the age . . . Is that enough?

INTERVIEWER: How do you think this style has changed since *On the Road*?

KEROUAC: What style? Oh, the style of *On the Road*. Well as I say, Cowley riddled the original style of the manuscript there, without my power to complain, and since then my books are all published as written, as I say, and the style has varied from the highly experimental speedwriting of *Railroad Earth* to the ingrown toenail packed mystical style of *Tristessa*, the *Notes from Underground* (by Dostoevsky) confessional madness of *The Subterraneans*, the perfection of the three as one in *Big Sur*, I'd say, which tells a plain tale in a smooth buttery literate run, to *Satori in Paris*, which is really the first book I wrote with drink at my side (cognac and malt liquor) . . . and not to overlook *Book of Dreams*, the style of a person half-awake from sleep and ripping it out in pencil by the bed . . . yes, pencil . . . what a job! Bleary eyes, insaned mind bemused and mystified by sleep, details that pop out even as you write them you don't know what they mean, till you wake up, have coffee, look at it, and see the logic of dreams in dream language itself, see? . . . And finally I decided in my tired middle age to slow down and did *Vanity of Duluoz* in a more moderate style so that, having been so esoteric all these years, some earlier readers would come back and see what ten years had done to my life and thinking . . . which is after all the only thing I've got to offer, the true story of what I saw and how I saw it.

INTERVIEWER: You dictated sections of *Visions of Cody*. Have you used this method since?

KEROUAC: I didn't dictate sections of *Visions of Cody*. I typed up a segment of taped conversation with Neal Cassady, or Cody, talking about his early adventures in L.A. It's four chapters. I haven't used this method since; it really doesn't come out right, well, with Neal and with myself, when all written down and with all the *ahs* and the *ohs* and the *ahums* and the fearful fact that the damn thing is turning and you're *forced* not to waste electricity or tape. . . . Then again, I don't know, I might have to resort to that eventually; I'm getting tired and going blind. This question stumps me. At any rate, everybody's doing it, I hear, but I'm still scribbling. McLuhan says we're getting more oral so I guess we'll all learn to talk into the machine better and better.

INTERVIEWER: What is that state of "Yeatsian semi-trance" which provides the ideal atmosphere for spontaneous writing?

KEROUAC: Well, there it is, how can you be in a trance with your mouth yapping away . . . writing at least is a silent meditation even though you're going a hundred miles an hour. Remember that scene in *La Dolce Vita* where the old priest is mad because a mob of maniacs has shown up to see the tree where the kids saw the Virgin Mary? He says, "Visions are not available in all this frenetic foolishness and yelling and pushing; visions are only obtainable in silence and meditation." Thar. Yup.

INTERVIEWER: You have said that haiku is not written spontaneously but is reworked and revised. Is this true of all your poetry? Why must the method for writing poetry differ from that of prose?

KEROUAC: No, first; haiku is best reworked and revised. I know, I tried. It has to be completely economical, no foliage and flowers and language rhythm, it has to be a simple little picture in three little lines. At least that's the way the old masters did it, spending months on three little lines and coming up, say, with:

> In the abandoned boat,
> The hail
> Bounces about.

That's Shiki. But as for my regular English verse, I knocked it off fast like the prose, using, get this, the size of the notebook page for the form and length of the poem, just as a musician has to get out, a jazz musician, his statement within a certain number of bars, within one chorus, which spills over into the next, but he has to stop where the chorus page *stops*. And finally, too, in poetry you can be completely free to say anything you want, you don't have to tell a story, you can use secret puns, that's why I always say, when writing prose, "No time for poetry now, get your plain tale." [*Drinks are served.*]

INTERVIEWER: How do you write haiku?

KEROUAC: Haiku? You want to hear haiku? You see you got to compress into three short lines a great big story. First you start with a haiku situation—so you see a leaf, as I told her the other night, falling on the back of a sparrow during a great big October wind storm. A big leaf falls on the back of a little sparrow. How you going to compress that into three lines? Now in Japanese you got to compress it into seventeen syllables. We don't have to do that in American—or English—because we don't have the same syllabic bullshit that your Japanese language has. So you say: Little sparrow—you don't have to say little—everybody knows a sparrow is little because they fall so you say

> *Sparrow*
> *with big leaf on its back—*
> *windstorm*

No good, don't work, I reject it.

> *A little sparrow*
> *when an Autumn leaf suddenly sticks to its back*
> *from the wind.*

Hah, that does it. No, it's a little bit too long. See? It's already a little bit too long, Berrigan, you know what I mean?

INTERVIEWER: Seems like there's an extra word or something, like *when*. How about leaving out *when*? Say:

> *A sparrow*
> *an autumn leaf suddenly sticks to its back—*
> *from the wind!*

KEROUAC: Hey, that's all right. I think *when* was the extra word. You got the right idea there, O'Hara! A sparrow, an autumn leaf suddenly—we don't have to say *suddenly* do we?

> *A sparrow*
> *an autumn leaf sticks to its back—*
> *from the wind!*

[Kerouac writes final version into a spiral notebook.]

INTERVIEWER: *Suddenly* is absolutely the kind of word we don't need there. When you publish that will you give me a footnote saying you asked me a couple of questions?

KEROUAC: *[writes]* Berrigan noticed. Right?

INTERVIEWER: Do you write poetry very much? Do you write other poetry besides haiku?

KEROUAC: It's hard to write haiku. I write long silly Indian poems. You want to hear my long silly Indian poem?

INTERVIEWER: What kind of Indian?

KEROUAC: Iroquois. As you know from looking at me. *[reads from notebook]*

> *On the lawn on the way to the store*
> *44 years old for the neighbors to hear*
> *hey, looka, Ma I hurt myself. Especially*
> *with that squirt.*

What's that mean?

INTERVIEWER: Say it again.

KEROUAC: Hey, looka, Ma, I hurt myself, while on the way to the store I hurt myself I fell on the lawn I yell to my mother hey looka, Ma, I hurt myself. I add, especially with that squirt.

INTERVIEWER: You fell over a sprinkler?

KEROUAC: No, my father's squirt into my Ma.

INTERVIEWER: From that distance?

KEROUAC: Oh, I quit. No, I know you wouldn't get that one. I had to explain it. *[opens notebook again and reads]*

> *Goy means joy.*

INTERVIEWER: Send that one to Ginsberg.

KEROUAC: [*Reads*]

Happy people so called are hypocrites—it means
the happiness wavelength can't work without
necessary deceit, without certain scheming and lies and
hiding. Hypocrisy and deceit, no Indians. No smiling.

INTERVIEWER: No Indians?

KEROUAC: The reason you really have a hidden hostility towards me, Berrigan, is because of the French and Indian War.

INTERVIEWER: That could be.

SAROYAN: I saw a football picture of you in the cellar of Horace Mann. You were pretty fat in those days.

STELLA: Tuffy! Here Tuffy! Come on, kitty. . . .

KEROUAC: Stella, let's have another bottle or two. Yeah, I'm going to murder everybody if they let me go. I did. Hot fudge sundaes! Boom! I used to have two or three hot fudge sundaes before every game. Lou Little . . .

INTERVIEWER: He was your coach at Columbia?

KEROUAC: Lou Little was my coach at Columbia. My father went up to him and said, "You sneaky long-nosed finagler . . ." He says, "Why don't you let my son, Ti Jean, Jack, start in the Army game so he can get back at his great enemy from Lowell?" And Lou Little says because he's not ready. "Who says he's not ready?" "I say he's not ready." My father says, "Why you long nose banana nose big crook, get out of my sight!" And he comes stomping out of the office smoking a big cigar. "Come out of here Jack, let's get out of here." So we left Columbia together. And also when I was in the United States Navy during the war—1942—right in front of the admirals, he walked in and says, "Jack, you are right! The Germans should not be our enemies. They should be our allies, as it will be proven in time." And the admirals were all there with their mouths open, and my father would take no shit from nobody—

my father didn't have nothing but a big belly about this big [*gestures with arms out in front of him*] and he would go POOM! [*Kerouac gets up and demonstrates, by puffing his belly out in front of him with explosive force and saying POOM!*] One time he was walking down the street with my mother, arm in arm, down the Lower East Side. In the old days, you know, the 1940s. And here comes a whole bunch of rabbis walking arm in arm . . . tee-dah teedah-teedah . . . and they wouldn't part for this Christian man and his wife. So my father went POOM! And he knocked a rabbi right in the gutter. Then he took my mother and walked on through.

Now, if you don't like that, Berrigan, that's the history of my family. They don't take no shit from nobody. In due time I ain't going to take no shit from nobody. You can record that.

Is this my wine?

INTERVIEWER: Was *The Town and the City* written under spontaneous composition principles?

KEROUAC: Some of it, sire. I also wrote another version that's hidden under the floorboards, with Burroughs.

INTERVIEWER: Yes, I've heard rumors of that book. Everybody wants to get at that book.

KEROUAC: It's called "And the Hippos Were Boiled in Their Tanks." The hippos. Because Burroughs and I were sitting in a bar one night and we heard a newscaster saying . . . "and so the Egyptians attacked blah blah . . . and meanwhile there was a great fire in the zoo in London and the fire raced across the fields and the hippos were boiled in their tanks! Goodnight everyone!" That's Bill, he noticed that. Because he notices them kind of things.

INTERVIEWER: You really did type up his *Naked Lunch* manuscript for him in Tangier?

KEROUAC: No . . . the first part. The first two chapters. I went to bed, and I had nightmares . . . of great long balonies coming out of my mouth. I had nightmares typing up that manuscript . . . I said, Bill! He said, Keep typing it. He said, I bought you a goddamn kerosene stove here in North Africa, you know. Among the Arabs . . . it's hard to get a kerosene stove. I'd light up the kerosene stove, and take some bedding and a little pot, or kif as

Peter Orlovsky, Jack Kerouac, Gregory Corso, and William Burroughs in Tangiers, 1957.

we called it there . . . or maybe sometimes hasheesh . . . there, by the way, it's legal . . . and I'd go toke toke toke toke and when I went to bed at night, these things kept coming out of my mouth. So finally these other guys showed up like Alan Ansen and Allen Ginsberg, and they spoiled the whole manuscript because they didn't type it up the way he wrote it.

INTERVIEWER: Grove Press has been issuing his Olympia Press books with lots of changes and things added.

KEROUAC: Well, in my opinion Burroughs hasn't given us anything that would interest our breaking hearts since he wrote like he did in *Naked Lunch*. Now all he does is that break-up stuff; it's called . . . where you write a page of prose, you write another page of prose . . . then you fold it over and you cut it up and you put it together . . . and shit like that. . . .

INTERVIEWER: What about *Junky*, though?

KEROUAC: It's a classic. It's better than Hemingway—it's just like Hemingway but even a little better too. It says: Danny comes into my pad one night and says, Hey, Bill, can I borrow your sap. Your sap—do you know what a sap is?

SAROYAN: A blackjack?

KEROUAC: It's a blackjack. Bill says, I pulled out my underneath drawer, and underneath some nice shirts I pulled out my blackjack. I gave it to Danny and said, Now don't lose it, Danny— Danny says, Don't worry I won't lose it. He goes off and loses it. Sap . . . blackjack . . . that's me. Sap . . . blackjack.

INTERVIEWER: That's a haiku: sap, blackjack, that's me. You better write that down.

KEROUAC: No.

INTERVIEWER: Maybe I'll write that down. Do you mind if I use that one?

KEROUAC: Up your ass with Mobil gas!

INTERVIEWER: You don't believe in collaborations? Have you ever done any collaborations, other than with publishers?

KEROUAC: I did a couple of collaborations in bed with Bill Cannastra in lofts. With blondes.

INTERVIEWER: Was he the guy that tried to climb off the subway train at Astor Place, in Holmes's *Go*?

KEROUAC: Yes. Yeah, well he says, Let's take all our clothes off and run around the block. . . . It was raining you know. Sixteenth Street off Seventh Avenue. I said, Well, I'll keep my shorts on—he says, No, no shorts. I said, I'm going to keep my shorts on. He said All right, but I'm not going to wear mine. And we trot-trot-trot trot down the block. Sixteenth to Seventeenth . . . and we come back and run up the stairs—nobody saw us.

INTERVIEWER: What time of day?

KEROUAC: But he was absolutely naked . . . about three or four A.M. It rained. And everybody was there. He was dancing on broken glass and playing Bach. Bill was the guy who used to teeter off his roof—six flights up, you know? He'd go—you want me to fall?— we'd say no, Bill, no. He was an Italian. Italians are wild, you know.

INTERVIEWER: Did he write? What did he do?

KEROUAC: He says, Jack, come with me and look down through this peephole. We looked down through the peephole, we saw a lot of things . . . into his toilet.

I said, I'm not interested in that, Bill. He said, You're not interested in anything. Auden would come the next day, the next afternoon, for cocktails. Maybe with Chester Kallman. Tennessee Williams.

INTERVIEWER: Was Neal Cassady around in those days? Did you already know Neal Cassady when you were involved with Bill Cannastra?

KEROUAC: Oh yes, yes, ahem . . . he had a great big pack of pot. He always was a pot happy man.

INTERVIEWER: Why do you think Neal doesn't write?

KEROUAC: He has written . . . beautifully! He has written better than I have. Neal's a very funny guy. He's a real Californian. We had more fun than five thousand Socony Gasoline Station attendants can have. In my opinion he's the most intelligent man I've ever met in my life. Neal Cassady. He's a Jesuit by the way. He used to sing in the choir. He was a choirboy in the Catholic churches of Denver. And he taught me everything that I now do believe about anything that there may be to be believed about divinity.

INTERVIEWER: About Edgar Cayce?

KEROUAC: No, before he found out about Edgar Cayce he told me all these things in the section of the life he led when he was on the road with me—he said, We know God, don't we Jack? I said, Yessir boy. He said, Don't we know that nothing's going to happen wrong? Yessir. And we're going to go on and on . . . and hmmmmmm ja-bmmmmmmmm . . . He was perfect. And he's always perfect. Everytime he comes to see me I can't get a word in edgewise.

INTERVIEWER: You wrote about Neal playing football in *Visions of Cody*.

KEROUAC: Yes, he was a very good football player. He picked up two beatniks that time in blue jeans in North Beach, Frisco. He said, I got to go, bang bang, do I got to go? He's working on the railroad . . . had his watch out . . . two-fifteen, boy I got to be there by two-twenty. I tell you boys drive me over down there so I be on time with my train . . . So I can get my train on down to—what's the name of that place—San Jose? They say, Sure kid and Neal says, Here's the pot. So—"We maybe look like great beatniks with great beards . . . but we are cops. And we are arresting you."

So, a guy went to the jailhouse and interviewed him from the *New York Post* and he said, Tell that Kerouac if he still believes in me to send me a typewriter. So I sent Allen Ginsberg one hundred dollars to get a typewriter for Neal. And Neal got the typewriter. And he wrote notes on it, but they wouldn't let him take the notes out. I don't know where the typewriter is. Genet wrote all of *Our Lady of the Flowers* in the shithouse . . . the jailhouse. There's a great writer, Jean Genet. He kept writing and kept writing until he got to a point where he was going to come by writing about it . . . until he came into his bed—in the can. The French can. The French jail. Prison. And that was the end of the chapter. Every chapter is Genet coming off. Which I must admit Sartre noticed.

INTERVIEWER: You think that's a different kind of spontaneous writing?

KEROUAC: Well, I could go to jail and I could write every night a chapter about Magee, Magoo, and Molly. It's beautiful. Genet is really the most honest writer we've had since Kerouac and Burroughs. But he came before us. He's older. Well, he's the same age as Burroughs. But I don't think I've been dishonest. Man, I've had a good time! God, man, I rode around this country free as a bee. But Genet is a very tragic and beautiful writer. And I give them the crown. And the laurel wreath. I don't give the laurel wreath to Richard Wilbur! Or Robert Lowell. Give it to Jean Genet and William Seward Burroughs. *And* to Allen Ginsberg and to Gregory Corso, especially.

INTERVIEWER: Jack, how about Peter Orlovsky's writings. Do you like Peter's things?

KEROUAC: Peter Orlovsky is an idiot!! He's a Russian idiot. Not even Russian, he's Polish.

INTERVIEWER: He's written some fine poems.

KEROUAC: Oh yeah. My . . . what poems?

INTERVIEWER: He has a beautiful poem called "Second Poem."

KEROUAC: "My brother pisses in the bed . . . and I go in the subway and I see two people kissing . . ."

INTERVIEWER: No, the poem that says "it's more creative to paint the floor than to sweep it."

KEROUAC: That's a lot of shit! That is the kind of poetry that was written by another Polish idiot who was a Polish nut called Apollinaire. Apollinaire is not his real name, you know.

There are some fellows in San Francisco that told me that Peter was an idiot. But I like idiots, and I enjoy his poetry. Think about that, Berrigan. But for my taste, it's Gregory.

Give me one of those.

INTERVIEWER: One of these pills?

KEROUAC: Yeah. What are they? Forked clarinets?

INTERVIEWER: They're called Obetrol. Neal is the one that told me about them.

KEROUAC: Overtones?

INTERVIEWER: Overtones? No, overcoats.

SAROYAN: What was that you said . . . at the back of the Grove anthology . . . that you let the line go a little longer to fill it up with secret images that come at the end of the sentence.

KEROUAC: He's a real Armenian! Sediment. Delta. Mud. It's where you start a poem. . . .

> As I was walking down the street one day
> I saw a lake where people were cutting off my rear,
> 17,000 priests singing like George Burns

and then you go on . . .

> *And I'm making jokes about me*
> *and breaking my bones in the earth*
> *and here I am the great John Armenian*
> *coming back to earth*

now you remember where you were in the beginning and you say . . .

> *Ahaha! Tatatatadooda . . . Screw Turkey!*

See? You remembered the line at the end . . . you lose your mind in the middle.

SAROYAN: Right.

KEROUAC: That applies to prose as well as poetry.

INTERVIEWER: But in prose you are telling a story . . .

KEROUAC: In prose you make the paragraph. Every paragraph is a poem.

INTERVIEWER: Is that how you write a paragraph?

KEROUAC: When I was running downtown there, and I was going to do this, and I was laying there, with that girl there, and a guy took out his scissors and I took him inside there, he showed me some dirty pictures. And I went out and fell downstairs with the potato bags.

INTERVIEWER: Did you ever like Gertrude Stein's work?

KEROUAC: Never interested me too much. I liked "Melanctha" a little bit.
     I should really go to school and teach these kids. I could make two thousand bucks a week. You can't learn these things. You know why? Because you have to be born with tragic fathers.

INTERVIEWER: You can only do that if you are born in New England.

KEROUAC: Incidentally, my father said your father wasn't tragic.

SAROYAN: I don't think my father is tragic.

Jack Kerouac taking a break at a poetry reading, surrounded by fans and groupies.

KEROUAC: My father said that Saroyan . . . William Saroyan ain't tragic at all . . . he's fulla shit. And I had a big argument with him. *The Daring Young Man on the Flying Trapeze* is pretty tragic, I would say.

SAROYAN: He was just a young man then, you know.

KEROUAC: Yeah, but he was hungry, and he was on Times Square. Flying. A young man on the flying trapeze. That was a beautiful story. It killed me when I was a kid.

INTERVIEWER: Do you remember a story by William Saroyan about the Indian who came to town and bought a car and got the little kid to drive it for him?

STELLA: A Cadillac.

KEROUAC: What town was that?

SAROYAN: Fresno. That was Fresno.

KEROUAC: Well, you remember the night I was taking a big nap and you came up outside my window on a white horse. . . .

SAROYAN: "The Summer of the Beautiful White Horse."

KEROUAC: And I looked out the window and said what is this? You said, My name is Aram. And I'm on a white horse.

SAROYAN: Moorad.

KEROUAC: My name is Moorad, excuse me. No, my name is . . . I was Aram, you were Moorad. You said, Wake up! I didn't want to wake up. I wanted to sleep. *My Name Is Aram* is the name of the book. You stole a white horse from a farmer and you woke up me, Aram, to go riding with you.

SAROYAN: Moorad was the crazy one who stole the horse.

KEROUAC: Hey, what's that you gave me there?

INTERVIEWER: Obetrol.

KEROUAC: Oh, obies.

INTERVIEWER: What about jazz and bop as influences rather than . . . Saroyan, Hemingway, and Wolfe?

KEROUAC: Yes, jazz and bop, in the sense of a, say, a tenor man drawing a breath and blowing a phrase on his saxophone, till he runs out of breath, and when he does, his sentence, his statement's been made. . . . That's how I therefore separate my sentences, as breath separations of the mind. . . . I formulated the theory of breath as measure, in prose and verse, never mind what Olson, Charles Olson says, I formulated that theory in 1953 at the request of Burroughs and Ginsberg. Then there's the raciness and freedom and humor of jazz instead of all that dreary analysis and things like "James entered the room, and lit a cigarette. He thought Jane might have thought this too vague a gesture . . ." You know the stuff. As for Saroyan, yes I loved him as a teenager, he really got me out of the nineteenth-century rut I was trying to study, not only with his funny tone but also with his neat Armenian poetic—I don't know what . . . he just got me . . . Hemingway was fascinating, the pearls of words on a white page giving you an exact picture . . . but Wolfe was a torrent of American heaven and hell that opened my eyes to America as a subject in itself.

INTERVIEWER: How about the movies?

KEROUAC: Yes, we've all been influenced by movies. Malcolm Cowley incidentally mentioned this many times. He's very perceptive sometimes: he mentioned that *Doctor Sax* continually mentions urine, and quite naturally it does because I had no other place to write it but on a closed toilet seat in a little tile toilet in Mexico City so as to get away from the guests inside the apartment. There, incidentally, is a style truly hallucinated, as I wrote it all on pot. No pun intended. Ho ho.

INTERVIEWER: How has Zen influenced your work?

KEROUAC: What's really influenced my work is the Mahayana Buddhism, the original Buddhism of Gautama Śākyamuni, the Buddha himself, of the India of old. . . . Zen is what's left of his Buddhism, or Bodhi, after its passing into China and then into Japan. The part of Zen that's influenced my writing is the Zen contained in the haiku, like I said, the three-line, seventeen-syllable poems written hundreds of years ago by guys like Bashō, Issa, Shiki, and there've been recent masters. A sentence that's short and sweet with a sudden jump of thought in it is a kind of haiku, and there's a lot of freedom and fun in surprising yourself with that, let the mind willy-nilly jump from the branch to the bird. But my serious Buddhism, that of ancient India, has influenced that part in my writing that you might call religious, or fervent, or pious, almost as much as Catholicism has. Original Buddhism referred to continual conscious compassion, brotherhood, the *dana paramita* meaning the perfection of charity, don't step on the bug, all that, humility, mendicancy, the sweet sorrowful face of the Buddha (who was of Aryan origin by the way, I mean of Persian warrior caste, and not Oriental as pictured) . . . in original Buddhism no young kid coming to a monastery was warned that "Here we bury them alive." He was simply given soft encouragement to meditate and be kind. The beginning of Zen was when Buddha, however, assembled all the monks together to announce a sermon and choose the first patriarch of the Mahayana church: instead of speaking, he simply held up a flower. Everybody was flabbergasted except Kāśyapīya, who smiled. Kāśyapīya was appointed the first patriarch. This idea appealed to the Chinese like the sixth patriarch Hui-Neng who said, "From the beginning nothing ever was," and wanted to tear up the records of Buddha's sayings as kept in the sutras; sutras are "threads of discourse." In a way, then, Zen is a gentle but goofy form of heresy, though there must be some real kindly old monks somewhere and we've heard about the nutty ones. I haven't been to Japan. Your Maha Roshi Yoshi is simply a disciple of all this and not the founder of anything new at all, of course. On the Johnny Carson show he didn't even mention Buddha's name. Maybe his Buddha is Mia.

INTERVIEWER: How come you've never written about Jesus? You've written about Buddha. Wasn't Jesus a great guy too?

KEROUAC: I've never written about Jesus? In other words, you're an insane phoney who comes to my house . . . and . . . all I *write about* is Jesus. I am Everhard Mercurian, General of the Jesuit Army.

SAROYAN: What's the difference between Jesus and Buddha?

KEROUAC: That's a very good question. There is no difference.

SAROYAN: No difference?

KEROUAC: But there is a difference between the original Buddha of India, and the Buddha of Vietnam who just shaves his hair and puts on a yellow robe and is a communist agitating agent. The original Buddha wouldn't even walk on young grass so that he wouldn't destroy it. He was born in Gorakhpur, the son of the consul of the invading Persian hordes. And he was called Sage of the Warriors, and he had seventeen thousand broads dancing for him all night, holding out flowers, saying you want to smell it, my lord? He says Git outta here you whore. He laid a lot of them you know. But by the time he was thirty-one years old he got sick and tired . . . his father was protecting him from what was going on outside the town. And so he went out on a horse, against his father's orders and he saw a woman dying—a man being burnt on a ghat. And he said, "What is all this death and decay?" The servant said that is the way things go on. Your father was hiding you from the way things go on.

He says, "What? My father!! Get my horse, saddle my horse! Ride me into the forest!" They ride into the forest; he says, "Now take the saddle off the horse. Put it on your horse, hang it on. . . . Take my horse by the rein and ride back to the castle and tell my father I'll never see him again!" And the servant, Kanthanka, cried, he said, "I'll never see you again. I don't care! Go on! Shoosh! Get away!!"

He spent seven years in the forest. Biting his teeth together. Nothing happened. Tormenting himself with starvation. He said, "I will keep my teeth bit together until I find the cause of death." Then one day he was stumbling across the Rapti River, and he fainted in the river. And a young girl came by with a bowl of milk and said, "My lord, a bowl of milk." [*Slurppp*] He said, "That gives me great energy, thank you my dear." Then he went and sat under the Bo tree. Figuerosa. The fig tree. He said, "Now . . . [*demonstrates posture*] I will cross my legs . . . and grit my teeth until I find the cause of death." Two o'clock in the morning, one hundred thousand phantoms assailed him. He didn't move. Three o'clock in the morning, the great blue ghosts!! Arrghhh!!! All *accosted* him. (You see I am really Scottish.) Four o'clock in the morning the mad maniacs of hell . . . came out of manhole covers . . . in New York City. You know Wall Street where the steam comes out? You know Wall Street, where the manhole covers . . . steam comes up? You take off them covers—yaaaaaahhh!!!!! Six o'clock, everything was peaceful—the birds started to trill, and he said, "Aha! The cause of death . . . the cause of death is birth."

Simple? So he started walking down the road to Banaras in India . . . with long hair, like you, see.

So, three guys. One says, "Hey, here comes Buddha there who, uh, starved with us in the forest. When he sits down here on that bucket, don't wash his feet." So Buddha sits down on the bucket. . . . The guy rushes up and washes his feet. "Why dost thou wash his feet?" Buddha says, "Because I go to Banaras to beat the drum of life." "And what is that?" "That the cause of death is birth." "What do you mean?" "I'll show you."

A woman comes up with a dead baby in her arms. Says, "Bring my child back to life if you are the Lord." He says, "Sure I'll do that anytime. Just go and find one family in Śrāvastī that ain't had a death in the last five years. Get a mustard seed from them and bring it to me. And I'll bring your child back to life." She went all over town, man, two million people, Śrāvastī the town was, a bigger town than Banaras by the way, and she came back and said, "I can't find no such family. They've all had deaths within five years." He said, "Then, bury your baby."

Then, his jealous cousin, Devadatta (that's Ginsberg you see . . . I am Buddha and Ginsberg is Devadatta), gets this elephant drunk . . . great big bull elephant drunk on whiskey. The elephant goes up—[*trumpets like elephant going up*] with a big trunk, and Buddha comes up in the road and gets the elephant and goes like this [*kneels*]. And the elephant kneels down. "You are buried in sorrow's mud! Quiet your trunk! Stay there!" He's an elephant trainer. Then Devadatta rolled a big boulder over a cliff. And it almost hit Buddha's head. Just missed. Boooom! He says, "That's Devadatta again." Then Buddha went like this [*paces back and forth*] in front of his boys, you see. Behind him was his cousin that loved him . . . Ananda . . . which means love in Sanskrit [*keeps pacing*]. This is what you do in jail to keep in shape.

I know a lot of stories about Buddha, but I don't know exactly what he said every time. But I know what he said about the guy who spit at him. He said, "Since I can't use your abuse you may have it back." He was great. [*Kerouac plays piano. Drinks are served.*]

SAROYAN: There's something there.

INTERVIEWER: My mother used to play that. I'm not sure how we can transcribe those notes onto a page. We may have to include a record of you playing the piano. Will you play that piece again for the record, Mr. Paderewski? Can you play "Alouette"?

KEROUAC: No. Only Afro-Germanic music. After all, I'm a square head. I wonder what whiskey will do to those obies.

INTERVIEWER: What about ritual and superstition? Do you have any about yourself when you get down to work?

KEROUAC: I had a ritual once of lighting a candle and writing by its light and blowing it out when I was done for the night . . . also kneeling and praying before starting (I got that from a French movie about George Frideric Handel) . . . but now I simply hate to write. My superstition? I'm beginning to suspect the full moon. Also I'm hung up on the number 9 though I'm told a Piscean like myself should stick to number 7; but I try to do nine touchdowns a day, that is, I stand on my head in the bathroom, on a slipper, and touch the floor nine times with my toe tips, while balanced. This is incidentally more than Yoga, it's an athletic feat, I mean imagine calling me "unbalanced" after that. Frankly I do feel that my mind is going. So another "ritual" as you call it, is to pray to

Jesus to preserve my sanity and my energy so I can help my family: that being my paralyzed mother, and my wife, and the ever-present kitties. Okay?

INTERVIEWER: You typed out *On the Road* in three weeks, *The Subterraneans* in three days and nights. Do you still produce at this fantastic rate? Can you say something of the genesis of a work before you sit down and begin that terrific typing—how much of it is set in your mind, for example?

KEROUAC: You think out what actually happened, you tell friends long stories about it, you mull it over in your mind, you connect it together at leisure, then when the time comes to pay the rent again you force yourself to sit at the typewriter, or at the writing notebook, and get it over with as fast as you can . . . and there's no harm in that because you've got the whole story lined up. Now how that's done depends on what kind of steeltrap you've got up in that little old head. This sounds boastful but a girl once told me I had a steeltrap brain, meaning I'd catch her with a statement she'd made an hour ago even though our talk had rambled a million light-years away from that point . . . you know what I mean, like a lawyer's mind, say. All of it is in my mind, naturally, except that language that is used at the time that it is used . . . And as for *On the Road* and *The Subterraneans*, no I can't write that fast anymore . . . Writing *The Subs* in three nights was really a fantastic athletic feat as well as mental, you shoulda seen me after I was done. . . . I was pale as a sheet and had lost fifteen pounds and looked strange in the mirror. What I do now is write something like an average of eight thousand words a sitting, in the middle of the night, and another about a week later, resting and sighing in between. I really hate to write. I get no fun out of it because I can't get up and say I'm working, close my door, have coffee brought to me, and sit there camping like a "man of letters" "doing his eight hour day of work" and thereby incidentally filling the printing world with a lot of dreary self-imposed cant and bombast, bombast being Scottish for pillow stuffing. Haven't you heard a politician use fifteen hundred words to say something he could have said in exactly three words? So I get it out of the way so as not to bore myself either.

SAROYAN: Do you usually try to see everything clearly and not think of any words—just to see everything as clear as possible and then write out of the feeling? With *Tristessa*, for example.

KEROUAC: You sound like a writing seminar at Indiana University.

SAROYAN: I know but . . .

KEROUAC: All I did was suffer with that poor girl and then when she fell on her head and almost killed herself . . . remember when she fell on her head? She was all busted up and everything. She was the most gorgeous little Indian chick you ever saw. I say Indian, pure Indian. Esperanza Villanueva. Villanueva is a Spanish name from I don't know where—Castile. But she's Indian. So she's half Indian, half Spanish . . . beauty. Absolute beauty. She had bones, man, just bones, skin and bones. And I didn't write in the book how I finally nailed her. You know? I did. I finally nailed her. She said, Shhhhhhhhhh! Don't let the landlord hear. She said, Remember, I'm very weak and sick. I said, I know, I've been writing a book about how you're weak and sick.

INTERVIEWER: How come you didn't put that part in the book?

KEROUAC: Because Claude's wife told me not to put it in. She said it would spoil the book.
   But it was not a conquest. She was out like a light. On M. M., that's morphine. And in fact I made a big run for her from way uptown to downtown to the slum district . . . and I said, Here's your stuff. She said, Shhhhhh! She gave herself a shot and I said, Ah . . . now's the time. And I got my little no good piece. But . . . it was certainly justification of Mexico!

STELLA: Here kitty! He's gone out again.

KEROUAC: She was nice, you would have liked her. Her real name was Esperanza. You know what that means?

INTERVIEWER: No.

KEROUAC: In Spanish, "hope." *Tristessa* means in Spanish, "sadness," but her real name was Hope. And she's now married to the police chief of Mexico City.

STELLA: Not quite.

KEROUAC: Well, you're not Esperanza—I'll tell you that.

STELLA: No, I know that, dear.

KEROUAC: She was the skinniest . . . and shy . . . as a rail.

STELLA: She's married to one of the lieutenants, you told me, not to the chief.

KEROUAC: She's all right. One of these days I'm going to go see her again.

STELLA: Over my dead body.

INTERVIEWER: Were you really writing *Tristessa* while you were there in Mexico? You didn't write it later?

KEROUAC: First part written in Mexico, second part written in . . . Mexico. That's right. Nineteen fifty-five first part, '56 second part. What's the importance about that? I'm not Charles Olson, the great artist!

INTERVIEWER: We're just getting the facts.

KEROUAC: Charles Olson gives you all the dates. You know. Everything about how he found the hound on the beach in Gloucester. Found somebody jacking off on the beach at . . . what do they call it? Vancouver Beach? Dig Dog River? . . . Dogtown. That's what they call it, "Dogtown." Well this is Shittown on the Merrimack. Lowell is called Shittown on the Merrimack. I'm not going to write a poem called Shittown and insult my town. But if I were six foot six I could write anything, couldn't I?

INTERVIEWER: How do you get along now with other writers? Do you correspond with them?

KEROUAC: I correspond with John Clellon Holmes but less and less each year; I'm getting lazy. I can't answer my fan mail because I haven't got a secretary to take dictation, do the typing, get the stamps, envelopes, all that . . . and I have nothing to answer. I ain't gonna spend the rest of my life smiling and shaking hands and sending and receiving platitudes, like a candidate for political office, because I'm a writer—I've got to let my mind alone, like Greta Garbo. Yet when I go out, or receive sudden guests, we all have more fun than a barrel of monkeys.

INTERVIEWER: What are the work-destroyers?

KEROUAC: Work-destroyers . . . work-destroyers. Time-killers? I'd say mainly the attentions which are tendered to a writer of "notoriety" (notice I don't say "fame") by secretly ambitious would-be writers, who come around, or write, or call, for the sake of the services which are properly the services of a bloody literary agent. When I was an unknown struggling young writer, as the saying goes, I did my own footwork, I hot-footed up and down Madison Avenue for years, publisher to publisher, agent to agent, and never once in my life wrote a letter to a published famous author asking for advice, or help, or, in Heaven above, have the nerve to actually *mail* my manuscripts to some poor author who then has to hustle to mail it back before he's accused of stealing my ideas. My advice to young writers is to get themselves an agent on their own, maybe through their college professors (as I got my first publishers through my prof Mark Van Doren) and do their own footwork, or "thing" as the slang goes . . . So the work-destroyers are nothing but certain *people*.

The work-preservers are the solitudes of night, "when the whole wide world is fast asleep."

INTERVIEWER: What do you find the best time and place for writing?

KEROUAC: The desk in the room, near the bed, with a good light, midnight till dawn, a drink when you get tired, preferably at home, but if you have no home, make a home out of your hotel room or motel room or pad: peace. [*Picks up harmonica and plays.*] Boy, can I play!

INTERVIEWER: What about writing under the influence of drugs?

KEROUAC: Poem 230 from *Mexico City Blues* is a poem written purely on morphine. Every line in this poem was written within an hour of one another . . . high on a big dose of M. [*Finds volume and reads*]

> Love's multitudinous boneyard of decay,

An hour later:

> The spilled milk of heroes,

An hour later:

> *Destruction of silk kerchiefs by dust storm,*

An hour later:

> *Caress of heroes blindfolded to posts,*

An hour later:

> *Murder victims admitted to this life,*

An hour later:

> *Skeletons bartering fingers and joints,*

An hour later:

> *The quivering meat of the elephants of kindness being torn apart by vultures,*

(See where Ginsberg stole that from me?)
An hour later:

> *Conceptions of delicate kneecaps.*

Say that, Saroyan.

SAROYAN: Conceptions of delicate kneecaps.

KEROUAC: Very good.

> *Fear of rats dripping with bacteria.*

An hour later:

> *Golgotha Cold Hope for Gold Hope.*

Say that.

SAROYAN: Golgotha Cold Hope for Cold Hope.

KEROUAC: That's pretty cold.

An hour later:

> *Damp leaves of Autumn against the*
> *wood of boats,*

An hour later:

> *Seahorse's delicate imagery of glue.*

Ever see a little seahorse in the ocean? They're built of glue. . . .
Did you ever sniff a sea horse? No, say that.

SAROYAN: Seahorse's delicate imagery of glue.

KEROUAC: You'll do, Saroyan.

> *Death by long exposure to defilement.*

SAROYAN: Death by long exposure to defilement.

KEROUAC: *Frightening ravishing mysterious beings concealing their sex.*

SAROYAN: Frightening ravishing mysterious beings concealing
their sex.

KEROUAC: *Pieces of the Buddha-material frozen and sliced*
microscopically
In Morgues of the North.

SAROYAN: Hey, I can't say that. Pieces of the Buddha-material
frozen and sliced microscopically in Morgues of the North.

KEROUAC: *Penis apples going to seed.*

SAROYAN: Penis apples going to seed.

KEROUAC: *The severed gullets more numerous than sands.*

SAROYAN: The severed gullets more numerous than sands.

KEROUAC: *Like kissing my kitten in the belly.*

SAROYAN: Like kissing my kitten in the belly.

KEROUAC: *The softness of our reward.*

SAROYAN: The softness of our reward.

KEROUAC: Is he really William Saroyan's son? That's wonderful!
Would you mind repeating that?

INTERVIEWER: We should be asking you a lot of very straight serious questions. When did you meet Allen Ginsberg?

KEROUAC: First I met Claude.* And then I met Allen and then I met
Burroughs. Claude came in through the fire escape . . . There were
gunshots down in the alley—Pow! Pow!—and it was raining, and
my wife says, Here comes Claude. And here comes this blond guy
through the fire escape, all wet. I said, What's this all about, what
the hell is this? He says, They're chasing me. Next day in walks
Allen Ginsberg carrying books. Sixteen years old with his ears
sticking out. He says, Well, discretion is the better part of valor! I
said, Aw shutup. You little twitch. Then the next day here comes
Burroughs wearing a seersucker suit, followed by the other guy.

INTERVIEWER: What other guy?

KEROUAC: It was the guy who wound up in the river. This was the
guy from New Orleans that Claude killed and threw in the river.
Stabbed him twelve times in the heart with a Boy Scout knife.
    When Claude was fourteen he was the most beautiful blond
boy in New Orleans. And he joined the Boy Scout troop . . . and
the Boy Scout master was a big redheaded fairy who went to
school at St. Louis University, I think it was.
    And he had already been in love with a guy who looked just
like Claude in Paris. And this guy chased Claude all over the
country; this guy had him thrown out of Baldwin, Tulane, and An-
dover Prep. . . . It's a queer tale, but Claude isn't a queer.

INTERVIEWER: What about the influence of Ginsberg and Burroughs? Did you ever have any sense then of the mark the three of
you would have on American writing?

* "Claude," Kerouac's pseudonym for Lucien Carr, is also used in *Vanity of
Duluoz*.

KEROUAC: I was determined to be a "great writer," in quotes, like Thomas Wolfe, see. . . . Allen was always reading and writing poetry. . . . Burroughs read a lot and walked around looking at things. The influence we exerted on one another has been written about over and over again. . . . We were just three interested characters, in the interesting big city of New York, around campuses, libraries, cafeterias. You can find a lot of the details in *Vanity* . . . in *On the Road*, where Burroughs is Bull Lee and Ginsberg is Carlo Marx, and in *Subterraneans*, where they're Frank Carmody and Adam Moorad, respectively. In other words, though I don't want to be rude to you for this honor, I am so busy interviewing myself in my novels, and have been so busy writing down these self-interviews, that I don't see why I should draw breath in pain every year for the last ten years to repeat and repeat to everybody who interviews me (hundreds of journalists, thousands of students) what I've already explained in the books themselves. It begs sense. And it's not *that* important. It's our work that counts, if anything at all, and I'm not too proud of mine or theirs or anybody's since Thoreau and others like that, maybe because it's still too close to home for comfort. Notoriety and public confession in the literary form is a frazzler of the heart you were born with, believe me.

INTERVIEWER: Allen once said that he learned how to read Shakespeare, that he never did understand Shakespeare until he heard you read Shakespeare to him.

KEROUAC: Because in a previous lifetime, that's who I was.

> *How like a winter hath my absence been from thee?*
> *The pleasure of the fleeting year . . . what freezings*
> *have I felt? What dark days seen? Yet Summer with his*
> *lord surcease hath laid a big turd in my orchard.*
> *And one hog after another comes to eat*
> *and break my broken mountain trap, and my mousetrap*
> *too! And here to end the sonnet, you must make sure*
> *to say, tara-tara-tara!!!!!!*

INTERVIEWER: Is that spontaneous composition?

KEROUAC: Well, the first part was Shakespeare . . . and the second part was . . .

INTERVIEWER: Have you ever written any sonnets?

KEROUAC: I'll give you a spontaneous sonnet. It has to be what, now?

INTERVIEWER: Fourteen lines.

KEROUAC: That's twelve lines with two dragging lines. That's where you bring out your heavy artillery.

> *Here the fish of Scotland seen your eye*
> *and all my nets did creak . . .*

Does it have to rhyme?

INTERVIEWER: No.

KEROUAC:

> *My poor chapped hands fall awry*
> *and seen the Pope, his devilled eye.*
> *And maniacs with wild hair hanging about my room*
> *and listening to my tomb*
> *which does not rhyme.*

Seven lines?

INTERVIEWER: That was eight lines.

KEROUAC:

> *And all the orgones of the earth will crawl*
> *like dogs across the graves of Peru*
> *and Scotland too.*

That's ten.

> *Yet do not worry, sweet angel of mine*
> *That hast thine inheritance*
> *imbedded in mine.*

INTERVIEWER: That's pretty good, Jack. How did you do that?

KEROUAC: Without studying dactyls . . . like Ginsberg . . . I met Ginsberg . . . I'd hitchhiked all the way back from Mexico City to

Berkeley, and that's a long way baby, a long way. Mexico City across Durango . . . Chihuahua . . . Texas. I go back to Ginsberg, I go to his cottage, I say, Hah, we're gonna play the music. He says, You know what I'm going to do tomorrow? I'm going to throw on Mark Schorer's desk a new theory of prosody! About the dactyllic arrangements of Ovid! [*laughter*]

I said, Quit, man. Sit under a tree and forget it and drink wine with me . . . and Phil Whalen and Gary Snyder and all the bums of San Francisco. Don't you try to be a big Berkeley teacher. Just be a poet under the trees . . . and we'll wrestle and we'll break holds. And he did take my advice. He remembered that. He said, What are you going to teach . . . you have parched lips! I said, Naturally, I just came from Chihuahua. It's very hot down there, phew! You go out and little pigs rub against your legs. Phew!

So here comes Snyder with a bottle of wine . . . and here comes Whalen, and here comes what's his name, Rexroth, and everybody . . . and we had the poetry renaissance of San Francisco.

INTERVIEWER: What about Allen getting kicked out of Columbia? Didn't you have something to do with that?

KEROUAC: Oh, no . . . he let me sleep in his room. He was not kicked out of Columbia for that. The first time he let me sleep in his room, and the guy that slept in our room with us was Lancaster who was descended from the White Roses or Red Roses of England. But a guy came in . . . the guy that ran the floor and he thought that I was trying to make Allen, and Allen had already written in the paper that I wasn't sleeping there because I was trying to make him, but he was trying to make me. But we were just actually sleeping. Then after that he got a pad . . . he got some stolen goods in there . . . and he got some thieves up there, Vicky and Huncke. And they were all busted for stolen goods, and a car turned over, and Allen's glasses broke, it's all in John Holmes's *Go*.

Allen Ginsberg asked me when he was nineteen years old, Should I change my name to Allen Renard? "You change your name to Allen Renard I'll kick you right in the balls!" Stick to Ginsberg . . . and he did. That's one thing I like about Allen. Allen *Renard*!!!

INTERVIEWER: What was it that brought all of you together in the fifties? What was it that seemed to unify the Beat generation?

KEROUAC: Oh the Beat generation was just a phrase I used in the 1951 written manuscript of *On the Road* to describe guys like Moriarty who run around the country in cars looking for odd jobs, girlfriends, kicks. It was thereafter picked up by West Coast Leftist groups and turned into a meaning like "Beat mutiny" and "Beat insurrection" and all that nonsense; they just wanted some youth movement to grab on to for their own political and social purposes. I had nothing to do with any of that. I was a football player, a scholarship college student, a merchant seaman, a railroad brakeman on road freights, a script synopsizer, a secretary . . . And Moriarty-Cassady was an actual cowboy on Dave Uhl's ranch in New Raymer, Colorado . . . What kind of beatnik is that?

INTERVIEWER: Was there any sense of "community" among the Beat crowd?

KEROUAC: That community feeling was largely inspired by the same characters I mentioned, like Ferlinghetti, Ginsberg; they are very socialistically minded and want everybody to live in some kind of frenetic kibbutz, solidarity and all that. I was a loner. Snyder is not like Whalen, Whalen is not like McClure, I am not like McClure, McClure is not like Ferlinghetti, Ginsberg is not like Ferlinghetti, but we all had fun over wine anyway. We knew thousands of poets and painters and jazz musicians. There's no "Beat crowd" like you say. . . . What about Scott Fitzgerald and his "lost crowd," does that sound right? Or Goethe and his "Wilhelm Meister crowd"? The subject is such a bore. Pass me that glass.

INTERVIEWER: Well, why did they split in the early sixties?

KEROUAC: Ginsberg got interested in left wing politics . . . Like Joyce I say, as Joyce said to Ezra Pound in the 1920s, "Don't bother me with politics, the only thing that interests me is style." Besides I'm bored with the new avant-garde and the skyrocketing sensationalism. I'm reading Blaise Pascal and taking notes on religion. I like to hang around now with nonintellectuals, as you might call them, and not have my mind proselytized, ad infinitum. They've even started crucifying chickens in happenings, what's the next step? An actual crucifixion of a man . . . The Beat group dispersed as you say in the early sixties, all went their own way, and this is my way: home life, as in the beginning, with a little toot once in a while in local bars.

INTERVIEWER: What do you think of what they're up to now? Allen's radical political involvement? Burroughs's cut-up methods?

KEROUAC: I'm pro-American and the radical political involvements seem to tend elsewhere. . . . The country gave my Canadian family a good break, more or less, and we see no reason to demean said country. As for Burroughs's cut-up method, I wish he'd get back to those awfully funny stories of his he used to write and those marvelously dry vignettes in *Naked Lunch*. Cut-up is nothing new, in fact that steeltrap brain of mine does a lot of cutting up as it goes along . . . as does everyone's brain while talking or thinking or writing. . . . It's just an old Dada trick, and a kind of literary collage. He comes out with some great effects though. I like him to be elegant and logical and that's why I don't like the cut-up which is supposed to teach us that the mind is cracked. Sure the mind's cracked, as anybody can see in a hallucinated high, but how about an explanation of the crackedness that can be understood in a workaday moment?

INTERVIEWER: What do you think about the hippies and the LSD scene?

KEROUAC: They're already changing, I shouldn't be able to make a judgment. And they're not all of the same mind. The Diggers are different. . . . I don't know one hippie anyhow. . . . I think they think I'm a truck-driver. And I am. As for LSD, it's bad for people with incidence of heart disease in the family [*knocks microphone off footstool . . . recovers it*].

Is there any reason why you can see anything good in this here mortality?

INTERVIEWER: Excuse me, would you mind repeating that?

KEROUAC: You said you had a little white beard in your belly. Why is there a little white beard in your mortality belly?

INTERVIEWER: Let me think about it. Actually it's a little white pill.

KEROUAC: A little white pill?

INTERVIEWER: It's good.

KEROUAC: Give me.

INTERVIEWER: We should wait till the scene cools a little.

KEROUAC: Right. This little white pill is a little white beard in your mortality which advises you and advertises to you that you will be growing long fingernails in the graves of Peru.

SAROYAN: Do you feel middle-aged?

KEROUAC: No. Listen, we're coming to the end of the tape. I want to add something on. Ask me what Kerouac means.

INTERVIEWER: Jack, tell me again what Kerouac means.

KEROUAC: Now, kairn. K (or C) A-I-R-N. What is a cairn? It's a heap of stones. Now Cornwall, cairn-wall. Now, right, kern, also K-E-R-N, means the same thing as cairn. Kern. Cairn. *Ouac* means "language of." So, Kernouac means the language of Cornwall. Kerr, which is like Deborah Kerr. Ouack means language of water. Because Kerr, Carr, etc., means water. And cairn means heap of stones. There is no language in a heap of stones. Kerouac. Kerwater, ouac-language of. And it's related to the old Irish name, Kerwick, which is a corruption. And it's a Cornish name, which in itself means cairnish. And according to Sherlock Holmes, it's all Persian. Of course you know he's not Persian. Don't you remember in Sherlock Holmes when he went down with Dr. Watson and solved the case down in old Cornwall and he solved the case and then he said, "Watson, the needle! Watson, the needle . . ." He said, "I've solved this case here in Cornwall. Now I have the liberty to sit around here and decide and read books, which will prove to me . . . why the Cornish people, otherwise known as the Kernuaks, or Kerouacs, are of Persian origin. The enterprise which I am about to embark upon," he then said, after he got his shot, "is fraught with eminent peril, and not fit for a lady of your tender years." Remember that?

MCNAUGHTON: I remember that.

KEROUAC: McNaughton remembers that. McNaughton. You think I would forget the name of a Scotsman?

—TED BERRIGAN
1968

Charles Olson

was born in Worcester, Massachusetts, in 1910. He began his career as a scholar, writing *Call Me Ishmael* (1947), a seminal study of Herman Melville's prose and a classic exploration of American culture and letters. During the Second World War, he briefly worked for the ACLU and the Foreign Language Information Service until turning to writing full time. In 1948, he published his first book of poetry, *Y & X*. The two works received major attention, winning him a position as a teacher and then rector of Black Mountain College—an experimental institution in North Carolina. There he joined forces with Robert Creeley to launch a free-verse "revolution" based on the kinetics of "projective verse." Olson's essay on the subject challenged poetic conventions; inspired by William Carlos Williams's defense of new verse forms, Olson advocated "open-field composition," poetry whose appearance and internal logic are governed by the spontaneity of the writing process.

Though Olson was well read and well educated (B.A., M.A. from Wesleyan, 1932 and 1933), he never thought of himself as bookish. For him, it was "awkward to call myself a poet or a writer. . . . This is the morning, after the dispersion, and the work of the morning is the methodology: how to use oneself, and on what. That is my profession. I am an archaeologist of morning."

Olson's most accomplished work, *The Maximus Poems*, is an epic collection that begins with a study of local politics in Gloucester, Massachusetts, and moves into a mythological investigation of world history. Published in sequence between 1953 and 1976, the poems champion the tradition of the extended narrative form initiated by Walt Whitman, Ezra Pound, and T. S. Eliot.

In 1970, Olson's short poems were collected in *Archaeologist of Morning*. He died later that year, leaving all his papers to the University of Connecticut.

I arrived at Annisquam, a village nearby Gloucester, on Sunday, April 13, about midday. I was the houseguest of the poet Gerrit Lansing whom I had met a few years previously in New York at a party given by the poet Kenward Elmslie. Early in the evening Gerrit and I decided to set out for the Cut. It was seven-thirty when we reached Charles Olson's flat to discover a note taped to the windowpane of the rear door, which read as follows: "Gerard: Best I can see is if another night will do me any good (if you can afford to try me again). Gerrit—Gerard—Have been in bed with some strange malady solidly since Saturday. This is to get you an immediate response." I answered the note stating that I would try again the following night to catch him at home.

Monday at five-forty-five P.M. Gerrit and I returned to the scene. The sun had just disappeared behind the village scattered among the hills across the Cut. I had my Uher 1000 Report Pilot strapped to my shoul-

*der. Upon reaching the door Gerrit and I discovered a second note
(Olson's notorious for his door memos), which read: "I shall try to see if
anything comes into my head—I actually mean if my head has any response itself—and either change this note or call you and Gerrit."*

*Returning to Gerrit's house I immediately phoned Mr. Olson with
whom I exchanged a few words and agreed that I should come by tomorrow at leisure without fixing a prescribed time.*

*The following day, Gerrit and I were met by Harvey Brown (pub-
lisher of Niagra Frontier Books) who, from nearby West Newbury,
joined us for lunch. Afterward, Gerrit, Harvey and I decided to see if
Olson was up and around. I didn't have my machine with me, so was
not expecting to begin an interview, having not planned to visit Mr.
Olson at this time.*

*A chance meeting with Mr. Olson on Tuesday beside the wooden
staircase leading to his second-story floorthrough apartment was a benediction. We had not met before, but upon seeing him, it was as if he had
been waiting for me to arrive the entire afternoon. I found him facing the
driveway and the bay, enjoying the sunlight and the breath of brine waft-
ing from the sea. His discourse was chiefly of the past; but he was not un-
mindful of current events nor was he unaffected by the picturesque
surroundings of his secluded abode. With seeing vision, acutest faculties,
and clearest utterance, Olson surveyed his little seaside hamlet and its
environs, interpreted the marvels all about him and shed the light of his
presence upon the common things of the sea and land always within
sight. An hour with this gentleman of the old school, in seclusion deepened and shadowed by hill, cliff, rock, tree, shrub, and vine, and sweet-
ened by the mingling odors of marsh and upland, was the beginning of
what turned out to be an all-night affair. Listening to him speak, long
after the sun went down and long after having run out of tape, until the
morning hours, was a deep and most enchanting experience.*

*When I awoke a few hours after the all-night conversation, I found
the flat empty. The cool blue sunlight of morning filtered through all the
southern-exposure windows of the flat. In the kitchen on a table cluttered
with beer cans, cigarette and cigar butts, and unanswered correspon-
dence, I found a draft of a new Olson poem scribbled on the back of an envelope, which read:*

To build out of sound the walls of the city
& display in one flower the wunderworld so that,
by such means the unique stand forth
clear itself shall be made known.

I slipped his words like a thief into the breast pocket of my coat. My eyes then caught sight of a note addressed to me from Mr. Olson which read: "Forgive me if I sleep until I wake up (?)—Like, like, why now? When— call??? Ever???? Ever??? P.S. Buy more tapes."

. . .

OLSON: Get a free chair and sit down. Don't worry about anything. Especially this. We're living beings and forming a society; we're creating a total, social future. Don't worry about it. The kitchen's reasonably orderly. I crawled out of bed as sick as I was and threw a rug out the window.

INTERVIEWER: Now the first question I wanted to ask you. What fills your day?

OLSON: Nothing. But nothing, literally, except my friends.

INTERVIEWER: These are very straight questions.

OLSON: Ah, that's what interviews are made of.

INTERVIEWER: Why have you chosen poetry as a medium of artistic creation?

OLSON: I think I made a hell of a mistake. That's the first confidence I have. The other is that—I didn't really have anything else to do. I mean I didn't even have enough imagination to think of something else. I was supposed to go to Holy Cross because I wanted to play baseball. I did, too. That's the only reason I wanted to go to Holy Cross. It had nothing to do with being a priest.

INTERVIEWER: Are you able to write poetry while remaining in the usual conditions of life—without renouncing or giving up anything?

OLSON: That's the trouble. That's what I've done. What I've caused and lost. That describes it perfectly. I've absolutely.

INTERVIEWER: Are the conditions of life at the beginning of a work . . .

OLSON: I'm afraid as well at the end. It's like being sunk in a cockpit. I read the most beautiful story about how Will Rogers and Wiley Post were lost; they stomped onto a lake about ten miles from Anchorage, Alaska, to ask an Indian if Anchorage was in that direction and when they took off, they plunged back into the lake. The poor boy was not near enough to rescue them, so he ran ten miles to Anchorage to get the people to come out. He said one of the men had a sort of a cloth on his eye and the guy then knew Post and Rogers were lost. Wiley Post put down on pontoons; so he must have come up off this fresh water lake and went poomp. Isn't that one of those great national treasures. I'll deal you cards, man. I'll make you a tarot.

INTERVIEWER: Does poetry constitute the aim of your existence?

OLSON: Of course I don't live for poetry; I live far more than anybody else does. And forever and why not. Because it is the only thing. But what do you do meanwhile? So what do you do with the rest of the time? That's all. I said I promised to *witness*. But I mean I can't always.

INTERVIEWER: Would you say that the more you understand what you are doing in your writing, the greater the results?

OLSON: Well, it's just one of those things that you're absolutely so bitterly uninterested in that you can't even live. Somehow it is so interesting that you can't imagine. It is nothing, but it breaks your heart. That's all. It doesn't mean a thing. Do you remember the eagle? Farmer Jones gets higher and higher and he is held in one of the eagle's claws and he says you wouldn't shit me would you? That's one of the greatest moments in American poetry. In fact, it is *the* great moment in American poetry. What a blessing we got.

INTERVIEWER: Does Ezra Pound's teaching bear any relevance to how your poems are formed on the page?

OLSON: My masters are pretty pertinent. Don't cheat your own balloon. I mean—literally—like a trip around the moon—the Jules Verne—I read that trip . . . it is so completely applicable today. They don't have any improvements yet.

INTERVIEWER: Do you write by hand or directly on the typewriter? Does either method indicate a specific way in which the poem falls on the page?

OLSON: Yeah. Robert Duncan is the first man to ask me the query. He discovered when he first came to see me that I wrote on the machine and never bothered to correct. There's the stuff. Give me half a bottle. Justice reigns.

INTERVIEWER: What about line units and indentations in your poems, particularly *The Maximus Poems*? Are they visual shapes before you set them down on paper via the typewriter?

OLSON: Wow, if I only knew I did it. It would be marvelous. Did I? Thank you. I read that piece of Jeremy Prynne's and he says everything right, accurately, I'm sitting here and thinking—isn't it terrible until somebody tells you. I didn't even know I did it though he says I did. I know I did what he said I did. Is that wonderful? Sad. So funny, because my vanity is so backfaced. I'm stuck with the other end. That's honest. That's honest.

INTERVIEWER: Would it be correct to say that your abbreviations derive from the device which Pound used in portions of the *Cantos*?

OLSON: I wish I had never done those damn things. I wish I had known enough to slip my head or something, because all that stuff isn't that interesting and it's the cheapest kind of nonattention to take a service mark for the whole thing. I think writing has gotten now to the point of AT&T or Western Union syntax.

INTERVIEWER: What is the distinction between your usage of the technique of quotation and that of Pound?

OLSON: To tell you the truth, I think both Pound and Eliot were after something rather different than us who came a little later, like myself, hip hip hip. All that matters is that the thing be the

A Charles Olson manuscript page.

thing of the thing—a cool thing which is like a river for the tiger of the river. To say it in language is like hard as hell. The greatest poetry profile that was made this side or the other side of the Atlantic Ocean is called the anacreontic award and I hereby now make it and it's pre-amanquiantic and it is absolutely way down below Atlantis and it has got no end, no end because it is like the stock of heaven and creation and it hasn't even been booed or had a crown yet, but it exists. And I know where it's playing—and I know

where it is planted and I know where it is and we all do too, and
we all know what we're talking about, because it is down on the
plantation under the trunk of that large cypress tree in all that goo
way down there in that rain swamp. . . .

INTERVIEWER: Yes. Would you define the nature of influence?

OLSON: That we are influenced, right? Yeah. That sounds too apho-
ristic. At all costs. Clear the air. Clear the air. The American advantage. Clear the air. Clear our equity.

INTERVIEWER: What is the distinction between influence and disci-
pleship?

OLSON: I don't really think these questions are, if you'll excuse me,
Gerard . . . I mean I *respect* you, but this is like when I was on
Canadian television—one of those feature programs with a lady
tiger from Tanganyika and buzz buzz and an American baseball,
or something. The Canadian voice is still too rustic. So therefore
only Englishmen can get announcers' jobs on Canadian broad-
casting. This English guy who had the notes never knew who I
was or what I was there for. I was there to represent poetry. Like as
against hunting in Tanganyika and playing sacred games. That's
very connective. Where did we go from? Was it an easy question I
botched?

INTERVIEWER: It's an easy question. You have to take these questions seriously.

OLSON: Well, are *you* in school, am *I* in school that I'm getting easy
questions? I mean like *jeez.* I thought when I didn't feel well for
two days at least Gerard will keep me interested. OK, I'm very
fresh. I just woke up.

INTERVIEWER: Do you enjoy telling young poets what they ought
to do?

OLSON: Oh, Jesus, God, if I ever did, may the Lord of the whole of
the seven saints of India and China Buddhaland, Ganges town,
and all takers this side of where the Tartars went—may they forgive me because like I am happy to have some friends here in the
kitchen. I mean, wow, I've been very lucky, very lucky. I'm sorry,
but I was born with a towel on my head.

INTERVIEWER: Let's say you were to meet a young poet whose work shows signs of influence from your own work . . .

OLSON: It's instantly as immaculate or as impeccable as the existence of something new and boom, boom, wang, doong, zip, toodle, deedo, etc., etc. Could you give me a light. I ain't got no light. I have to answer that you don't help people. You don't help poor people in your poems. I'm afraid of teasing you, but don't worry. I been trying to help people all my life—that's been the trouble. My sense of responsibility. Otherwise I'm a free man, that's a big eighteenth-century problem. I'm absolutely trying to climb up both walls at once. That beautiful Blake who is like four feathers of a raven caught down in a chasm of which we're just later birds, but like, oh, he's like a frozen four-winged raven, shrieking for the light—not frozen, but *ahead* of us. Like a box kite. We're all moving, movie, moving, move. Isn't it nice?

INTERVIEWER: What poet do you think you have had a lasting influence upon?

OLSON: Oh, wow, a lasting influence—my God. This indicates everything I've ever done that might possibly have had influence upon some of the men who I really feel connected to, and how! Wow. I mean if I could get drafts with reds, black, and ribbons I'd be a collector!

INTERVIEWER: Don't you have the fear of being reduced to conformity by having too many other poets understand and imitate what you are doing?

OLSON: Oh, God, are you kidding? I mean, do you think I could be? Do you think I'm empty? I mean I got about five people who have given me evidence that they know what I said.

INTERVIEWER: Five, who were the five?

OLSON: Well, that would be really to create quite a successful society. In fact, very successful; from my point of view with that five, wow! But no, that's literary history. And I'd have no interest in it whatsoever.

INTERVIEWER: Yes, but the people of *The Paris Review* want to know.

OLSON: Well, I know, but light a rock under *The Paris Review*. You are moved by the fact that another person sees what it is that you have done, which is like coming to the shore—like I fell off the big rowboat, and I carried the flag with me, and I swam ashore. I mean that kind of a marvelous result. It is that the other person somehow will say something relevant to what you have gotten yourself involved in. It is so important that it is like love, whatever that is. I mean if I can claim five persons who give me the sense that I'm where I was—then I'm still living. That's as big as I know it to be. And that's what's so great.

INTERVIEWER: Would you say that the *Black Mountain Review* helped to systematize your ideas about "projective verse"?

OLSON: I'd written it long before the review—four years before the review appeared.

INTERVIEWER: What are the basic differences between projective verse and the objectivist movement established by the American poet Louis Zukofsky?

OLSON: Do you want me to educate you? It is like I mentioned earlier about being on Toronto TV and the announcer comes on and says, "Mr. Olson, what do you think of imagism?" And I said, "What?" I mean that's the same sort of question as the indissoluble union of Mr. Pound and myself at the Pratagiano or something—of the skin of being which is as true in poets' loves for each other and in parenthood as it is in the whole forms of life—trees, ferns, and eventually fair rocks in the earth.

INTERVIEWER: How do you account for the change of trend in American poetry today from experiment and technique to subject matter? Do you think projective verse helped to bring this literary revolution about? Or is there little doubt that this type of poetry would have eventually been written without you?

OLSON: Same reason why this nation is going to hell right now—because it finally got caught up with itself. The tail got caught in the mouth, or something. I tried to answer this once. In Toronto a marvelous ex-wrestler poet named Harry Moscowitch, I think, used to be mad at me and after I finished reading, he said, "Why don't you write like William Butler Yeats?" There was this protest from the audience, like modern new gangsterism—William Butler Yeats? Well, I didn't know what to say. Moscowitch. Harry Moscowitch. I really didn't know. I mean I felt so peculiar—what could I do?

INTERVIEWER: Why is it that so many poets tend to shy away from writing about nonpoetic things like the mass media or things that aren't considered poetic or proper poetic subjects?

OLSON: You know what the answer is—so simple—because they're not. They're social secondary matters which we have the government to take care of. I mean we have no interest in such servile mechanisms. That's why Mr. Foreman figures in the home. Our control of the planets as well as those machines is just vulgar matter. And in fact is based upon vulgar matter. It is simply an improvised condition of vulgar matter and will continue until somebody says this and really hears it because the thing is literally as old.

INTERVIEWER: Well, would you say that it is not poetic to glamorize things like mass media in poetry?

OLSON: That it is not poetic to glamorize? What's that connection to poetry? Mass media? I think it is a waste of energy—yeah, like a newspaper, because obviously in five years we will have won it all back. That is what I mean—that we *won't* want it all back. No, that's not fair, I guess.

INTERVIEWER: Why would we want it all back?

OLSON: No, I got you. I got you. I got you. I got you. I mean we want what's been suddenly disallowed.

INTERVIEWER: Were *The Maximus Poems* or the *Mayan Letters* written out of your emotions or do they represent a state of consciousness?

OLSON: I hope so. Altogether the question satisfied me completely.

INTERVIEWER: Have you ever found yourself struggling with existing ideas in a poem without being able to find a direction for new ideas?

OLSON: I don't, like I said in the *Maximus,* I didn't know there were any ideas. Ask me another question, immediately, on the same point.

INTERVIEWER: Do you find that one new word that comes to mind alters the whole picture, and you are obliged to rebuild the poem completely?

OLSON: I do think that's true absolutely—on the instant I begin a poem. But you know I am a little bit like Plutarch, or somebody. I write a poem simply to create a mode of a priesthood in a church forever, so that a poem for me is simply the first sound realized in the modality of being. If you want to talk about actuality, let's talk about actuality. And it falleth like a doom upon us all. But it falleth from above, and if that's not straight the whole thing is doodled and if straight then you can modality all you want. You can do anything, literally. Right? That I think is one of the exciting possibilities of the present. Modal throughout—that's what I love about today's kids. I like them because I think they're modaled throughout. I don't think their teachers are at all. I mean I'm almost like astringent here. I sit back in my lollipop Gloucester and don't do anything. A dirty lousy cop-out. I remember way back when I was young, ten years ago. I was lobbing 'em in. Now it's the Vietnam War. Dig? You follow me? It was marvelous. Playing catch, if I may say that—with a European audience as well. But I mean catch—we were playing catch. And he's a goddamn nice fielder. All that Jewish Bronx shit. I don't mean because it's Jewish. It's this late Jewish, late east Bronx literature which to a geologist like me is just uninteresting. A geochronologist geologist. The world machines—that's what they got now. The world machines. When will government cease being a nuisance to everybody.

INTERVIEWER: Do you find, when in the act of writing a poem, or reworking—

OLSON: Do I? Give me some more. Go ahead.

INTERVIEWER: Do you find in the act of writing a poem or reworking it afterwards that intensified observation brought about by self-remembering always has an emotional element?

OLSON: An emotional what?

INTERVIEWER: Emotional element.

OLSON: Yeah, I know. Here I defer to all those other American poets who for some reason I both envy and admire. I do. I mean, I

Charles Olson writing The Maximus, *1951.*

never have rewritten almost anything. . . . [*long pause*] Where was I? I was going to create this diamond we were going to run. The suitor diamond, the sutra diamond. The Sutra diamond for the superstar. Superstar. You know that's kind of an impressive thing. It's like those comics that are in now, that marvelous "Caper Comix" in the *Georgia Straight*. Those grotesque big-footed creatures. "Head Comics." God Jesus! You know this is just like "Head Comics." I was thinking reading the *Georgia Straight* the other night that I know this stuff like I know Jess Collins's revisions of Dick Tracy. You know that color thing? That's the incunabula of the twentieth century. It's absolutely monkish.

INTERVIEWER: I first saw Jess Collins's Sunday comic strip of Dick Tracy back in September 1963. I do think, though, that Jess is in a very unfortunate position.

OLSON: Why?

INTERVIEWER: Because the whole pop art thing is over and done with and Jess is going to be totally crushed. . . .

OLSON: Maybe, but maybe Dick Tracy won't be. Like the heroes of the present will retreat to the imitation they are anyhow. And both the comic and the photographic and the antiquarian figures behind each one of those comics. What was your word just now? What was your verb just now?

INTERVIEWER: Jess is in a very bad position.

OLSON: No. That's not what you were saying. That's not the point. What was your verb, because I want to get that verb in because that's the whole thing. I have to. That's what's so nice. It's like that dipple-dopple bird in a box. You're the one that starts. Once it gets some water, it has to take water.

INTERVIEWER: Right, that's it.

OLSON: God, isn't it beautiful? I mean that's after Newton. I tell you the truth. If you do treat the sacred drugs sacredly you discover that they really yield what everybody else finds. God does, love does, life does, they do. The problem is not the quality.

INTERVIEWER: If you write down what you actually recall of some particular episode in your past, do you discover how little you remember?

OLSON: No. On the contrary. I rush immediately, because I know about 99 percent.

INTERVIEWER: What are the techniques and attitudes that you require in order to create your poetry?

OLSON: Anything I can find. What do you mean? I mean—the yachts, piazza with the yachts' quarter flags flying and some chap in Tyre and some chap in the White House cometh. I have no idea, the green grass. I sound like Homer. I mean Winslow Homer. But I do sound like Homer, because really I'm sure he was talking about the same thing. Like a painting. Like a beautiful French painting—that thing that sold recently. You know, that great cat Monet. Come in, *Paris Review*, come in. Paris; the God of Streets.

INTERVIEWER: Are objectivity and directness very significant principles for your poetry?

OLSON: I shouldn't think so. I would think quite the opposite— that I'm the most devious nonobjective, coolest, plural subjective son of a bitch this side of the wind. In fact, I can confess it all now.

INTERVIEWER: Could you explain—

OLSON: He's calling me back. Really I could have finished that in seven stanzas—not in seven stanzas but in seven choruses. We just have horses prancing, singing horses, walking horses. It's like the guy who photographed that marvelous, primary, primitive head. Did you see his photographs of an elephant walking in the field—you know the guy I mean? I'll have to look at it again.

INTERVIEWER: Could you explain the degrees of consciousness or unconsciousness with which you create a poem?

OLSON: Sounds like I'm in a hell of a trap, Gerard. I wouldn't even know. It's so radical that it's not even news.

INTERVIEWER: I was speaking with John Wieners on the phone the other day and he asked me to ask you, "To what dissent do you participate in guarding your forebears in literature?"

OLSON: How about that? I complained about this to—beautiful! It's said the right way. That's the first question. That's like the plum or the lemon or the orange on the vice machine. Oh Johnny, you've done it again. I agree, entirely. What do you want me to do? Talk like a slot machine? I can pay off punch punch punch. No kidding because that's the only answer to that kind of question. It's so sexual that it's—it's between you and me . . . oh Johnny, oh Johnny. Remember I told you about those slot machines. I play alone like in a mirror.

INTERVIEWER: What is your personal aim about what you want to attain?

OLSON: I got the question, give me the answer. Propose, propose the answer.

INTERVIEWER: I don't know. That's why I'm asking you the question. Why is it that a poem will produce different impressions on people of different levels?

OLSON: Because of the vulgarity of all classes. I never thought I could be the ultimate. I didn't know there was a snob beyond snobs, right? It's new.

INTERVIEWER: Do you feel you will be able to write what you want to?

OLSON: What? I mean I'm already too old even to have arrived at that stage, and now I got to do something new. I mean something unheard of. I blew my time. I didn't earn it. I spent it, I blew it. So now I got to, why are you asking me? I ain't got no time. What are you talking about? Read that question again.

INTERVIEWER: Do you feel that when the time comes to write what you want to, you must know what it is?

OLSON: Oh wow, I see, it's like school. Instruction. I think it's like instruction. It's in three parts—sort of—it's like the beginning, the middle, and the end. It's that discourse, syntax question, if you'll allow me to say so. It's a devil and you know it. I mean how many times has this happened. This is the first time in my kitchen that we've been able to sit here. What the hell are we getting out of this? We ought to treat this as in sort of a negative.

INTERVIEWER: How can a poet learn to *feel* more if he lives so much in his head?

OLSON: Oh man. That's been the bearing. I hope you're representing the devil's advocate. All these questions have all of the leading errors and none of the relevant. I mean if there's anything I did that's interesting then it ought to be interesting. Otherwise it's a waste of time. This question—questions generally speaking—is like the Canadian broadcaster asking in 1963 what do you think about imagism in writing in 1913, right? I just read about it the other night. I don't mean to jump from this but I mean we can go over this question like a million times. This is a kind of tomato ketchup question, tomato juice, the US Banana Company.

INTERVIEWER: How can a poet tell whether he has established something for himself that will take him further in his work?

OLSON: I don't know. Belief, conviction, experience. The decision, the suddenness—whatever it is, whatever the initial thing that is the exact opposite of the universal. The whole living thing of creation is that moment when you know what you feel or do.

INTERVIEWER: Is it true that there is a definite rule regarding the writing of poetry—that when a poet writes he doesn't have to disguise what he writes because he cannot avoid using the same language in which he has learned to speak?

OLSON: So true, so completely true and now so evident by either the law of persona or the law of psyche. You can read everybody. It's not even interesting to tell the truth because to some extent it's false. This socializes the practice.

INTERVIEWER: Is the poet's responsibility towards craftsmanship that of exercising taste and discretion in deciding on the final form of his poem?

OLSON: Wow, that's very aesthetic. Say that again.

INTERVIEWER: Is the poet's responsibility towards craftsmanship that of exercising taste and discretion in deciding on the final form of his poem?

OLSON: Oh, utterly, in and throughout, like I once said in 1950. But let's be very insistent—I was very, very conservative from 1950 through seven different temporal changes and one major speech.

INTERVIEWER: Is distance a substitute for imaginative apprehension of a reality?

OLSON: My Gods, may I answer saying, "Look, I'm not a shaman, but shamans are." That question is answered completely by the utter human ability to transport itself where it is wanted and needed and has to be—so the answer is that it's bullshit to use the word *distance* as opposed to what I meant in *The Distances*, which is what *distance* always has meant to anyone who looks beyond the horizon. Well, I didn't mean to sound like Eugene O'Neill. . . . Would you call Mrs. Tobin? I tried to. I forgot to get the liquor. 283-420, I think it is, and get her to send over the usual.

INTERVIEWER: We should read the telephone directory—you could read it.

OLSON: No, no, no. I got a friend who does that. Let's finish off where we were. Because otherwise this diamond is going to break. Do you understand who the diamond is? Chin-chin. Some ancient unburied or unrecovered Tibetan low-mountain style we get from Upsbridge—where Frank O'Hara and I were born. Let's go on the road—like they say. The other night I saw a picture of Dylan looking absolutely la-da-da. Oh, magnificent—back when Poland was Poland. What's his new recording?

INTERVIEWER: *Nashville Skyline.*

OLSON: That's right. That's the one. Another lovely Hasidim, laughing Jew. He is just beautiful. It has nothing to do with Woody or any of that shit. He is just an absolutely delicate thing. That incredible whatever it is—not the power of the benediction of God, but the fortune of the sidereal realm that the Jews come out with— the crescent of this question—if there is such a question.

INTERVIEWER: Did you write *The Maximus Poems* independently of any influence?

OLSON: Yes. I sure did. Like that's an *answer* to that question. But how can I prove it. I don't know. I mean I, Tyre of Gloucester. I don't know how much *Maximus* is, of course, a verb.

INTERVIEWER: The divine inspiration of poetry? I would have expected you to say Pound or Williams because everything is structure.

OLSON: Well, no. It is not structure. That's ignorance, if you'll excuse me. Ignorance of your own, baby, time. Because I'm one of the clichés that has grown up. In fact, it was created to put me out of business, as well as my friend, the lovely Dr. Williams, as well as Mr. Pound; because there is a goddamn funny thing going on in this century though I certainly don't believe in conspiracy. I mean the amount of connection that any one of those three people mentioned would feel to the other is highly questionable. . . .

INTERVIEWER: Would you have written *The Maximus Poems* as you did without knowing Pound's or Williams's works?

OLSON: That's like asking me how I could have written without having read. You read the nearest at hand.

INTERVIEWER: Is there any similarity between the views of Pound on history and your own?

OLSON: None whatsoever. Ezra's are optative; mine are decisive. I love Ezra for all the boxes he has kept. He really is a canto-maker. I couldn't write a canto if I sat down and deliberately tried. My interest is not in cantos. It's in another condition of song, which is connected to mode and has therefore to do with absolute actuality. It's so completely temporal.

INTERVIEWER: Would you say that your inclusion of the subject of economics in *The Maximus Poems* is a revival of that very same effort found in the *Cantos*?

OLSON: Mr. Pound, I think, comes of a family which had means enough to take Ezra across the Atlantic. So he had the advantage of a European situation. I was born in south Worcester. That's a very important thing. I finally got pissed off at Ezra's pissing on Dr. Williams because one portion of Williams was Jewish—about $\frac{1}{16}$, $\frac{1}{18}$, $\frac{1}{9}$, $\frac{1}{8}$, $\frac{1}{4}$, $\frac{1}{7}$, $\frac{1}{17}$ . . .

INTERVIEWER: Would you make a specific distinction between poets whom you could imitate and poets from whom one could learn?

OLSON: Oh boy, I mean *learn* anything. Like my palm I've forgotten what it sounded like. Wow! I mean like just flash me again, what was that signal?

INTERVIEWER: Would you make a specific distinction . . .

OLSON: Yeah, yeah. Yeah.

INTERVIEWER: . . . between poets whom you yourself . . .

OLSON: Yeah. Yeah. Yeah. Yeah.

INTERVIEWER: . . . or anyone could imitate and poets from whom one could learn?

OLSON: That's not the whole question. You've gone on.

INTERVIEWER: No, no, I haven't.

OLSON: Say that question you asked me just now again.

INTERVIEWER: Would you make a specific distinction between poets whom you yourself or anyone could imitate and poets from whom one could learn?

OLSON: Is that what you said? That's too much. That's damn interesting. You've got your answer, you *had* your answer. Father Pound, that was beautiful, father of me. That's too much. Beautiful. That's way out.

INTERVIEWER: Is one of the ways by which contemporary poetry has tried to escape the rhetorical, the abstract, the moralizing—is it to concentrate its attention upon trivial or accidental or commonplace objects?

OLSON: I think you're an agent of a foreign power. A series of questions even the FBI . . . never in all my life in court or in secret have I known such questions! Who wrote this, did you? If so, leave my house! If not, then please, own up the ownership. Mr. Malanga, Signor Malanga, I will expose you to your nation.

INTERVIEWER: I will expose myself. Anyway, no one escapes the media, least of all you.

OLSON: I will send you back to Málaga to raise more raisins. The raisins are good. Grapes are good. Those are dry questions. I would like you to repeat that raisin of a question once more so that the whole world via *The Paris Review*—which is the Gorgon or Medusa instead of the present—can be spoken to through a comic mask.

INTERVIEWER: I'll try another. Do you find it useful to collect opinions of friends about your work? Do you feel this often helps in discovering points to improve your work that you would normally not discover on your own?

OLSON: You mean my friends? It's not enough, they don't say enough. Did you? Did you? I mean like Emperor Jones—not only LeRoi, but Mr. O'Neill's—walking through the forest—scared to death.

INTERVIEWER: What constitutes a school of poetry?

OLSON: Total change, like the man said; one doesn't look like boopeedeboop—of course. Carry on, destroy film, take another giant step backwards. Málaga. Take one step backwards. Now, ask me some decent questions.

INTERVIEWER: Is the function of a literary—

OLSON: That sounds dirty as hell. Maybe we can take that to the Supreme Court. Yeah, I heard you. Continue without repeating it.

INTERVIEWER: Is the function of a—

OLSON: He's already conditioned. It's like a reflex. Atlantis will arise again. Go ahead. God's with this boy.

INTERVIEWER: Is the function of a literary movement primarily to secure publication of the poets connected with that movement or doesn't a literary movement or school present a different function or advantage?

OLSON: That's a dumb sort of block historical question, if I may say so, and typical sort of a Columbia twentieth-century question.

INTERVIEWER: A school is a place where one can learn something. Can a school lose by giving away its knowledge?

OLSON: Oh boy, that's beautiful. That's a lovely question. It's really such a lovely question. Jesus God. I see it. Right through the solar plexus as the pantheon of Black Mountain pharaoh of the exile . . . We all went on to the other fields, other Bull Runs. It's a marvelous question, though.

INTERVIEWER: Would you say Black Mountain College's sole existence depended on the part of those artists who took part in the
building of it?

OLSON: Oh no. I think, in fact, the man who built it wonderfully
enough was not an artist at all, but a man from Charleston—a rare
bird.

INTERVIEWER: Is a school of poetry necessary in order to gain attention for a group of poets' work or is it a handicap?

OLSON: I don't think it's relevant.

INTERVIEWER: I'm talking about schools of poetry in terms of such
as the so-called New York school of poetry, if you'll pardon the
expression.

OLSON: All right, so name them. Poets have no reason to be in the
marvelous ITT thing or Inter-World Aviation.

INTERVIEWER: Do you see the prospect of a definitive practical guide
in the form of an anthology of the Black Mountain school of poets?

OLSON: Well, I certainly don't. If the fuckers don't get along down
the trail I'll kick their fucking asses for them. I'm an old trail man
from the woods and if the goddamn stuff doesn't come down the
trail to my satisfaction, until I'm beaten, I'm still boss.

INTERVIEWER: Would you say that your life as a by-product is existing without you?

OLSON: Oh, that's mad!!! Having rolled in all the way from—
boom, boom! We're just back to the whole landing on the barren
coast of North America. Fantastic. I think for the audience of Europe. This is one of them bawdy questions that don't come off
anymore—really bawdy question like that. But listen to this, man,
what's that story when the joke is at the end—what do you call
that—so boom! The ending. OK? I'm afraid you've got a problem.
A very normal problem. And you will take care of it. I hope. At
one point much earlier in this tape, something sounded good
enough, sounded like Hawaiian—can't make anything out of *this*
stuff. It's only shredded wheat.

INTERVIEWER: What about our country?

OLSON: There is a grace of life which is still yours, my dear Europe. Oh! As against this abusive, vulgar, cruel, remorseless and youthless country, the United States of America. May she perish in these five years, simply not because of any wish—any radical wish at all, but that she would get out of our way, and leave us alone. And leave things alone which she has harmed and harmed and harmed. And for what? For nothing. For something which she herself no longer values and will buy her nothing. We will all be in the same boat with all the leaks of this filthy system which has purchased all of our lives at its cost. Not really, thank God. God damn her soul, because she didn't have enough strength to win us. But my God, when I think of two centuries which did play her game, whistle to her tune.

INTERVIEWER: There was no skipper.

OLSON: I don't have a skipper. I'm no skipper either. This country has been unconscious, and it's got to awake and that's my belief. And that's why I've spent so much time just painting her nails and sails or something. I mean—the piper of a sleeping nation. It's so stupid. It's awake all the time and it's never awake for a minute. It's the deadest sleep that ever was, to talk like Blake. I don't think Blake could have imagined it.

INTERVIEWER: What do you spend your money on?

OLSON: Oh, wow. Jesus, like any poor citizen; in fact, pay my bills. Go out and tear the town apart. I mean if we can't eat, let's fuck the place tonight—dump her in the ocean. Let's. We deserve something; this is crazy.

—GERARD MALANGA
1970

(The editors wish to express their thanks to Harvey Brown for his great assistance in preparing the interview.)

Andrei Voznesensky and Allen Ginsberg: A Conversation

A ndrei Voznesensky was one of the leaders of the poetic renaissance in Soviet literature in the early 1960s. His works include *Parabola* (1960), *Nostalgia for the Present* (1978), and *An Arrow
in the Wall: Selected Poetry and Prose* (1988).

Peter Orlovsky met Ginsberg in 1954 while staying with
painter Robert LaVigne in San Francisco. The pair immediately
took to one another, beginning a thirty-year romance that eclipsed
Orlovsky's fame as a poet. His books include *Clean Asshole Poems
and Smiling Vegetable Songs: Poems, 1957–1977* and *Straight Heart's
Delight: Love Poems and Selected Letters, 1947–1980.*

*The following are fragments of a conversation held in New York
City on December 28, 1978. The dialogue was taped at the Chelsea Hotel;
in the rear of a taxicab; on the streets of the West Village. That week,
Ginsberg had been asked by the Modern Language Association to read
before an assembly of American literature scholars. In order to demonstrate the oratorical style common to their work, he had invited Voznesensky and Orlovsky to join him.*

. . .

GINSBERG: You ever heard Hart Crane?

VOZNESENSKY: No.

ORLOVSKY: Oh, you've got a surprise coming.

GINSBERG: He is a great oratorical poet. He committed suicide
around 1932. Tomorrow I will be reading Crane.* You want to hear
some? What this sounds like in English? This is very high, powerful. The howl in my style comes from the power—like Shelley.
Very hard to understand, but you can decipher. It is about the

---

* At the MLA Convention, Hilton Hotel, NYC.

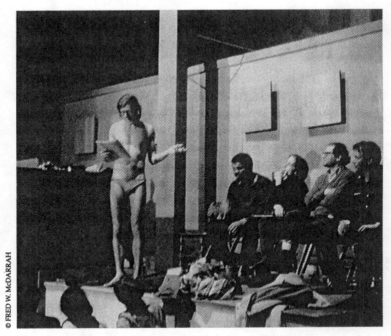

© FRED W. McDARRAH

Peter Orlovsky reading his "Clean Asshole Poems," 1964.

Brooklyn Bridge, linking present to future. Science. Like your poem to the airport. His vision of the Brooklyn Bridge in 1920. A long poem, made of many parts.

ORLOVSKY: Very condensed, and no fat.

GINSBERG: I'll begin with just this small invocation to Brooklyn Bridge; then I'll read you the grand chorale at the end. It ends . . . big ecstasy. Begins:

> *How many dawns, chill from his rippling rest*
> *The seagull's wings shall dip and pivot him,*
> *Shedding white rings of tumult, building high*
> *Over the chained bay waters Liberty—*

[*continues reading*]

VOZNESENSKY: Very good, very good.

GINSBERG: This is where Robert Lowell got much of his iron. You know he has some iron-clang rhyme? Very beautiful parts on the rail tracks with old bums. Big American panorama, like Kerouac, who loved him.

ORLOVSKY: What is a "prayer of pariah"?

GINSBERG: A pariah is like an outcast, a beggar. Prayer of pariah.

VOZNESENSKY: Very good, yes.

GINSBERG: But the great moment is the "Atlantis." I won't read it for sense, just for sounds. The pure rhythm sounds. It's like a Bach fugue. It rises, comes like this, rises again, comes like this, and then comes. And then post-coitus, you know? After . . .

> *Through the bound cable strands, the arching path*
> *Upward, veering with light . . .*

[*continues reading*]

VOZNESENSKY: Fantastic.

GINSBERG: Great. Like Shelley. Like Shelley's "Ode to the West Wind."

ORLOVSKY: What is "sidereal phallanx"?

GINSBERG: Sidereal. The starry assemblies of the bridge. Very . . . somewhat technical language. *Kinetic of white choiring wings.*

VOZNESENSKY: Very good.

GINSBERG: It's mouthfuls. Of tremendous vowels, end, *Oh, Answerer of all!* . . . bom-bom-bom-da-pa-da!

VOZNESENSKY: Very good, very good.

GINSBERG: This was published in 1930. This volume was given to me by William Burroughs in 1946. I've had it all these years. The poem was written, I think, in the late twenties. What year did Mayakovsky go to the Brooklyn Bridge?

VOZNESENSKY: I think '29.

GINSBERG: William Carlos Williams went to Greenwich Village, he told me, and he went to a reading of Mayakovsky's . . . a small hall, a few people, poets. But good poets, like Williams, the avant-garde. After it was over, Williams went up to Mayakovsky and said, "You laid an egg." Now in English it's funny. To lay an egg means to smell . . . bad thing. But what he meant with Maya-kovsky was "You put something solid on the table." Laid an egg.

ORLOVSKY: Something real. Something you could see.

GINSBERG: That will grow, give birth. He laid an egg, he said. Williams told that story.

VOZNESENSKY: But Mayakovsky did not understand it?

GINSBERG: I think Williams said he was not sure; they had to translate it over and over again. Because it also means something terrible. Like a show "lays an egg." But Williams turned it upside down.

VOZNESENSKY: It was a small room, like for friends?

GINSBERG: In America there were no big poetry readings then. Except Vachel Lindsay. Do you know him? He tried to write syncopated jazz poetry. He wrote one about the blacks, called "The Congo," that goes:

> *Fat black bucks in the wine-barrel room,*
> *Barrel-house kings, with feet unstable,*
> *Sagged and reeled and pounded on the table,*
> *Beat an empty barrel with the handle of a broom,*
> *Hard as they were able,*
> *Boom, boom, BOOM.*
> *With a silk umbrella and the handle of a broom.*

> . . . . . .

THEN I SAW THE CONGO, CREEPING THROUGH
   THE BLACK,
CUTTING THROUGH THE FOREST WITH A GOLDEN
   TRACK.

[*continues reciting*]

ORLOVSKY: Kettle drums.

GINSBERG: There is a recording of him. He was the first twentieth-century-on-the-road-bard. He wrote *Rhymes to Be Traded for Bread.* Out on the road he'd offer to recite poems for a piece of pie. And he lectured like we do. Went to clubs. "The Chautauqua Circuit," in those days. It was a circuit of educated clubs.

[*Voznesensky takes a phone call, speaking in Russian.*]

GINSBERG: Something terrible happened at the Academy.

VOZNESENSKY: What?

GINSBERG: I sent in the proposed names to, I guess the literary department. And they voted. When we got the final ballot yesterday: neither Burroughs nor Snyder was on it.

VOZNESENSKY: Was Brodsky?

GINSBERG: Brodsky was on it. John Hollander was on it. Many others, younger people, let us say, than Burroughs. Or Snyder. It's amazing. I can't imagine. Brodsky is all right. But Burroughs is like this vast international presence.

VOZNESENSKY: Certainly.

GINSBERG: So I was thinking of resigning, but I don't know. That won't cure ignorance either. What apparently happened is that the Battle of Anthologies, as they called it, between the academic poets, the university poets, and the open-form poets—post-Williams, post-Whitman—is continuing; there really continues to be a kind of establishment. I thought because I was in the Academy it didn't exist anymore. But to exclude Burroughs is scandalous, actually.

ORLOVSKY: Gary Snyder, too.

GINSBERG: And Gary Snyder, yes. The poets they chose may be worthy but they are not of equal power, or originality, or influence, or accomplishment.

VOZNESENSKY: How many?

GINSBERG: Well, they had eight poets, I think, that they could vote for. The expected ones were proposed and seconded by William Meredith, William Jay Smith, Richard Wilbur, with a few eccentrics proposed by Richard Eberhart or Muriel Rukeyser. And the totally eccentric proposed by me! So when that man said he thought I should resign, at that supper we had there, I thought, well, he's just talking drunk. But it probably represents the majority, for all I know.

ORLOVSKY: And they want you to resign?

GINSBERG: Every year. Every time some of the old people die, the *alte kockers*—you know, the Yiddish phrase, old farts—the *alte kockers* elect some newer people, there is hope. Hollander is an old friend from Columbia, we went to school together. He wrote a terrible attack on *Howl* when it was put out, calling it a vulgar little book, but he's changed his mind. And he introduced me at Yale last year. What they must think of Burroughs I have no idea. They probably think he's some kind of outrageous madman.

ORLOVSKY: Monster, monster.

GINSBERG: It's just their own stupidity, or insensitivity, or hatred. I'm supposed to be a beatnik but I'm a member of the Academy! And it's almost a dishonor to be a member of an Academy where Burroughs, who is my teacher, is not a member. When I was young I read in stories of history about how great artists were neglected, and how the academies were always stupid. And I said, "When I grow up things will not be like that. If I am a member of an academy, I won't let these things happen." And now it is happening.

VOZNESENSKY: One woman came to you and saw your black suit, your black, very elegant coat and said, "Oh, how do you happen to be dressed like this?"

GINSBERG: Well, when I was elected I always had dungarees and the day that I was installed I wore dungarees. But afterwards, I dressed up to be polite, to talk about Burroughs. It is a basic American problem. It's like plutonium, poisoning everybody through their ignorance. But how do you communicate with . . .

people doomed to their ignorance? It's perplexing to know what to do in a situation like that. Do you have a similar situation in Russia?

VOZNESENSKY: No.

GINSBERG: But then you must have geniuses that can't get in.

VOZNESENSKY: In general, I think there are no geniuses.

GINSBERG: Was Mandelstam a member of the Writer's Union when he was killed?

VOZNESENSKY: No.

ORLOVSKY: Who killed him?

VOZNESENSKY: Stalin. Not Stalin personally but his camp system. Mandelstam wrote a poem against Stalin, when he was in exile. After he returned from exile he wrote a poem *for* Stalin. After several years, they put him in jail but he was very weak, and he died in a hard-labor camp.

GINSBERG: How do people get elected to the Writer's Union in Russia?

VOZNESENSKY: There are several steps. First, you have three recommendations. After, if you are a poet, you are elected by a poetry group in Moscow, Leningrad, or some other place.

GINSBERG: How long does that take?

VOZNESENSKY: About a year, too long.

GINSBERG: You can publish without being a member?

VOZNESENSKY: Certainly, but it is impossible to be a member if you have not two or three books. You can publish and certainly not be a member. With one book they can invite you to come, or two books. But usually two or three is the minimum.

GINSBERG: Are there any sort of intelligent writers that are not in, that are blackballed?

VOZNESENSKY: Yes. Some of them now have been expelled. Some of them are now in emigration.

GINSBERG: I've been getting headaches lately. Too much work. Too many hours over the desk, too many hours on the telephone, too many hours answering mail, running around to the Chelsea Hotel in taxi-cabs, going uptown tonight to the Modern Language Association meeting.

VOZNESENSKY: What will be tonight?

GINSBERG: Tonight will be very interesting. I'm not sure of the function, but the heads of the departments of English come together for a convention once a year. They have a president and they have committees. Part of it is a Hart Crane Association. They have a Hart Crane newsletter. Some scholarly work. But mostly it is a meat market for young Ph.D. instructors trying to get jobs as professors. They go there hungrily, looking for their fate. To find a job teaching in Iowa or in Hartford or in some small college in South Carolina. It's a job market. So now, with inflation, there are too many teachers and Ph.D.s, and very few jobs. Everybody wants a good job. Otherwise, they'll have to go rob a bank or wash tables in cafeterias, mop, go on relief, sell gas, chop wood, or go back to the forest. So they're all going to congregate there tonight and tomorrow, mainly looking for jobs. And tonight we're going to be the comic relief in this tragedy! We'll actually present some poetry.

VOZNESENSKY: Do you like Elvis Presley?

GINSBERG: Not particularly.

VOZNESENSKY: I was not a great admirer of his but when he died I said something important had died with him.

GINSBERG: That was a little excessive. A little bit. Too much. It sounds like you are naïve and think he is the only originator. But actually, Presley imitated the blacks. He was the first white man to imitate the blacks.

VOZNESENSKY: He was white or black?

GINSBERG: White.

VOZNESENSKY: No? All white? Not half-white?

GINSBERG: No. That was his remarkable cultural contribution—that he was the first white man to sing like a black man, what was called in those days R 'n' B, rhythm-and-blues, southern style. He picked it up, with the physical gestures of the hips—fuck gestures of the hips—along with the sexuality attributed to the black soul singers, and he put black soul into a white body and white mouth and white words. The famous song, "Hound Dog," is basically black southern blues, rapping.

So he did break through. But then he was commercialized and capitalized on and used as a patriotic symbol. And finally . . . he took a lot of drugs and drank a lot. Finally, he was perhaps somewhat crazed. He walked to the White House in a cape.

ORLOVSKY: In a purple cape.

GINSBERG: And showed up at the gate and wanted to see Nixon. To lick Nixon's ass. To ask Nixon to give him a badge as a narcotics agent. He must have been paranoid. There's a famous photograph of him and Nixon standing there, Nixon presenting him with a narc's badge, promising that he could work with the police. Afterwards, he used to ride around with the police to bust people who were taking dope. But he himself, according to his autopsy, apparently was taking all kinds of dope, including, I believe, codeine, opiates, and downers and uppers. That's what he died of, overdoses of too much. Ice cream and dope. And patriotism. So he had become somewhat of a hulk. He's known in Russia?

VOZNESENSKY: Well, we know him more like a symbol. Because you needed more than his records, you needed to see him.

GINSBERG: Well, the disks were good, too.

VOZNESENSKY: Smile and tease.

GINSBERG: That's the key. He sang black. He sang like a black. He had a great career. Then after the army he came out and made very dumb movies that were popular and made a lot of money. He sang less and improvised less. Finally, he was working for the Mafia in Las Vegas, that is to say the gambling nightclubs in Las

Vegas. Making millions of dollars. And very popular. But retired from the world. You read about his end? His last years?

ORLOVSKY: He died in the bathroom. Going to take a shit.

VOZNESENSKY: Heart attack?

ORLOVSKY: I think it was a heart attack.

GINSBERG: And congestion of all different drugs.

ORLOVSKY: Malfunction of the kidney, or the liver. They found thirteen drugs in his blood, thirteen different kinds of drugs.

GINSBERG: Medicines, prescribed by doctors: valium for sleeping, sleeping pills, some codeine, some opiates. I read in the newspaper a very interesting thing about drugs the other day. Remember Senator Joe McCarthy, the famous symbol? He was a morphine addict. He had an arrangement with Harry Anslinger, the commissioner of the Federal Bureau of Narcotics, to get a prescription for illegal morphine, secretly. Anslinger tells about it in his book, but recently there's been a little exposé . . . that the name of the person was Joe McCarthy. So Joe McCarthy, the famous anticommunist, was actually a morphinomaniac.

GINSBERG: You were not in the public eye when Stalin was alive, were you?

VOZNESENSKY: No. Only Yevtushenko published. His first book.

GINSBERG: Did Stalin and Yevtushenko meet . . . ?

VOZNESENSKY: No. Stalin was too big to meet a small poet. No. Yevtushenko was only beginning, and he was writing like everybody else then. At that time, everybody wrote about Stalin. Everybody wrote that he was a genius. It was a way of thinking. Really. I was a schoolboy. I didn't write because I was not a poet. I didn't write that Stalin is great. But I thought so . . . everybody said he was great, and that he saved our country during the war, that he saved the country before the war. He was the greatest revolutionary, and greatest friend of Lenin. I read all these things— all lies. I read them and I didn't know anything else.

GINSBERG: When did you get the Fear?

VOZNESENSKY: Fear of what?

GINSBERG: Capital F. When did the change come over you?

VOZNESENSKY: Oh, very late. After his death.

ORLOVSKY: What year was that?

VOZNESENSKY: In 1953. I was twenty.

GINSBERG: How did you begin to learn that the historical truth you'd learned at school was . . .

VOZNESENSKY: Oh, I . . . in the university, from the Khrushchev reports, and when people returned from the labor camps and they started talking. [*telephone conversation*]

GINSBERG: We were sitting with a painter, Russian-born, Raphael Soyer, and we said we were seeing you. I gave him *Nostalgia for the Present* and he had a book of Yevtushenko. He's very old, seventy-nine. So I asked him what he thought. He had some criticism. You want to hear?

VOZNESENSKY: Does he understand Russian?

GINSBERG: He reads Russian. He said he liked Yevtushenko. Said he was plain, straightforward. He thought you were equal. But he said he thought you flirted too much. You know flirt?

VOZNESENSKY: Yeah. Too public?

GINSBERG: With "ideas," or "modernity," or beatnik . . . you know, the "mode," flirted. It was very interesting from an old man, seventy-nine.

VOZNESENSKY: He's a painter?

ORLOVSKY: For sixty years.

VOZNESENSKY: He's a very good painter?

GINSBERG: Very good, but not modern. You know the Ashcan school? George Bellows. He ascends from that. Very good portraits. Too bad we didn't go there together—maybe get our portrait painted. Classic style. Old-fashioned classic, but very, very good. He does not like Jasper Johns or Robert Rauschenberg or Kandinsky. Who else didn't he like? He didn't even like Cézanne! No, he likes Cézanne's subject matter.

VOZNESENSKY: I think, for him, my language and way of thinking is not understandable because Russia has changed. But he doesn't understand the change and he thinks I am playing the clown. Yevtushenko is certainly good, but for an old man he is easier to understand.

GINSBERG: I think that's what Soyer likes. Because it was so down, so grounded, or so plain . . . the Russia he knows.

VOZNESENSKY: In my poetry he misses the language and grammar of his time.

GINSBERG: It was interesting to hear an old man say that. It was the only time I've heard anybody give criticism of you that I thought, that's interesting, maybe to think about and tell you. People criticize me a lot. Why are you always doing this about politics, why drugs, why punk rock? Why nonpoetic exhibiting? And I take it to heart.

VOZNESENSKY: Did this ever embarrass you, this criticism . . .

GINSBERG: I take it seriously. I get angry sometimes. Once there was a critic [A. Alvarez] in England, very formalist, I forget his name, a friend of Sylvia Plath's, who reviewed "Kaddish" in the 1961 London Times Literary Supplement, and denounced it as being a fake poem and terrible. Insincere. Bad writing. Beatnik. It belonged to psychiatry, not to poetry. I got so angry, one of the very few times—maybe five times—I wrote the critic a letter, privately, saying, I forbid you ever to write about my work again, you're an evil creep, you're a nut. But then I regretted writing, because I was just angry. And his judgment later proved, among his peers, like Robert Lowell, to be so erroneous! And then he himself later began writing about suicide poetry! With Sylvia Plath. And got all entangled in that area that he was denouncing to me.

[*Following a discussion about where to eat*]

GINSBERG: So the key in American poetry that I got from Kerouac and that he got from Lucien Carr, was this pronunciation of the *tones* of key words in sentences. That comes somewhat from the exaggerated style of barroom conversation among newspaper reporters. Do you have that tradition in Russia? That journalists drink a lot?

VOZNESENSKY: Oh yes.

GINSBERG: Well, everybody drinks a lot. The American myth is that newspaper men, in their bars, drink all the time. Which is partly true.

VOZNESENSKY: Because they travel a lot and meet new friends and . . .

GINSBERG: And there's a peculiarly aggressive, cynical quality to their conversation. So you get that rhythmic run of ba-ba-ba-BA-BA-ba. "Well, *you say* you heard that, but I don't believe that." "*You say* you saw that guy murder that guy I don't believe it." "*You say* you're innocent but I don't believe it." So you get a da-DA-da-da-da. So that actually provides a set of vocal tones which can be applied to emphasize the meaning of any sentence.

Like a sentence, a simple sentence: "I just gave him *the key.*" Ta-ta-ta-TA-TA.

Ezra Pound has very interesting advice for poets: to "follow the tone leading of the vowels"—a, e, i, o, u. The open sounds in English. To follow the *tone* leading of the vowels.

VOZNESENSKY: Fantastic. Very good.

GINSBERG: To be conscious of that. He inherited his consciousness from his study of Greek meters. Because in Greek they also had tones measured. Part of Greek meter was pitch or tone.

VOZNESENSKY: Yes, I know that.

GINSBERG: So part of their measure of the line was perhaps a line with three high tones, two low tones. I don't know Greek meter. But since Pound, many American poets have been conscious of the tones, as well as the rhythm, in stress—da, da, da, da-da. As well as the length of the vowel. And Pound measures his poetry in length of vowel, I think we talked about this one time.

VOZNESENSKY: In a plane. I remember this conversation. We were going to Boston, I think?

GINSBERG: Yes.

VOZNESENSKY: You didn't tell me about your reading in a café and singing in Boston [at Passim's Coffeehouse].

GINSBERG: I lost my voice. Friday night all the lights in Harvard went out, and so no more sound system. I was singing with Peter and with a guitar; so we moved the stage to the steps . . . because there was one light on the steps, sort of an emergency light, and did it without loudspeaker, singing. My voice is still a little rough from that. Otherwise it's good. Business was not so good because many, many snowflakes fell that weekend. But it was enough to pay our way and make money and pay for the . . . actually $2,000 for four nights, two shows. A lot of work. But intimate and fun.

VOZNESENSKY: Tell me, Harvard students are not the same as in the whole United States?

GINSBERG: Well, they're the same except the environment is different and they realize their environment is elite.

[On a walk through the Village, following Voznesensky's reading]
GINSBERG: Cunt will always get you confused. You must never let cunt come before art! Or cock! That's why I try to arrange to read earlier. In big readings I always, often, get put last. And by that time everybody is strained and tired and has headaches and wants to go to the bathroom and wants to eat, is hungry. So this time I said, well, maybe we go second.

VOZNESENSKY: Are the love odes typical for you? You read in a very intimate and touching way.

GINSBERG: I have four poems that style. Different affairs. From now on, every affair I will write poems about . . . new adventures. New adventures in the heart.

ORLOVSKY: He has not read his S&M poem yet, how he likes to be spanked!

GINSBERG: I brought "Punk Rock"—to wake them up. Then, once woken, to bring them serious, from heart love poems, then some intellectual stuff, with that "Fake Saint" and then . . . What I can't understand is, how, after all these years, there are still poets who read with that sing-song, a dying fall they call it. *Momma, why don't you give me your* . . . —reading different poems with the same tone, as if there were no different emotion, no different situation.

VOZNESENSKY: Yeah. Nothing happened.

GINSBERG: The text was not bad . . . the young man's [at the MLA reading]. Good things . . . *cows knee-deep in muck by the barn.* Clear. But he said it flat-voiced: "cows-knee-deep-in-muck-by-the-barn."

VOZNESENSKY: Very sentimental.

GINSBERG: Just one voice-tone.

ORLOVSKY: Fragile.

GINSBERG: Fragile, sentimental. It is the old tradition of the artificial.

VOZNESENSKY: And impossible to understand where a poem is finished. He wanted to take his handkerchief out . . .

GINSBERG: You have the same thing in Russia?

VOZNESENSKY: Yes.

GINSBERG: What is the old-fashioned style in Russia?

VOZNESENSKY: The same. Very simple.

GINSBERG: But they have the tradition of chants.

VOZNESENSKY: Tradition . . . Mayakovsky was one. But there are a thousand poets in other style.

ORLOVSKY: My father said there was a poet in Russia who dressed up like a cat and recited his poems. Do you know his name?

VOZNESENSKY: No. It's not important, I think. There is one now who wears a mask, a black mask. He was in the war and was blinded. And he's very popular because he was a hero and there is an aura of mystery about him. Very romantic, when he came with velvet black mask, and girls leaping.

GINSBERG: But are there imitators of Mayakovsky and Yesenin who shout their poetry?

VOZNESENSKY: A lot like Mayakovsky. Mayakovsky was very sincere.

[*In restaurant*]
GINSBERG: You had a good object lesson tonight.

VOZNESENSKY: What for?

GINSBERG: To see the two styles. You see American poetry was not involved with vocalization.

VOZNESENSKY: You are like from another planet. They are from another planet. But you are full of blood. . . .

ORLOVSKY: When did you first start booming out your voice?

VOZNESENSKY: I guess from the beginning. From the beginning, 1958. I think it was because I was so shy.

GINSBERG: Did your voice change over the years?

VOZNESENSKY: Yes, very much. Because I had a very high voice, a young voice. And a slightly different style, not like now. Not childish but boyish.

GINSBERG: When did it begin changing?

VOZNESENSKY: I think maybe . . . around the time I came to the States.

GINSBERG: When you came to the States?

VOZNESENSKY: Not because of the trip but because something had changed inside me. It was after a terrible period in my life and my poetry. Before, I had been more naïve and lyrical and romantic. It's very strange to hear the records I made in those days.

GINSBERG: From 1963 my voice went down, lower, lower, lower, from mantra chanting, Hare Krishna, OM . . . AH . . . HŪM . . .

VOZNESENSKY: Did you read your "Plutonian Ode" in another style before?

GINSBERG: Every time different. The times you heard me I read it in a loud voice. Then I lost my voice in Cambridge, like I told you . . . the loudspeaker failed, so I shouted.

VOZNESENSKY: That happens in the United States.

GINSBERG: All the time. One day there was a giant blackout all over the Eastern seaboard. Remember? So I began to read "Plutonian Ode" very personally. Without shouting. And I realized that I had been shouting too much. Using too much aggression. And that the poetry was strong enough that it could be delivered more in ordinary speech-voice.

VOZNESENSKY: But today it was addressed to everyone personally. Each person.

GINSBERG: That was because I was ashamed of the way I had read it before in front of you—too loud, not sensitive enough. Also because Robert Cordier was there and he never heard it. He had translated my poetry into French, and didn't know that I had written a big poem this year. Also because some of the poets there I knew, and some of the teachers. I was hoping to communicate. You know, if you have a lover in the audience . . .

VOZNESENSKY: Oh yes, you read better.

GINSBERG: Then you've had that experience?

VOZNESENSKY: Certainly.

GINSBERG: Peter's quality of voice is amazing. He is one of the few poets who could read in a railroad station or in a factory and be heard. Like a farmer's voice calling hogs!

VOZNESENSKY: But how they understand you? Did they like you, these farmers, when you read to them?

ORLOVSKY: No, he said I could read . . . well, when I'm out in the farm fields, making a garden, planting trees, I sing a lot. Sing all day long. I sing for two days, nonstop. And I sing very loud. I yodel very loud. So it builds up the strength of the voice. And then there are herbs to make your voice strong. Licorice.

VOZNESENSKY: What kind of songs?

ORLOVSKY: Songs about birds, green grass, living to be 118, soil, tasting the soil, good soil, poor soil. Different-colored plants— some light green, some dark green. Anything that comes into my head. As fast as it comes into my head, I sing it out.

GINSBERG: Who else in Russia has not a strong voice but a real voice? From heart?

VOZNESENSKY: Have you heard Bella Akhmadulina?

GINSBERG: Very bell-like.

VOZNESENSKY: Yes. Everybody has his own style, Martynov has his own, Bella her own.

ORLOVSKY: How old is Bella?

VOZNESENSKY: She was born in 1937. She is forty. I think forty.

GINSBERG: I learned from Bob Dylan. A singer. He completely becomes one with the wind coming from his body. And bends the wind a lot. Long breath.

VOZNESENSKY: How is his poetry now?

GINSBERG: Better. Better and better. More realistic. More disillusioned. He said, talking about art, that what he wants to do is to stop time. To be so intensely in the moment that he stops time. And he also said, quoting Henry Miller, "the artist innoculates the society with his disillusionment."

VOZNESENSKY: Fantastic.

GINSBERG: No illusion. Just sees straight reality.

VOZNESENSKY: Very good.

GINSBERG: Kerouac said if Russia and America ever went to war, he'd commit suicide. Because Kerouac read all Dostoevsky and he wept for the Russian soil.

ORLOVSKY: He said he'd get up in the trees and shoot the Reds.

GINSBERG: No, that was later, when he was drunk, he was talking about the Chinese Reds, Mao. But earlier, I said what if we live long enough to see Russia and America get into war? He said, "Oh, I'd commit suicide. That would be the end of everything." Very sweet then. That was 1960.

VOZNESENSKY: Where is Burroughs?

GINSBERG: Burroughs? He went back to Boulder. He has a little apartment and one telephone. And his telephone rings in New York, but he is out there in Colorado. And his secretary or somebody answers it in New York. And he works all the time, writing. Every day he gets up at eight o'clock, he writes for two or three hours, takes a walk, comes home. He has finished one great, huge long novel in the last five years, including work from ten years ago.

ORLOVSKY: Five hundred pages.

GINSBERG: *Cities of the Red Night.* His magnum opus—big work— of the seventies, maybe his greatest work, is about a world plague. It's like an invasion of a virus, maybe from outer space, maybe launched by the KGB-CIA. And a characteristic of the plague is that all the citizens' buttocks and loins and genitals turn bright red like a bikini, and they get sexually aroused into frenzy and they die in orgasms. But they contaminate each other and they die spurting semen all over, attacking and raping everybody. And the only people exempt from the plague are the ex-junkies, the junkies, and heroin addicts—because perhaps the heroin has subdued their sexual appetite and made them disillusioned. So the police and the army are all opiomanes and the army is paid with heroin and with opium. They get very sentimental with each other about being in the army, and very patriotic. The conversations between the old sergeant and the private are, "Sarge, could you give me a little extra pay for the weekend? I want to go out for the weekend; I need a little extra fix."

VOZNESENSKY: Are they very weak?

GINSBERG: Actually, no. It's like Chinese rickshaw drivers. They go on the nod sometimes.

VOZNESENSKY: But tell me, what is in fashion now? Is it cocaine?

GINSBERG: What is it now? The rich people take cocaine, maybe the Rockefellers. It is more and more in vogue. Because it makes you feel brilliant. Have you ever tried it?

VOZNESENSKY: No.

GINSBERG: No? I've had cocaine lots. It's like amphetamines, Benzedrine, you know? Uppers . . .

VOZNESENSKY: Yeah, yeah.

GINSBERG: It gives you a feeling of great power, magnanimity.

ORLOVSKY: White light in your brain, sexual extra power, extra thrill.

GINSBERG: Also vocal, also intellectual. The sounds you hear echo and rebound from the ceiling. So sensitive. But also puts you in this egomaniac, big universe of your own.

ORLOVSKY: You're the only one in the world.

GINSBERG: I was with Dylan years ago on tour, and there was a lot of white powder around. So he said, "You've got to come with us for the rest of the tour and we'll go around the world forever, singing, I'm a minstrel." I said, "My father is dying, I have to go home, I've got to go home for a month or two, take care of my father." He said, "Bring your father!" I said, "What about me, when I'm dying." He said, "We'll take care of you when you're dying." But then the next morning he was glum and he didn't remember, or we didn't talk about it. And I'd gone up to my room, thinking he was going to take care of me for the rest of my life! I didn't realize that his munificence was engorged with snow. You know the word *snow*?

VOZNESENSKY: No.

GINSBERG: *Snow* is the slang for cocaine. Snow.

VOZNESENSKY: Oh yes, I know.

GINSBERG: I remember in Paris I had a lot of cocaine. And I stayed up one whole night thinking, I'm going to write a great prose work. And I typed all night. And at the end it was this prose work about beating up a slave, a sexual slave!

ORLOVSKY: Gives you an octopus mind. Your mind goes in many directions all at once.

GINSBERG: Really antisocial. It is not for organic community. So that on the rock 'n' roll tour where we were, at the beginning, it was family and friends and community, but then when the cocaine entered, everybody went off into their own rooms to brood over their destiny.

ORLOVSKY: Didn't talk much.

GINSBERG: Everybody became Napoleon.

ORLOVSKY: Stopped talking in the hallways and the buses. They became quiet.

GINSBERG: Everybody became paranoiac Napoleons.

VOZNESENSKY: Not aggressive?

GINSBERG: Yeah, some aggression comes out.

ORLOVSKY: Some of them broke mirrors on walls. Got drunk, broke mirrors.

GINSBERG: It's not bad, for fun. But then some people think maybe it's real power. It's a power drug.

ORLOVSKY: Too much, no good. Once . . .

GINSBERG: Try it sometime.

ORLOVSKY: Once in a while it's all right.

GINSBERG: What happened to you when I gave you that STP pill?

VOZNESENSKY: I don't remember.

GINSBERG: You took it? I made the mistake, I got to confess to you, I had never tried it and I gave it to you. I told you before. Peter took it.

VOZNESENSKY: What happens with STP?

ORLOVSKY: I was crawling on the floor, near the radiator, and I saw a spark, a blue spark fly from the radiator. And a very brilliant light, bright light, colors. Got very excited. And I think I fell asleep. And I shit in my pants!

GINSBERG: And what happened to you? I gave it to you by mistake, thinking it was LSD and thinking I was going to influence the course of Russian poetry.

VOZNESENSKY: It was in the Chelsea.

GINSBERG: I thought you took it back to Russia and took it.

VOZNESENSKY: No, no, no. In the Chelsea. After you left me. It was the first and last time.

ORLOVSKY: What year?

VOZNESENSKY: I don't remember what year!

GINSBERG: Destroyed your brain?

VOZNESENSKY: No, no, no. It was '67. And something happened, I think, with my memory for about five days. Because I remember the beginning of this, but I don't remember what happened. I am told that I didn't eat for, I think, two days. Is that possible?

GINSBERG: That was one of the worst things I've ever done. Ignorance. Ambitious.

ORLOVSKY: We have some good LSD.

VOZNESENSKY: I am afraid; I am very afraid for my brain.

ORLOVSKY: We all take it together. We go out in the country, with a little meditation, get nice, bright colors.

GINSBERG: LSD is much milder than STP. LSD, you don't get a habit. Well, some young people think they are going to chase God down to the end of eternity, so they take it every day. But Gregory Corso says that "LSD shows you more of what isn't there." You see your own projections. If you think a cloud looks like the face of Rembrandt, then, after a while, the idea solidifies and you start pointing it out to other people. They can't see it and they think you're crazy.

ORLOVSKY: My father told me in Siberia they used to take Siberian mushrooms; the monks and the head monk would eat the mushrooms because there was a scarcity of mushrooms and the lower monks would drink the urine of the head monk. They would pass on the urine cup.

GINSBERG: I have a big book at home, all about it, with all the anthropological documents. By Gordon Wasson. In English and French. There are many studies of it.

VOZNESENSKY: I've never read about it.

GINSBERG: The urine passes through the body and can be recycled. In central Siberia there are many stories of the shamans using that.

ORLOVSKY: Morarji Desai, the prime minister of India, drinks one glass, eight ounces, of his urine every morning.

GINSBERG: His own or cow's urine?

ORLOVSKY: His own urine. Because he said, in *Time* magazine, in the People section, it makes him feel good every day.

GINSBERG: It's an old Indian tradition. Peter was drinking his piss the other day.

ORLOVSKY: But not every day, no.

GINSBERG: Experimenting.

VOZNESENSKY: One of our poets had a name, "Uran." Not a bad poet. But for him his name sounded too atomic, too modern. He has changed his name to "Urine." He thinks it sounds better.

[*seeing the Empire State building in the distance*]
GINSBERG: Empire State—red, pink, and green for Christmas. Do they light up buildings in Moscow?

VOZNESENSKY: No, not with colored lights. White. In my building they do. I live in a skyscraper. Very fine light. You know, Moscow's a lot cleaner. Very clean, very clean city.

GINSBERG: Washington, San Francisco, everywhere. Denver is terrible, Denver is the second worst, Los Angeles is up front.

VOZNESENSKY: But I was in Los Angeles and did not notice.

GINSBERG: But when you come down, in a plane, you notice this color, that haze—you know what color that is? Brown. What does it look like? Shit brown.

VOZNESENSKY: Yeah, shit brown.

GINSBERG: Shit smear. Because it is the shit of the cities, the gas, the fart of the cities.

1980

Paul Bowles

was born in New York City on December 30, 1910. He periodically attended the University of Virginia, taking time off to work for the *Herald-Tribune* in Paris. There and in Berlin, he studied musical composition with Aaron Copland, Virgil Thomson, and Nadia Boulanger. He returned to New York in the mid-thirties to become one of the preeminent composers of American theater music, writing scores for William Saroyan's *Love's Old Sweet Song*, Lillian Hellman's *Watch on the Rhine*, and Tennessee Williams's *The Glass Menagerie* and *Horse Eats Hay*, directed by Orson Welles for the Federal Theater Project.

In 1938, Bowles married Jane Auer who, under her married name, became an accomplished author. They spent much of their married life traveling throughout the world. In the late 1940s, they made Tangier, Morocco, their permanent home. Following the publication of his wife's novel, *Two Serious Ladies*, Bowles wrote his first novel, *The Sheltering Sky*, in 1949. In 1990, the novel was adapted for the screen in a film starring Debra Winger and John Malkovich.

Bowles has written numerous works of fiction and prose, including *Let It Come Down* (1952), *The Spider's House* (1955), *Too Far from Home* (1991), and an autobiography, *Without Stopping* (1972). His short-story collections include *The Delicate Prey and Other Stories* (1950), *The Time of Friendship* (1967), *Things Gone & Things Still Here* (1977), *Unwelcome Words* (1988), and several story translations from Moghrebi Arabic, most notably those of Mohammed Mrabet.

Bowles's travels in Europe and North Africa occasioned encounters with some of the most intriguing literary figures of his day: Gertrude Stein, André Gide, Jean Cocteau, Ezra Pound, and Alfred Chester. Inspired by his nomadic eccentricities, Stein once remarked to Bowles, "If you were typical, it would be the end of civilization. You're a manufactured savage."

Bowles continued to reside in Tangier until returning to the States in 1997.

COURTESY OF BLACK SPARROW PRESS

*Like any romantic, I had always been vaguely certain that some-
time during my life I should come into a magic place which, in dis-
closing its secrets, would give me wisdom and ecstasy—perhaps
even death.*

—*Paul Bowles in* Without Stopping

*T*he Tangier that once greeted Bowles in 1931, promising "wisdom
and ecstasy," bears little resemblance to the Tangier of the 1970s.
The frenetic medina, with its souks, its endless array of tourist bou-
tiques, its perennial hawkers and hustlers is still there, of course, though
fifty years ago it had already been dwarfed by the European city and its
monuments to colonialism: the imperious French Consulate, the Café de
Paris, luxury hotels in the grand style (the Minzah, the Velasquez, the
Villa de France), the now forlornly abandoned Teatro Cervantes, and the
English church with its cemetery filled with the remains of knight com-
manders, baronets, and the prodigal sons of former empires. The days of

Tangier as the wide-open international city of intrigue are gone forever. Today it is simply one city of a third-world country in flux, slowly but steadily coming to grips with the twentieth century.

For those of a romantic bent, however, the power of Tangier to evoke images of the inscrutable East remains potent, despite the ravages of modernity. It still seems an appropriate place to find Paul Bowles. Any American who comes to Tangier bearing more than a casual curiosity about Morocco and a vague concern for music and literature considers a visit with Bowles an absolute must; for some, it even assumes the reverential character of a pilgrimage. In no way, however, does Bowles see himself as an object of special interest. Indeed, such an attitude strikes him as being amusingly naïve, if not downright silly.

He lives in a three-room apartment in a quiet residential section of Tangier. His flat, located in a fifties-futuristic building in sight of the American consulate, is comfortably unimposing, though it does testify to his days as a world traveler: souvenirs from Asia, Mexico, black Africa; a bookcase lined with personally inscribed volumes by Burroughs, Kerouac, Ginsberg, Vidal; an entryway in which vintage trunks and suitcases are stacked shoulder high, as if a voyage of indefinite length were perpetually in the offing.

Our first meeting took place in the summer of 1976. I arrived at his door in the early afternoon. I found him newly awakened, his thick white hair tousled and pale blue eyes slightly bleary; he was obviously surprised that anyone would come to call at that hour of the day. As he finished his breakfast and lighted up his first cigarette, his thin, somewhat wiry frame relaxed noticeably. He became increasingly jovial.

Evidently, however, my timing hadn't been particularly good. The tape recorder had just begun to roll when a series of visitors announced themselves with persistent rings of the doorbell: his chauffeur, his maid, a woman friend from New York, an American boy who'd taken the apartment downstairs, and, eventually, Mohammed Mrabet. Handsome in a rugged and brooding way, Mrabet asked me to bring him, on my return to Tangier, a pistol with nine chambers as there were apparently nine people upon whose elimination he was intent at that time.

As it turned out, I had reason to be grateful for his and the other interruptions. They enabled me to return and talk at length with Bowles that evening, the next day, and two more times over the following year and a half.

• • •

INTERVIEWER: For many people, the mention of your name evokes romantic images of the artist's life in exotic, faraway places. Do you see yourself as a kind of consummate expatriate?

BOWLES: I'm afraid not. I don't see myself as a consummate anything. I don't see myself, really, I have no ego. I didn't find the United States particularly interesting and once I found places that were more interesting I chose to live in them, which I think makes sense.

INTERVIEWER: Was this decision to leave the United States an early one?

BOWLES: I made it at seventeen, so I guess you'd say it was an early decision. Some people absorb things more quickly than others, and I think I had a fairly good idea of what life would be like for me in the States, and I didn't want it.

INTERVIEWER: What would it have been like?

BOWLES: Boring. There was nothing I wanted there, and once I'd moved away I saw that all I needed from the States was money. I went back there for that. I've never yet gone there without the definite guarantee of making money. Just going for the pleasure of it, I've never done.

INTERVIEWER: Since your contact with foreign places has so obviously nurtured your writing, perhaps you would never have been a writer if you had stayed in the States.

BOWLES: Quite possibly not. I might have gone on as a composer. I cut the composing cord in 1947, when I moved here, although, as I say, I went back several times to write scores for Broadway.

INTERVIEWER: Did you cut the composing cord because writing and music were getting in each other's way?

BOWLES: No, not at all. You do them with separate parts of the brain, I think. And you derive different kinds of pleasure from them. It's like saying, "Is it more fun to drink a glass of water when you're thirsty or eat a good meal when you're hungry?" I gave up composing professionally simply because I wanted to leave New York. I wanted to get out of the States.

INTERVIEWER: Did giving up an entire career because you disliked life in America leave you feeling hostile toward the place?

BOWLES: No, no. But when you say "America" to me, all I think of is New York City where I was born and brought up. I know that New York isn't America; still, my image of America *is* New York. But there's no hostility. I just think it's a great shame, what has happened there. I don't think it will ever be put right; but then again, I never expect anything to be put right. Nothing ever is. Things go on and become other things. The whole character of the country has changed beyond recognition since my childhood. One always thinks everything's got worse—and in most respects it has—but that's meaningless. What does one mean when one says that things are getting worse? It's becoming more like the future, that's all. It's just moving ahead. The future will be infinitely "worse" than the present; and in *that* future, the future will be immeasurably "worse" than the future that we can see. Naturally.

INTERVIEWER: You're a pessimist.

BOWLES: Well, look for yourself. You don't have to be a pessimist to see it. There's always the chance of a universal holocaust in which a few billion people will be burned. I don't hope for that, but it's what I see as a probability.

INTERVIEWER: Can't one also hope for things like a cure for cancer, an effective ban on nuclear arms, an upsurge of concern for the environment, and a deeper consciousness of being?

BOWLES: You can hope for anything, of course. I expect enormous things to happen in the future, but I don't think they'll be things which people born in my generation will think are great and wonderful. Perhaps people born in 1975 will think otherwise. I mean, people born in 1950 think television is great.

INTERVIEWER: Because American technology has already contributed so much to making what you regard as an inevitably undesirable future, I guess it's understandable that living outside your indigenous culture became almost a compulsion with you.

BOWLES: Not almost; it was a *real* compulsion. Even as a small child, I was always eager to get away. I remember when I was six years old, I was sent off to spend two weeks with someone—I don't know who it was or why I was sent—and I begged to stay longer. I didn't want to go home. Again, when I was nine and my father had pneumonia, I was sent off for a month or two and I kept writing letters asking, "Please, let me stay longer." I didn't want to see my parents again. I didn't want to go back into all that.

INTERVIEWER: In *Without Stopping*, you were quite frank about your feelings toward your parents in describing the fondness you had for your mother and your estrangement from your father.

BOWLES: I think most boys are fond of their mothers. The hostility involved with my father was very real. It started on his side and became reciprocated, naturally, at an early age. I don't know what the matter was. Maybe he didn't want any children. I never knew the real story of why he was so angry with me, although my maternal grandmother told me it was simply because he was jealous. She said he couldn't bear to have my mother pay attention to this third person, me. It's probably true.

INTERVIEWER: Did this negative relationship with your father affect your becoming a traveler and an artist?

BOWLES: Probably, I don't know. I've never really gone over it in my mind to see what caused what. I probably couldn't. It's obvious that a shut-in childhood is likely to make an introverted child and that an introverted child is more likely to be "artistic."

INTERVIEWER: Your parents weren't enthusiastic about your going off to Europe when you were only eighteen?

BOWLES: It wasn't a matter of their being enthusiastic or not, inasmuch as they knew nothing about my going. I had the money for my passage to France, plus about twenty-five dollars.

INTERVIEWER: Were you running away from something?

BOWLES: No, I was running toward something, although I didn't know what at the time.

INTERVIEWER: Did you ever find it?

BOWLES: Yes, I found it over the years. What I was ultimately running toward was my grave, of course: "The paths of glory lead but to the grave."

INTERVIEWER: You began studying with Aaron Copland not long after your return from that first trip abroad. How would you describe your experience with Copland?

BOWLES: It couldn't have been better. He was a wonderful teacher.

INTERVIEWER: Apparently Copland was able to compose professionally outside of New York, yet you say that you weren't.

BOWLES: No, because I had to make a living at writing music. If I'd had a private income I could have composed anywhere, as long as I'd had a keyboard. A few composers don't even need that, but I do. Aaron and I had a very hard time the first summer here in Tangier, in 1931. Gertrude Stein had told us that it would be easy to get a piano, but it wasn't. Nowadays it's impossible, but in those days you still could if you really looked. We finally found one. It wasn't very good, and the problem of getting it up the mountain to the house we'd rented was horrendous. The road wasn't paved so it had to come up on a donkey. Just as it was going through the gate the piano fell off with a WHAM!!! and I thought, "That's the end of our summer." It worked out all right, eventually. Aaron was writing a short symphony and although he couldn't finish it, he was able to do some work on it. Of course, he worked constantly.

INTERVIEWER: Weren't you as diligent a worker as Copland?

BOWLES: I wouldn't say so, no. When we were in Berlin, it seemed that I was always going somewhere else. Aaron was rather annoyed by that. I was supposed to be studying, but instead I would set out for Austria or Bavaria.

INTERVIEWER: What was your impression of Berlin back then?

BOWLES: Well, I wasn't there for very long, only four months; one whole spring. But it was crazy. Really crazy. It was like a film of Fritz Lang's. You had the feeling that all of life was being directed by Lang. It was sinister because of the discrepancy between those who had and those who didn't, and you felt it all very intensely. The "haves" were going hog-wild while the "have-nots" seethed with hatred. There was a black cloud of hatred over the whole east end of the city. It was that summer that the Disconto-Gesellschaft failed. You felt the catastrophe coming, which gave an uncomfortable tinge to everything that happened. Christopher Isherwood was living it rather than writing about it then.

INTERVIEWER: How did you react when Isherwood gave your name to his best-known character creation?

BOWLES: Sally Bowles? I thought it was quite natural, really. We'd all been there together through the whole season and we used to eat lunch together every day. He didn't want to use her real name, Jean Ross, so he used mine. Where he got "Sally," I don't know.

INTERVIEWER: From your recollection, did the real Jean Ross much resemble the character she had inspired?

BOWLES: I'd say so. Yes. She was very attractive, and also very amusing. Christopher was always with her. They lived in the same rooming house on the Nollendorfplatz. I lived on Güntzel-strasse, in a room with a balcony, I remember. Aaron took a flat that belonged to an American poet named Alfred Kreymborg on the Steinplatz, so I would go there for my lessons every day. We'd have lunch with Stephen Spender, Christopher, and Jean. We always had that nucleus. We generally ate at the Café des Westens opposite the Kaiser Gedächtnis Kirche.

INTERVIEWER: Did you know that you were observing the genesis of *Goodbye to Berlin?*

BOWLES: How would I? I had no idea that he was going to write a book. One was just concerned with living each day as it came. I met some of the people in *The Berlin Stories,* but I never suspected they were going to be "immortalized."

INTERVIEWER: Have you ever felt any professional antagonism toward other artists?

BOWLES: No, I've never been like that at all. I refuse to play. I told you I don't have much of an ego. I meant it. To take part in such games, you have to believe in the existence of your personality in a way that I don't. And I couldn't do it. I could pretend, but it wouldn't get me very far.

INTERVIEWER: When you were a young man making the acquaintance not only of other young writers such as Isherwood and Auden but also getting to know more established writers, like Stein and Cocteau, were you consciously attempting to become part of an artistic community? Were you looking to be nurtured by contact with other artists?

BOWLES: I was never aware of wanting to become part of a community, no. I wanted to meet them. I suppose I simply felt that I was taking pot shots at clay pipes. Pop! Down goes Gertrude, down goes Jean Cocteau, down goes André Gide. I made a point of those things—meeting Manuel de Falla, for example—for no reason at all. I went to Granada, found his door, knocked, went in, and spent the afternoon. He had no idea who I was. Why I did that, I don't know. Apparently I thought such encounters were important or I wouldn't have bothered, because it involved a lot of work and sometimes a sacrifice of something I cared about. But exactly how I felt I can't remember, because it wasn't an intellectual thing. It was "unthought," and it's hard for me to recall the reason for it. Of course, I've never been a thinking person. A lot seems to happen without my conscious knowledge.

INTERVIEWER: Has it always been that way, or has it developed over the years?

BOWLES: It was always like that. All through my late teens, from sixteen on, I was writing surrealist poetry. I read André [Breton], who explained how to do it, and so I learned how to write without being conscious of what I was doing. I learned how to make it grammatically correct and even to have a certain style without the slightest idea of what I was writing. One part of my mind was doing the writing, and God knows what the other part was doing. I suppose it was bulldozing the subconscious, dredging up ooze. I don't know how those things work, and I don't want to know.

INTERVIEWER: It sounds as though Breton served to inspire your early writing. Did you have many "inspiration" writers?

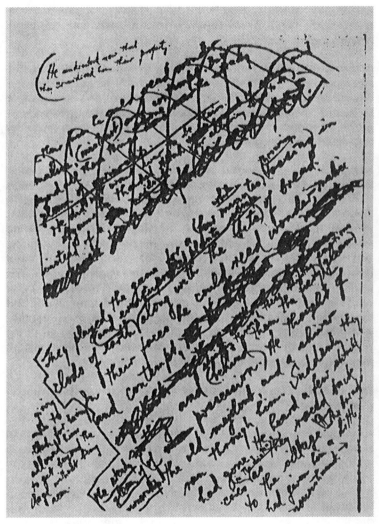

A Paul Bowles manuscript page.

BOWLES: Not really. During my early years in Europe, I was very much taken with Lautréamont. I carried him with me wherever I went, but I got over that and didn't supplant him with anyone else. You may have such enthusiasms when you're very young, but you don't usually have them when you get older, even a few years older. There were many writers whom I admired, and if they were living I tended to seek them out: Stein, Gide, Cocteau, many others.

INTERVIEWER: Your autobiography, *Without Stopping,* seemed to overflow with the names of artists, writers, famous people in general, whom you'd met.

BOWLES: And yet I cut many of them out. I saw when I was finished that it was nothing but names, so I cut out fifty or sixty. The reason for all that was that Putnam wanted the book to be a roster of names; they stressed that at the beginning, before I signed the contract. If they'd just left me alone without all the stipulations, I think I could have done something more personal. Actually, I think the first half was personal enough, but the last half was hurried. Time was coming to an end and I had to meet the deadline. They'd already allowed an extra year in the contract, so I just rushed it off. I'd never do another book like that, under contract. A full year after I'd signed the contract I still hadn't begun to write. It took me that length of time to recall events and sequences. I had no diaries or letters to consult, so I had to go back over my entire life, month by month, charting every meaningless meander of its course. And as I say, that took more than a year.

INTERVIEWER: You've never been a diarist?

BOWLES: No. I had no letters or documents to go on at all.

INTERVIEWER: Was that intentional? Would a diary have hindered your spontaneity?

BOWLES: I don't know about that. It was just the facts of life. I never bothered. I felt that life itself was important, each day. I didn't see any reason to keep a diary. Then again, I never thought I'd be writing an autobiography.

INTERVIEWER: How do you write?

BOWLES: I don't use a typewriter. It's too heavy, too much trouble. I use a notebook, and I write in bed. Ninety-five percent of everything I've written has been done in bed.

INTERVIEWER: And the typing?

BOWLES: The typing of a manuscript to send out is another thing. That's just drudgery, not work. By work I mean the invention of something, the putting down, the creation of a page with words on it.

INTERVIEWER: Did you write any of your novels under a deadline?

BOWLES: No. When I finished them, I sent them in and they were published. I couldn't write fiction under pressure. The books wouldn't have been any good; they'd have been even less good than they were.

INTERVIEWER: You don't seem to have a particularly high regard for your talent as a writer.

BOWLES: No, no. I haven't.

INTERVIEWER: Why not?

BOWLES: I don't know. It doesn't seem very relevant.

INTERVIEWER: Haven't people encouraged you along the way, telling you that you were good?

BOWLES: Oh, yes. Of course.

INTERVIEWER: You just didn't believe them?

BOWLES: I believed that they believed it, and I wanted to hear them say they liked this or disliked that, and why. But I was never sure of their viewpoint, so it was hard to know whether they understood what they were liking or disliking.

INTERVIEWER: Would you say that it was easier for a serious young writer to get published twenty or thirty years ago?

BOWLES: I doubt that getting "serious" writing published was ever easy. But judging from the quantity of nonwriting that gets into print today, I'd deduce that today there are fewer young authors writing with the intention of producing serious work. To quote Susan Sontag: "Seriousness has less prestige now."

INTERVIEWER: In reading your work, one doesn't expect to be led to some conclusion through a simple progression of events. One has the sense of participating in a spontaneous growth of events, one on top of another.

BOWLES: Yes? Well, they grow that way. That's the point, you see. I don't feel that I wrote these books. I feel as though they had been written by my arm, by my brain, my organism, but that they're not necessarily mine. The difficulty is that I've never thought anything belonged to me. At one time, I bought an island off Ceylon and I thought that when I had my two feet planted on it I'd be able to say: "This island is mine." I couldn't; it was meaningless. I felt nothing at all, so I sold it.

INTERVIEWER: How big an island was it?

BOWLES: About two acres. A beautiful tropical forest on an island. Originally it had been owned by a French landscape gardener. Sixty or seventy years ago he'd brought back trees, shrubs, vines, and flowers from all over Southeast Asia and the East Indies. It was a wonderful botanical display. But as I say, I never felt I owned it.

INTERVIEWER: Was writing, for you, a means of alleviating a sense of aloneness by communicating intimately with other people?

BOWLES: No. I look on it simply as a natural function. As far as I'm concerned it's fun, and it just happens. If I don't feel like doing it, I don't do it.

INTERVIEWER: One is struck by the violence in your work. Almost all the characters in *The Delicate Prey*, for example, were victimized by either physical or psychological violence.

BOWLES: Yes, I suppose. The violence served a therapeutic purpose. It's unsettling to think that at any moment life can flare up into senseless violence. But it can and does, and people need to be ready for it. What you make for others is first of all what you make for yourself. If I'm persuaded that our life is predicated upon violence, that the entire structure of what we call civilization, the scaffolding that we've built up over the millennia, can collapse at any moment, then whatever I write is going to be affected by that assumption. The process of life presupposes violence, in the plant world the same as the animal world. But among the animals only man can conceptualize violence. Only man can *enjoy* the *idea* of destruction.

INTERVIEWER: In many of your characterizations, there's a strange combination of fatalism and naïveté. I'm thinking in particular of Kit and Port Moresby in *The Sheltering Sky*. It seemed to me that their frenetic movement was prompted by an obsessive fear of self-confrontation.

BOWLES: Moving around a lot is a good way of postponing the day of reckoning. I'm happiest when I'm moving. When you've cut yourself off from the life you've been living and you haven't yet established another life, you're free. That's a very pleasant sensation, I've always thought. If you don't know where you're going, you're even freer.

INTERVIEWER: Your characters seem to be psychologically alienated from each other and from themselves, and though their isolation may be accentuated by the fact that you've set them as foreigners in exotic places, one feels that they'd be no different at home, that their problems are deeper than the matter of locale.

BOWLES: Of course. Everyone is isolated from everyone else. The concept of society is like a cushion to protect us from the knowledge of that isolation. A fiction that serves as an anaesthetic.

INTERVIEWER: And the exotic settings are secondary?

BOWLES: The transportation of characters to such settings often acts as a catalyst or a detonator, without which there'd be no action, so I shouldn't call the settings secondary. Probably if I hadn't had some contact with what you call "exotic" places, it wouldn't have occurred to me to write at all.

INTERVIEWER: To what degree did the character of Kit resemble your wife, Jane Bowles?

BOWLES: The book was conceived in New York in 1947, and 80 percent of it was written before Jane ever set foot in North Africa in 1948, so there's no question of its being related to experience. The tale is entirely imaginary. Kit is not Jane, although I used some of Jane's characteristics in determining Kit's reactions to such a voyage. Obviously I thought of Port as a fictional extension of myself. But Port is certainly not Paul Bowles, any more than Kit is Jane.

INTERVIEWER: Have you ever written a character who was supposed to be Jane Bowles, or a character who was *directly* modeled after her?

BOWLES: No, never.

INTERVIEWER: Yet couldn't one say that you both exerted a definite influence on each other's work?

BOWLES: Of course! We showed each other every page we wrote. I never thought of sending a story off without discussing it with her first. Neither of us had ever had a literary confidant before. I went over *Two Serious Ladies* with her again and again, until each detail was as we both thought it should be. Not that I put anything into it that she hadn't written. We simply analyzed sentences and rhetoric. It was this being present at the making of a novel that excited me and made me want to write my own fiction. Remember, this was in 1942.

INTERVIEWER: You hadn't had that strong an interest before?

BOWLES: Oh, I'd written before, of course, although of the fiction I saved only one short story. All during my childhood I was writing, and that means from the age of four on. Even at four it gave me a very special kind of pleasure to make up my own stories and print them on paper. They were always about animals and barnyard fowl. My memory doesn't go back to a time when I couldn't read. I remember being ridiculed by my grandfather because I couldn't pronounce the word "clock." I said, "Tlot," but I indignantly spelled it out for him to prove that I knew the word. I must have spelled it "c-l-o-c-tay."

INTERVIEWER: You learned to read at an unusually early age?

BOWLES: Three, I guess. I learned from wooden blocks that had letters of the alphabet carved on them. Toys weren't encouraged. They gave me "constructive things," drawing paper, pencils, notebooks, maps and books. Besides, I was always alone then, never with other children.

INTERVIEWER: Tell me, would you please, about Jane Bowles.

BOWLES: That's an all-inclusive command! What can I possibly tell you about her that isn't implicit in her writing?

INTERVIEWER: She obviously had an extraordinary imagination. She was always coherent, but one had the feeling that she could go off the edge at any time. Almost every page of *Two Serious Ladies*, for example, evoked a sense of madness although it all flowed together very naturally.

BOWLES: I feel that it flows naturally, yes. But I don't find any sense of madness. Unlikely turns of thought, lack of predictability in the characters' behavior, but no suggestion of "madness." I love *Two Serious Ladies*. The action is often like the unfolding of a dream, and the background, with its realistic details, somehow emphasizes the sensation of dreaming.

INTERVIEWER: Does this dreamlike quality reflect her personality?

BOWLES: I don't think anyone ever thought of Jane as a "dreamy" person; she was far too lively and articulate for that. She did have a way of making herself absent suddenly, when one could see that she was a thousand miles away. If you addressed her sharply, she returned with a start. And if you asked her about it, she would simply say: "I don't know. I was somewhere else."

INTERVIEWER: Can you read her books and see Jane Bowles in them?

BOWLES: Not at all; not the Jane Bowles that I knew. Her work contained no reports on her outside life. *Two Serious Ladies* was wholly nonautobiographical. The same goes for her stories.

INTERVIEWER: She wasn't by any means a prolific writer, was she?

BOWLES: No, very unprolific. She wrote very slowly. It cost her blood to write. Everything had to be transmuted into fiction before she could accept it. Sometimes it took her a week to write a page. This exaggerated slowness seemed to me a terrible waste of time, but any mention of it to her was likely to make her stop writing entirely for several days or even weeks. She would say: "All right. It's easy for you, but it's hell for me, and you know it. I'm not you. I know you wish I were, but I'm not. So stop it."

INTERVIEWER: The relationships between her women characters are fascinating. They read like psychological portraits, reminiscent of Djuna Barnes.

BOWLES: In fact, though, she refused to read Djuna Barnes. She never read *Nightwood*. She felt great hostility toward American women writers. Usually she refused even to look at their books.

INTERVIEWER: Why was that?

BOWLES: When *Two Serious Ladies* was first reviewed in 1943, Jane was depressed by the lack of understanding shown in the unfavorable reviews. She paid no attention to the enthusiastic notices. But from then on, she became very much aware of the existence of other women writers whom she'd met and who were receiving laudatory reviews for works which she thought didn't deserve such high praise: Jean Stafford, Mary McCarthy, Carson McCullers, Anaïs Nin. There were others I can't remember now. She didn't want to see them personally or see their books.

INTERVIEWER: In the introduction that Truman Capote wrote for the collected works, he emphasized how young she'd been when she wrote *Two Serious Ladies*.

BOWLES: That's true. She began it when she was twenty-one. We were married the day before her twenty-first birthday.

INTERVIEWER: Was there something symbolic about the date?

BOWLES: No, nothing "symbolic." Her mother wanted to remarry and she had got it into her head that Jane should marry first, so we chose the day before Jane's birthday.

INTERVIEWER: Did your careers ever conflict, yours and your wife's?

BOWLES: No, there was no conflict of any kind. We never thought of ourselves as having careers. The only career I ever had was as a composer, and I destroyed that when I left the States. It's hard to build up a career again. Work is something else, but a career is a living thing and when you break it, that's it.

INTERVIEWER: Did you and Jane Bowles ever collaborate?

BOWLES: On a few songs. Words and music. Any other sort of collaboration would have been unthinkable. Collaborative works of fiction are rare, and they're generally parlor tricks, like *Karezza* of George Sand and who was it: Alfred de Musset?

INTERVIEWER: How did she feel about herself as an artist—about her work?

BOWLES: She liked it. She enjoyed it. She used to read it and laugh shamefacedly. But she'd never change a word in order to make it more easily understood. She was very, very stubborn about phrasing things the way she wanted them phrased. Sometimes understanding would really be difficult and I'd suggest a change to make it simpler. She'd say, "No. It can't be done that way." She wouldn't budge an inch from saying something the way she felt the character would say it.

INTERVIEWER: What was her objective in writing?

BOWLES: Well, she was always trying to get at people's hidden motivations. She was interested in people, not in the writing. I don't think she was at all conscious of trying to create any particular style. She was only interested in the things she was writing about: the complicated juxtapositions of motivations in neurotic people's heads. That was what fascinated her.

INTERVIEWER: Was she "neurotic"?

BOWLES: Oh, probably. If one's interested in neuroses, generally one has some sympathetic vibration.

INTERVIEWER: Was she self-destructive?

BOWLES: I don't think she meant to be, no. I think she overestimated her physical strength. She was always saying, "I'm as strong as an ox," or "I'm made of iron." That sort of thing.

INTERVIEWER: Considering how independently the two of you lived your lives, your marriage couldn't really be described as being "conventional." Was this lack of "conventionalism" the result of planning, or did it just work out that way?

BOWLES: We never thought in those terms. We played everything by ear. Each one did what he pleased—went out, came back—although I must say that I tried to get her in early. She liked going out much more than I did, and I never stopped her. She had a perfect right to go to any party she wanted. Sometimes we had recriminations when she drank too much, but the idea of sitting down and discussing what constitutes a conventional or an unconventional marriage would have been unthinkable.

INTERVIEWER: She has been quoted as saying, "From the first day, Morocco seemed more dreamlike than real. I felt cut off from what I knew. In the twenty years I've lived here, I've written two short stories and nothing else. It's good for Paul, but not for me." All things considered, do you think that's an accurate representation of her feelings?

BOWLES: But you speak of feelings as though they were monolithic, as though they never shifted and altered through the years. I know Jane expressed the idea frequently toward the end of her life, when she was bedridden and regretted not being within reach of her friends. Most of them lived in New York, of course. But for the first decade she loved Morocco as much as I did.

INTERVIEWER: Did you live with her here in this apartment?

BOWLES: No. Her initial stroke was in 1957, while I was in Kenya. When I got back to Morocco about two months later, I heard about it in Casablanca. I came here and found her quite well. We took two apartments in this building. From then on, she was very ill, and we spent our time rushing from one hospital to another, in London and New York. During the early sixties she was somewhat better, but then she began to suffer from nervous depression. She spent most of the last seven years of her life in hospitals. But she was an invalid for sixteen years.

INTERVIEWER: That's a long time to be an invalid.

BOWLES: Yes. It was terrible.

INTERVIEWER: Before that, though, your life together had been as you wanted it?

BOWLES: Oh, yes. We enjoyed it. We were always busy helping each other. And we had lots of friends. Many, many friends.

INTERVIEWER: What is life like for you in Tangier these days?

BOWLES: Well, it's my home. I'm settled here and I'm reasonably content with things as they are. I see enough people. I suppose if I had been living in the States all this time I'd probably have many more intimate friends whom I'd see regularly. But I haven't lived there in many years, and most of the people I knew are no longer there. I can't go back and make new acquaintances at this late date.

INTERVIEWER: All those trunks you've got stacked in your entry-way bear testament to your globe-trotting days. Don't you miss traveling?

BOWLES: Not really, surprisingly enough. And Tangier is as good a place for me to be as any other, I think. If travel still consisted of taking ships, I'd continue moving around. Flying to me isn't travel. It's just getting from one place to another as fast as possible. I like to have plenty of luggage with me when I start out on a voyage. You never know how many months or years you'll be gone or where you'll go eventually. But flying is like television: you have to take what they give you because there's nothing else. It's impossible.

INTERVIEWER: Tangier is nothing like the booming international city it once was, is it?

BOWLES: No, of course not. It's a very dull city now.

INTERVIEWER: Things were still happening here in the sixties when Ginsberg, Burroughs, and that group were here. To what degree were you involved with them?

BOWLES: I knew them well, but I wasn't involved with their work. I think Bill Burroughs came to live in the medina in 1952. I didn't meet him until 1954. Allen Ginsberg came in '57 and began to supervise the retrieving of the endangered manuscript of *Naked Lunch*, which was scattered all over the floor of Bill's room at the Muniriya. The pages had been lying there for many months, covered with grime, heelmarks, mouse-droppings. It was Alan Ansen who financed the expedition, and between them they salvaged the book.

INTERVIEWER: Was Gregory Corso here then?

BOWLES: No. He came when Ginsberg returned in 1961.

INTERVIEWER: What was Tangier like back then?

BOWLES: By the sixties, it had calmed down considerably, although it was still a good deal livelier than it is these days. Everyone had much more money, for one thing. Now only members of the European jet set have enough to lead amusing lives, and everyone else is poor. In general, Moroccans have a slightly higher standard of living than they did, by European criteria. That is, they have television, cars, and a certain amount of plumbing in their houses, although they all claim they don't eat as well as they did thirty years ago. But nobody does, anywhere.

INTERVIEWER: Moroccan life seems to be so incongruously divided between Eastern and Western influences—the medinas and *nouvelles villes*, djellabas and blue jeans, donkey-carts and Mercedes—that it sometimes seems downright schizophrenic. I wonder where the Moroccan psyche really is.

BOWLES: For there to be a Moroccan psyche there'd have to be a national consciousness, which I don't think has yet come into being. The people are much more likely to think of themselves as members of a subdivision: I'm a Sousse, I'm a Riffi, I'm a Filali. Then there are those lost souls who privately think of themselves as Europeans because they've studied in Europe. But the vast majority of Moroccans have their minds on getting together enough money for tomorrow's meal.

INTERVIEWER: Through the years that you've been here, have you ever had feelings of cultural estrangement, or even superiority?

BOWLES: That wouldn't be very productive, would it? Of course I feel apart, at one remove from the people here. But since they expect that in any case, there's no difficulty. The difficulties are in the United States, where there's no convention for maintaining apartness. The foreigners who try to "be Moroccan" never succeed and manage to look ridiculous while they're trying. It seems likely that it's this very quality of impenetrability in the Moroccans that makes the country fascinating to outsiders.

INTERVIEWER: But isn't there a special psychological dimension to the situation of a foreigner living in Morocco? It seems to me that a foreigner here is often looked upon automatically as a kind of victim.

BOWLES: Well, he *is* a victim. The Moroccans wouldn't use the word. They'd say "a useful object." They believe that they, as Muslims, are the master group in the world, and that God allows other religious groups to exist principally for them to manipulate. That seems to be the average man's attitude. Since it's not expressed as a personal opinion but is tacitly accepted by all, I don't find it objectionable. Once a thing like that is formulated you don't have to worry about the character of the person who professes it. It's no longer a question of whether or not he agrees with it as part of his personal credo.

INTERVIEWER: Doesn't this rather limit the nature of a relationship between a Moroccan and a non-Muslim?

BOWLES: It completely determines the nature of a relationship, of course, but I wouldn't say that it limits it, necessarily.

INTERVIEWER: You've never met a Moroccan with whom you felt you could have a Western-style relationship in terms of depth and reciprocity?

BOWLES: No, no. That's an absurd concept. Like expecting a boulder to spread its wings and fly away.

INTERVIEWER: Coming to this realization must have been a frustrating experience.

BOWLES: No, because right away when I got here I said to myself, "Ah, this is the way people used to be, the way my own ancestors were thousands of years ago. The Natural Man. Basic Humanity. Let's see how they are." It all seemed quite natural to me. They haven't evolved the same way, so far, as we have, and I wasn't surprised to find that there were whole sections missing in their "psyche," if you like.

INTERVIEWER: Can Morocco be described as a homosexual culture?

BOWLES: Certainly not. I think that's one thing that doesn't exist here. It may be putting in an appearance now in the larger cities, what with the frustrations of today's urban life. I would expect it to, since that's the world pattern. They're undifferentiated, if you like, but they don't have a preference for the same sex. On the contrary.

INTERVIEWER: I suppose there are advantages to living in a sexually "undifferentiated" society.

BOWLES: There must be, or they wouldn't have made it that way. The French *colons* found it an unfailing source of amusement, of course.

INTERVIEWER: Isn't it paradoxical, though, because of the restrictions of Islam?

BOWLES: But religion always does its utmost to restrain human behavior. The discrepancy between religious dogma and individual behavior is no greater here than anywhere else.

INTERVIEWER: What do you know about Moroccan witchcraft?

BOWLES: *Witchcraft* is a loaded word. To use it evokes something sinister, a regression to archaic behavior. Here it's an accepted facet of daily life, as much as the existence of bacteria is in ours. And their attitude toward it is very much the same as ours is toward infection. The possibility is always there, and one must take precautions. But in Morocco only what you'd call offensive magic is considered "witchcraft." Defensive magic, which plays the same game from the other side of the net, is holy, and can only be efficacious if it's practiced under the aegis of the Koran. If the *fqih* uses the magician's tricks to annul the spell cast by the magician, it doesn't necessarily follow that the *fqih* believes implicitly in the existence of the spell. He's there to cure the people who visit him. He acts as confessor, psychiatrist, and father image. Obviously some of the *fouqqiyane* must be charlatans, out to get hold of all the money they can. But the people get on to the quacks fairly fast.

INTERVIEWER: One hears a lot about the legend of Aicha Qandicha. Who is she?

BOWLES: You mean who do I think she really is? I'd say she's a vestigial Tanit. You know when a new faith takes over, the gods of the previous faith are made the personification of evil. Since she was still here in some force when Islam arrived, she had to be reckoned with. So she became this beautiful but dreaded spirit who still frequented running water and hunted men in order to ruin them. It's strange; she has a Mexican counterpart, La Llorona, who also lives along the banks of streams where there's vegetation, and who wanders at night calling to men. She's also of great beauty, and also has long tresses. The difference is that in Mexico she weeps. That's an Indian addition. In Morocco she calls out your name, often in your mother's voice, and the danger is that you'll turn and see her face, in which case you're lost. Unless, unless. There are lots of unlesses. A series of formulas from the Koran, a knife with a steel blade, or even a magnet can save you if you're quick. Not all Moroccans consider Aicha Qandicha a purely destructive spirit. Sacrifices are still made to her, just as they are to the saints. The Hamadcha leave chickens at her sacred grotto. But in general she inspires terror.

INTERVIEWER: The Moroccans have had an extremely violent history, and even now it seems that there's an innate belligerence in their character, a constant undercurrent of violence. Do you think that's true?

BOWLES: As far as I can see, people from all corners of the earth have an unlimited potential for violence. The Moroccans are highly emotional individuals. So naturally in concerted action they're formidable. There's always been intertribal violence here, as well as the age-old rustic resentment of the city dwellers. Until 1956 the country was divided officially into two sectors: *blad l-makhzen* and *blad s-siba*, or, in other words, territory under governmental control and territories where such control couldn't be implanted. That is, where anarchy reigned. Obviously violence is the daily bread of people living under such conditions. The French called *blad s-siba* "La Zone d'Insécurité." As an American you were just as safe there as anywhere else in Morocco, but it wasn't the security of Americans that the French were thinking of.

INTERVIEWER: One also feels, don't you think, that the concept of time is completely different here?

BOWLES: Well, yes, but it's partially because one lives a very different life. In America or Europe the day is divided into hours and one has appointments. Here the day isn't measured; it simply goes by. If you see people, it's generally by accident. Time is merely more or less, and everything is perhaps. It's upsetting if you take it seriously. Otherwise it's relaxing, because there's no need to hurry. Plenty of time for everything.

INTERVIEWER: How did your association with Mohammed Mrabet come about?

BOWLES: I began to translate from Moghrebi Arabic twenty-five years ago, when I'd notate stories Ahmed Yacoubi told me. Shortly afterward, tape recorders arrived in Morocco and I went on translating, but from tapes. I did the novel *A Life Full of Holes,* by Layachi, and some things by Boulaich. When I met Mrabet I knew that there was an enormous amount of material there, and fortunately he wasn't averse to exploiting it. On the contrary, he's been telling tales into a microphone now for thirteen years, all from Arabic. The only difficulty with Mrabet is getting everything onto tape. I've lost some wonderful tales merely because at the moment he told them there was no way of recording them.

INTERVIEWER: Isn't Mrabet continuing an oral tradition which is well established here?

BOWLES: He's very much aware of it. From his early childhood he preferred to sit with elderly men, because of the stories they told. He's impregnated with the oral tradition of his region. In a story of his it's hard to find the borderline between unconscious memory and sheer invention.

INTERVIEWER: Why isn't he more popular within Morocco?

BOWLES: It's not a question of being popular or not being popular. He's practically unknown in Morocco. His books are all in English, though there are a few things in French, Italian, and Portuguese. What little notice he's received here has been adverse. There have been a few unpleasant articles about him in the newspapers, but probably only because it was I who translated him. But since, at the moment, I'm the sole possible bridge between him and the publishers, I go on doing these books, even though the local critics may take a dim view of them. They feel that a foreigner can present a Moroccan only as a performing seal. They scent neocolonialism in a book translated directly from *darija.* At first they wrote that he didn't exist, that I'd invented him. Then they accused me of literary ventriloquy. I'd found some fisherman and photographed him so I could present my own ideas under the cover of his name, thinking that would give them authenticity. What they seem to resent most of all is not that the texts were taped, but that they were taped in the language of the country which, by common consent, no one ever uses for literary purposes. One must use either Classical Arabic or French. Moghrebi is only for conversational purposes. Then they object to the subject matter. For them contemporary prose must be political in one way or another. They don't conceive of literature as such, only as ammunition to implement their theories about economics and government. Most Moroccan intellectuals are confirmed Marxists, naturally. The same pattern as in other third-world countries. I can see clearly why they'd execrate the very concept of such a phenomenon as Mrabet. His books could as easily have been written under the colonial regime as during independence, and this strikes the local critics as tantamount to intellectual treason.

INTERVIEWER: Are you still taping storytellers whom you meet in cafés?

BOWLES: There aren't any more. All that's completely changed. There's a big difference just between the sixties and seventies. For instance, in the sixties people still sat in cafés with a *sebsi* [pipe] and told stories and occasionally plucked an *oud* or a *guimbri*. Now practically every café has television. The seats are arranged differently and no one tells any stories. They can't because the television is going. No one thinks of stories. If the eye is going to be occupied by a flickering image, the brain doesn't feel a lack. It's a great cultural loss. It's done away with both the oral tradition of storytelling and whatever café music there was.

INTERVIEWER: The music here is supposed to have a mesmerizing effect on its listeners. Is this true?

BOWLES: That's one of its functions, but not the only one. If you're an initiate of certain religious groups, it can induce trancelike conditions. In less evolved cultures music is always used for that. But something similar exists in many parts of the world, perhaps even in our own. Strobe lights, acid rock, and so on, I think all that's meant to alter consciousness.

INTERVIEWER: Has your involvement with Moroccan music been a means of maintaining your contact with the music world at large?

BOWLES: How could it be? It's just a natural interest which I've had since I first came.

INTERVIEWER: What are your future plans, as regards writing?

BOWLES: I don't think much about the future. I've got no plans for future books. The book of stories I'm writing at present takes up all my attention. More tales about Morocco. If an idea were to come to me which required the novel form, I'd write a novel. If it happens, it happens. I'm not ambitious, as you know. If I had been, I'd have stayed in New York.

—JEFFREY BAILEY
1981

Ken Kesey

was born on September 17, 1935, in La Junta, Colorado. His father, a rancher and outdoorsman, moved the family to Oregon in 1943. Kesey attended the University of Oregon where he became a champion wrestler. After graduating, he received a Stegner Fellowship from Stanford to study fiction under Malcolm Cowley, Wallace Stegner, and Frank O'Connor. His classmates included Ken Babbs, Larry McMurtry, and Robert Stone.

In the fifties Kesey enlisted as a paid volunteer for government drug experiments in a California hospital where he later worked as an attendant. With these experiences in mind, Kesey wrote his first successful novel, *One Flew over the Cuckoo's Nest* in 1962. Recounting the terrors imposed upon the inmates of an Oregon psychiatric ward, the novel covertly indicted the sterile and suffocating politics of a nation at war. The vitality and anarchist-sway of its hero, Randle McMurphy, struck a chord with the reading public. Together with *Sometimes a Great Notion* (1964), the two novels established Kesey's reputation as a social rebel.

During the sixties, Kesey became the ringleader of an itinerant group of hippies, the Merry Pranksters, who toured the country on a bus driven by Neal Cassady. Described in Tom Wolfe's *The Electric Kool-Aid Acid Test*, the troupe staged a variety of shows and psychedelic-drug experiments that led to Kesey's arrest on marijuana charges, his escape to Mexico, and eventually his serving three months in jail.

Kesey has written two books for children, *Little Tricker the Squirrel Meets Big Double the Bear* (1990) and *The Sea Lion* (1992). In full Native American dress, he gives readings from these works at children's hospitals and schools. In 1994, Kesey completed his first major novel in twenty-eight years, *Sailor Song*. In 1995, he and Ken Babbs teamed up to write a play, *Twister*, and a western dime novel, *Last Go Around*.

Joining forces with Jane's Addiction, the Rock 'n' Roll Hall of Fame, and others, Kesey continues to stage festivals for amateur performers across the country.

© CHRIS FELVER

*A*t the center of Kesey's work are what he calls "little warriors" battling large forces. Over the years, some critics have praised his work
for its maverick power and themes of defiance; others have questioned his
wild and paranoid vision. He has been dubbed a renegade prophet, a sub-
versive technophile, a spiritual junkie—characterizations that Kesey
does little to discourage.

He lives in a spacious barn that was built in the thirties from a Sears
Roebuck catalog. It is decorated in bright Day-Glo colors. The stairs as-
cending to his loft-study are covered in streaks of neon green and pink,
recalling the psychedelic designs made famous by Kesey's bus, **Furthur**.
Inspired by these visual remnants of the sixties, Kesey works late into the
night, observed, as he points out, by a parliament of owls.

This interview was conducted during several visits with Kesey at
his Oregon farm in 1992 and 1993.

. . .

INTERVIEWER: Your only formal studies in fiction were as a fellow in Wallace Stegner's writing program at Stanford. What did you learn from Stegner and also from Malcolm Cowley?

KEN KESEY: The greatest thing Cowley taught me was to respect other writers' feelings. If writing is going to have any effect on people morally, it ought to affect the writer morally. It is important to support everyone who tries to write because their victories are your victories. So I have never really felt that bitter cattiness writers feel toward their peers.

INTERVIEWER: Yet you had a difficult relationship with Stegner. What were the differences between you?

KESEY: Shortly after *Cuckoo's Nest* came out, I did an interview with Gordon Lish for a magazine called *Genesis West*. I don't remember exactly what I said about Stegner, but it made him angry. When I heard he was angry I tried to see him, but his secretary wouldn't let me in. We never spoke again after that. Wally never did like me. At one point, I read that he had said he found me to be ineducable. I had to stew for a long time over what Stegner didn't like about me and my friends. We were part of an exceptional group, there's no doubt about it. There was Bob Stone, Gurney Norman, Wendell Berry, Ken Babbs, and Larry McMurtry. All of us who were part of that group are still very much in contact; we all support each other's work. Stegner was the great force that brought us all together. He put together a program that ruled literature in California and, in some ways, the rest of the nation for a long time. Stegner had traveled across the Great Plains and reached the Pacific but, as far as he was concerned, that was far enough. Some of us didn't believe that it *was* far enough, and when we went farther than that, he took issue with it, especially when it was not happening in the usual literary bailiwicks that he was accustomed to. I took LSD, and he stayed with Jack Daniel's; the line between us was drawn. That was, as far as he was concerned, the edge of the continent, and he thought you were supposed to stop there. I was younger than he was, and I didn't see any reason to stop, so I kept moving forward, as did many of my friends. Ever since then, I have felt impelled into the future by Wally, by his dislike of what I was doing, of what we were doing. That was the kiss of approval in some way. I liked him, and I actually think that he liked me. It was just that we were on different sides of the fence. When the Pranksters got together and headed off on a bus to deal with the future of our synapses, we knew that Wally didn't like what we were doing, and that was good enough for us. A few years ago, I taught a course at the University of Oregon. I began to appreciate Wally much more after I had been a teacher. Every writer I know teaches—at some point, even if you don't need the money, you have to teach what you were taught, especially if you were taught by a great coach.

INTERVIEWER: Did your experience at Stanford drive you to an anti-intellectual stance?

KESEY: The reason you read great authors—Thomas Paine, Jefferson, Thoreau, Emerson—is not because you really want to teach them, though that's one of the things you find yourself doing because you know it's important that they be taught. You study literature because you're a scholar of what's fair. It's just a way of learning how to be what we want to be. We go to concerts to hear a piece by Bach not because we want to be intellectuals or scholars or students of Bach, but because the music is going to help us keep our moral compass needle clean.

INTERVIEWER: What connection is there between Ken Kesey the magician-prankster and Ken Kesey the writer?

KESEY: The common denominator is the joker. It's the symbol of the prankster. Tarot scholars say that if it weren't for the fool, the rest of the cards would not exist. The rest of the cards exist for the benefit of the fool. The fool in tarot is this naïve innocent spirit with a rucksack over his shoulder like Kerouac, his eyes up into the sky like Yeats, and his dog biting his rump as he steps over the cliff. We found one once at a big military march in Santa Cruz. Thousands of soldiers marching by. All it took was one fool on the street corner pointing and laughing, and the soldiers began to be uncomfortable, self-conscious. That fool of Shakespeare's, the actor Robert Armin, became so popular that finally Shakespeare wrote him out of *Henry IV*. In a book called *A Nest of Ninnies*, Armin wrote about the difference between a fool artificial and a fool natural. And the way Armin defines the two is important: the character Jack Oates is a true fool natural. He never stops being a fool to save himself; he never tries to do anything but anger his master, Sir William. A fool artificial is always trying to please; he's a lackey. Ronald McDonald is a fool artificial. Hunter Thompson is a fool natural. So was the Little Tramp. Neal Cassady was a fool natural, the best one we knew.

INTERVIEWER: Neal Cassady was a muse to the Beats and became one to you as you started writing. When did you first encounter him?

KESEY: It was 1960. He had just finished the two years he served in the pen. He showed up at my place on Perry Lane when I was at Stanford. He arrived in a Jeep with a blown transmission, and before I was able to get outside and see what was going on, Cassady had already stripped the transmission down into big pieces. He was talking a mile a minute, and there was a crowd of people around him. He never explained why he was there, then or later. He always thought of these events as though he was being dealt cards on a table by hands greater than ours. But that was one of my earliest impressions of him as I watched him running around, this frenetic, crazed character speaking in a monologue that sounded like *Finnegans Wake* played fast forward. He had just started to get involved in the drug experiments at the hospital in Menlo Park, as I had. I thought, "Oh, my God, it could lead to this." I realized then that there was a choice. Cassady had gone down one road. I thought to myself, are you going to go down that road with Burroughs, Ginsberg and Kerouac—at that time still unproven crazies—or are you going to take the safer road that leads to John Updike. Cassady was a hero to all of us who followed the wild road, the hero who moved us all.

INTERVIEWER: Were there literary influences as well?

KESEY: Many of us had read Ginsberg's "Howl," Kerouac's *On the Road*, Kenneth Rexroth's work, Ferlinghetti's. I knew their work when I was a student at the University of Oregon. I had a tape of Ferlinghetti saying, "I'm sitting now outside of my pool hall watching the hipsters come by in their curious shoes." I wanted to go down to the North Beach area and see Mike's Pool Hall. That's where I met Ken Babbs and Bob Kaufman, a great poet and a casualty of exploration of the synapses.

INTERVIEWER: Do you think the drug experimentation produced mostly casualties? Do you think Cassady was one?

KESEY: I think most artists who, as the saying goes now, "push the envelope," wind up as casualties. If you think about the history of writers and artists, the best often don't end up with pleasant, comfortable lives; sometimes they go over the edge and lose it. I've been close to enough casualties to learn how to avoid that pitfall. Some critics like to argue that some of the Beats had a death wish. Cassady certainly didn't have a death wish. He had a more-than-life wish, an eternity wish. He was trying to recapture, as Burroughs says, the realities he had lost. He was storming the reality studio and trying to take the projector from the controllers who had been running it. When that happens you are bound to have some casualties.

INTERVIEWER: How did Cassady become the driver of your bus, *Furthur*?

KESEY: Cassady was around us often. There was one incident in particular when he truly impressed me not only as a madman, genius, and poet but also as an avatar—someone in contact with other powers. He took me to a racetrack near San Francisco. He was driving and talking very fast, checking his watch frantically, hoping we would get to the track on time. If we got to the track just before the last three races, we'd get in free. We made it just in time, and we bet on the last two races. Cassady had a theory about betting he'd learned in jail from someone named Knee-Walking Jackson. His theory was that the third favorite at post time is often the horse most likely to upset the winner and make big money. Cassady's strategy was to step up to the tellers at the ticket booths just at post time. He'd glance up to see who was third favorite and put money on that horse. He didn't look at the horses, the jockeys, or the racing sheets. He said to me, "This is going to be the one, I can feel it." He asked me for ten bucks, and I gave it to him. He put three dollars down with my ten. Given the odds we would have made some good money. We went right down to the line to watch, and it was a close race, neck and neck. I'm no horse fan, but I was getting into it because it looked like the third favorite could win. There was a photo finish and Cassady suddenly tore up his tickets and left. I followed him back to the car and could hear the announcement: "We have a photo finish, and the winner is . . ." It turned out to be the favorite. Neal was so confident of his vision that if he lost he never waited around or looked back.

Cassady was a hustler, a wheeler-dealer, a conniver. He was a scuffler. He never had new clothes, but was always clean, and so were his clothes. He always had a toothbrush and was always trying to sell us little things and trying to find a place where he could wash up. Cassady was an elder to me and the other Pranksters, and we knew it. He was literally and figuratively behind the

Kesey in front of Further II.

wheel of our bus, driving it the way Charlie Parker worked the sax-ophone. When he was driving he was improvising an endless monologue about what he was seeing and thinking, what we were seeing and thinking, and what we had seen, thought, and remem-bered. Proust was his literary hero, and he would quote long pas-sages from Proust and Melville from memory, lacing his revelations with passages from the Bible. He was a great teacher, and we all knew it and were affected by him.

INTERVIEWER: What did you learn from Cassady?

KESEY: I've listened to the tapes from the bus trip and reread his letters and autobiography—*The First Third*—for years. I've tried to distill his teachings as best I can. The most important lesson is also the most ironic: most of what is important cannot be taught except by experience. His most powerful lesson behind the rap was not to dwell on mistakes. He used the metaphor of driving. He believed that you got into trouble by overcorrecting. A certain sloth, he thought, lets you veer into a ditch on the right side of the road. Then you overcorrect and hit a car to your left. Cassady believed you had to be correcting every instant. The longer you let things go, the longer you stayed comfortable, the more likely the case that you would have to overcorrect. Then you would have created a big error. The virtue of continual, engaged experience—an endless and relentless argument with the self—that was his lesson.

INTERVIEWER: What do you think of Wolfe's account of you and the Pranksters in *The Electric Kool-Aid Acid Test*?

KESEY: When the galleys came out, we all read through them in one session. I had no major problems with the book then, though I haven't looked at it since. When he was around us, he took no notes. I suppose he prides himself on his good memory. His memory may be good, but it's *his* memory and not mine.

INTERVIEWER: You met Jack Kerouac and Allen Ginsberg at a party in Manhattan during the bus trip. What happened at that encounter?

KESEY: That was the first time I had met Kerouac. It was an important moment for me. I'd known Ginsberg and Dick Alpert—before he became Ram Dass—back at Perry Lane. Ginsberg was good friends with Vik Lovell, the guy who got me involved in the Menlo Park hospital and to whom I dedicated *Cuckoo's Nest*. Ginsberg and Alpert were part of IFIF, the International Federation for Internal Freedom. That was the Millbrook psychological experiment group that included Timothy Leary. Our group on the bus was known as ISIS, the Intrepid Search for Inner Space.

I have thought about that meeting hundreds of times since then. We wanted Kerouac to be the same way he was when he wrote *On the Road*. I find the same thing happening to me when people show up and expect me to be the way I was twenty-five years ago. Kerouac seemed offended by our wildness, particularly by the way we were wearing American flags draped around our heads. He thought we were being derisive of the United States. But we weren't. We just liked the look of dressing in the flag. I was disappointed in myself for not going up to him and sincerely expressing how much his work meant to me. But it wasn't the right time, and I needed to say it in a letter.

After Kerouac died, his agent gave me a letter from his wife, Stella. She was very bitter that people had passed Jack by and instead were looking at people like me as the new literary lions. I wrote her back and told her that I couldn't hold a candle to him. His life's work will stand for centuries. I can't say that about Mailer or Updike or Kosinski. But I believe that people will be reading *On the Road* centuries from now as the true lens into our time.

In his writing Kerouac was true to his vision to the end. He believed there were drama and glory in the most mundane parts of our lives. And all things—running across a football field, the smell of leaves, the sound of a car—became charged with romance in Kerouac's imagination. Kerouac didn't have to have much money, and he didn't have to be famous. But he was part of the ongoing exploration of the American frontier, looking for new land, trying to escape the dust bowls of existence. He had a deep connection to the American romantic vision. Kerouac was a giant to the end, a sad giant. But then giants are usually sad.

Kesey in the San Mateo County Jail in 1967. Shortly after painting this op-art mural on the wall of the tailor shop where he worked, he was demoted to ditch digging.

INTERVIEWER: How much of Neal Cassady went into the making of Randle P. McMurphy?

KESEY: He's part of the myth. The Irish names—Kesey, Cassady, McMurphy—were all together in my mind as well as a sense of Irish blarney. That's part of the romantic naïveté of McMurphy. But McMurphy was born a long time before I met Neal Cassady. The character of McMurphy comes from Sunday matinees, from American Westerns. He's Shane that rides into town, shoots the bad guys, and gets killed in the course of the movie. McMurphy is a particular American cowboy hero, almost two-dimensional. He gains dimension from being viewed through the lens of Chief Bromden's Indian consciousness.

INTERVIEWER: You were working at the Veterans Administration Medical Center in Menlo Park participating in experiments with psychedelic drugs. How much did those drugs affect you or help you to write *Cuckoo's Nest?*

KESEY: I was taking mescaline and LSD. It gave me a different perspective on the people in the mental hospital, a sense that maybe they were not so crazy or as bad as the sterile environment they were living in. But psychedelics are only keys to worlds that are already there. The images are not there in the white crystals in the gelatin capsule. Drugs don't create characters or stories any more than pencils do. They are merely instruments that help get them on the page.

INTERVIEWER: Do you use LSD or other drugs when you sit down to write?

KESEY: It's impossible for me to write on LSD—there are more important things to think about. Hunter Thompson can do it, but I can't. It's like diving down to look at coral reefs. You can't write about what you've seen until you're back up in the boat. Almost every writer I know drinks to ease the burden of being out on the cliffs, so to speak. But writing under the influence of drugs is a little like a plumber trying to fix the pipes without being able to work the wrench.

I did write the first several pages of *Cuckoo's Nest* on peyote, and I changed very little of it. It had little effect on the plot, but the mood and particularly the voice in those first few pages remained throughout the book. There were also some sections of *Sometimes a Great Notion* written when I was taking mushrooms. Again, the effect is more on mood and voice than on vision. But for the most part, I don't write under the influence of LSD or other drugs.

INTERVIEWER: Do you take notes when you use LSD or other hallucinogens?

KESEY: Yes, sometimes I use a little tape recorder for notes. There's often a big difference between what you think you wrote under the influence and what you actually recorded. One time a friend of mine and I were taking LSD and thought we had written "The History and Future of the Universe." What we actually wrote down was something on the order of "If you pick your nose long enough the world will unravel." But often when I am taking LSD, there is an accessing of a universal pool of images, forms that I often find, for example, in Indian art. By the time I started taking peyote and LSD, I had already done a great deal of reading about mysticism—the Bhagavadgītā and Zen and Christian mystical texts. They helped me to interpret what I was seeing, to give it meaning. You don't just take the stuff and expect understanding. It's also important not to be in a hellish place with LSD or it can be a hellish experience. You need to be in a secure setting.

INTERVIEWER: Do any of the visions you have using LSD get translated into your writing?

KESEY: I'm fond of computer analogies. There are visions written on those programs that are hard to access or convert to the writing programs. I like to take it mostly for the spiritual experience.

INTERVIEWER: Do you recommend LSD as a tool for writing?

KESEY: No.

INTERVIEWER: To go back to *Cuckoo's Nest*, it seems that Chief Bromden's perspective is crucial. What was the origin of his character?

KESEY: Some have described Bromden as schizophrenic. But his is a philosophical craziness, not a clinical illness. I knew Indians who would eat mushrooms and sit and stare at the beach until the beach stared back at them. They're not unlike Baudelaire twisting

SONG   21   kulnak

"contrite and quiet. The day after that, if she stayed out of the
~Alice
bar, Milly was once again shy and soft-spoken and half-way
social.
But
A bar with Angry Alice socially drinking in it was only a
dormant potential battleground, an impending jungle, a yawning pit, because it
could quickly become a Such a bar could
bar with Alice wide-open full-ass drunk in it could find itself

emptied of all patrons in a matter of minutes, and remain empty

until the management either closed down or kicked her out.

    Closing down was easier. You could always wait fifteen or

twenty minutes until she reeled off on her way to her next out-

rage, then open back up. If you kicked her out you ran the risk

of giving her anger focus. She might be right back, with a

snowcloud to put a through your window, or shit in your pick-up

seat. after being ejected from the Sand Bar into a ten

below midnight, she stacked the garbage cans into a precarious

scaffolding at the rear of the place so she could climb up on the
when she was able to
roof and kick off the galvanized stove pipe and pee down into the

oildrum stove. Within seconds the street was full of weeping

customers, wept weeping like they'd gassed.

    If you called the cops and Lieutenant Barnhardt got around

to actually hailing her off and locking her up for a week or so,

you could expect trouble from some of the other Deaps, who Many
One December
secretly admired her spirit. Once, after an absolute

unconditional expulsion from the Crabbe Pot, some sly band of

carpenters pried all the nails almost all the way out of the
clearly was
aluminum panels that sided the building. It had to be done by

more than one nail-puller; More than three-quarters the siding

A manuscript page from Ken Kesey's Sailor Song.

himself so that he could look at flowers in a different way. They're
still flowers, and he knows they're flowers but he also sees them
as eyes, looking back at him. That's what Chief's craziness is all
about. The idea is to regain control of reality so it's no longer presented by public relations people or funneled through a Coca-
Cola bottle. The reaction against control is often violent and

destructive and lashes out in all directions, even against things that are beneficial. If a man doesn't have a little madness, he never breaks the control lock that gets placed on reality. It's facing the vast ocean alone, without the safety of land or boat.

My father used to take me to the Pendleton Roundup in northern Oregon. He would leave me there for a couple of days. I spent time hanging around the Indians living in the area. I used to take the bus back down through the Columbia River Gorge where they were putting in The Dalles Dam to provide electricity to that part of Oregon so the fields could be irrigated. But it was also going to flood the Celilo Falls, an ancient Indian fishing ground along the Columbia. The government was using scaffolding to build the dam. When I first came to Oregon, I'd see Indians out on the scaffolds with long tridents stabbing salmon trying to get up the falls. The government had bought out their village, moved them across the road where they built new shacks for them. One

Ken Kesey reading galleys for One Flew over the Cuckoo's Nest, *1961.*

© HANK KRANZLER

time, as we got closer to this dam project, we were pulled over by the cops. We were in a big line of traffic. The bus driver got out and walked up to see what was happening. He came back and told us, "One of them crazy drunk Indians took a knife between his teeth and ran out into the highway and into the grill of an oncoming diesel truck, which was bringing conduit and piping to the dam project." I thought, "Boy, that's far out." Finally, he couldn't take it anymore. He just had to grab his knife, go out into a freeway, and run into a truck. It was really the beginning of *Cuckoo's Nest*—the notion of what you have to pay for a lifestyle. It started an appreciation in me for the Indian sense of justice and drama. I mean, it's dumb and nasty, but that's class, and the fact that he had the knife between his teeth, that's style. So this Indian consciousness has been very important in all of the stuff that I write. It's not just in *Cuckoo's Nest*. The character Indian Jenny in *Sometimes a Great Notion* is very close to the character of Alice in *Sailor Song*. It is the dispossessed Indian spirit that's trying to reconnect with the white male spirit.

INTERVIEWER: In describing the Native American who hurled himself at the truck, you said he had both class and style. How do you distinguish between class and style?

KESEY: A woman who was a circus acrobat did one act for thirty years. She climbed atop of a 180-foot aluminum pole and stood on her head as her brother balanced her. One day she fell and died, and I remember reading about it in the paper. She fell, the pole fell, because it got too far over, and her brother couldn't keep up with it; he probably stepped on a peanut. She began to fall but she held her pose the whole way down and didn't scream. And of course she must have thought about it thousands of times, "What am I gonna do if it ever gets to the point where I know I can't stop it, it's going to go all the way over and I'm going to die. Can I hold my pose and not scream?" She did, and that's class. Paul Krassner, who was there, told me, "Yeah, but the fact that when she hit, she did the splits, that's style." So class is more important than style, but they're connected.

INTERVIEWER: What authors and works do you consider strong embodiments of class and style?

KESEY: Hemingway, because he built his work very rigidly and structured it with a lot of muscle. But Faulkner is so much better.

In "The Bear," the prose just tumbles out like water out of a spring, especially in that primeval moment when we see a man posed on the back of the bear with the knife, hugging and hanging on. There is class in the character and class in the style. This takes training and discipline beyond anything Hemingway could imagine. This is Faulkner being true to a very deep source and letting it run, letting it go, not perverting it. Hemingway's prose holds up a mirror. He walks around in front of it and works on style. Faulkner's prose doesn't have time for a mirror. It's tumbling and tumbling, and this takes trusting and courage.

Eudora Welty has tremendous class, not just in her work, but in the way she walks, the look in her eyes, the way she has conducted her life. Kerouac had lots of class—stumbling drunk in the end, but read those last books. He never blames anybody else; he always blames himself. If there is a bad guy, it's poor old drunk Jack, stumbling around. You never hear him railing at the government or railing at this or that. He likes trains, people, bums, cars. He just paints a wonderful picture of Norman Rockwell's world. Of course it's Norman Rockwell on a lot of dope.

Jack London had class. He wasn't a very good writer, but he had tremendous class. And nobody had more class than Melville. To do what he did in *Moby-Dick*, to tell a story and to risk putting so much material into it. If you could weigh a book, I don't know any book that would be more full. It's more full than *War and Peace* or *The Brothers Karamazov*. It has Saint Elmo's fire, and great whales, and grand arguments between heroes, and secret passions. It risks wandering far, far out into the globe. Melville took on the whole world, saw it all in a vision, and risked everything in prose that sings. You have a sense from the very beginning that Melville had a vision in his mind of what this book was going to look like, and he trusted himself to follow it through all the way.

INTERVIEWER: What do you see as evil in the world and how do you depict it?

KESEY: In my novels and stories, evil is always the thing that seems to control. In *Cuckoo's Nest*, it's the combine. In *Sometimes a Great Notion*, it's the symbol of the river, eating away, leveling, trying to make that town the same. In *Demon Box*, the villain is entropy. That natural running-down of energy is the fear that the refrigerator is going to be empty, that we're not going to have enough of something; that fear makes you vulnerable to every kind of scam artist trying to sell a solution. But the real villain is not entropy. It's the notion that entropy is the only choice. And there are a lot of other choices that we can find in religion, philosophy or art.

INTERVIEWER: In *Cuckoo's Nest*, Big Nurse is often regarded as the embodiment of evil. Do you think that is an accurate representation of her?

KESEY: Recently, I was over in Newport, at the opening of the Oregon Coast Aquarium, which has been seven years in the making. I was performing *The Sea Lion* in the Newport Performing Arts Center. Afterwards a white-haired old woman approached me and said, "Hey, you remember me?" I looked her over, and I knew I remembered her, but had no idea who she was. She said, "Lois." It still didn't click. She said, "Lois Learned, Big Nurse," and I thought, Oh my God. She was a volunteer at Newport, long since retired from the nursing business. This was the nurse on the ward I worked on at the Menlo Park hospital. I didn't know what to think, and she didn't either, but I was glad she came up to me. I felt there was a lesson in it, the same one I had tried to teach Hollywood. She's not the villain. She might be the minion of the villain, but she's really just a big old tough ex-army nurse who is trying to do the best she can, according to the rules that she has been given. She worked for the villain and believed in the villain, but she ain't the villain.

INTERVIEWER: Do you believe that individuals have to be held accountable for evil, even if they are not the ultimate source?

KESEY: I may, as they say in jail, hang the jacket on them, but I'm not the judge. I can expose something, but as you get older and hopefully wiser, you find that blame and punishment beget only more blame and punishment. I'm probably, from another person's point of view, the Big Nurse in somebody else's story. The thing that changes as you get older is your belief that certain people are bad forever or good forever. We're not. It wouldn't make any sense to write if we were. With blame, you either resist it or you pick up rocks and throw them at who's to blame. Wendell Berry talks about that when he says we all have the capacity to do evil but we have to learn to forbear it. What keeps us from being monsters are Emerson and Thoreau and the Beatles and Bob Dylan— great artists who teach us to love and hold off on the hurt. The hurt is inside of us, and of course we can always randomly hurt something, but a great artist will teach you to love a thing and not want to possess it or alter it—just to love it. You finally have to love Big Nurse. It's the symbol behind her, the combine, that makes her do what she does. You've got to fight that, but finally you have to love them all—the poor, broken human beings, even the worst of them.

INTERVIEWER: Your novels have been popular in eastern Europe and translated in the former communist-bloc countries. How do you account for that?

KESEY: They were allowed in all the communist-bloc countries because the authorities considered them anti-American. Totalitarians never see themselves as being totalitarians; they always see that in the other guys. And *Cuckoo's Nest* is, to some extent, anti-American. It's about American terror. Big Nurse works for an American bad guy, the combine, the inhuman part of American industrialism.

INTERVIEWER: Why did you break off from writing the screenplay for *Cuckoo's Nest*?

KESEY: I was contracted to do the screenplay, but they wanted me to do it a certain way, leaving out the narrative thread of Chief's perspective and making Big Nurse the center of evil. And there were other disputes.

INTERVIEWER: What do you think of the movie?

KESEY: I've never seen it. We were arguing with lawyers, and the issue was whether I had been paid adequately. I was fussing with them. They said, "Why are you coming on like that, you'll be the first in line to see that movie." I said, "I swear to God I'll never see that movie." I did it in front of the lawyers, and I'd hate to go to heaven and have these two lawyers calling me on it. I mean, to lie to a lawyer, that's low.

INTERVIEWER: Do you see the inhuman evil present in nature?

KESEY: No, evil is part of the human consciousness. A baboon may get a harem and rape and hurt, then some other baboon will tear that baboon up eventually. It's part of baboonery, and it's gonna be there. The evil force isn't interested in baboons or daisies. The evil force wants to hang human souls on its walls for some reason, and I don't think of it as satanic. It's lukewarm. As Christ says, hot and cold are cool, but evil is lukewarm, and it's a drag.

When I see bad-looking bikers with black leather studs on their wrists hanging out at the Oregon Country Fair, I take it as a sign of health. No, I don't want them hanging around, but trying to eliminate them all, arrest them all, legislate against them all—that's evil. I have asked feminists, "If you could, would you eliminate all male chauvinist pigs? If you could come up with some kind of spray to spray in the air and do away with them, would you? Would you do away with all scorpions and rattlesnakes, mosquitoes?" Mosquitoes are part of the ecosystem. So are male chauvinist pigs. You've got to fight them, but you don't try to exterminate them. A purifying group or system that would eliminate them all—that would be an evil force. Anytime you have a force that comes along and says, "We will eradicate these people," you have evil. Looking back in history, what has seemed the worst turns out not to be the worst. Imagine how the Catholics must have talked about Galileo, how he must have seemed a great evil to them. But as time went on, it turned out that he was not only a good human being but good for the Catholic Church.

INTERVIEWER: Your heroes are often little warriors against big enemies. If the writer is a "warrior," who is his enemy?

KESEY: When I begin to try to follow the money, as they say in *All the President's Men*, up the evil ladder, past the businessmen, past the Mafia, past the leaders in the state, I ask, "Who is doing the stuff, who is pulling the cords?" It looks an awful lot like God. It's the big fascist in the sky. But all of this religion, government, and civilization bending towards God is dangerous. There's nothing worse for a forest than to have all the trees be the same. So you think, well maybe this isn't God. Maybe this is the famous Antichrist who's been the bad guy all along. The good guys, the real God, are hippies in tie-dyes out at the Oregon Country Fair, who are providing a sprinkle of mischief and chaos to keep things from becoming mud all over. As Burroughs says, the job of the writer is that of an exterminator. You're trying to battle the evil bugs that have crawled into our works and get in the way of exploring the hollow. Zora Neale Hurston and Louise Erdrich are good examples of warriors. So is Tom Robbins. People laugh and point at him, but that's just because he's on the West Coast, and he won't dress up in the right clothes. His prose is like that motley that the fool wears, and it's easy to be impatient with him, but he's a warrior the same way that old Hunter Thompson is a warrior.

INTERVIEWER: Are there other contemporary evils for which you believe the writer has to account?

KESEY: In Kurt Vonnegut's book *Cat's Cradle* the worst thing that ever happens to a marine is mud, and there is a thing called *ice-nine* that you can add to mud to solidify it. But then all the mud around the world starts to go solid. We have to try to fight anything that is going to create solid mud worldwide.

INTERVIEWER: *Sometimes a Great Notion* begins and ends with the image of Henry Stamper's amputated arm with its middle finger extended. Did you structure the book around this image?

KESEY: The image of the amputated arm came to me before I knew whose arm it was. Writing the book was the way to figure out who belonged to the arm and why. In writing the book I figured out what the symbol meant. First, I thought that Stamper was the hero, fighting the union's attempt to control the family. But in retrospect, the river is the controlling force the family is battling. The Stamper brothers, Hank and Lee, are matching wills and egos over Vivian. When Vivian leaves at the end, she leaves the people she loves for a dark future, but one in which she isn't controlled. Mother Nature throws off the forces that try to control her. Old feminism, women's lib, had something to do with that, but I didn't know it at the time.

INTERVIEWER: *Sometimes a Great Notion* is much more ambitious than *Cuckoo's Nest*. Do you think it is as successful?

KESEY: It's my best work, and I'll never write anything that good again. It's a question of time spent on it. I worked on *Notion* for two years without interruption, exploring symbols and characters and letting the narrative take its own way.

INTERVIEWER: Did you have a model for the narrative experimentation in *Sometimes a Great Notion*?

KESEY: Orson Welles's film *The Magnificent Ambersons* influenced *Sometimes a Great Notion* quite a lot in its ability to move narrative along by going from situation to situation with just a few lines of dialogue by one of the characters. Someone would say the next thing we needed to know, and there would be a cut to that shot. The first part of *The Magnificent Ambersons* covers quite a long period in a very short time, and you get to see the characters in a structured, stylized way—they step out on stage and deliver lines that help with the exposition. That influenced me in terms of structure.

INTERVIEWER: After *Sometimes a Great Notion*, you set out on the bus, *Furthur*. What did you want to explore?

KESEY: What I explore in all my work: wilderness. I like that saying of Thoreau's that "in wildness is the preservation of the world." Settlers on this continent from the beginning have been seeking that wilderness and its wildness. The explorers and pioneers were out on the edge, seeking that wildness because they could sense that in Europe everything had become locked tight with things. The things were owned by all the same people, and all of the roads went in the same direction forever. When we got here there was a sense of possibility and new direction, and it had to do with wildness. Throughout the work of James Fenimore Cooper there is what I call the American terror. It's very important to our literature, and it's important to who we are: the terror of the Hurons out there, the terror of the bear, the avalanche, the tornado—whatever may be over the next horizon. It could be the biggest, most awful thing in the world. As we came to the end of the continent, we manufactured our terror. We put together the bomb. Now even that bomb is betraying us. We don't have the bomb hanging over our heads to terrify us and give us reason to dress up in manly deerskin and go forth to battle it. There's something we're afraid of, but it doesn't have the clear delineation of the terror the Hurons gave us or the hydrogen bomb in the cold war. It's fuzzy, and it's fuzzy because the people who are in control don't want you to draw a bead on the real danger, the real terror in this country.

INTERVIEWER: What is the "real terror" in America?

KESEY: When people ask me about LSD, I always make a point of telling them you can have the shit scared out of you with LSD because it exposes something, something hollow. Let's say you have been getting on your knees and bowing and worshiping; suddenly, you take LSD, and you look, and there's just a hole, there's nothing there. The Catholic Church fills this hole with candles and flowers and litanies and opulence. The Protestant Church fills it with hand-wringing and pumped-up squeezing emotions because they can't afford the flowers and the candles. The Jews fill this hole with weeping and browbeating and beseeching of the sky: "How long, how long are you gonna treat us like this?" The Muslims fill it with rigidity and guns and a militant ethos. But all of us know that's not what is supposed to be in that hole. After I had been at Stanford two years, I was into LSD. I began to see that the books I thought were the true accounting books—my grades, how I'd done in other schools, how I'd performed at jobs, whether I had paid off my car or not—were not at all the true books. There were other books that were being kept, real books. In those real books is the real accounting of your life. And the mind says, "Oh, this is titillating." So you want to take some more LSD and see what else is there. And soon I had the experience that everyone who's ever dabbled in psychedelics has. A big hand grabs you by the back of the neck, and you hear a voice saying, "So you want to see the books. Okay, here are the books." And it pushes your face right down into all of your cruelties and all of your meanness, all the times that you have been insensitive, intolerant, racist, sexist. It's all there, and you read it. That's what you're really stuck with. You can't take your nose up off the books. You hate them. You hate who you are. You hate the fact that somebody has been keeping track, just as you feared. You hate it, but you can't move your arms for eight hours. Before you take any acid again you start trying to juggle the books. You start trying to be a little better person. Then you get the surprise. The next thing that happens is that you're leaning over looking at the books, and you feel the lack of the hand at the back of your neck. The thing that was forcing you to look at the books is no longer there. There's only a big hollow, the great American wild hollow, that is scarier than hell, scarier than purgatory or Satan. It's the fact that there isn't any hell or there isn't any purgatory, there isn't any Satan. And all you've got is Sartre sitting there with his momma—harsh, bleak, worse than guilt. And if you've got courage, you go ahead and examine that hollow. That's the wilderness that I've always wanted to explore, and it's connected to the idea of freedom, but it's a terrifying freedom. I'm working on a book called *The Seven Prayers of Grandma Whittier*. The idea is to take someone who is a very strong, very devout Christian and put her into a situation in which she loses her faith and show how she wrestles and comes back from this hollow. And so my grandma, who's a hundred years old this year, and I are in some way linked in an excursion into her dark hole of Alzheimer's. You know she must *be* something even though she can't remember the Lord's Prayer or read the Bible anymore. She's alive, but that's it. You can go into that hollow and still come out of it and have a positive life.

INTERVIEWER: And that hollow is, for you, the new wilderness?

KESEY: That's the new wilderness. It's the same old wilderness, just no longer up on that hill or around that bend, or in the gully. It's the fact that there is no more hill or gully, that the hollow is there and you've got to explore the hollow with faith. If you don't have faith that there is something down there, pretty soon when you're in the hollow, you begin to get scared and start shaking. That's when you stop taking acid and start taking coke and drinking booze and start trying to fill the hollow with depressants and Valium. Real warriors like William Burroughs or Leonard Cohen or Wallace Stevens examine the hollow as well as anybody; they get in there, look far into the dark, and yet come out with poetry.

INTERVIEWER: Have you ever felt that you were going too far into void, getting too twisted to come out?

KESEY: Many times I feel I have been way out, but I always come back. I have my family, my wife, Faye, the farm, chickens, and cows. The earthly world calls out to you in clear voices that you must come back. Those earthly voices are far better than anything I've heard crying in the night.

INTERVIEWER: After *Sometimes a Great Notion*, you seem to have grown dissatisfied with the novel as a medium. Do you prefer public performance?

KESEY: Yes. The first rule—whether you are a writer or a dancer or a fiddle player or a painter is—don't bore people. My dad used to say that good writing ain't necessarily good reading. A lot of people think good writing is like the compulsories in figure skating; it goes round in circles and doesn't go anywhere. If I'm going to skate, I'm going to race.

At one point, I was trying to write an illuminated novel with pictures and different kinds of print, experimenting with visual form as well as prose form. It's not right yet. But I haven't felt like

I have taken a vacation from my work. I feel that I am continuing to probe into that big hollow, but the traditional form of the novel won't do. My metaphor has been that I've been dating Emily Brontë, and the old dame just ain't putting out like she used to. The novel is a noble, classic form but it doesn't have the juice it used to. If Shakespeare were alive today he'd be writing soap opera, daytime TV, or experimenting with video. That's where the audience is. The audience is there even if there's a lot of mediocrity in the writing. I have just completed a play, *Twister*. Writing drama for a live audience is exciting, almost addictive.

INTERVIEWER: What do you think of when you think of an audience?

KESEY: I was in a quandary about my audience when I was working on *Notion* until I realized that I'm not writing for the East Coast literary establishment. I am writing for Mountain Girl and Jerry Garcia's oldest girl, Annabelle—she's a great Stephen King fan. She just reads and reads. She likes something that's got a little zip to it. At one point, I realized that's whom I'm writing for. If Annabelle Garcia reads this book, gets excited, and grins about it, then I have hit my audience, and all the rest just ricochets.

INTERVIEWER: Some of your most recent works have been children's stories, *Little Tricker the Squirrel Meets Big Double the Bear*, as well as *The Sea Lion*, which also appears as part of your recent novel, *Sailor Song*. What are the attractions and challenges of writing for children?

KESEY: When you go into the arena before a group of kids you don't care what Christopher Lehmann-Haupt said about you in previous reviews in *The New York Times*. Your strokes are broader, because all the little fine brush lines are lost on a kid. But the message beneath them has to be clearer. In a kid's story like *Pinocchio* the message is clearly communicated—if you lie your nose gets bigger. In a novel you have to conceal it, or you're accused of being too obvious. When you're writing for kids all you have to have is a good story; it will be accepted. Also, you can tell whether it works when you read it to a kid. It's hard for a writer to tell when a novel works.

INTERVIEWER: When you were five your maternal grandmother, Grandma Smith, told you the original story of Little Tricker.

KESEY: What I remember most about the way she told the story are the repetitions, the series of threes in the events, the alliteration in the language. She taught me the speech rhythms that are essential to being a good storyteller. There is a drumbeat, in which you have to get your idea across in a breath. She also taught me a great deal about irony. When you think of irony you've got to think of an outside force looking in. Irony doesn't exist without a god of some kind. Irony is not a trait many kids learn. It's not just God sitting up there laughing at you; there's the whole universe sort of grinning wryly at you. The main point she taught me is how essential wonder is to a storyteller. The storyteller himself has to feel wonder in order to communicate it. Somehow I don't think that sense of mystery can be taught to you by your parents. It has to be taught by your grandparents or perhaps your aunts and uncles.

INTERVIEWER: Did Grandma Smith inspire you to become a writer?

KESEY: It was all part of doing magic shows when I was a kid. For one thing, you have to talk, explain things as you go along. I would go to farm producers' meetings with my dad and perform tricks for farmers and their kids. I always found a mean little redheaded kid in the audience. I would get him up on the stage and announce that I was going to tell a story about the pasteurization of milk. Chuck, my brother, helped me with an ice pick and a funnel. I pretended to bore a hole in the top of this kid's head with the ice pick, explaining that you had to use redheads because they are a whole lot more hotheaded than most people, and I poured the milk on top of his head, letting it run past his eyes, and explaining how when it comes down out your elbow, it's pure. Then I'd pump the milk out the elbow. A story went with each magic act, and the stories enhanced the act. This is what a shaman does; he has a little story, and a few tricks along with it, a dance, some drumbeats, a painted set, and some beads strung together. Writing is just one of those parts. It has been elevated to the point that people think it is the "thing." It isn't. Shakespeare doesn't come alive until it's on stage. It's about performance.

INTERVIEWER: *Sailor Song* is your first novel in twenty-eight years. Do you consider it a comeback?

KESEY: Michael Douglas said to me when we were talking about doing a stage version of *Cuckoo's Nest*, "Oh yeah, this would be a great comeback." I said, "Good God, I didn't know I'd gone anywhere." I feel what I did with the bus, what I'm doing with my new play *Twister*, the political activity around here, reading these stories in children's hospitals, is all part of the same work. You put on a different costume. But you're always a shaman. The fire pit changes its shape. The fire gets more civilized when you're doing a reading back at the St. Mark's Church in the Bowery, but you're still a shaman. I haven't slacked off at all. But it has been really important and tremendously gratifying for me to finish a big book because no matter what you say, every writer knows that the novel is the bear and, as Faulkner says, every so often the dog has to go against the bear just to keep calling itself the dog. I set out to do this book in the early 1980s but got dragged away, mainly when my son Jed was killed. That really took the wind out of my sails. During that time I did a lot of other things that were just ways of avoiding this book. I brought out *Demon Box*, a compilation of stories about the farm and the bus in what I think of as the comedown years—my gonzo time. But Viking wanted me to use my name and everybody's real names. *Demon Box* is fiction, although not many people would appreciate the fact that some of the stories happened and some of them didn't. "The Further Inquiry," a screenplay about the bus, turned up in a box back at Viking. *Caverns*, a collaborative novel from a writing class I taught at the University of Oregon, was brought out. So these books came out as I was trying to avoid getting back to *Sailor Song*.

INTERVIEWER: What was the genesis of *Sailor Song*? You published *The Sea Lion*, the children's story which appears in *Sailor Song*, before the novel. Did one precede the other or did they evolve together?

KESEY: When I began *Sailor Song* I didn't have the story thought out, just the vision of what happens when a movie company comes to a little Alaskan town and takes it over. I needed a story within the story; I wanted it to be an ancient-seeming story, around which the larger tale could be folded. Then, as Larry McMurtry says, it was the job of the fiction writer to make stuff up, so I made up *The Sea Lion*. Although the two stories pretty much evolved together, the ideas behind *The Sea Lion* began when my brother and I went up to see an Indian storyteller in Washington up on the slopes of Mount Saint Helens. A family called Laluska makes masks up there. Those Northwest Indian images are tremendously powerful and as yet pretty much unused. They haven't been bled dry like many of the images from the Plains Indians and from the Ojibwa art back on the east coast. I saw that there was a terrific power to these faces and masks, especially the eyes. You could see that it came from the way wood knotholes are worked by surf, giving them the look of leather. They have taken it and styled it beautifully so that you can see that surf-worn quality more clearly. This was in some way connected to the story. You can't really separate the mask and the look from the story and the performance. Just hanging a mask on the wall makes it a piece of art in the museum, but if you put it on and use it as part of a story, then the story comes alive; the mask comes alive. The look of these masks was the way I wanted my work to look in the reader's mind. Fiction is when you twist what's out in front of you and stylize it so it's more clearly seen by the reader— just the same way that the Indian carvers can create an eye that looks more like an eye than an eye—a fictional eye that enables you to see better than the true eye did. That's what good fiction is always about. Reading *Moby-Dick*, you see a whale more clearly than you could see him by going over to the coast and watching through a pair of binoculars. It's the stylization of the whales that lets you see inside and outside of them, their mythical as well as their mundane qualities.

INTERVIEWER: In the title essay of *Demon Box*, you express remorse about the intrusion of the filmmaker and the artist's eye into both private suffering and uncorrupted wilderness. The effect of Hollywood on an Alaskan town is the dramatic center of *Sailor Song*. Have you come to view the film industry as an evil?

KESEY: Well, writers have always had a real love-hate relationship with Hollywood. Even if your book sells really well, you don't make that much money out of it unless Hollywood picks it up. So you want Hollywood's attention, yet you don't want it. There's a saying, often attributed to Hemingway, that sums up my feeling about having your novel turned into a film: "I don't like to see my bull turned into a bullion cube." In *Sailor Song*, I'm not really trying to put Hollywood down. It's just another force moving on this earth. It has its benefits and it's a nuisance. We know movies better than novels. Most writers have seen more movies than they've read books. It is the common denominator, two hours of story. Sometimes you'll get something that will go well into a miniseries like Larry McMurtry's *Lonesome Dove*. The miniseries is not a bad form because the story can be developed in a leisurely way.

INTERVIEWER: Has the vanishing of the frontier and wilderness changed what it means to create an American hero?

KESEY: In Western novels, especially Zane Grey novels, there is a code of the West that the hero and most of the characters in the novels adhere to. It has to do with fairness, courage, but in a lot of ways I think it mostly has to do with forgiveness. A guy in a Zane Grey novel can be a real bad outlaw, running with the bad bunch, but he comes up against a woman who changes his heart and his ways, and the good guys who have been after him accept him back into the fold. The code of the West is that you may have done a lot of bad stuff in the past but you can always turn over a new leaf at any point and change. The problem now is that the good guys aren't the good guys anymore. You don't want to turn over a new leaf and become part of society because you've seen society's dirty underwear, and it isn't much better than the bad guys' dirty underwear. Then you drop out of the hero business.

INTERVIEWER: In *Sailor Song* there is a conflict about how to read the Indian story, "The Sea Lion." One character sees it as meaningless for American audiences looking for symbols and plots. Do you believe stories should have a discernible meaning?

KESEY: I'm for mystery, not interpretive answers. When I was working on *Caverns*, I found out that one of the problems was that students kept looking for the answers to symbolic riddles and believed that modern fiction is supposed to supply you with the answer. The answer is never the answer. What's really interesting is the mystery. If you seek the mystery instead of the answer, you'll always be seeking. I've never seen anybody really find the answer, but they think they have. So they stop thinking. But the job is to seek mystery, evoke mystery, plant a garden in which strange plants grow and mysteries bloom. The need for mystery is greater than the need for an answer.

INTERVIEWER: How did the class show its desire to provide an answer?

KESEY: One student tried to tie *Caverns* up in a Buddhistic bag. There were thirteen of us contributing to the book. Without telling any of us, he introduced into the last chapter four pages of material that was pure Diamond Sutra; it came from the Rajneesh. He was a disciple all along, and he had been keeping this in his mind.

His answer was the same kind of dogma that people spout when they think the answer is Christ or environmental awareness. Anytime they do that they're already joining with the forces of *ice-nine*-hard mud.

INTERVIEWER: What was your response to the student writer?

KESEY: After his reading, the class was just ready to string him up. He had violated one of the most important taboos in writing fiction. "What are you gonna do to him?" someone asked. I said, "We're not going to do anything. We're not gonna talk about it. We won't speak of it. We will not ever speak again of this to him at all." He came in the door and he said, "What do you think of my new piece?" So we didn't speak of it. The last week of class went on, and he began to get a strange look in his eyes. We had sent him to some kind of literary Coventry. It had to be taken care of because what I had told the class in the beginning of the year was that I was going to try to teach them the job of the serious writer in modern America as best I could. It was my last day of class, and I was trying to give some kind of closing lecture to tie this up in a little package they could take home with them. I told them they had all read and studied, that they could all write. They knew fiction far better than I did. If there had been a test, they'd have just walked all over me because they knew the history of literature and the history of style better than I did. But I told them, "So you guys can write, and well enough that one of these days you're going to have a visitation. You're going to be walking down the street and across the street you're going to look and see God standing over there on the street corner motioning to you, saying, 'Come to me, come to me.' And you will know it's God, there will be no doubt in your mind—he has slitty little eyes like Buddha, and he's got a long nice beard and blood on his hands. He's got a big Charlton Heston jaw like Moses, he's stacked like Venus, and he has a great jeweled scimitar like Mohammed. And God will tell you to come to him and sing his praises. And he will promise that if you do, all of the muses that ever visited Shakespeare will fly in your ear and out of your mouth like golden pennies. It's the job of the writer in America to say, 'Fuck you, God, fuck you and the Old Testament that you rode in on, fuck you.' The job of the writer is to kiss no ass, no matter how big and holy and white and tempting and powerful. Anytime anybody says come to me and says, 'Write my advertisement, be my ad manager,' tell him, 'Fuck you.' " The job is always to be exposing God as the crook, as the sleazeball.

Nelson Algren says the job of the writer in America is to pull the judge down into the docket, get the person who is high down where he's low, make him feel what it's like where it's low.

INTERVIEWER: Do you believe that an author imposes his own cultural vision on his readers in this way?

KESEY: I think that the artist should feel obligated to force whatever he can upon his audience and be the authority because if he doesn't, some advertising man will. Ronald McDonald will be out there telling people what to think. The cynic who says, "Oh, none of this counts anymore," is wrong. I can remember when I thought that too. But the older you get, the more you see people in the past who have thoughts that last. Things you think you're saying for the first time ever, have been said better before by Shakespeare, though they may need saying again. As Faulkner says, there are the old verities. Revenge is about the same as it always was.

—ROBERT FAGGEN
1994

The Craft of Poetry:
A Semester with Allen Ginsberg

The news that Allen Ginsberg was going to be teaching at New York University was passed around campus like a joint, making some people giddy and euphoric, others mildly confused, and still others paranoid—teachers and students alike. The waiting list to get into the class was extraordinary not only in length, but for the sheer number of times students eagerly checked it to see if they had moved up. As a graduate student in the creative writing program I was given first dibs. I was curious to meet Ginsberg, curious to see how he would commandeer the Craft of Poetry class, which in the past had been taught by Galway Kinnell and William Matthews. The following excerpts were culled from a diary I kept during the semester.

· · ·

January 25

It's hard to think of Allen Ginsberg as "Professor Ginsberg." His work, as well as his ubiquitous persona, breed a kind of familiarity, not only because you may have sat next to him as he ate pierogi at the Veselka Coffee Shop or seen him at St. Mark's Bookshop, but because he's a pop icon and his work (and there's a lot of it) is classically American.

Ginsberg is smaller and grayer and older than I expected, much more conservative looking, nay professorial in his gray flannel jacket and dark blue knife-creased trousers. His eyeglasses are clear plastic, his salt-and-pepper beard is neatly trimmed. He is wearing what seem to be thick-soled Rockport walking shoes, sensible shoes. Although he is sixty-nine he manifests few overt signs of old age. Perhaps it is the company he keeps—young attractive men who seem to be talismans against aging. I remember someone telling me that when Ginsberg was a mere youth he slept with someone who slept with Walt Whitman, the degree of sexual separation between those two bawdy bards was that close.

The tiny classroom is cramped—full of people who have dropped in as if it were a coffeehouse. Those who can't find a desk sit on the floor. I haven't seen most of these students anywhere else on campus, not in Victorian Lit. or even the Derrida lectures.

There are the ubiquitous poetesses in flowing gauze skirts who write in purple ink and the self-serious poets with their smudgy eyeglasses and ravel-sleeved blazers. There is also a sprinkling of pseudo-Beats in black berets and uniform goatees and kohl-eyed women in black stretch leggings, and though it's cold outside, Diane Di Prima sandals.

Professor Ginsberg sits behind his wide desk frowning up at the low ceiling as though the harsh fluorescent light were assaulting him. Without further ado he begins to take roll. Somehow I thought it would be a hey, drop-in-drop-out-whenever-the-mood-suits-you kind of arrangement. As he calls off the names, I realize that half of the people crammed into this tiny room aren't even enrolled in the class. They're just here to catch a glimpse of Ginsberg, to get some kind of Beat benediction.

Then to confuse those of us who thought this class would be beating on bongos and barking haiku into the ether, he passes out the standard old literature class standby—a syllabus. In fact, there are *two*, one a "Survey of Historical Poetics from Pre-Literate Oral

Allen Ginsberg self-portrait, 1985.

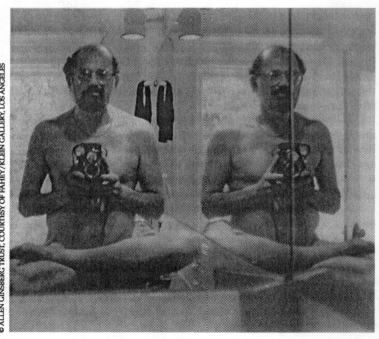

Traditions to Multiculti Poetics," the other a "Conversational Syllabus" dated spring 1994, which surprisingly only lists the first seven weeks of classes—only half the classes scheduled. The "Conversational Syllabus" instructs the student to "Read as much as you can of book titles bibliographed above. Consult photocopied anthologies by Allen Ginsberg when you can't find or finish books. Look up your English language anthologies for authors mentioned in passing. Use your research head for others not so obvious: Kalevala, Cavafy, Sappho, Cavalcanti, Bunting, Catullus, etc. Check out whatever you can, but take it easy. You can't do everything."

After passing out the papers Ginsberg lays out the nuts and bolts of the class. We are responsible for a term paper ("I don't want no academic jargon, just tell me what's on your mind"), plus five pages of our own poetry ("No more or I'll never get through them"), a bibliography of outside reading that relates to the class. Eyes flicker hungrily at the suggestion that Ginsberg will actually read our work.

Ginsberg announces his office hours: "My office is over in the English Department. Everyone should sign up for an interview. So, whenever you feel like it come by my office, we can talk poetry, we can rap, we can make love . . ." at this a few raised eyebrows and titters.

"So," he continues, "Gregory Corso will be teaching class on February 23. He is provocative, he might try to push your buttons." He grins. Someone jokes that Corso, one of Ginsberg's longtime chums, will try to get us to take our clothes off. Ginsberg enigmatically smiles, then says, "Bone up on Homer, and the *Iliad*."

He continues: "Gregory Nunzio Corso . . . Annuncia or 'the announcer of the way' Corso. Poetry is the seeking of the answer. . . . Let's start with Corso's theory of oxymorons—the yoking together of opposites. Corso takes very ordinary archetypes and plays with pop-art ideas, takes a one-word title and explores all the kinds of thoughts about it. He uses stereotypes and turns them inside out. He combines disparate ideas to make a little firecracker—he is not one of those high teacup poets."

Ginsberg then reads aloud some of Corso's work from *The Happy Birthday of Death*. He tells us that the title poem was written from notes Corso took after blacking out from laughing gas. Thanks to a cousin who was a dentist, Ginsberg has also experimented with laughing gas. He then reads a poem he refers to as Corso's most famous poem, "Marriage."

"In this poem he takes a one-word title and explores all the kid thoughts about it, you know—rice, lobby zombies, Niagara Falls—

everybody knowing what's going to happen on the honeymoon. This is a very anthologized poem, it's an easy poem, it's *cornball*, it's like trenchmouth, one anthology passes it on to the next."

Class breaks up; half the students file out into the hall. The other half, mostly attractive adolescent boys with wispy suggestions of facial hair, loiter and circle his desk, some in a rather proprietary way. Some hold out books to be signed, others just gaze as Ginsberg politely fields their attentions.

February 15

Tonight class meets in the same squalid little room. The ceiling is poked full of holes where kids have been whipping sharpened pencils up into the cork panels of the ceiling. I've brought my tape recorder; a few other students have done the same. Tonight he's in a blue shirt, red necktie, and a dark blue wool blazer. He looks like a very tidy union organizer, or a podiatrist. There are fewer gawkers.

"Today we'll continue with Corso and Creeley and more on oxymoronic poems, the notion of poetics as a poet's magical ability to hypnotize people," he says. He interrupts himself as a straggler tries to sneak quietly into the back row. "Are you in the class?"

"Yes."

"Are you going to be late often?"

"Uh, no."

"If you can make it, try and be on time. Otherwise there's this constant interruption of people drifting in late, and I have to find them on the roster."

He looks up to spot yet another latecomer. "What is *your* name?" he asks in irritation, peering over the top of his glasses.

"Joe."

"Are you in the class?"

"No."

"*Please* try and come on time because I constantly have to interrupt the discourse to accommodate your lateness. It's not like we've got that much time, it's just a measly hour and a half."

At this grouchy outburst, everyone sits staring down at their notebooks. Ginsberg sounds more like a high school gym teacher than the Dharma Lion.

He hands out a copy of "Mind Writing Slogans." The subhead is a quote from William Blake, "First thought is best in Art, Second in other matters." Then comes a wild array of aphorisms:

I. *Ground* (Situation or Primary Perception)
"My writing is a picture of the mind moving."
—Philip Whalen
"My mind is open to itself."—Gelek Rinpoche
"Catch yourself thinking."—AG

II. *Path* (Method or Recognition)
"The natural object is always the adequate symbol."
—Ezra Pound
"Show not tell."—Vernacular
"Only emotion objectified endures."
—Louis Zukofsky

III. *Fruition* (Result of Appreciation)
"What's the face you had before you were born?"
"The purpose of art is to stop time."—Bob Dylan
"Alone with the alone."—Plotinus

Ginsberg starts with Corso's later work, reminiscing about the notorious 1959 Columbia University poetry reading where Corso, Orlovsky, and Ginsberg were put down rather condescendingly in a long essay by Diana Trilling in the *Partisan Review.* They were invited back sixteen years later, and Corso wrote a poem about it, called "Columbia U Poesy Reading 1975" which Ginsberg describes as "a sort of retrospective of the Beat generation that presents its own personal and medical history."

"What a sixteen years it's been since last sat I here with the Trillings . . . sixteen years ago we were put down for being filthy beatnik sex commie dope fiends . . . Well I guess I'll skip ahead"—there is laughter—*"Bill's ever Bill even though he stopped drugging . . . Dopey-poo, it be a poet's prerogative. . . .*

"A lot of Corso's poems are pieces of mind candy, a jawbreaker; you really can't figure them out any more than you can figure out Einstein's theory of relativity—is it inside or outside? Is the external phenomenal world inside or outside? It's the classic proposition. It goes back thousands of years and is a subject of Buddhist discourse."

A student pokes her hand up, then seeming to think the gesture too formal, slowly lowers it, her ears pinkening in embarrassment. "So, what is Corso's method? How does he work?"

"Corso's method is to write on a typewriter with two fingers, one phrase at a time, breath-stop in the lines, a mental or physical breath. Spontaneous composition, little revision. It makes incremental sense verse to verse, so there are surprises to the reader as well as to him. You can see his mind working line by line. Corso composes out of an idea or a conception turned inside out."

He goes on, "He stays a lot at home, and thinks. He tends to critique a convention and refine the idea over and over again until he finds exactly the right formulation of it. He had this idea that he worked with for about ten years, 'I'll never die, because when I'm dead I won't know it. Only other people die but I'll never die.' It's built on the paradox of subject-object again, external or internal, phenomenal or whatever. He then works on them, again taking classic abstractions and turning them on their heads like the thing Heracleitus did—'Everything is flowing. You can't step in the same river twice.' Right? Corso altered it to, 'You can't step in the same river once.' " He pauses for a moment to let this sink in.

"What Corso tries to do is to bring abstraction down to an idiom comprehensible to the man in the street . . . living language rather than a literary language. Most contemporary poetry is under the spell of the more elegant—and in some respects inauthentic—living speech of Wallace Stevens rather than William Carlos Williams's spoken vernacular. So in Corso there's an element of street wisdom mixed with classical references and philosophy and common sense."

The door opens and a face peers in briefly. Wrong class.

"There's an old American tradition from Thoreau saying, Most men lead lives of quiet desperation. Well there are millions of poems of quiet desperation and they are all published in *The New Yorker.*" Ginsberg chuckles derisively. "So, on to Creeley."

Then out of the blue he says, "Let's take five breaths."

What's this about? Weren't we all in fact just breathing? One person is even sleeping and actually breathing rather deeply. Ginsberg closes his eyes and instructs us, "Follow your breath from the tip of your nose until it dissolves for five breaths."

The thought crosses my mind that this deep-breathing exercise is like a metaphysical sorbet, a brain palate cleanser. I shut my eyes, then open them as I hear Ginsberg draw his first deep inhalation through his nose. Most of the class have their eyes shut, the rest are, like me, furtively peeking out from under their lashes, looking away in embarrassment when our eyes meet.

Ginsberg finally breaks the uneasy silence. "Robert Creeley was born in 1926. He was a northeastern poet; his style is kind of minimal, in short verse lines, haltingly slow. He was very much influenced by Miles Davis's phrasings on the trumpet, early Davis of the forties. He's from New England so there's a kind of reticence like in Emily Dickinson, not wanting to overstate his case . . . minimalism not *my* bullshit.

"The other influence on Creeley was Thomas Campion; he was the Bob Dylan of poetry of the Renaissance. Performing lyric poems on his tortoiseshell lyre, he created a renaissance all over Europe. Lyric poems should be performed with a musical instrument, or else they lose their muscle. They become lax without that kind of exquisite, delicate hovering accent."

Ginsberg recites some Campion from heart. "All Whitman is 'I celebrate myself, and sing myself.' It's self-empowerment. He's not scared of his own body there in the midst of nature. Campion does the same thing.

"There's an undercurrent of abrasiveness, a kind of turn-the-apple-cart-over in Creeley's work. Generally he types the figure a phrase at a time, until the next phrase comes to him, so there's a kind of break in the line or breath stop as he calls it. Like Corso, each line he writes modifies or alters the previous line, so he doesn't know what he's going to say until he's said it. His method, like Kerouac's, is that of spontaneous composition, and relatively little rearrangement or revision."

Wrapping up class, Ginsberg reminds us that next week he is reading at the DIA Center downtown and that he's gotten free tickets for the class. He also reminds us, "If you don't have, or can't find any of the writers on the syllabus, or any of these books, let me know and I'll lend you my own books." There is a pervading sense that he is a kind of poetry pusher, the intellectual candy man.

The DIA Center Reading

Allen reads a poem that includes a line about getting out of bed after having sex with a young man who has turned his body to face the wall. There are two attractive guys sitting in front of me, neither of whom I've ever seen in class. One turns to the other: "Is that Billy he was talking about?"

"No," the guy proudly replies, "that's me."

February 23

Tonight we are liberated from our dinky classroom, upgraded to a small amphitheater in the Main Building. Once again a bunch of odd people have turned up in the class; perhaps they've heard through the groovy grapevine that Corso is at the helm tonight.

Corso slouches into class with the quick anxious step of the hunted man, a man unhappy to have left his apartment. His long snaggly gray hair is pulled back in a low ponytail. He sits down, and hunching over the desk, nervously tugs and strokes his little beard. He's wearing a blue denim work shirt, khakis, and a ratty black jacket. He *looks* like a Beat poet. One of the boys perpetually buzzing around Ginsberg passes around an attendance sheet.

By way of introduction Corso begins with a question, "Does anyone know where the Trojan horse is from? The Cassandra myth?"

No one says a word.

"Big big man Mr. Homer. Homer is the daddy of all mythology. You should have read Homer, there is no excuse for it, if you haven't. No excuse for not embracing Homer. If you haven't gone through Homer . . ." He throws up his hands in dismay.

"Homer wrote the *Odyssey* at the base of Mt. Olympus. He wrote the *Iliad* right on top. He wrote about the bickering of men, like the bickering of gods. Here was a man who dealt with the *gods*, who put his own voice in the mouth of gods—quite fantastic. Big big man Mr. Homer. Hindu gods don't bicker." Corso strokes his chin and fidgets in his chair. I have the feeling he isn't accustomed to lecturing. "What do you want to talk about?" he asks, nervously drumming his fingers upon the desktop.

The room is silent.

In a heartbeat he launches back in on Homer. "It is just basic knowledge for a writer; you should *all* know your Homer."

No one says a word.

"I find somebody dumb who doesn't know Homer—that's how I feel. Check him out; he brought the Greek gods on the scene, that is for sure. But then again I just happened to be reading that book that afternoon when Ginsberg called. We don't have to be stuck with the *Iliad*. There are insights in that book that are stupendous." He rocks in his chair and checks his wrist for a nonexistent watch. "How long have I been here?"

"Twenty minutes."

"That's a long time man!" He sighs in exasperation. "Let's get on to something else."

There is an uneasy silence in the room. Nervous giggling. No one knows what to do, least of all Corso. "Take a look at the Greeks and their hell," he says desperately. "Their hell was like their weather. Their weather was not too cold, not too warm, it was *moderate*. Look at the Gilgamesh hell—that was a funny hell. That hell is a desert. Different kinds of hells for different seasons."

"Where is your hell?" someone calls out from the crowd. "Right here, believe me." He laughs uncomfortably. The class laughs along with him.

"I always figured a guy who is a philosopher would never go and tell people he was a philosopher," he says lighting on a new topic. "Others had to tell him he was a philosopher. But a poet has to tell people he's a poet. If you don't, they don't know. It's like Anne Waldman, whom I love, who made the mistake once of showing me a poem. She asked, 'Is this a poem?' And I said, 'Hell no.' She hasn't forgiven me for *ten* years. I don't want her wrath on me. I never expected poets to be that sensitive," he says rolling his eyes. "I thought you could screw around with them. My god. I made it worse by trying to apologize. I tried, and oh, I was so embarrassed. I didn't mean it, really. One day she will see. That shows you how careful you have to be of what you say.

"I think as a poet you have to have certain things under your belt—the Cassandra myth, the Trojan horse. You've got to have the essentials in your head; even if they aren't essential, they're at least beautiful. I'd rather have a little bit of knowledge than a whole lot of faith. I'd rather have knowledge, an encyclopedic head. Of course to be a poet you don't have to know nada."

This seems to cheer the class.

"You've said poetry was a saving grace to you, how so?" a student asks.

"Because it educated me. Poetry is a study of the head. You use your head for pondering and worrying, working things out. I was alone. I didn't have some of the people others have, like parents—so I worked it out for myself. Then poetry came along."

Corso seems noticeably more at ease answering questions than lecturing.

"When did you realize you were a poet?" someone inquires.

"I realized I was a poet around fourteen, fifteen. I never got a chance to be rejected. I said I was a poet—so I was. First poem I wrote was about my mother. I used to ask people what happened to her. Sometimes they said she had died, other times they told me she was a whore, or that she just disappeared. To this day I don't know. So I took the disappearance, and figured she went back to Italy, a shepherdess in Calabria, tending sheep around the lemon trees. That was my mother. The poem was called 'Sea Chanty.' " He recites it, "My mother hates the sea / my sea especially / I warned not to / it was all I could do / . . . Upon the shore I found a strange / yet beautiful food / I asked the sea if I could eat it / and the sea said I could . . .

"You know it would be easier to be a painter," he laments. "You have to show your ass in writing. It is embarrassing when you have to face people and read poems; they see how you look, they see you—*oh my god*." He raises his hand to his cheek in mock horror. "Whereas a painter just puts his stuff in a gallery and walks away."

"How do you work?"

"I get a certain poem-feeling in my gut. I watched Tennessee Williams once in Greece when I was staying at his house. He'd get up every morning at seven and pull down the shades and play schmaltzy music on tapes he had from America and start typing away. The time I usually work is when people are sleeping; it is always in the middle of the night, the hour of the wolf, while the world is asleep. Not that I do it every night, but I like the dark, I don't like the bright sunlight. I'd rather be in the shade."

"How do you feel about rewriting?"

"At the time of writing I don't rewrite. First thought best thought. We were always into that. You know, first words that are down, best words that are down. The first thought is the purest thought. The purest stuff is spontaneous. But sometimes I do rewrite. Why not make it better? Why not?"

"Do you share work with other writers?"

"I've read poems on the phone to Ginsberg. He read me 'Howl.' Sharing the work is good. Why hoard your words? Poetry is *hard*," he says with a grimace.

"Do you like to read work aloud?" someone in the back calls out.

"You get more out of reading a poem than from hearing it read to you. You get more out of me in print than in a reading, yeah. Because usually I don't read the heavyweight stuff that I write. I just can't bear it. It would take too much out of me. So I read the light stuff, the funny stuff. To make them laugh. Oh boy, they love you when you make them laugh. I've got to have a couple of drinks before I do it. To face this horde, this is like death, this is the darkest nights of our souls, it is horrific, and then there is Ginsberg up there like it's a great come-on. Oh boy, he can be like a clown up there." He pauses. "It diminishes poetry, I think. It diminishes poetry by reading it and playing the clown, or entertainer. But I've done it to make money. I prefer the nice quietude of poetry. For me poetry comes from here." He points to his sternum. "If not, it doesn't mean anything—it don't mean nada. You can't sneak the miracle. There is no way that you're going to write a better poem just because you want to be remembered for it.

"As a kid I knew when I grew old I'd always have poetry. Old age didn't bother me because I'd always have poetry to go to—it was a standby. Whenever you have pain, or trouble, or things upsetting you, try to write poetry, it will be your greatest friend. In many ways poetry benefits you, and it could benefit others. It's a good thing. It doesn't hurt anybody en masse."

Having made this proclamation Corso rises to his feet as if to leave. A clock watcher calls out, "Uh, you've got forty-five minutes left."

Corso groans and sinks back in his seat. "I can't get out of here!"

The class cracks up. No one wants him to stop talking.

An addled-looking blond woman stands up in the back. "Do you ever have anybody else read your poetry out loud?"

"No. I never have, but I bet they have. Why, you wanna read one?"

"Yeah."

"Which one?"

"I want to do the one about the stains. The stains. I really like the thing about stains, you know that one?"

Corso knits his brow and rubs his forehead in contemplation. "Do you know the one I'm talking about?"

Corso shrugs. "*You* don't know the poem you're talking about?" He laughs.

"I remember the *concept*," she says. "I don't remember the words. You don't remember it?"

"I don't remember my poetry that well, other than that sea chant. Who recites American poetry by memory? No one does that anymore," he says.

"Do you read criticism of your work?" a man with a shaved head asks, as the blond woman slides, as if in slow motion, back down into her chair.

"I don't see much of it. The message is either going to be heavily down, or all the way for it. They don't know how to handle it. But I have no doubts, I mean if I died now, I wouldn't feel that I wasn't accomplished.

"I could write a volume of poetry in a week—if it hit me. But I don't want to throw out poetry like that, one after another. People say, 'People are going to forget you.' I don't give a damn, I'm not a movie star. I'm a poet. Today poets have all got to be famous. It's all changed, the ball game has changed. It is only a new thing that's happened with poetry that poets are known while they are alive. Allen Ginsberg got it, nailed it so well. He knows how to handle it and put it to good use. Check it out. The man has been *beneficial* to people. If I look at history, I can't see where poets have caused any hurt en masse—I can't see where a drop of blood's been spilled, except among themselves. Verlaine with Rimbaud shooting him in the wrist, okay, Villon cutting the priest's neck because the priest wanted to seduce him, well okay—family quarrels.

"I'm facing old age," he says gently nodding his head. "I'm sixty-three. I hope poetry will stand by me. Look at Blake. Before he died, he was singing in his bed to his wife Kate, dying and just singing. The years they go like that. I saw my nine-year-old kid the other day and I didn't recognize him.

"Poetry is when you are all alone in a little room and you have to write the fucker down." He pauses for emphasis. "It's all there. Remember, it's a game being a writer; you are taking a gamble there. I really admire people who do it, even hack writers, I admire them, because they can create attitudes, time spans." He nods. Then, rising to his feet for the last time, he signs off, "I hope I gave you something."

Corso left the class twenty minutes early. Nobody seemed to notice.

March 1

Tonight's class is greatly diminished. The regular core plus one or two stalkers. Ginsberg unloads a pile of books from a tote bag. He seems anxious to hear about last week's class. "Anybody take any notes?" he asks, rubbing his hands together gleefully. "I'd be curious to see what happened. What did he have to say?"

"He spoke about growing old and the Trojan horse," a student in her seventies says.

"We talked about his *craft*," murmurs a kohl-eyed woman in long dangly earrings.

"It was *great!*" says an eager note-taker in the front row. Ginsberg nods in satisfaction.

"Today I want to talk about Creeley, his growing older, middle-aged poems, and his realization of aging. So, we'll begin with 'Self-Portrait,' his realizations about himself:

> He wants to be
> a brutal old man,
> an aggressive old man,
> as dull, as brutal
> as the emptiness around him,

He doesn't want compromise,
nor to be ever nice
to anyone. Just mean,
and final in his brutal,
his total, rejection of it all.

"It's a rare and brutal self-portrait, and it is very much him. It reflects his recollections of his earlier life, when he did drink quite a bit, and was quite mean to people when he got drunk. Some drunken people are very sweet, some are dopey, some are maudlin—some get really really mean. Fortunately, he never turned it on me, but I've seen him in that situation. He is actually alcohol-free now, I think.

"Incrementally, almost monosyllabically, the meaning of a Creeley poem accumulates, changing everything that goes before it. His method of writing is to put paper in the typewriter and begin with whatever phrase or insight he started with, a retroactive small instance of feeling, and then accumulate detail and reach for common ground."

Ginsberg reads aloud Creeley's poem "Memories":

Hello, duck
in yellow

Cloth stuffed from
inside out,

Little
pillow

"That's all there is," he laughs, then reads it aloud again. "It's very *intimate* poetry. Some people say it's incomprehensible, but I don't think so. If you look long enough it will make sense. The work couldn't be more real or concrete. Like the duck—it's a real baby cloth duck. It is a play of pure language, but there is always some substantive matter there."

"What do you think when people call him abstract?" someone asks.

"Well, it *is* abstract. I wouldn't want to write that way myself, so abstractly, except I really dig it when I read it. I'm almost crying it is so cool.

" 'Go' is another minimal one," Ginsberg says, then reads aloud:

Push that little
thing up and the
other right down.
It'll work.

"It sounds like instructions for a baby toy, doesn't it? It is also slightly erotic; it might read as some suggestion about the whole process of creation, Push that little thing up." He laughs uproariously. "It's so beautiful! It is actually the memory of a child's toy but it is also parallel to God, or a divine messenger telling man, *Push that little thing up, it will work.*" He trembles with laughter. "It is your generic instructions for existence, or am I reading too much into it? It *is* there," he insists. "If anybody here doesn't get it, it's all right. It took me forever to get them myself."

Next we read "Age," which is from Creeley's collection *Windows.* It's the most explicit poem we've read. Ginsberg begins to crack up over the line, "probe into your anus." He has to stop at "roto-rooter-like device" to catch his breath, and by the time he reaches "like a worn out inner tube" his voice is a high-pitched squeak, and he's laughing hysterically at the line "to snore not unattractively." After he wipes the tears from his cheeks he continues, "I guess what I like about his poems is that they are a trip. It's really the mind laid bare. He may do some tinkering, but I think his method is if it doesn't work, it doesn't work and he throws it away. This poem is like a mind trap in a way. Creeley's poems are like jokes that crack themselves."

After he has composed himself Ginsberg adds, "Creeley takes from Campion the rhythmical subtlety, the musicality characteristic of English song and lyric poetry. The delicate cadence in Creeley comes from Campion. His care for the syllable is like the poets of the Black Mountain School, who composed their work conscious of every syllable and how it fits into the cadence."

The subject of cadence and rhythm leads us to Sappho, whom Ginsberg refers to as "the first Rimbaud." We listen to him read some of Sappho's most famous poems like "Invocation to Aphrodite" and some other fragments.

"Sappho invented a number of stanza forms, like the sapphic stanza," he says, then begins to chant, "Trochee trochee dactyl trochee trochee." He waits for a second as if expecting us to jump in, but the class is speechless. The woman next to me whispers, "Is he having some kind of flashback?"

"Okay," he says in his best patient-Cub-Scout-leader voice, "let's do it together!" and leads the whole class in a chorus of sapphic stanza form. At first we are timorous and shy, then after a few rounds our voices become loud, even celebratory. This singing makes class seem more like day camp than a literature class.

"These are dance steps," Ginsberg tells us. "Ed Sanders and The Fugs use these. These have a cadence so powerful and inevitable that they outlasted Troy—the monuments of marble, brass, and iron—and the Parthenon—and they're good for love poetry, good for poems of *yearning*. They're not far from the blues in terms of structure. Actually, they're very similar to twelve-bar blues.

"For next week," he calls out as everyone gathers up their books, "I want you to write a sapphic poem!" As we file out of class I can hear people humming trochee trochee dactyl trochee trochee . . .

March 8

I'm early for class. Ginsberg hasn't arrived yet. The woman next to me is visibly peeved. She's riffling through some papers and sighing in exasperation. I can see that they're sheaves of poetry which have been corrected in cramped handwriting—I think it's Ginsberg's hand. She looks over at me and rolls her eyes.

"Have you had your meeting with him yet?" I ask.

"Oh, *yeah* . . ." she says, sucking in her breath and raising her eyebrows. "I got completely clobbered. He hated it. He was *so* critical—I don't think he likes women. At least he sure doesn't like my work, it's too *girly* for him."

I confess to her that I'm nervous about my meeting. She smirks. "You should be. I couldn't wait to get out of there. I know these are good, I've workshopped one of them even," she says, sliding the poems out of my sight and into a purple folder.

One on One with Ginsberg

I sit in the hall outside of Ginsberg's office, along with several other students. A platinum-haired boy with a black goatee scribbles in his journal. A woman with long black Medusa locks twirls a snake of dark hair around her finger, looking pained as she reads a slender volume of Sappho. I can see, through the crack in the door, a boisterous fellow in cowboy boots sitting in the chair alongside Ginsberg's desk. He is leaning across the desk jabbing his finger into what I suspect is his poem. In his lap is a large pile of papers, more poems I assume. I can't hear the conversation, but as I watch I can see the man slowly deflating, his gestures becom-

ing larger as he struggles to explain the intention behind his art. I
feel sick. I read over my own poems, stumbling over obvious
metaphors and silly turns of phrase. I want to flee. I can hear Ginsberg's voice, "Okay," he says in a wrapping-it-up voice, "there are
other people waiting." My heart is pounding. The man bounds
out of the office.

Ginsberg looks down at his sign-up sheet. "Schappell?" he
asks, peering over the rims of his clear plastic glasses. I nod and
shut the door tightly behind me, I don't want anyone to witness
my artistic evisceration. He waves me into the chair next to his
desk. My heart is pounding as I hand over my work.

He reads silently, tipping back in his chair. Then he leans forward across the desk and smiles. To my surprise he is incredibly
generous and complimentary. Perhaps my contemporaries have
just worn him down so his critical faculties are muted. Perhaps
he's just in a good mood. He makes insightful comments, and
does a quick edit that vastly improves my poem. He suggests a
few writers for me to read and asks me questions about my poem,
which is about my experiences with olfactory hallucinations. He's
curious about them and nods as I tell him about the strange and
unsettling phenomena of smelling smoked meat and alcohol
when none are in evidence. He writes down the name of a neurol-
ogist who might be interested in my case and suggests I stop by
again. I leave his office feeling greatly relieved, and a bit elated.

March 29

When I show up for class, the amphitheater is full of strange faces.
Another class has hijacked our room. Ginsberg looks annoyed.
Tonight he's wearing a hand-knitted dark blue, white, and red
cardigan with chunky hand-wrought silver buttons. It looks like a
Tibetan Perry Como sweater.

"Just sit down and let's get going," he says in irritation, and
gestures at the floor for us to sit down. "We have a lot to do." At
his bidding people sit cross-legged on the floor just outside the
open door of the amphitheater as though in peaceful protest. The
other class peers out the door at us. Just as Ginsberg starts to take
roll, a uniformed security guard appears and sternly informs us
that there are too many of us to sit in the hall. *We're a fire hazard.*
Ginsberg insists he has the paperwork needed for the room, and
pats his pockets as though he carries the documents with him. The
guard disappears, then reappears a few minutes later saying he
has found another room for us. We move en masse to an audito-

rium on another floor. The new room is a lecture hall for the sciences, its main source of decoration being an enormous periodic table of the elements.

Without waiting for the stragglers to find seats, Ginsberg plants himself on the edge of the stage and starts in on John Wieners. "Wieners is the great gay poet of America. He's in hardly any anthologies, but he's so emotional and truthful." Ginsberg reads us "A Poem for Trapped Things" in a voice that is full of intense appreciation.

"Wieners is like Cavafy, a Greek modern poet of the twentieth century who died in the twenties or thirties. His work gives us glimpses into his love life, his homosexual bent . . . it's a similar aesthetic to Whitman's poetry."

He quotes from Wieners's tragic American poem "The Acts of Youth": "*I have always seen my life as drama, patterned after those who met with disaster or doom*," then reads the poem in its entirety. Ginsberg compares Wieners with Hart Crane, who he describes as "a doomed powerful poet whose low self-esteem led him to commit suicide."

Ginsberg reads more Wieners, interjecting comments on his sexual infatuation with Robert Creeley and how this pissed off Creeley's wife. He tells us of Wieners's time spent in and out of various asylums, his shock treatments and awful nightmares, and how he experimented with peyote and "locoweed," which makes you lose your memory and then your mind. "He had been over the abyss before," Ginsberg says and pauses. "There's a thread of Marlene Dietrich glamour in Wieners's poetry."

He describes Wieners's trips to New York to do poetry readings. "Sometimes he would just read one," Ginsberg recalls. "He'd read one, sit down, and wait until they applauded and he was called back onto the stage. Then he'd get up and read another, then go sit back down. Sometimes he would read the gossip columns as poetry. He wrote some of his poetry under the nom de plume Jackie O."

Class ends too soon. "For next week think about Kerouac and vowel delicacy, meditation, and poetics," he cries out.

April 5

Tonight we're in yet another classroom—a cramped but bright little space with many more chairs than students, so people are fanned out all over the room, mostly lingering in the back. This seems to annoy Ginsberg, who insists, "Come closer, come closer,

I don't want to yell." We pull our chairs up in a circle and surround him like disciples.

"What was the face you had before you were born?" Ginsberg asks. "That question, the theme of a Zen poem, is the heart of Beat poetry. It could be called the 'golden ash' school, as Kerouac said, 'A dream already ended, the golden ash of dream.' "

"Has anyone ever heard of the Prajnaparamita Sutra?" he asks. Everyone shakes their head no.

Someone jokes, "Isn't that like the Kama Sutra?" The class giggles.

"This is the basis of much Eastern thought, particularly in the Buddhist world through Indo-China, Burma, Ceylon, Tibet, and China itself. This is a translation by Shunryu Suzuki Roshi, a Zen master from San Francisco who was a big deal in the fifties and sixties. It was tinkered with by myself and a Tibetan lama to make it maybe a little clearer. Generally it's chanted in a monotone, so I'll chant it."

Ginsberg chants the Prajnaparamita Sutra in a strangely pretty monotone.

"First time I ever heard anything about Buddhism was Kerouac crooning the Buddha refuge vows; he was singing these, crooning them like Frank Sinatra." Ginsberg, with his eyes downcast sings the refuge vows, repeating them three times.

Allen Ginsberg, John Wieners, and Gregory Corso, 1986.

He describes the four vows of the bodhisattva then chants them for us. This is all to prepare us for Kerouac. Of the books *On the Road*, *Visions of Cody*, and *Doctor Sax*, all published in a three-year period, Ginsberg believes that *Visions of Cody* contains some of his best writing. "By then he had discovered his method of spontaneous writing. He'd written the huge novel *On the Road* and had rethought it. He decided he would do it even better and bigger, by going back over the same characters, same plot, not making it a chronological narrative, but according to epiphanous moments. He'd write a series of discrete epiphanous moments, then string them together. Different experiences and moments popping up in whatever order would be the structure of the book. It wouldn't have the linear quality of a regular novel, with a beginning, middle, end. It would be as the mind sees a cubist painting. Cody Pomeray is Dean Moriarty is Neal Cassady, all based on a real person, all real happenings but fictionalized.

"His next book, *Doctor Sax*, was written on marijuana, so it has an elaborate marijuana openness. Doctor Sax was the Shadow, a bogeyman, the shrouded stranger, the figure you see through your window at night who follows you down the street and makes you want to run home fast after it gets dark. He even made a drawing of him, a comic strip. Like science fiction, he emerges out of the docks of the Brooklyn waterfront; he comes up out of the water with his hair long and glistening in a shroudy cape, and goes to the Pyramid club and dances on the bar. So here's the situation, little Jacky Kerouacky from Lowell, Mass., at the age of twelve or thirteen is befriended by Doctor Sax, the bogeyman. In the daytime he's a football coach, but at night he puts on his shrouded cape and goes around the city performing miracles, and the big plot of this is that the millennium is approaching, the apocalypse, or Armageddon, and at Snake Hill in Lowell, Mass., the great snake of the world is going to emerge and devour the planet. This is a recording of Jack reading *Doctor Sax* made in 1961 on an old tape recorder at his house."

Ginsberg pushes down the play button and Kerouac's voice booms out of the battered tape recorder as if possessed. Despite the scratchy static his voice is clear and mesmerizing, his nasal New England accent rattling the room, his cackle electric. The whole class is rapt. Ginsberg's face softens and gets a little dreamy-looking.

"That's beautiful, isn't it?" He repeats and savors Kerouac's sentences, biting the consonants and mouthing the vowels, emphasizing the oral qualities and rhythms. "It has a subtlety of both language and ear that comes from a virginal, or rather somewhat youthful, marijuana fantasy.

"The writing of *Visions of Cody* was influenced by Thomas Wolfe, Thomas Mann, Proust's madeleine and tea, and Joyce's *Finnegans Wake*. It has the extended sentences, panoramic awareness and interesting narrative like *On the Road*." Ginsberg then reads us bits of *Visions of Cody*. He thankfully doesn't try to sound like Kerouac, or read like him.

"These are sort of Whitmanic descriptions, aren't they?" he points out. "This is an experimental, exuberant book. It's broken down into sections like jazz sessions. It might mean one sentence, or it might mean pages. Each section is written in a session of writing like a jazz musician. It's like blowing until the energy is gone. Gertrude Stein also did this. She'd write it all out in a focus of attention. Kerouac didn't always write it all down. It was mostly babbling in bars or under the Brooklyn Bridge. We used to walk under the Brooklyn Bridge and improvise a lot, trading lines, riffing poetry. There are a couple specimens between me and Kerouac and Peter Orlovsky. They're not all that interesting," Ginsberg confesses, but he shares them anyway. " '*Pull my daisy / tip my cup / all my doors are open.*' Burroughs and Kerouac did a collaborative novel back in the forties, set in the St. Louis zoo. It was called *And the Hippos Were Boiled in Their Tanks*."

This recollection gets Ginsberg on to the subject of Burroughs. "Burroughs thinks in pictures—he spends long sessions just sitting at the typewriter, seeing images moving against the dark. He sits with his hands hovering over the typewriter thinking about *hands pulling in nets in the dark* like in 'Interzone.' He does cut-ups and revises a lot. He follows his dreams, follows them visually like a movie camera and writes the images down. His material often comes from dreams or visual daydreams, and are filed according to subject matter in manila folders. All writing is spontaneous, you don't know what the next word is going to be until you write it, unless you're like the Russians who work it all out in their heads."

Ginsberg ends class by reading Kerouac's mea culpa in *Visions of Cody*. In the middle of it he nearly begins to weep. "I never thought it would be published."

April 12

Ginsberg is eager to start class today. "We'll begin with a recording of blues and haiku done by Kerouac in 1959 with Al Cohn and Zoot

Sims, two vanguard hard bop white saxophonists. Kerouac would pronounce the haiku and they would make up a little saxophone haiku. With the push of a button Kerouac is alive reciting haikus accompanied by slithery sax music that complements the verse:

> *In my medicine*
> *cabinet the winter fly*
> *has died of old age.*

"Nice, huh?" Ginsberg nods appreciatively. "Did you notice his enunciation? It's like real mature mouthing. I mentioned last week that the master of intonation and enunciation, Frank Sinatra, was actually an influence on Kerouac. Sinatra, I think, learned his technique from Billie Holiday. So the lineage is Billie Holiday through Sinatra to Kerouac."

> *Drunk as a hoot owl writing letters by thunderstorm.*

"I've a series of poems of my own, which instead of calling haiku I've called 'American sentences.' The trouble with most of the traditional haiku is the way they're synthesized into English; they're not a complete sentence. They sort of hang in the air. The advantage of *In my medicine cabinet the winter fly has died of old age* is it's a straightforward active sentence with a subject, verb, and object. It just goes right into your head without that *arty* sound of *translationese.*

"The next recording is 1959, a time when Steve Allen, then a popular television personality, *somewhat* literate, really dug Kerouac and understood that he was a little better than the beatnik image given in the press. He actually made friends with him. He asked him to come into the recording studio. It was lucky that Steve Allen had that intuition because there are not so many recordings of Kerouac. He made some on his own home machine like the *Doctor Sax* that I played you last week, but that's quite rare and not issued. There's another I have of him reading *Mexico City Blues,* but he's really *completely* drunk and the timing is not good, though it's still him.

"At the time of *Mexico City Blues* Jack was reading a book called the *Buddhist Bible*. Did we ever do sitting practice and meditation here?" he suddenly asks us.

"That might be interesting to do that. So you know what Kerouac's talking about when he talks about Buddhism and meditation and all that crap. So if you will sit forward in your seats with your hands on your knees, *sit up straight*. The reason I say sit *forward* is to keep your spine straight so that you're not slumping over, you're *erect*. Okay, top of the head supporting heaven (so to speak), so it's not quite marine military; the chin is down, somewhat more relaxed, eyeballs relaxed, so you're not staring at any specific point, but letting the optical field hang outside of your skull, looking through your skull at the outside. We are led to believe a lie when we see with not through the eye, says William Blake, so you're looking through the eye, with *perhaps* awareness of the periphery of the optical field.

"We're *not* leaving the world, we're *here*; we're just resting within the phenomenal world and appreciating it. Shoulders relaxed, nose in line with belly button, ears in line with your shoulder blades. Sitting forward actually on the edge of the chair is best, balanced on your feet, hands resting on thighs. Mouth closed, putting the tongue toward the teeth and roof of your mouth, *eliminating the air pocket* so you won't be disturbed by an accumulation of saliva forcing you to swallow. Gaze tending toward the horizon, resting in space, or, if it's too bright, at a forty-five degree angle down in front of you toward the floor. So the basic classical practice is paying attention to the breath leaving the nostril and following the breath until it dissolves, not *controlling* the breath, just any regular old natural breath that comes along will do. What you are adding is your *awareness* of the breath rather than any control. On the *in* breath you can let go of your observation, maybe check your posture; if you're slumped you will tend to be daydreaming, if you are upright you will tend to be alert. So, let's try that. Don't ignore other parts of the mind. When you notice you are thinking, label it thinking and take a friendly attitude toward your thoughts. That is the nature of the mind to think thoughts, but when you become aware of it observe it, acknowledge it, notice it, then return your attention back to the breath, and it will restore your focus."

We sit on the edge of our seats, hands on our knees. If someone were to peek through the window in the door, they would see what I am sure looks like an army of zombies awaiting instructions. The room hums with silence. A smoker begins to hack, everyone else sits still, drawing deep breaths.

"Okay," Ginsberg says, disturbing our pleasant revery. "*Mexico City Blues*. In 'Chorus 63' Kerouac's commenting on his own poetics, 'Rather gemmy, Said the King of Literature Sitting on a davenport at afternoon butler's tea.' " Ginsberg guffaws, the class laughs too. Ginsberg's reading it in a very funny high-tone sniffy

British voice. " 'Rather gemmy *hmmm* . . . always thought these sonnets of mine were rather gemmy as you say, true perfect gems of lucid poetry, poetry being what it is today, rather gemmy . . .'

"It's sort of like a midtown intellectual ninny or somebody reading *The New Yorker*," he says. "Kerouac was really a master of camp. Very few people realize that a lot of Kerouac is campy voices, or getting into other people's heads, very common archetypal people like a *New Yorker* reader, or Burroughs, or W. C. Fields, very often he goes into W. C. Fields mode.

"Kerouac is often accused of being naive macho but this is very sophisticated camp he's laying down." Ginsberg then reads "Chorus 74," which he recites in a lockjawed English accent he confesses is Gore Vidal's.

"I think Jack had slept with Gore Vidal by this time, or so Gore Vidal said. Why, I don't know. Kerouac wasn't really gay, but on the other hand I think he dug Vidal as a sort of ultra-sophisticated person and wanted some of it to rub off, or maybe it was just drunken lust, but I think it was more a sort of envious inquisitiveness and curiosity and amusement."

Ginsberg starts the "Chorus 64," " 'I'd rather die than be famous,' " he reads, then mutters, under his breath, "Fat chance." .

He moves on to another point about *Visions of Cody*. "The first forty-two pages are a series of little sketches. A friend, Ed White, who studied architecture at Columbia when Kerouac was hanging around there in 1948 to 1949, told him what he ought to do is go out with a pencil, a sketch pad and make verbal sketches just like painters make sketches, little quick sketches, little salient lines, to capture the motif or subject, to capture the ephemera of the moment . . . sketch. It's actually quite a good exercise. Sit in front of a window and sketch what you see within the frame of the window. It ain't so easy, but it ain't so hard either. So that's your homework. Jack died, I believe, sitting in a chair verbally sketching the action on a TV quiz program. Making a little prose poem sketch of what was going on."

April 19

Despite the overcast gray sky it feels like spring. The consensus is to have class out of doors. This evening there's a journalist from *The New Yorker* in our class. She's doing a piece for their upcoming fiction issue. Like some ragtag tribe following a prophet, we are led outside to the Leonard Stern business building. Ginsberg sits down in the lotus position on the walkway beneath an overhang and takes off his shoes. His socks are dark blue with no holes in the toes or heels. We sit around him on the pavement and grass. A few students try to imitate his pretzel-pose. He is the only one who looks remotely comfortable, especially when it begins to drizzle, forcing us all to huddle under the cement lip of the building where there's a decidedly dank odor of urine and wet dog.

"This week or next I'd like to lay down the materials for Kerouac's rules for writing—because that is essential to the writing aspect of the Beat generation. It is also essential to understand in relation to earlier work like Gertrude Stein's and see how it reflects back into Shakespeare."

Ginsberg reads a few of Kerouac's verses from *Mexico City Blues*, 104, "I'd rather be thin than famous," and 110 and 111, which deal with Buddhism. "Is this making sense at all? Or is it gobbledygook? Is there anyone who feels this is totally unclear? I confess I don't always know what the hell Kerouac is talking about in his poetry."

"It seems like a totally different attitude than *On the Road*," comments a guy in a baseball cap.

"Well this *is* five years later. In *On the Road* you'll also find moments of perception of the whole phenomenal world as delusion also. In *On the Road* there's one point where he's coming out of Mexico or into Texas and he sees an old lonely shrouded stranger walking the road looking like death or God or a prophet and his prophetic word is *Wow.* I am so glad we're having this class out of the building so I have this vast space to point to—endless space, going beyond the sky, beyond what we can see, beyond the clouds, galaxies. . . . Everybody has already accomplished their existing in vastness, or some form of eternity whether they know it or not; everybody is already a Buddha in infinity, already placed in the infinite, so it's a question of whether they know they're in the infinite, or they're just stuck with their nose in a bank book, or somebody's cunt or whatever. . . . There's no attainment because there's no nonattainment. It's already happened, it's already *here.* The ordinary mind in the place of transcendental mind if you catch on, which is the purpose of sitting and the practice of meditation, to catch on to that. To catch on to the vastness of your own mind, to see that inside space is the same as outside space, so therefore everything is ignorant of its emptiness."

As it continues to rain, Ginsberg discusses meditation at some length. Most of us are a bit befuddled.

"So when you meditate you're trying *not* to think?" someone asks shyly.

"No. You're observing the thought, you observe the breath. Let's do that for just a moment now. I was going to do it inside, but now that we've got the open space . . . I don't know how comfortable you can get. It doesn't require a straight back. Just relax your mind, and maybe focus attention on the out breath, out through the nose if you can, unless you've got problems. . . . Follow your breath if you can, then as you find yourself thinking, or conceptualizing, notice it, touch on it, like anger when you notice it; it dissolves, then you're back here in the space where you are, and then latch on to your out breath again, which should keep your mind here in this space until it drifts again. So it's a question of observing your thought, rather than stopping it. Trying to stop your thought is only another thought. You can go into an infinite regress of thought. The only way is to actually switch your attention to the breath, become conscious of breath and soon your mind is out there in space. The formula is mixing breath with space, mixing mind with breath, mixing mind with space. Let's go for four minutes."

We sit up straight. I remember to think of balancing heaven on the top of my head. We close our eyes, and breathe deeply through our noses, trying to filter out the yipping dogs and the chatter of sorority girls.

We sit and meditate, some of us more deeply than others. The journalist from *The New Yorker* falls deeply asleep, her mouth hanging gently agape. She doesn't rouse herself until a good fifteen minutes have passed. Ginsberg looks amused and a little annoyed.

To wrap up Kerouac we look at a handout, composed by Kerouac in his own unique shorthand, perhaps intended as a letter.

Belief & Technique for Modern Prose a List of Essentials

1. Scribbled secret notebooks, and wild typewritten pages, for yr own joy
2. Submissive to everything, open, listening
3. Try never get drunk outside yr own house
4. Be in love with yr life
5. Something that you feel will find its own form
6. Be crazy dumbsaint of the mind
7. Blow as deep as you want to blow
8. Write what you want bottomless from bottom of the mind

9. The unspeakable visions of the individual
10. No time for poetry but exactly what is
11. Visionary tics shivering in the chest
12. In tranced fixation dreaming upon object before you
13. Remove literary, grammatical and syntactical inhibition
14. Like Proust be an old teahead of time
15. Telling the true story of the world in interior monolog
16. The jewel center of interest is the eye within the eye
17. Write in recollection and amazement for yourself
18. Work from pithy middle eye out, swimming in language sea
19. Accept loss forever
20. Believe in the holy contour of life
21. Struggle to sketch the flow that already exists intact in mind
22. Dont think of words when you stop but to see picture better
23. Keep track of every day the date emblazoned in yr morning
24. No fear or shame in the dignity of yr experience, language, & knowledge
25. Write for the world to read and see yr exact pictures of it
26. Bookmovie is the movie in words, the visual American form
27. In Praise of Character in the Bleak inhuman Loneliness
28. Composing wild, undisciplined, pure, coming in from under, crazier the better
29. You're a Genius all the time
30. Writer-Director of Earthly movies Sponsored & Angeled in Heaven

As ever,
Jack

April 26

"How many of you write some form of open verse? Most of you. Well, for you kids who want to write it there are some rules and regulations. Now, Robert Frost, he made one notorious comment that writing free verse was like playing tennis without a net. And

I think T. S. Eliot was quoted as saying no verse is really free. Ezra Pound has endless suggestions for experimenting with verse forms. William Carlos Williams's effort was to find an 'American measure' as he called it, or a variable measure. Nobody seems to know what that is. So at one point or another I began toting up all the different considerations that might be weighed in the balance in laying out your verse lines on the page, and I'd like to go through some of them. Does anybody know Marianne Moore's method of composition of the stanza? Well, you know her stanzas are kind of cute, like butterfly wings, or very irregular, but they all have some kind of shape when you look at them, like the famous poem 'Poetry' which begins, 'I, too, dislike it. . . .' Let's look at that poem."

It becomes apparent no one in class has a Marianne Moore book with them. A few people are lugging their Norton anthologies of modern poetry, but most of the class is either empty-handed or have brought their Kerouac books. According to our "Survey of Historical Poetics" we are to be looking at *Post-literate Oral Tradition: Preacher, Spirituals, Hymns, Blues, Calypso, improvisation; Signifying Monkey, Rap, African-American and Caribbean poetics, Bop.* What book should one presume to bring to class for "Signifying Monkey"? The class has been proceeding organically, for want of a better word, growing and evolving along the ecstatic tributaries of Ginsberg's passions and obsessions. There is no schedule. From week to week we have no idea what he is going to do; this free-associative format can be confusing, but it's also exciting.

Ginsberg sighs in exasperation. "Oh man, how can I teach if you're all spaced out."

"You said this week we were doing Kerouac," someone offers in our defense.

"We're not doing Kerouac."

"We just never know," says a nervous-looking poet who gnaws his pencils.

"Okay . . . I just wish you would always bring your fucking books," he says ruefully, "because I'm trying to improvise to *some* extent and have it *real* rather than just a rote thing."

Ginsberg begins to discuss the ways Marianne Moore constructed her verse and laid it out on the page. "The basic principle is that each verse, stanza to stanza, maintains the same number of syllables, or can be divided arbitrarily into syllables with no particular significance to the count of the syllables line by line except to make an interesting look, like a butterfly's wing on the page; or there may be some counter rhythm the way the line runs."

Ginsberg then gives a long explanation of how various poets lay their work out on the page according to syllables, accents, breath stop, units of mouth phrasing and division of mental ideas. In a burst of inspiration Ginsberg springs to his feet and goes to the blackboard.

"You might begin a poem on, uh, hair. Let's do that. Let's write a poem on . . . bald heads." He turns to the board and begins to compose on the board, improvising aloud. He first writes "Bald Heads."

> *My own with a fringe of gray*
> *Corso's mop salt and pepper*
> *Eisenhower's dome*

"Now something just occurred to me relating to Eisenhower, so I'll put it over here on the board. That will lead on to other skulls,

> *Alas poor Yorick*
> *Nixon's skull-to-be*

"Do I want Yorick or first thought, best thought, or should I say alas poor Lincoln, or alas poor who? . . . Alas, poor Warren Harding!" He laughs as he scribbles it on the board. "And his girlfriend's skull, or mistress. Harding was famous for having a mistress, wasn't he? Remember that? What was her name? I knew it once.

> *and his Lilly's skull*
> *Again my own*

"You see, one thought comes from another thought, so that this opens up like a telescope along the line. What is the next thought I have? It is that movie star, Johnny Depp, has long hair, so I go back to the margin: *Johnny Depp has long hair.* You just diagram your thought out. So this is division of mental ideas.

"No." He scowls and erases the line about Johnny Depp, "That doesn't work. Anyway these were the ideas that came to me while I was standing here at the blackboard. So I was laying them out, with a space in between each idea as it arose, maybe making a line. But if I had two thoughts coming together fast like Corso's mop salt and pepper, I left them on one line. It is like diagramming your mind. But you have to focus your mind on the subject, exhausting all the variations that arise in your mind." He turns to the board and reads his poem. "Not bad," he shrugs. "So you can divide the lines the way they are spoken or the way you think them up. Sometimes it's simultaneous and identical, sometimes it might not be."

"When you changed Yorick to Warren Harding, do you think that you lost any of the sort of electricity of your natural thought process?" someone asks.

"Maybe, but I think it was an even trade. Yorick, it's too formulaic. . . . I was on Eisenhower: Nixon and Warren Harding made it more common, universalized it in a way, unexpected. You were fresh from the drama of Eisenhower, Nixon, and Warren Harding is not very dramatic at all; he's very ordinary, but it brings it back to the ordinary skull; so does his Lilly's skull, his girlfriend's skull . . . it means it's *everybody's* skull and that leads again to my own."

"So is it a combination of a natural thought process and control?" the student asks.

"Well, it's a natural thought process and then something quick, shrewd, swift." Ginsberg laughs. "Spontaneity. I mean how did I get to Warren Harding? *He rose up.* So it's sort of a nimble skill during the time of composition in making substitutions and hopping it up a little bit."

"Is this how it really happens with you?" someone else asks incredulously.

"Yeah. I wouldn't mind copying that down and having a little poem out of it. Some little magazine asks me for a poem, I could send them that 'Bald Heads.' " Everyone laughs. "A little meditation on bald heads." He shrugs and grins. We believe him.

Towards the end of class—after we have discussed the aesthetics of laying work out according to typographical topography, original notation, and pure chance—someone asks about Ginsberg's punctuation.

"There are some dashes here and there. The first person to get rid of punctuation, the first modern poet was Apollinaire, who went over the proofs of his book which included the poem 'Zone' and eliminated all the punctuation to get it a little closer to his stream of thought. I tend not to punctuate too much. One thing I really avoid for some reason or another is being too finicky. I rarely use a semicolon in a poem, sometimes a colon, but a semicolon? I don't get it. It just sounds like a lot of extra spaghetti. I don't know exactly what spoken idiom or cadence would require a semicolon in actual speech. That's my own prejudice. George

Bush doesn't like broccoli, and I don't like semicolons. Maybe semicolons are good for you. Maybe semicolons help you avoid radiation sickness.

"Another matter we should look into is how to revise poems written in the principle of absolutely spontaneous verse. How do you revise poems? A total contradiction in terms." Ginsberg chuckles gleefully. He takes out the handout we received the first day. Things are actually coming full circle.

Fourteen Steps for Revising Poetry

1. Conception
2. Composition
3. Review it through several people's eyes
4. Review it with eye to idiomatic speech
5. Review it with eye to the condensation of syntax (blue pencil and transpose)
6. Check out all articles and prepositions: are they necessary and functional?
7. Review it for abstraction and substitute particular facts for reference (for example: "walking down the avenue" to "walking down 2nd Avenue")
8. Date the composition
9. Take a phrase from it and make up a title that's unique or curious or interesting sounding but realistic
10. Put quotations around speeches or referential slang "so to speak" phrases
11. Review it for weak spots you really don't like, but just left there for inertial reasons
12. Check for active versus inactive verbs (for example: "after the subway ride" instead of "after we rode the subway")
13. Chop it up in lines according to the breath phrasing/ideas or units of thought within one breath, if any
14. Retype

Ginsberg explains, "Well, you have the conception of the poem, then the composition of the poem, which we just had. Then the next thing I generally do is read it through a lot of different people's eyes. I have a new book out. I spent several times reading it once with Burroughs's eyes, once with Bob Dylan's eyes, once through my stepmother's eyes, various people's. I see what will hook them into the poems and see what flaws the poems have according to people's intelligence I am familiar with and which have been imprinted on me. For instance, reading my own poetry through Burroughs's eyes I get much more cynical and much less tolerant of sentimentality. Reading it through Dylan's eyes I'm wondering if it's surprising enough or if it's pedestrian. Looking through Corso's eyes I wonder if it's condensed enough and tailored interestingly so that I'm not prosaic. Reading it through the eyes of the editorialist at *The New York Times*, I wonder does it make some political sense. . . . Intuitively I end up reading my work through several hundred people's skulls. It's a way of accumulating a lot more intelligence than your own, because what you are doing, to the extent that you are sensitive to other people's swiftness, and intelligence and sensitivity, is empathizing with them as you're reading your own poems to improve them and figure out where your poems are weak. Take the highest intelligences you know, the people you most admire and read it through their eyes. The people you really *dig*, the people you really want to please or communicate to, and then go through it with an eye to *could you say this out loud to your mother or your friend without sounding poetic, or arch, or literary or artificial?* and without sounding like you are copping a poetic attitude of some sort. Review the whole thing through idiomatic speech. Can you say it without embarrassment either to an audience, or your best friend, or to your mommy? Intense emotionally charged fragments of idiomatic speech people won't question, but emotionally charged moments that sound highfalutin or literary or hand-me-down literary, people will suspect the genuineness and sincerity of it. So review it with an eye to idiomatic speech and that will correct the whole attitude of the poem. Then the next is condensation of syntax. Let's look at my poem," he says hopping up and going back to the blackboard, this time with an eraser. He snuffs out the words "with a" from the first line.

" '*My own gray fringed*' . . . that's better. I don't need all those syllables.

" '*Corso's mop salt and pepper,*' that's impeccable, '*Eisenhower's dome,*' '*Nixon's skull-to-be,*' that's all right, '*Alas, poor Warren Harding,*' do I need *and* there? Nah—comma *his Lilly's skull,* I don't know that I need *again*? Maybe dash *my own.* So I would review it. Do I need all the articles, the conjunctions, connectives, *the*'s, *them*'s, *of*'s. . . . *Of* particularly, you can often get rid of the *of* which is more French. You examine every single syllable, especially the small ones, the monosyllables that have no substantive information, and see if you can transpose and reconnect things a little more solidly without the extra articles and particles. Don't reduce it to Chinese laundry talk where you eliminate all the articles, you don't want to do that. . . .

"Next, I generally review for abstraction. Nailing the thing down, grounding the generalizations. Very often generalizations are like a blank in a form that you can fill in.

"Okay, next week is our last class, we'll do the other steps. And be prepared to do Shelley's 'Ode to the West Wind'!"

May 3

I wondered if class might start off with some acknowledgment that this is our final class, or perhaps some hash brownies and jug wine. Instead class begins in a pedestrian way with Ginsberg passing out copies of open form poems. He takes roll, of course, then launches into the texts.

A guy walks in late. Ginsberg in typical fashion asks the late-comer, "What's your name? Are you in the class?" The guy has been in the class since the first day.

Ginsberg takes us through the process of how poets such as Philip Whalen, Gary Snyder, Lawrence Ferlinghetti, and William Carlos Williams lay their poems on the page. He then eagerly passes out copies of Shelley's "Ode to the West Wind."

"There was one other thing that I wanted to do that we hadn't done, which was to do a choral recitation of this poem. My suggestion is that we read it together. Pay attention to the punctuation, so that where you have a comma, a colon, a parenthesis, an exclamation point, a period that indicates a pause, you take a pause and breathe so that we will all be doing it at the same time. We'll do *everything* at the same time or it will be chaos . . . with some people stopping and some people going on. The run-on lines, where there's no punctuation, read as run-on lines. But where there's punctuation, please observe it as a sign of breath. This poem is about the subject of breath, or wind. He's asking the west winds to enter him and let the spirit of the west wind be his spirit, meaning the breath of the west wind be his own breath, and that using the breath of that wind and his own breath make the poem immortal, so that other people after he's dead can chant the same poem using the same periods of breath that he employs in the poem itself. The subject is spirit or breath (spirit means breathing in Latin), his observation is of his breath, the means of vocalization is breath, and if you do that you can get high, you can get a little buzz out of this poem, quite literally if you follow his breaths. It's like taking a pill . . . where you internalize the actual breathing that Shelley has set out for you. All you have to do is follow his notational instructions and you'll get a hyperventilated buzz." Ginsberg laughs. "So we'll just do it all together. One two three . . . 'O wild West Wind, thou breath of Autumn's being . . .' "

We start off in sync and go in and out of it as the poem progresses. I feel decidedly lightheaded, and a little giddy. It's not exactly a party trick, but it is a pleasant experience. As soon as we finish people begin clapping.

"Well, I got a buzz!" He laughs. "It's really a terrific piece. To get to, 'Drive my dead thoughts over the universe/Like withered leaves to quicken a new birth!' you have to do some abdominal breathing to get that whole line through, because that's a long, long breath. How many have read Shelley?" A couple of students grudgingly raise their hands. "Well, how was it?" he asks the way one might ask a first time drug-user how the trip was. Judging by the laughter and murmurs the experiment was a success.

"Better late than never, I guess." He sighs. "Shelley is supposed to be the acme of romantic expostulation in poetry."

Seeing how turned on everybody is by the reading he launches in on Hart Crane's *The Bridge,* focusing particularly on the "Atlantis" section, which he describes as "one of the great rhapsodies in the English language." He reads it aloud with gusto. After he finishes, his face is flushed, his eyes gleaming.

"It tends to rise, then come to a plateau, then drop a bit in tone, then rise again, then drop a bit in tone, then rise all the way up to a sort of prayer in ecstasy and then kind of *come* in an orgasmic series of breaths, then a coda, or post-coitus triste, the end. Basically an iambic pentameter eight-verse stanza."

The class sits in amused shock. Did he say "come"? Perhaps we appear unconvinced or maybe Ginsberg is just enjoying himself, but he rereads what I imagine to be the "come" part with great drama—"white seizures!" he cries out, then says professorially, "So you get some kind of power breath there, like in the 'Ode to the West Wind.' It's one of the best pieces of music of this century, I think, in terms of a machine that begins to levitate and finally take off. I think probably to some extent *The Bridge* is almost a substitute for Eros in a way. . . . Ultimately, I think, this mouthing is a variety of cocksucking. It's the same emotional devotional adorational impulse displaced into musical language. Crane was gay and also into sailors (like Genet, sort of), but this is almost the acme of sublimated eros into poetry. When this was published, his good friends, Yvor Winters and Allen Tate, both academic poets, objected that there was no object that could contain his emotions, that it was an idealism that had no location . . . so much adoration, so much emotion, so much buildup, so much orgasmic mouthing—so to speak—that they denounced the poem as a great failure. It kind of broke Crane's heart. He found himself not only a pariah, but as a gay in a time when to be gay was to be somewhat of a pariah in those circles of academic poets who were all tending toward Eliotic conservatism and undemonstrative cool poetry. That general rejection of his feelings was one of the elements that I think led him to jump off the rear of an ocean liner and drown himself two years later. I also think the constriction of the form didn't allow him full play of all of the emotions that he kept in a kind of emotional and mental prison. I think he would have survived better if he had opened up the form and taken in more detail like William Carlos Williams. He certainly was a great ear, a great poet, and I think that *The Bridge* is one of the great long poems of the century, certainly a big influence on my own work and Kerouac and other writers. One of the most exciting pieces of music in the last fifty to sixty years. Pound's 'Uzura' has some of that excitement, and so do the *Cantos*, and Dylan Thomas's 'Fern Hill.' You have to go back to when T. S. Eliot is kidding with *'OOO, that Shakespeherian Rag— / It's so elegant / So intelligent'* . . . that has a little bit of the rhythmical excitement in it. You get it in other languages, you might get it in some blues, you might get it in Ma Rainey in that long extended spiritual breath, but it's rare, and that is what Shelley is noted for particularly. You get it in Kerouac certainly, and I try to imitate it in the Moloch section of 'Howl.'

"It is an aspect of poetry that really people don't pay too much attention to. Of course the sound poets do. You'll find it in Dada poetry and in Bob Dylan. Actually 'A Hard Rain's Gonna Fall' has a buildup like that." Ginsberg recites the song from memory.

"So this is, you know, our last meeting—I had started last time on the fourteen steps for revising and left midway at number seven, and so I'll just say a few more things about that then leave some time open for conversation.

"Wherever you find yourself generalizing or in abstraction, you can examine it for generalization. If you can tell the difference between particularity and generalization, if you can tell the difference between minute particulars and vague reference, it might do to check for elements that have no special pictorial value or special sound value, just general moo, moo, moo. Of some suggestion of smell, like Resnikoff's 'A pot of fish was boiling on the stove. Sometimes the water bubbled over and hissed. The smell of fish filled the cellar,' or some sort of tactile, sight, smell, sound, taste, touch, anything palpable. You can find a lot of Latinate words that have no sensory suggestion. They're like blanks in a bureaucratic form to be filled in with particulars. What were you really referring to when you spoke of being lonesome in the city? What city? On the roof? Where in your bedroom? Can you particularize a little?

"I myself date compositions so that I know where the origin was, when I first thought something up; if I work on it a long time, I'll put a date showing the finish. If it's your ambition to be a great poet, you'll want to help your scholars and professors a hundred years from now. They're all lazy. If you date it yourself, they won't have to shuffle through all your papers. Dating your work means there'll be a greater accumulation of term papers on your work, master's theses, graduate theses, which means that you'll get more attention in the future. So, if you want to be immortal, date your mortality."

The class laughs, not sure if he really means what he is saying.

"The question of getting a title. Usually I go through a poem and I find two interesting words that combined together might give the gist of the poem. The title actually begins to magnetize or get people into your poem.

"Then one interesting thing I found really useful is that in reading my work aloud I'll tend to hasten through parts that are not quite so interesting till I get to the meat of the poem, to the parts I *really* like. If you can detect that difference, you might examine the weaker parts and perhaps eliminate them altogether. If they bore you, they might bore other people too. It might be a little phrase, a whole sentence, or even a section of the poem that isn't as good . . . so why not just eliminate that and get to the point fast? Williams's phrase for that was 'one active phrase is more valuable than pages of inert writing.' Reading aloud is a good bullshit detector. I read poetry aloud a lot. I may read a poem a hundred times before it's published in a book, and I found after many years that was a really good way of editing. So get rid of the cool parts and leave yourself a hot fragment, like in Sappho. Readers might never get to your great fragment because they got stuck with the first ten lines.

"So now the floor is open—does anybody have anything they want to talk about, as we are in our last breaths here?"

"Why would you want to be immortal?" asks one of the boys who periodically shows up in class.

"Remember that line from Zukofsky," Ginsberg replies. *"Nothing is better for being eternal/nor so white as the white that dies of a day.* Well, if the purpose of your poetry is to assuage your suffering or relieve the sufferings of others, then you want to build a machine which will operate after your death. In a way you could say that Poe did that by liberating consciousness once and for all to experience its own paranoia and feedback, and to experience guilt and conscience, to articulate it so clearly that everybody thereafter would have their minds opened up. What is the purpose of Christ laying down the Golden Rule, or the Sermon on the Mount, or Buddha or Allah? Their function is not so much that they are immortal but that their spirit, their gentility, generosity, openness can be more widespread. Poetry is not an ego trip that preserves your ego in the amber of the poem, but rather that you've made your own ego transparent, conquered it. Your battle against selfishness begins with yourself, to enlighten others to the techniques of liberating yourself from your ego.

"In Yeats's books it is really interesting to see the progression of his mind from beginning to end, and how he ends up with Crazy Jane and very spare things. His last poem actually turns out to be, *How can I . . ./My attention fix/. . . on Russian/Or on Spanish politics? . . . But O that I were young again/And held her in my arms.* The final thought that he wanted to leave behind. It's interesting to know that's where he concluded and to see how he got there. It's interesting to know in what part of Keats's life, what sequence those poems came on, how he developed and at what point he got to that last little poem 'This Living Hand.' Do you know that? It's to Fanny Brawne, his girlfriend, and he knew he was dying. It's really kind of uncanny. It's one of Gregory Corso's favorite poems. Well, when you know it's the last poem it adds a dramatic flair, as well as a kind of ghoulish presence."

Someone calls out, "How do you reconcile your mind-writing slogan—first thought best thought—with rewriting?"

"I don't know. As I get older, I get more schizophrenic about it," Ginsberg confesses, then quotes Whitman, *"Do I contradict myself? Very well then I contradict myself, I am large, I contain multitudes.* The answer is embedded in what I said before about dating. If the poem, the original skeleton of the poem, retains its integrity, that's it.

"Kerouac allows for revision, for certain afterthoughts or mistakes. I don't feel as sure of myself as Kerouac, and maybe his assurance came from his vow not to return to the poem. So that it pushed him to the limit during the time of writing, but I don't feel the same absoluteness, or courage, and yet I like it in him. And what *is* the first thought? The first thought isn't necessarily the first thought you notice, it's the first thought you subnotice. People edit their awareness of what is underneath their minds.

"I remember when I was a boy in grammar school my brother and I had a chemistry set. One of the mysterious miracles of grammar school chemistry was sodium. If it's pure, a little fragment of sodium in water fizzes, burns, gives off hydrogen which will pop, or explode if you put a match next to it. We had a whole pound of sodium which we kept in a bucket of kerosene. While cleaning the chemistry set, I got some water in the kerosene. My father had to carry the whole thing steaming and bubbling out of the house just before it exploded. Why that arose in my mind right now, I don't know. I was looking for a first thought . . . an early significant thing that I remember at least once a month, maybe three times a month, because it was a moment that I got away with something. I was lucky. I could have blown the house apart.

"If I wanted to write it as a poem I might want to recall how the water got into the bucket. I think it was some stupid attempt to clean up the whole pantry shelf where we kept all our chemicals. It would pertain to the first thought. Second thought would be, Young kids do foolish things around the house. Third or fourth would be the generalization: Parents are always there to rescue their kids who do foolish things around the house. Or something wittier like, Wise father puts out the son's fire. First thought does not necessarily mean don't correct at all, it just means that your model should be the interior form that you glimpse, rather than the superficial level of mind. If the mind is shapely the art will be shapely."

With that final pronouncement the semester formally ends. There's an awkwardness. No one knows what to do—everyone seems to be waiting for something else to happen. Finally someone calls out, "What about our paper, our poetry?"

"Oh yeah, yes," Ginsberg answers loudly as though he had almost forgotten to collect them. "I'll take them all now if you have them," he says clearing a space on the edge of the cluttered desk for the proliferation of colored folders and slim sheaves of cream-colored paper. Students linger around the desk, hands extending books to be signed, notebooks to be autographed.

"Your name again?" Ginsberg asks with a hint of embarrassment, as he signs his name, then doodles inside the flyleaf, a sun and a crying hot dog. A few students dawdle, backs pressed up against the wall like they're waiting to be asked to dance. Slowly the class filters out, and Ginsberg bundles up his books and papers. As he starts to shuffle out of class, one last student reaches out to touch his elbow.

—ELISSA SCHAPPELL
1995

Gary Snyder

was born in San Francisco in 1930. Shortly thereafter, he moved to the Pacific Northwest where he worked on his parents' farm and seasonally in the woods. While attending Reed College, he held jobs as a logger, seaman, and fire lookout for the U.S. Forest Service. In 1951, he graduated with degrees in literature and anthropology. After a semester of linguistics study at Indiana University, he transferred to the University of California at Berkeley to study Oriental languages. There, he became actively involved in the burgeoning West Coast poetry scene.

In the summer of 1955, Snyder worked on a trail crew in Yosemite National Park and began to write the first poems he felt were truly his. At the Six Gallery reading in San Francisco, he debuted his poem, "A Berry Feast," inspiring an interest in Zen Buddhism that became a hallmark of Beat writing. In 1956, he left the United States for what was to become a twelve-year residence abroad, spent largely in Japan. In Kyoto he pursued an intensive Zen Buddhist practice. During this period, he also worked in the engine room of a tanker traveling along the Pacific Rim, and then spent six months in India with Allen Ginsberg. Together, they had a notable discussion of hallucinogens with the Dalai Lama. In 1959, his first book of poetry, *Riprap*, was published in Japan, followed by *Myths and Texts* (1960) and two pamphlets in 1965 that gained him a wide readership: *Riprap and Cold Mountain Poems* and *Six Sections from Mountains and Rivers Without End*. His most notable nonfiction works include *Earth House Hold* (1969), *The Old Ways* (1979), and *The Real Work* (1980). In 1975 he won the Pulitzer Prize for his poetry collection *Turtle Island*.

Snyder returned to the United States in 1969 to build a house in the foothills of the northern Sierra Nevada, where he lives today. Since 1985, he has taught at the University of California at Davis, where he helped develop a new academic discipline based on studies of nature and culture. As a spokesperson for "those without voice—the trees, rocks, river and bears—in the political process," Gary Snyder has become, as U.S. poet laureate Robert Hass put it, "a major poet and ethical voice" in American letters.

© RAKU MAYERS

G ary Snyder is a rarity in the United States: an immensely popular *poet whose work is taken seriously by other poets. He is America's primary poet-celebrant of the wilderness, poet-exponent of environmentalism and Zen Buddhism, and poet-citizen of the Pacific Rim—the first American poet to gaze almost exclusively west toward the East, rather than east toward Western civilization. A Snyder poem is instantly recognizable, and often imitated badly: an idiosyncratic combination of the plain speech of Williams, the free-floating, intensely visual images of Pound, and the documentary information of both; the West Coast landscape first brought to poetry by Robinson Jeffers and Kenneth Rexroth; the precise and unallegorized observation of everyday life of the classical Chinese poets; and the orality of Snyder's fellow Beats.*

He may well be the first American poet since Thoreau to devote a great deal of thought to the way one ought to live and to make his own life one of the possible models. In person, he is full of humor and surprisingly undogmatic, with the charisma of one who seems to have already considered long and hard whatever one asks him. Snyder is an encyclopedia of things both natural and artificial: what they are, how they were made, what they are used for, how they work. Then he quickly places each thing into a system that is ecological in its largest sense. Now in his mid-sixties, he would be a likely choice for a personal sage: sharp, wise, en-thusiastic, and an unexpectedly good listener.

The interview took place before an audience at the Unterberg Poetry Center of the 92nd Street Y in New York City on October 26, 1992, and was later updated. What the transcript doesn't show is how often the conversation was punctuated by laughter.

. . .

INTERVIEWER: When Jerry Brown of California was running for president, people were kidding you that if he were elected, you would be named secretary of the interior. Now, the thing that interests me about this is that you are the only poet in America for whom there is any scenario, no matter how far-fetched, of actually entering into real political power. Is this something you think poets ought to do? Would you do it?

SNYDER: I've never thought seriously about that question. Probably not, although I am foolish enough to think that if I did do it, I'd do it fairly well, because I'm pretty single-minded. But you don't want to be victimized by your lesser talents. One of my lesser talents is that I am a good administrator, so I really have to resist being drawn into straightening things out. The work I see for myself remains on the mythopoetic level of understanding the interface of society, ecology, and language, and I think it is valuable to keep doing that.

INTERVIEWER: But it is abnormal for poets not to be involved in the state. The United States remains an exception to most of the rest of the world, where poets commonly have served as diplomats or as bureaucrats in some ministry.

SNYDER: Oh true. The whole history of Chinese poetry is full of great poets who played a role in their society. Indeed, I do too. I am on committees in my county. I have always taken on some roles that were there for me to take in local politics, and I believe deeply in civic life. But I don't think that as a writer I could move on to a state or national scale of politics and remain a writer. My choice is to remain a writer.

INTERVIEWER: Let's get on to the writing and go back forty years or so. One of the amazing things about your work is that you seemed to burst on the scene fully formed with *Riprap* and *Cold Mountain Poems*, which were published in 1959 and 1958 but written earlier in the fifties when you were in your twenties. The poems in both books are unmistakably Snyder poems, and apparently, unlike the rest of us, you are not embarrassed by the work of your youth, for you picked eighteen of the twenty-three poems in *Riprap* for your *Selected Poems*.

SNYDER: Actually the poems in *Riprap* are not the poems of my youth. Those are the poems that I've kept because those were the ones I felt were the beginning of my life as a poet. I started writing poems when I was fifteen. I wrote ten years of poetry before *Riprap*. Phase one: romantic teenage poetry about girls and mountains.

INTERVIEWER: You're still writing that!

SNYDER: I realized I shouldn't have said that as soon as the words were out of my mouth. I would like to think that they are not romantic poems but classical poems about girls and mountains. The first poet that touched me really deeply, as a poet, was D. H. Lawrence, when I was fifteen. I had read *Lady Chatterley's Lover* and I thought that was a nifty book, so I went to the library to see what else he had written, and there was something called *Birds, Beasts and Flowers*. I checked that out. I was disappointed to find out that it wasn't a sexy novel, but read the poems anyway, and it deeply shaped me for that moment in my life.

And then phase two, college. Poems that echoed Yeats, Eliot, Pound, Williams, and Stevens. A whole five years of doing finger exercises in the modes of the various twentieth-century masters. All of that I scrapped; only a few traces of that even survive. I threw most of them in a burning barrel when I was about twenty-five.

So when I wrote the first poems in *Riprap* it was after I had given up poetry. I went to work in the mountains in the summer of 1955 for the U.S. Park Service as a trail crew laborer and had already started classical Chinese study. I thought I had renounced poetry. Then I got out there and started writing these poems about the rocks and blue jays. I looked at them. They didn't look like any poems that I had ever written before. So I said, these must be my own poems. I date my work as a poet from the poems in *Riprap*.

INTERVIEWER: What got you back to poetry at that moment? Was it primarily the landscape?

SNYDER: No, it just happened. What got me back to poetry was that I found myself writing poems that I hadn't even intended to write.

INTERVIEWER: And what poets were important to you then? Who were the masters at this point?

SNYDER: When I was twenty-two or twenty-three, I began working with Chinese and found myself being shaped by what I was learning from Chinese poetry, both in translation and in the original. And I had been reading Native American texts and studying linguistics.

INTERVIEWER: What were you finding in Chinese poetry at that time?

SNYDER: The secular quality, the engagement with history, the avoidance of theology or of elaborate symbolism or metaphor, the spirit of friendship, the openness to work, and, of course, the sensibility for nature. For me it was a very useful balancing force to set beside Sidney, *The Faerie Queene*, Renaissance literature, Dante. The occidental tradition is symbolic, theological, and mythological, and the Chinese is paradoxically more, shall we say, modern, in that it is secular in its focus on history or nature. That gave me a push.

INTERVIEWER: Were you getting the ideogramic method from Pound or from the Chinese poetry directly?

SNYDER: From the Chinese poetry directly. I could never make sense of that essay by Pound. I already knew enough about Chinese characters to realize that in some ways he was off, and so I never paid much attention to it. What I found in Pound were three or four dozen lines in the *Cantos* that are stunning—unlike anything else in English poetry—which touched me deeply and to which I am still indebted.

INTERVIEWER: Pound as a landscape poet?

SNYDER: No, as an ear. As a way of moving the line.

INTERVIEWER: Since we are talking about Chinese poetry I wanted to ask you about the Han Shan translations, Cold Mountain Poems. It is curious because Chinese poetry is so canonical, and Han Shan is not in the canon. I think at the time there were people who thought that you made him up. I wondered how you discovered him?

SNYDER: Well, he is only noncanonical for Europeans and Americans. The Chinese and the Japanese are very fond of Han Shan, and he is widely known in the Far East as an eccentric and as possibly the only Buddhist poet that serious Far Eastern litterateurs would take seriously. They don't like the rest of Buddhist poetry—and for good reason, for the most part.

To give you an example: in 1983 I was in China with a party of American writers—Toni Morrison, Allen Ginsberg, Harrison Salisbury, William Gass, Francine du Plessix Grey, and others—and we were introduced to some members of the Politburo upstairs in some huge building. The woman who was our simultaneous interpreter introduced me to these bureau members—I am embarrassed to say I don't remember who these impressive Chinese persons were—by saying, "He is the one who translated Han Shan." They instantly started loosening up, smiling and quoting lines from Han Shan in Chinese to me. He is well known. So whose canon are we talking about?

INTERVIEWER: You haven't continued to translate much. Was this just something you felt you should do at the moment but that later there was too much other work to do?

SNYDER: There is a line somewhere—is it Williams who says it?— "You do the translations. I can sing." Rightly or wrongly, I took that somehow, when I ran into it, as a kind of an instruction to myself, not to be drawn too much into doing translation. I love doing Chinese translations, and I have done more that I haven't published, including the longest shih in Chinese, the Ch'ang-hen ko, "The Long Bitter Song" of Po Chü-i. So I am not just translating these tiny things. I am working right now on finishing up the P'i-p'a hsing, the other long Po Chü-i poem about the woman who plays the lute. And I've done a few Tang poems. Maybe someday I'll get to doing more Chinese translations.

INTERVIEWER: Getting back to the early poems: it's interesting that the American West is essentially invented in literary American poetry by two of your immediate predecessors, Robinson Jeffers and Kenneth Rexroth. Did you feel that they opened it up for you somehow, made it acceptable to write about?

SNYDER: Definitely. Jeffers and Rexroth both, as you say, were the only two poets of any strength who had written about the land-scapes of the American West, and it certainly helped give me the courage to start doing the same myself.

INTERVIEWER: What about the community of poets at the time? Philip Whalen, Lew Welch, Allen Ginsberg, Michael McClure, Robert Duncan, among others. One gets the sense that this was the only community of poets in which you were an active participant, that since that time you've been involved in other things. How important is a community of poets to you or to any poet? And what has happened since?

SNYDER: I think that rather than the term *community* it would be more accurate to speak of a *network* of poets. *Community* is more properly applied to diverse people who live in the same place and who are tied together by their inevitable association with each other, and their willingness to engage in that over a long period of time. But that is just a quibble.

When you are in your twenties, in particular, and you are a working, dissenting intellectual and artist, you need nourishment. Up in Portland, where I went to college, there were only a couple of other people you could talk to about poetry—Philip Whalen and Lew Welch and William Dickey. We started hearing little echoes of things in California and ended up there, all of us—for the comrade-ship, for the exchange of ideas. That was before the Beat generation broke onto the scene. I met Jack Spicer, Robin Blaser, Robert Duncan, Madeline Gleason, Tom Parkinson, Josephine Miles, William Everson, Kenneth Rexroth—that whole wonderful circle of San Francisco Renaissance people, such brilliant minds, such dedication to the art, and such unashamed radical politics. Most of them were conscientious objectors in World War II, had rejected Stalinism early on, and with Kenneth Rexroth had formulated an antistatist, neo-anarchist political philosophy, anarcho-pacifism, which at that time in American history made great sense. I was proud to be part of that circle at that time.

That group was enlarged when Allen Ginsberg and Jack Kerouac came onto the scene and the phenomenon that we are more commonly aware of as the San Francisco Beat generation poetry emerged. But it came out of that group of Duncan, Spicer, Rexroth, and Blaser that was already eight or ten years old—it wasn't just created by Allen and his friends. Through Allen I began to meet people from the East Coast. I met Kenneth Koch, Ed Sanders, Anne Waldman, Jerome Rothenberg, Don Hall, James Laughlin, Robert Creeley, Ed Dorn, and many others. I still keep in touch with many of them. A wonderful circle.

INTERVIEWER: Has the Beat thing been a burden for the rest of your life? Are you tired of hearing about the Beats?

SNYDER: I was for a while, but nobody has been beating me on the head with it lately.

INTERVIEWER: I am surprised that very young people now are so fascinated by the Beats, compared to the hippie movement. As an old hippie I think we're much more interesting. What do you think they see in the Beats?

SNYDER: Gee, I don't know if I should say this to you. When I look at the differences, one that emerges is that the political stance of the West Coast Beats was clear. They were openly political and, in terms of the cold war, it was a kind of a pox-on-both-your-houses position. Clearly our politics were set against the totalitarianism of the Soviet Union and China, and at the same time would have no truck with corporate capitalism. Today you might say, "Okay, what else is new? Do you have any solutions to suggest?" I understand that, of course, but at that time the quality of our dissent alone was enough to push things in a slightly new direction. What it led to in the poetry was a populist spirit, a willingness to reach out for an audience and an engagement with the public of the United States. This swell of poetry readings, going to all of the college towns and the big cities, which started around 1956, transformed American poetry. It was a return to orality and the building of something closer to a mass audience.

I do feel that there was a visionary political and intellectual component in the hippie phenomenon, but it is harder to track out what it is. It wasn't so clearly spoken and it was outrageously utopian, whereas the Beat generation's political stance was in retrospect more pragmatic, more hardheaded, easier to communicate, and it didn't rely on so much spiritual rhetoric. So that might be one reason, just as the punks rejected hippie spiritual rhetoric and went for a harder-edged politics, well, the Beat generation had a harder-edged politics.

INTERVIEWER: As long as we're talking about hippies, what about drugs? Obviously in the fifties and sixties you experimented with hallucinogens. Did it help or hurt the writing? Tear down obstacles or erect new ones? Or was it ultimately irrelevant?

SNYDER: That's a whole topic in itself, that deserves its own time. I'll just say that I am grateful that I came to meet with peyote, psilocybin, LSD, and other hallucinogens in a respectful and modest frame of mind. I was suitably impressed by their powers, I was scared a few times, I learned a whole lot, and I quit when I was ahead.

INTERVIEWER: Going back—you basically left the scene in 1956 to go to Japan.

SNYDER: In May of 1956 I sailed away in an old ship, headed across the Pacific for Japan.

INTERVIEWER: Why did you go? It seems like it was an exciting moment in America when you left.

SNYDER: Well, exciting as the scene was looking in 1956, I was totally ready to go to Japan. I had laid plans to go to the Far East, oh, three years prior to that, and had had several setbacks. The State Department denied me a passport for some of my early political connections.

INTERVIEWER: Would you have gone to China if the political situation had been different at the time?

SNYDER: I certainly would have.

INTERVIEWER: It would have completely changed the course of the rest of your life.

SNYDER: I'm sure it would have changed my life, although I don't know just how much, because my focus in going to the Far East was the study of Buddhism, not to find out if socialism would work, and the only Buddhists I would have found in China would have been in hiding at that time and probably covered with bruises. So it wouldn't have been a good move.

INTERVIEWER: I get the sense that you are much more attracted to Chinese poetry than Japanese poetry.

SNYDER: To some extent that's true. It is a karmic empathy that is inexplicable. I love Japanese literature and Japanese poetry too, but I feel a deep resonance with Chinese poetry.

INTERVIEWER: You stayed in Japan for ten years?

SNYDER: I was resident in Japan for about ten years, and I maintained residence there for twelve. I was away part of the time working on oil tankers and teaching at the University of California–Berkeley for a year.

INTERVIEWER: And how many years were you in the monastery . there?

SNYDER: I was in and out of the monastery. That was where my teacher lived, and I was resident in it for *sesshin*—for meditation weeks—and then out, then in again. I had a little house that I rented just five minutes walk from the Daitoku-ji monastery.

INTERVIEWER: Are you still a practicing Buddhist? Do you sit every day?

SNYDER: Almost every day. *Zazen* becomes a part of your life, a very useful and beautiful part of your life—a wonderful way to start the day by sitting for at least twenty, twenty-five minutes every morning with a little bit of devotional spirit. My wife and I are raising a thirteen-year-old adopted daughter. When you have children you become a better Buddhist too, because you have to show them how to put the incense on the altar and how to make bows and how to bow to their food and so forth. That is all part of our culture, so we keep a Buddhist culture going. My grown sons say, when they are asked what they are, because they were raised that way, "Well, we are ethnic Buddhists. We don't know if we really believe it or not, but that is our culture."

INTERVIEWER: What does *zazen* do for the poetry? Do you feel that there is a relation there that helps somehow in the writing?

SNYDER: I was very hesitant to even think about that for many years, out of a kind of gambler's superstition not to want to talk too much or think too much about the things that might work for you or might give you luck. I'm not so superstitious anymore, and to demystify *zazen* Buddhist meditation, it can be said that it is a perfectly simple, ordinary activity to be silent, to pay attention to your own consciousness and your breath, and to temporarily stop listening or looking at things that are coming in from the outside. To let them just pass through you as they happen. There's no question that spending time with your own consciousness is instructive. You learn a lot. You can just watch what goes on in your own mind, and some of the beneficial effects are you get bored with some of your own tapes and quit playing them back to yourself. You also realize—I think anyone who does this comes to realize—that we have a very powerful visual imagination and that it is very easy to go totally into visual realms where you are walking around in a landscape or where any number of things can be happening with great vividness. This taught me something about the nature of thought and it led me to the conclusion—in spite of some linguists and literary theorists of the French ilk—that language is not where we start thinking. We think before language, and thought-images come into language at a certain point. We have fundamental thought processes that are prelinguistic. Some of my poetry reaches back to that.

INTERVIEWER: You've written that language is wild, and it's interesting that, in your essays and in some of the poems, you track down words as though you're hunting or gathering. But do you believe that language is more a part of nature than a part of culture?

SNYDER: Well, to put it quite simply, I think language is, to a great extent, biological. And this is not a radical point of view. In fact, it is in many ways an angle of thought that has come back into serious consideration in the world of scientific linguistics right now. So, if it's biological, if it's part of our biological nature to be able to learn language, to master complex syntax effortlessly by the age of four, then it's part of nature, just as our digestion is part of nature, our limbs are part of nature. So, yes, in that sense it is. Now, of course, language takes an enormous amount of cultural shaping, too, at some point. But the structures of it have the quality of wild systems. Wild systems are highly complex, cannot be intellectually mastered—that is to say they're too complex to master simply in intellectual or mathematical terms—and they are self-managing and self-organizing. Language is a self-organizing phenomenon. Descriptive linguistics come after the fact, an effort to describe what has already happened. So if you define the wild as self-managing, self-organizing, and self-propagating, all natural human languages are wild systems. The imagination, we can say, for similar reasons, is wild. But I would also make the argument that there is a prelinguistic level of thought. Not always, but a lot of the time. And for some people more than other people. I think there are people who think more linguistically, and some who think more visually, or perhaps kinesthetically, in some cases.

INTERVIEWER: Getting back to Buddhism for a second. For many poets, poetry is the religion of the twentieth century. And I'm curious what you get, in that sense, from Buddhism that you don't get from poetry?

SNYDER: I had a funny conversation with Clayton Eshleman, the editor and poet, many years ago while he was still in Kyoto. Clayton was talking, at length and with passion, about poetry. And I said to him, "But Clayton, I already have a religion. I'm a Buddhist." It's like the Pope telling Clare Boothe Luce, "I already am a Catholic." I don't think art makes a religion. I don't think it helps you teach your children how to say thank you to the food, how to view questions of truth and falsehood, or how not to cause pain or harm to others. Art can certainly help you explore your own consciousness and your own mind and your own motives, but it does not have a program to do that, and I don't think it should have a program to do that. I think that art is very close to Buddhism and can be part of Buddhist practice, but there are territories that Buddhist psychology and Buddhist philosophy must explore, and that art would be foolish to try to do.

INTERVIEWER: So you mainly draw that line on ethical grounds?

SNYDER: Well, there's ethics, there is philosophy, there is the spirit of devotion, and there is simply its capacity to become a cultural soil, a territory within which you transmit a way of being, which religion has a very strong role in. And then there is the other end of religious practice and Buddhist practice, which is to leave art behind. Which is to be able to move into the territory of the completeness and beauty of *all* phenomena. You really enter the world, you don't need art because everything is remarkable, fresh, and amazing.

INTERVIEWER: So how do you keep writing?

SNYDER: Because you don't want to live in that realm very much of the time. We live in the realm of forms, we should act in the realm of forms. Jim Dodge and I once went to a Morris Graves exhibit in

Oakland, where he was arguing with me about this Buddhist position in regard to art. I was saying, "You don't need art in a certain sense, Jim." So he went to the Morris Graves exhibit looking at the Morris Graves paintings, and I went through it looking at the spaces between the paintings with as much attention, and pointing out wonderful little hairline cracks in the plaster, the texture of the light, and so forth. There is a point you can make that anything looked at with love and attention becomes very interesting.

INTERVIEWER: So you think people should read the margins of your books?

SNYDER: This is an oral art. They should listen to the unsaid words that resonate around the edge of the poem.

INTERVIEWER: Just as Chinese poetry is full of empty words, deliberately empty words for the *ch'i*, the sort of breath, to circulate through. In 1970 you moved back to the Sierra Nevadas, and you've been there ever since. I think from that moment on, when you finally settle down, you're talking much more about a poetry rooted in place.

SNYDER: Certainly a number of the poems written since 1970 reflect the position of being in a place, a spot in the world to which I always return. A lot of poems, however, do come out of my hunting and gathering trips to other territories. The idea of being a person of place never excludes the possibility of travel. To the contrary, it reminds people of place—everybody else in the world except Canadians, Australians, and Americans—that they know where they come from. They have a place to go back to. They have no difficulty answering the question "Where are you from?" But Americans often can't answer that question. They say, "Well, do you mean where I was born or where I went to high school, or where my parents live now, or where I went to college, or where my job is, or where I'm going to move next year?" That's an American dilemma. So having a place means that you know what a place means. And if somebody asks you, "What folk songs do you sing where you come from?" you have a song you can sing to them. Like in Japan, say, where you're always being asked to sing a song from your native place.

INTERVIEWER: Yes. Ours is "I Love New York in June." Do you think that sense of place is primary for the poetry?

SNYDER: Not in any simple or literal way. More properly I would say it's a sense of what *grounding* means. But place has an infinite scale of expansion or contraction. In fact, if somebody asks me now, "What do you consider to be your place?" my larger scale answer is, "My place on earth is where I know most of the birds and the trees and where I know what the climate will be right now, roughly, what should be going on there on that spot on earth right now, and where I have spent enough time to know it intimately and personally." So that place for me goes from around Big Sur on the California coast all the way up the Pacific coast through British Columbia, through southeast Alaska, out through southwest Alaska, out onto the Aleutian chain, and then comes down into Hokkaido and the Japanese islands, and goes down through Taiwan. Now that's the territory I have moved and lived in and that I sort of know. So that's my place.

INTERVIEWER: Since we're talking about your map of the world, people have wondered about the general absence of European civilization—or at least Europe after the Paleolithic—in your work. To me it's no more shocking than the absence of Asia—not to mention Africa—from everyone else's work. But still the question comes up. Is this a deliberate criticism of Eurocentrism or merely just the track your interest followed?

SNYDER: It's true that I haven't visited Europe much, but it isn't totally absent from my poetry, and there are some key points in my work that connect with occidental cultural insights that are classical, if not Paleolithic. The scholar Robert Torrance even wrote a little paper on the occidental aspect of my work. Much of the value I find in the West is in the pre-Christian, the pagan, and the matrifocal aspects, however. And I track things like connections I fancy that I can see from Greek poetics to the Arabic poetry of Spain, in turn to Lorca, in turn to Jack Spicer. And the Bogomils, Waldenses, Albigenses, shepherds of Montaillou, Anabaptists, Quakers, Luddites, Amish, and Wobblies have my gratitude, of course. And now that I'm getting old enough to enjoy hotels as well as camping I think I'll start visiting Europe. I loved Spain—I went there recently.

INTERVIEWER: I want to change gears and talk about the word *work*, which is central to all of your writing. You've written, to take one of many examples, "Changing the filter, wiping noses, going to meetings, picking up around the house, washing dishes, check-

Gary Snyder at work, 1994.

ing the dip stick, don't let yourself think these are distracting you from your more serious pursuits." What does this mean for a writer who would feel that her or his "real work" is the writing, and that all these other things are overwhelming?

SNYDER: If one's real work is the writing and if one is a fiction writer, I guess one's work as a writer really holds one to the literally physical act of writing and visualizing and imagining and researching and following out the threads of one's project. However, if one is a nonfiction prose writer or a poet, one is apt to be much more closely engaged with daily life as part of one's real work, and one's real work actually becomes life. And life comes down to daily life. This is also a very powerful Buddhist point: that what we learn and even hopefully become enlightened by is a thorough acceptance of exactly who we are and exactly what it is we must do, with no evasion, no hiding from any of it, physically or psychologically. And so finding the ceremonial, the almost sacramental quality of the moves of daily life is taught in Buddhism. That's what the Japanese tea ceremony is all about. The Japanese tea ceremony is a model of sacramental tea drinking. Tea drinking is taken as a metaphor for the kitchen and for the dining room. You learn how to drink tea, and if you learn how to drink tea well, you know how to take care of the kitchen and dining

A manuscript page from Gary Snyder's Mountains and Rivers Without End.

room every day. If you learn how to take care of the kitchen and the dining room, you've learned about the household. If you know about the household, you know about the watershed. *Ecology* means house, *oikos*, you know, from the Greek. *Oikos* also gives us economics. *Oikos nomos* means "managing the household." So that's one way of looking at it. I understand that there are other lines and other directions that poets take and I honor them. I certainly don't believe there's only one kind of poetry.

INTERVIEWER: I have a line from Auden here that "the goal of everyone is to live without working." And basically what he's saying in the rest of the passage is that work is something that other people impose on us.

SNYDER: I would agree with Auden. The goal of living is not to consider work work, but to consider it your life and your play. That's another way of looking at it.

INTERVIEWER: But how is that different from Calvinism, in the sense of extolling the virtues of work?

SNYDER: Well, work per se does not bring about salvation, nor is it automatically virtuous. It has more the quality of acknowledgment and recognition and making necessity charming. And it's not always charming, and nothing I've said should lead us to think that an oppressed worker should swallow and accept the conditions of his life without fighting back. It's none of that really. Your question catches me a little bit by surprise because I am so far removed from being a puritan in any way, and so is Buddhism, incidentally. There is a very funny quality in Buddhism, which is enjoying and acknowledging badness. So you can be bad and still be a good Buddhist. So everything I say has its reverse. "I hate work," you know, let it all go. Or as W. C. Fields once said, "If a thing is worth doing at all, it's worth doing poorly."

INTERVIEWER: Speaking of the doing of things, let me ask you about your mechanics of writing. I gather you have some complicated system of file cards, even for the poems. Can you describe that?

SNYDER: Most writers I know, and certainly prose writers, have a well-organized shop. There are moves in longer poetic projects that are very like the work of researchers. I tell young would-be poets not to fear organization, that it won't stultify their scope. I use some systems I learned from anthropologists and linguists. Now I use a computer too. A friend who's a professional hydrologist gives a good caution, "Write up your field notes at the end of each day!" And then get them into your hard disk fairly soon and always back that up. The main thing though is to give full range to the mind and learn to walk around in memory and imagination smelling and hearing things.

INTERVIEWER: Your poems are notable both for their extreme condensation and their musicality. Do the lines come out in such compact form? Are the poems initially much longer and then chipped away? Do you consciously count syllables or stresses, or do you mainly write by ear?

SNYDER: There is one sort of poem I write that is highly compressed and has a lot of ear in it. As a poem comes to me, in the process of saying and writing it, the lines themselves establish a basic measure, even a sort of musical or rhythmic phrase for the whole poem. I let it settle down for quite a while and do a lot of fine-tuning as part of the revision. Doing new poems at readings brings out subtle flaws in the movement or music to be immediately noted. I don't count syllables or stresses, but I discover after the fact what form the poem has given itself, and then I further that. Of course I write other sorts of poems as well—longer, less lyrical, formal, borrowings or parodies, and so forth. I am experimenting with switching back and forth between a prose voice and a lyric voice in some of the work I'm doing now.

INTERVIEWER: I gather that, unlike many writers, you publish very slowly—allowing things to sit for years before they're brought out in the world. Why is that? And what works are currently hanging up to dry?

SNYDER: Well, I have found that if you let a poem sit around long enough, you come to see and hear it better. Not that a poem in progress doesn't reach a point of being pretty much finished. So I don't rush it—it's a matter of allowing intuition and taste to come into play; you choose to hold on to a piece, waiting for some little turn of insight. This is true of prose writing, too. But letting it wait might be a kind of luxury sometimes because there are often urgent reasons to get things into the world, especially essays dealing with current issues. I recently finished a project I called *Mountains and Rivers Without End*—a series of longish poems that I have been working at for decades. And I'm glad I let it wait that long, it is more tasty.

INTERVIEWER: Why do you think it took so long?

SNYDER: Well of course when I launched myself into this in 1956, having just finished the book-length poem *Myths and Texts*—which only took three years—I thought it would be wrapped up in five or six years. I started studying the Lotus Sutra and some geomorphology and ecology texts as a bit of beginning research, and also I set sail for Japan. It all got more complicated than I had predicted, and the poems were evasive. So I relaxed, and thought, However long it takes. I kept my eye on it, walking, reflecting, and researching, but didn't make any big demands on the mountain-goddess muse. So it worked out to about one section a year for forty years.

INTERVIEWER: How does it feel, having completed a forty-year-long project like *Mountains and Rivers Without End*?

SNYDER: How does it feel to finish it? I'm truly grateful. Now I have further work with it though—I'm learning how to read it aloud, and I'm still learning more about its workings.

INTERVIEWER: As with Pound and the *Cantos,* did you find it impossible to tear yourself away from *Mountains and Rivers* to work on other things?

SNYDER: As I say, I was pretty relaxed about results for a long time. But I did keep a really sharp focus going, never neglected it. Through those years I also wrote and published fifteen or sixteen books. Then, between 1992 and 1996, seeing the shape of the whole forming up, I put *Mountains and Rivers* ahead of everything else—stopped all other sorts of writing, neglected the garden, let the pine needles pile up on the road, quit giving poetry readings, didn't answer mail, quit going to parties, my old truck quit running—till it was done.

INTERVIEWER: Working on a book for forty years, do you carry the germ of your next project? What *are* you going to do next?

SNYDER: What I want to do next is restart the garden and the truck, go out with the young people to some deserts and rivers and maybe cities, and reengage with a bunch of old friends. And then back to prose and the thorny problems of our time.

INTERVIEWER: You're one of the few poets whose work is accessible to a non-poetry-reading public. Yet somewhere you say—

you're talking about Robert Duncan—that it's the poetry you never fully comprehend that most engages you. I was wondering whether you consciously strike out obscurities, thinking of the general reader, to make the poetry accessible?

SNYDER: Semiconsciously. I've written a number of different sorts of poems and there's a percentage of my poetry—maybe twenty-five percent, maybe forty—that is accessible. I think partly that has been a function of my regard for the audience, my desire to have some poems that I knew that I could share with people I lived and worked with. Certainly a number of the work poems, and poems of travel and poems of place, are works that I could and did share with neighbors or with fellow workers on the job. I've always enjoyed that enormously. At the same time there are territories of mind and challenges that are not easily accessible. I've written a number of rather difficult poems. I just don't read them at poetry readings as a rule.

INTERVIEWER: Let me quickly ask you about your book of selected poems. *No Nature*, as a title, obviously takes many aback. It seems apocalyptic until you realize that it's a kind of Buddhist joke: the true nature is no nature, the nature of one's self is no nature. Is that correct?

SNYDER: Yes, and it's also a critical-theory joke.

INTERVIEWER: In what sense?

SNYDER: In that some folks hold that everything is a social construction, and I add that society is a natural construction, including the industrial and the toxic.

INTERVIEWER: It's interesting that, for someone involved as much as you are in the environmental movement, your work is surprisingly without disasters. There's very little bad news in the poetry—no Bhopals, no Chernobyls. Are you setting positive examples? Or are you just cheerful?

SNYDER: There are several poems that have some very bad news in them. Going all the way back to a poem written in 1956 called "This Tokyo." And the poem that I wrote as an op-ed piece for *The New York Times* in 1972 called "Mother Earth: Her Whales." However, I feel that the condition of our social and ecological life is so serious that we'd better have a sense of humor. That it's too serious just to be angry and despairing. Also, frankly, the environmental movement in the last twenty years has never done well when it threw out excessive doom scenarios. Doom scenarios, even though they might be true, are not politically or psychologically effective. The first step, I think, and that's why it's in my poetry, is to make us love the world rather than to make us fear for the end of the world. Make us love the world, which means the nonhuman as well as the human, and then begin to take better care of it.

INTERVIEWER: Many are surprised to discover that you're not a vegetarian and not a Luddite, but rather a carnivore with a Macintosh. This sets you apart from, on the one hand, many Buddhists, and, on the other, from a certain branch of the environmental movement. Any comments?

SNYDER: Come, come, I'm not a carnivore, I'm an omnivore. Carnivores have ridiculously short intestines! I am a very low-key omnivore at that, as are most of the Third World people who eat very little fish or meat, but who certainly wouldn't spurn it. I did a whole discussion of this question—for Buddhists—in a recent issue of *Ten Directions*, from the Zen Center of Los Angeles. The key is still the first precept: "Cause least harm." We have to consider the baleful effects of agribusiness on the global environment, as well as have concern for the poor domestic critters. Ethical behavior is not a matter of following a rule, but examining how a precept might guide one, case by case.

Now, as for environmentalists, my Earth First! and Wild Earth friends are pretty diverse, but one thing they all share is that they are not prigs or puritans. They do ecological politics as a kind of contact sport. I'm all for that.

As for computers: the word processor is not the agent of transformation, it's language that is the agent. The word processor is just a facilitating device. Keep your eye on the ball!

AUDIENCE MEMBER: I was on the phone this afternoon with my teacher, who is a Lakota. I mentioned that I was going to see Gary Snyder. And she said, "Oh, Gary Snyder. He's an Indian. Ask him if he knows it." Do you know that you are an Indian? A Native American.

SNYDER: That was very kind of her to say that. I don't know if I know I'm an Indian or not. However, I do know that I'm a Native

American. Here again is a Turtle Island bioregional point. Anyone is, metaphorically speaking, a Native American who is "born again on Turtle Island." Anyone is a Native American who chooses, consciously and deliberately, to live on this continent, this North American continent, with a full spirit for the future, and for how to live on it right, with the consciousness that says, "Yeah, my great-great-grandchildren and all will be here for thousands of years to come. We're not going on to some new frontier, we're here now." In that spirit, African Americans, Euro-Americans, Asian Americans, come together as Native Americans. And then you know that those continents that your ancestors came from are great places to visit, but they're not home. Home is here.

INTERVIEWER: But do you think that the myths that come out of here belong to everyone?

SNYDER: They belong to the place, and they will come to belong to those who make themselves members of this place. It's not that easy, however. It takes real practice.

INTERVIEWER: I'm just playing devil's advocate for a moment. I know in the seventies there were Native Americans who were criticizing you—I don't think rightly—essentially saying, "Hey, white boy, keep your hands off our coyote."

SNYDER: You know, coyote—the trickster image—is found all over the globe. In myth and world folklore, it blankets the planet from forty thousand years ago on. It is totally cosmopolitan, and we know this. So, in that sense, mythology and folklore are archaic international world heritages. The question is to understand what to do with them and how to respond to them. The stories about Coyote Old Man are in fact genuinely something that came out of Native American experience, broke through the civilization-history time barrier, and are now fully rooted in twentieth-century literature. That's something that has come across. It's quite amazing. And I'm sure that other things will prove in time to have come across like that. You can't be against it. It makes both worlds, the old and new, richer, and it testifies to the openness of the imagination.

AUDIENCE MEMBER: There are a lot of things that are splitting the country apart nowadays. Does this scare you?

SNYDER: Well, along with everyone else, I have very troubled moments about the future of the United States and our society. And it would be foolish to say that I've got any easy answers. For those who can do it, one of the things to do is not to move. To stay put. Now staying put doesn't mean don't travel. But it means have a place and get involved in what can be done in that place. Because without that we're not going to have a representative democracy that works in America. We're in an oligarchy right now, not a democracy. Part of the reason that it slid into oligarchy is that nobody stays anywhere long enough to take responsibility for a local community and for a place.

AUDIENCE MEMBER: In a radio interview several years ago, you were asked about your politics and you responded that you were an anarchist. Can you explain that, and how that really works?

SNYDER: You know I really regretted saying that on the radio. That was on *Fresh Air*. I try not to say that on the radio. In fact, I try not to even use the word *anarchist* because it immediately raises the question that you just raised, which is, "Can you explain that?" The term shouldn't be used, it has too many confusing associations. Anarchism should refer to the creation of nonstatist, natural societies as contrasted with legalistically organized societies, as alternative models for human organization. Not to be taken totally literally, but to be taken poetically as a direction toward the formation of better and more viable communities. Anarchism, in political history, does not mean chaos, it means self-government. So a truly anarchist society is a self-governing society. We all need to learn better how to govern ourselves. And we can do that by practice, and practice means you have to go to meetings, and going to meetings means you'll be bored, and so you better learn how to meditate.

INTERVIEWER: The tao of bureaucracy.

SNYDER: That's right. The tao of bureaucracy. Anybody who meditates knows how to handle boredom so then you can go to meetings. That's how I got into politics.

AUDIENCE MEMBER: You've had to submit to a very rigorous discipline in your religious practice, learning of languages, and study of poetry. Do you find your students now willing to submit to that kind of discipline?

SNYDER: You know, I never felt like I was submitting to discipline. Since I was about sixteen or seventeen, I've never done anything I didn't want to do. It was always my own choice. When I was studying Chinese, it was what I wanted to do. I could have left at any time, nobody was paying me to do it, and I didn't have any parents insisting that I do it. So, I don't know how to answer that. I've always operated from my own free choice. However, I certainly would say that a highly motivated person, willing to engage intensely with something, is not easy to find among the students I've run into. But there are always a few that have some sort of fire under them.

AUDIENCE MEMBER: What would you tell sixteen-year-olds with the world before them, what should they do?

SNYDER: This is one of the occupational hazards of being a poet. You're asked questions that you really don't know an answer for. I'd say the same thing that I say to my eighteen-year-old step-daughter: you're going to have to get a lot of formal education. And don't think that a four-year education is the end of it. Nowadays you have to go on a little bit farther or it isn't going to mean a whole lot. But even while doing education, don't think it makes you superior to uneducated people or illiterate people, because there's a tremendous amount of cultural wisdom and skill out in the Third World, out in the preliterate world that is intrinsically every bit as viable as anything that Euro-American society has created. And then the fundamental ethical precept: whatever you do, try not to cause too much harm.

—ELIOT WEINBERGER
1996

Barney Rosset

was born in Chicago in 1922. His formative years were spent in the Francis Parker School, where several politically radical teachers introduced him to socially conscious literature and to organizations like the American Student Union. After serving in the Signal Corps during World War II, commanding a photographic unit in China, he produced a feature film, *Strange Victory*, in 1948.

In 1951, he bought a fledgling literary publishing company, Grove Press, named after the Greenwich Village street where it began. For the next thirty-three years he ran it from various locations in the same neighborhood, developing Grove into a critical part of the downtown New York firmament and one of the most influential publishers of its day.

Always undercapitalized, Grove often paid low advances. But writers came to the press because it championed their work in an often hostile environment. In the fifties, repressive obscenity laws made it illegal to publish D. H. Lawrence's *Lady Chatterley's Lover* and Henry Miller's *Tropic of Cancer*. Rosset deliberately set out to overturn these laws, publishing and defending these books, and others, in court.

As the Beat generation gave way to the counterculture, Grove became the principal home for writers who challenged the American mainstream. In addition, Grove produced a magazine, *Evergreen Review*, distributed art films, and, by the late sixties, added a book club and two film theaters to its modest conglomerate. But when the sixties ended, the press abruptly hit hard times and implemented drastic cutbacks. Rosset continued the company for another fourteen years before selling it in 1985. He left the following year after disputes with the new management.

In 1988, the PEN American Center presented Rosset with its Publisher Citation for "distinctive and continuous service to international letters, to the freedom and dignity of writers and to the free transmission of the printed word across barriers of poverty, ignorance, censorship and repression."

© ASTRID MYERS

*O*n the strength of his personal tastes and left-wing convictions, Barney Rosset has developed an impressive list of authors. Attracted to
books that in some way—through their form or content—challenged the
assumptions of the status quo, Rosset published writers other presses
passed up because they were too far out, too experimental, or violated the
prevailing mores of the day. Among them were the Beats, the postwar
European avant-garde, the New American poets of the fifties, and the
playwrights of the Theater of the Absurd. Indeed many Grove writers,
who were considered iconoclasts in their day, are now regarded as central
figures in our culture: Samuel Beckett, Jack Kerouac, William S. Burroughs, Malcolm X, Frantz Fanon, Octavio Paz, Pablo Neruda, LeRoi
Jones, Alain Robbe-Grillet, Marguerite Duras, Jean Genet, Eugene
Ionesco, Frank O'Hara, Kenneth Koch, Charles Olson, Harold Pinter,
Tom Stoppard, Michael McClure, Kenzaburō Ōe, Kathy Acker, and
David Mamet.

Rosset is a wiry man with strong hands. His hair is neatly trimmed.
He speaks with a clipped staccato rhythm that communicates a charged
enthusiasm. He has a shy, introspective smile that lends him much of his
considerable charm.

The interview was culled from over a dozen conversations held between 1993 and 1996 in Rosset's East Village loft—a long, comfortable

space with a pool table in the center and Beckett play posters on the walls. On several occasions, Fred Jordan, my father and a close friend of Rosset's, who began work at Grove in 1956 and stayed for most of the next thirty years, attended the conversations.

· · ·

INTERVIEWER: When did you first read *Lady Chatterley's Lover?*

BARNEY ROSSET: When I was already at Grove. I didn't know much about that book, and actually it didn't interest me that much—only in terms of how it might help us to publish Henry Miller's *Tropic of Cancer.* It seemed to me that D. H. Lawrence was a more respected figure than Miller, that he had a higher hit on the ratings scale, so he would be easier to present as "literature" in the courts.

INTERVIEWER: What did you think of the book?

ROSSET: I didn't really like it. It affronted me in certain odd ways. It was written from a very class-conscious point of view, which didn't particularly appeal to me. Lawrence's blood-and-thunder thing really did not excite me either—he regarded sex and death as mythological. The book was also about industrialization, which he detested.

INTERVIEWER: Wasn't the use of the word *fuck* a major issue?

ROSSET: Well, there was a very graphic description of sex in the book. It wouldn't be considered graphic now, but at the time it was. When he talked about his prick he called it "John Thomas." It was like a detached person. "What does John Thomas want today?" "Oh, well he wants *you* . . . !" Ultimately it's a good book. I like it better now than I did then. I mean, politically I did not go for it, but it was there, and it had to be published. And it led to *Tropic of Cancer.* Henry Miller did not have the kind of reputation that Lawrence did. He was thought of as a sort of bum, an early Kerouac.

INTERVIEWER: The Grove edition of *Chatterley* came out in 1959. If you started the process to publish it in 1954, why did it take so long before the book came out?

ROSSET: We prepared very carefully. We decided the best thing to do was send the book through the mail so it would be seized by

the post office. We thought this would be the best way to defend
the book. The post office is a federal government agency, and if
they arrest you, you go to the federal court. That way you don't
have to defend the book in some small town. If we won against
the post office, then the federal government was declaring that
this book was not objectionable. That was the idea, and it worked
out in exactly that way. The post office has its own special court,
where the judge and the prosecutor are the same man. We brought
in all these famous writers. Malcolm Cowley was a witness. He
was particularly good because he was deaf and couldn't hear the
questions of the prosecutor—so he gave a lecture. Alfred Kazin
was another witness. Picked him up from the New School, where
I'd taken a course with him. Horace Gregory. The judge, if you
could call him that, ruled against us. We lost. Even so, I felt a great
wave of sympathy coming from him, the way he stated things and
the fact that he let us put all this evidence into the record. Getting
things into the record was really important, because the judge
who rules on the appeal only looks at what's in the record. No
new evidence was allowed.

INTERVIEWER: What happened on appeal?

ROSSET: For the appeal Cy Rembar wrote a very good brief explaining why the book was a piece of literature. He appealed
specifically on the issue of what is obscene. They had tried to ban
Lady Chatterley because they said it "appeals to prurient interests"—which meant it caused "itching" as far as we could tell. Finally we won the appeal on that basis—that the book had literary
merit. I still don't like that idea. It seems like a compromise to me.
But without my really noticing it at the time, that's what the defense became, and we won.

INTERVIEWER: You went through this with *Lady Chatterley's Lover*
just to publish *Tropic of Cancer* in the U.S. Why was Henry Miller
so important to you?

ROSSET: I first went to college at Swarthmore, and that's where I
discovered Henry Miller. *They* didn't discover him—he certainly
wasn't being taught in English class. I read *Tropic of Cancer*, which
I bought at Steloff's Gotham Book Mart on Forty-seventh Street.
Who told me about it, I don't know, but I liked it enormously and
I wrote my freshman English paper about both it and *The Air Conditioned Nightmare*. My paper was anti–United States—it was all

about what a lousy country we live in. My professor said, "Perhaps the jaundice is in the eye of the beholder," meaning my eyes and Miller's. He gave me a B minus.

At Swarthmore I got to hate Quakers. Detest them. They were anti-Semitic at Swarthmore, and there were no blacks, not one. They had fraternities! I say it with venom because I hated the idea. I was most certainly not going to join a fraternity—and nobody asked me. I really got disgusted by the whole place and was desperately unhappy. After I read *Tropic of Cancer*, I left—decided to go to Mexico. Because the book had influenced me so much, I left in the middle of the term. But I ran out of money. I never got to Mexico; I got as far as Florida and I came back. Four weeks had gone by. They had reported me missing to the United States government. My family didn't know where I was. I came back, sort of sadly. At Swarthmore if you missed two classes you automatically flunked. So I went to the dean. He said, "Well, nobody's ever done this before"—there was no precedent for it—"so let's pretend it never happened!" But you know what, I was not happy. It did not make me like him. It didn't change my mind a bit.

That paper, by the way, helped me a great deal years later. At the Chicago trial over *Tropic of Cancer* the prosecutor said, "You don't care about Henry Miller, you're only publishing him for the money." So I took this paper, written in 1940, out of my pocket and started reading it. It made a big point.

INTERVIEWER: When you published *Tropic of Cancer* in 1961, the post office didn't seize the book?

ROSSET: No, they didn't come after us, unfortunately. You can't force them to. After *Lady Chatterley*, they never got involved in obscenity suits again. They learned their lesson, I think.

But if the post office doesn't arrest you, there are still many other possibilities for arrest. The local police can go into a store and say, "Take this book off the shelves," and arrest the bookseller. In Brooklyn they came after *me*, the publisher, and charged me with conspiracy. They claimed that Henry Miller and I conspired to have him write *Tropic of Cancer*—that I commissioned him to write it *in Brooklyn* in 1933! That was a mistake, right? I would have been ten years old, and anyway he wrote the book in Paris. It was insane. Then John Ciardi wrote a two-page editorial in the *Saturday Review* blasting the government, absolutely ridiculing the district attorney. In the course of blasting them, he told the history of the book, and that really helped us. I was brought before a grand jury. It was a big room. The jury looked like nice people. The district attorney got up and said, "I understand that the children of these people on the grand jury are able to buy *Tropic of Cancer* at their local newsstand." I said, "Well, that's very good. And if their children bought that book and read it all the way through, then those parents should be congratulated!" The district attorney just got laughed out of there by the grand jury. All the cops in America had settled on page seven or something as *the* page that made the book arrestable. It's the page where the woman is shitting five-franc pieces out of her cunt, and there are wild chickens running around—the DA asked me to read it aloud. I did, and that's when the jury *really* started laughing. And then *he* started laughing. And so they dropped it. The grand jury would not indict me. That was only one of hundreds of cases, all over the country, in *every* state—literally.

INTERVIEWER: Did Henry Miller ever testify in any of those trials?

ROSSET: No, he wouldn't. He was afraid. He considered himself out of that business. He was not excited about the whole thing. It took years to convince him even to let us publish the *Tropic*s. He wasn't such a great crusader. He wrote me a letter in which he said: Now people come to Paris to buy the book, and they bring it back, and each book that gets into the United States is read by fifty people. What happens if you publish it and we actually win the case? In five years they'll assign it in college courses and no one will want to read it!

INTERVIEWER: How did you convince him to let you do it?

ROSSET: First I went to his house in Big Sur, this crazy, strange place at the top of a mountain, with a couch out on the lawn overlooking a cliff—which gave me vertigo. He was out, but his wife was there, and she was very friendly, and lovely. Miller was off seeing a daughter who was in a mental institution from a much earlier marriage. His wife told me, "When he gets here he's not going to be friendly about this. I think you should publish it, but I will pretend I'm against it, because anything I say, he disagrees with me." They divorced not too long thereafter. Sure enough, he came back and we spoke. He was very cool, noncommittal. I did my best. His wife disagreed with me. She did what she said she would do. But he was much more interested in a book he was doing then with an American painter, Abraham Rattner, who lived in East Hampton, *The Smile at the Foot of the Ladder.* He wanted to talk about that. It was not a very successful meeting. So I had to go, defeated, down the mountain and drive out of there. Afterwards nothing happened. I appealed to Jay Laughlin of New Directions. Nothing worked.

INTERVIEWER: Laughlin didn't want to do it himself?

ROSSET: He was afraid. You know, he never went to court about anything. I had always admired New Directions. But Laughlin was dilettantish to a degree that I didn't think was acceptable. Why wouldn't he publish *Tropic of Cancer*? He was very important to Miller, kept him alive, but then he wouldn't do the guy's work.

INTERVIEWER: How did you finally get permission to go ahead with *Tropic of Cancer*?

ROSSET: I got a telegram from Maurice Girodias and Henry Rowohlt in Hamburg: "Come, Henry Miller is here." Girodias was the publisher of Olympia Press in Paris; his father had published Miller in his Obelisk Press. Rowohlt was Miller's publisher in Germany. They had spoken to Miller on our behalf and were instrumental in getting his approval. I got right on a plane and went. There he was. He was in a very different mood. Much better. We played Ping-Pong. He signed the contract.

INTERVIEWER: What had Grove Press published at the time you bought it?

· ROSSET: When I bought Grove they had done three books, all paperbacks: *The Confidence Man, The Verse in English of Richard Crashaw,* and *The Selected Writings of the Ingenious Mrs. Aphra Behn* (the first English female professional writer).

INTERVIEWER: What was it that attracted you to Richard Crashaw?

ROSSET: Nothing.

INTERVIEWER: Then why did you buy the company in the first place?

ROSSET: I was doing nothing at the time and thought, This might be interesting. I think I paid fifteen hundred dollars for half—

which included the inventory. I took the inventory to my apartment on Ninth Street, all of it, in three suitcases.

INTERVIEWER: You had never done anything like this before. Did you have any business or publishing experience?

ROSSET: Well, I wasn't such a kid. I'd produced a feature film, *Strange Victory*. I'd been in the army. I was already in my late twenties.

INTERVIEWER: How did you meet Joan Mitchell?

ROSSET: I grew up with her, in Chicago. Her father was a famous doctor there, and her mother was the editor of *Poetry* magazine— her mother was a snob.

INTERVIEWER: But your family and her family were friends?

ROSSET: My father somehow made friends with them, but I couldn't. To them, I was a Jew. My Irish Catholic half didn't count. I mean, they were snobs.

Then in the late forties Joan and I lived together in the south of France near Cannes on the Riviera. I was very depressed. I'd just sit there and look out the window—it was very pretty. At night we would play bridge with this couple; they were real estate dealers. Joan knew how to play. I didn't. This guy did. His wife didn't—but she was very beautiful. So I'd sit and look at her.

INTERVIEWER: Would you say Joan was important to you in your early development, intellectually and artistically?

ROSSET: Oh, artistically, totally. Not politically. I mean I almost destroyed her, made *her* into a communist. For a painter that was bad news, because that meant socialist realism. But you couldn't keep her down.

INTERVIEWER: Her sense of aesthetics was something that she must have conveyed to you and opened your eyes to art.

ROSSET: Oh, it was an incredible experience. I had watched her change from being a realist to an abstractionist. Day by day. It was very exciting. The figures faded away. The Tour de France, the great bicycle race, went through our little town. We went and watched it

Rosset with his first wife, painter Joan Mitchell. Painting described in text.

and then chased it in a car. She did a beautiful painting. The bicycles all merged. The bicycle wheels went around together. If you saw it now you wouldn't think it was so abstract, but it was like Marcel Duchamp's *Nude Descending a Staircase*. It was absolutely key to her development, and I thought it was fantastic. Then she became more and more abstract, but that painting was key. Later I asked her about that painting, a number of times, and she said, "Don't worry, I know where it is." It was in her parents' apartment. I have a photograph of us standing in front of it. It's the only evidence I have of that goddamn painting. I don't know what happened to it.

While all this was going on we were totally isolated. But Joan had heard about the New York painters, Hans Hofmann and a little bit about Pollock. Hofmann had a school on Eighth Street, and I just felt maybe that's where she ought to be. I knew it was where I ought to be. So I said, finally, "We'd better go home." She said, "Who's going to carry my paintings—they're big!" I said, "I will, but only if you marry me." Big mistake! She said okay. We got married by the mayor. The ocean liner came and anchored offshore. The paintings went out by rowboat. All those goddamn paintings. We lived here, first on Eleventh Street, way west, almost to the White Horse Tavern—a little house in the back, a dollhouse. Later we lived on Ninth Street. Then Joan left.

INTERVIEWER: She walked out?

ROSSET: She walked out and moved to Tenth Street, where she had a studio. I waited for her to come back. I said, "Joan, you've got to come back—if you don't come back, I'm going to get divorced." "Don't get divorced," she said, "I'll come back." I waited one year. So I finally said, "I'm going to Chicago." In Illinois they have extremely liberal divorce laws if you're a resident, which we were not exactly. But *her* father, *my* father . . . So I went to Chicago. I called her. I said, "Joan, I'm getting divorced tomorrow." I charged her with desertion, and she agreed it was true. One paragraph was the whole divorce thing, and one other sentence. She kept the right to use her maiden name. That's all she wanted! That was the whole settlement.

INTERVIEWER: You got involved with many of her painter friends—Franz Kline, de Kooning, Jackson Pollock, and so on. . . .

ROSSET: All through her. Very inarticulate people. They didn't talk much. Motherwell did, but he couldn't paint so well. He had no passion. He was an academic. He talked and published books; he was a good teacher. I bought Motherwell's house in East Hampton after he had moved out. I lived there for thirty years. There were things in the house he'd left behind—including his family Bible. Didn't interest him. But he had left a little cup by Matisse, with a little erotic drawing. I told him that, and he jumped—*Where is it?* His own family Bible for generations didn't interest him. De Kooning had used his studio as his teaching place, so there were all these rolled up de Koonings. I wish I knew what happened to *them.*

INTERVIEWER: You mentioned that you had tried to get Joan to paint in a socialist-realist manner. Could you speak a little about your involvement with left-wing politics when you were younger?

ROSSET: When I grew up in Chicago, communism was my idea of personal freedom. Especially freedom to make love, right? Actually "free love" was a huge slogan used *against* the communists. I never heard the communists use it themselves—but it was implicit in communism, because Lenin said "sex should be like having a glass of water."

After the war I joined the party in Chicago. Each member of the party was supposed to sell fifty copies of the *Daily Worker* a week. I would take mine and throw them in the garbage can! I mean, the idea of going through the South Side of Chicago among all these black families and selling them the *Daily Worker* took more courage than I had! So I threw them away. Then I was voted the *Daily Worker*'s best salesman. I had the best record. I paid for them out of my own pocket. They were five cents each. Cheap. Then in 1948 Joan and I traveled to Czechoslovakia to show the film I had produced, *Strange Victory*. We were disgusted by what we saw. We got there just after the communists had taken over. It was not for the good. It was frightening. You could see the regimentation everywhere. That was the last straw. We didn't say anything, we just got the hell out and went back to France to be decadent, bourgeois slobs. That was the end of it for me.

INTERVIEWER: The theme of personal freedom, of your trying to extend your own personal freedom, was in effect the thread that runs through all the activities of Grove Press. Grove really was an extension of your personality, the defining of yourself as you published books, right? How did Samuel Beckett fit into your political vision, because he's really the opposite of an engaged political writer.

ROSSET: Absolutely. But you have to remember he was Irish. To me, that meant a lot. While he may not have been overtly political, he was very liberal, though sometimes it bothered me that he wasn't left enough.

INTERVIEWER: On the other hand, his drama was so radical it really upset the status quo.

ROSSET: They banned him in the Soviet Union. *Waiting for Godot* was not allowed. Neither was Henry Miller. The Soviets condemned them both. Miller would have been used as an example of decadence, being a very good analyst of how terrible and monstrous American culture was. That they liked, but they wouldn't publish him. I guess it must have been the sex. With Beckett, it must have been the hopelessness.

INTERVIEWER: How did you first hear of *Waiting for Godot*?

ROSSET: Sylvia Beach, who was Joyce's publisher in Paris and the owner of the Shakespeare & Co. bookstore, called me. She knew about Grove, one way or another, and she thought maybe we would like to publish *Godot*. I admired her very much; I was really struck by her effort, and she bolstered my involvement with the play a great deal. Beckett had already been turned down by Simon & Schuster. All of the established publishers would have had a much better chance at doing Beckett than Grove, right? They could have paid five times as much, but nobody wanted it. Nobody was interested.

The same was true of Ionesco. *The Bald Soprano* was put on in Paris and got a lot of attention. Don Allen, who was an important editor at Grove in the beginning, liked Ionesco very early. Beckett and Ionesco were on the scene together. They liked each other. I never heard one say anything bad about the other. At a much later date, I think Ionesco became jealous because he never achieved the same level of acclaim as Beckett . . . and he became a nasty son of a bitch, very reactionary as he got older. But they did admire each other. You have to remember that they both wrote in French, though neither one had French as his native language. Both were not that young when they started to get recognition. Both were struggling to make it in the theater, blasting away at the existing structure.

INTERVIEWER: Do you remember when you met Beckett?

ROSSET: I remember the exact moment. It was in the bar of the Pont Royal Hotel, which is next door to Gallimard. And at that time Sartre hung out there, as did Camus, and so on. I was with Loly, my wife at the time, and we were to meet Beckett at six for a drink. This very handsome gentleman walked in wearing a raincoat and said, "Hi, nice to meet you. I've only got forty minutes." He was all set to get rid of us! At four that morning he was buying us champagne.

INTERVIEWER: So you hit it off very well.

ROSSET: Right away. He was so gentle and charming. Kind.

INTERVIEWER: Beckett was extremely loyal to Grove Press, and you became close friends. How did Beckett feel about the other books that Grove published—writers like the Beats, Henry Miller?

ROSSET: I took him to lunch with Henry Miller after we won the *Tropic of Cancer* verdict in Chicago. They had known each other from the thirties; they did not like each other. Everything that you read about these two would tell you that they were not easy peo-

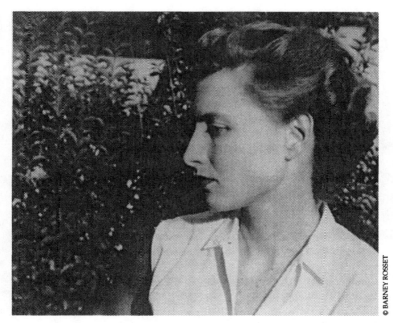

© BARNEY ROSSET

Loly Rosset.

ple to get along with. But when I brought them together, each of them told me afterwards, "Boy, has he changed! He's so nice now." I don't know what Beckett thought about Miller's writing. In one of his very early letters he asked if I had read J. D. Salinger's *Catcher in the Rye*. He said he really liked it.

William Burroughs was a writer he particularly didn't understand. There is a famous anecdote about a meeting between Burroughs and Beckett, which took place in Maurice Girodias's restaurant. I remember sitting next to Sam, while Burroughs, who worshiped Beckett, was explaining to him how you do cut-ups. Beckett said to Bill, "That's not writing, that's plumbing." Allen Ginsberg and Burroughs were very unusual in the sense that they understood that Beckett was important at that time. They wanted him, almost desperately, to recognize them, and he just didn't seem to connect. It wasn't dislike, it was just . . . nontogetherness. He just didn't get it. If he had read anything of Burroughs before he started doing the cut-ups maybe he'd have gotten it. But the Beats didn't impinge upon his consciousness. Trocchi did. Anything of Alex Trocchi's.

INTERVIEWER: When you published *Godot* you couldn't have thought of it as a potentially popular title.

ROSSET: We only printed something like a thousand copies, and the first year it sold about four hundred. It wasn't until the play was produced on Broadway a couple of years later—with Bert Lahr playing Estragon—that the book started to sell, though the production only lasted six weeks in New York. The audience walked out and Walter Winchell denounced it as the new communist propaganda. But that production made it famous.

INTERVIEWER: How many copies of *Godot* did Grove end up selling?

ROSSET: Well over two million.

INTERVIEWER: Not bad for a play so widely panned when it opened. Were there other eventual successes that you turned down?

ROSSET: I had the genius to turn down Lawrence Durrell's *Justine*. I thought it was shit.

INTERVIEWER: The title should have attracted you.

INTERVIEWER: It did, but when I read it I was very disappointed. I didn't see the connection between his *Justine* and Sade's, which we *did* publish at Grove. The story went back and forth in time. I have a real block against that. Science fiction or wandering between the centuries never appealed to me. But I tell you, if I knew how it was going to sell, I would have bought it. And if I knew how Tolkien, who was offered to me, was going to sell, you better believe I'd have published it. But I couldn't understand a word of it. I mean, I didn't object to it. It wasn't like it was a fascist tract.

INTERVIEWER: Another book Grove published in the U.S. was Jean Genet's *Our Lady of the Flowers*.

ROSSET: I discovered Genet at the Gotham Book Mart in 1940. I have a beautiful blue leather edition of *Our Lady of the Flowers* done by a French publisher in English. But Genet was impossible. He was a thief and a scoundrel and a crook. We met him in Montmartre. We were forewarned that Genet was a kleptomaniac. That night Loly was wearing very lovely earrings. We ate at a restaurant at the top of Montmartre, and Genet took us to the window.

He said, "Can you see the view, and all the things going on down there?" The whole time Loly has her hands over her ears because Genet was trying to get the earrings off! But not a word was spoken about it. Jean Genet was a thief, but he was a *real* thief. He was a thief from the inside out. Like Sartre said, he was a saintly thief.

INTERVIEWER: You're known in publishing circles to be the only publisher who would say no to a book because another publisher wanted to do it. If you were told that Knopf wanted a book, you'd say, "Let them have it."

ROSSET: Well, that makes sense, because if Knopf could publish it, then it was a Knopf book not a Grove book. Many of the books that we did were rejected by thirty or forty publishers. Some of the best books, in fact.

INTERVIEWER: Do you think that it's possible for a young publisher to do something like Grove again today?

ROSSET: In terms of editorial judgment, yes. If you had enough money. I told a friend the other night that if you want to be a publisher, you should inherit a lot of money. If you don't inherit it, then you should marry a very rich girl. Preferably both! If you don't have either, forget it. That's the history of good American publishing. It was true for Knopf, Viking, New Directions, Scribner. Marshal Field financed Simon & Schuster when they were almost broke. He was a *good* capitalist: he bought Simon & Schuster when it was at a low ebb, and when it got successful he sold it back to them for what he paid for it.

INTERVIEWER: It's also true that the success of *Lady Chatterley's Lover* and *Tropic of Cancer* brought in a lot of revenue that small publishers normally wouldn't have.

ROSSET: Today you'd have to do it very differently than we did. I don't know how you would do it with only hardcover books. That would really puzzle me. Paperback I think would be your chance, but you would have to hook it on to something special.

INTERVIEWER: Recently the Whitney Museum put on a large show dedicated to the Beat generation, to the writers and artists who were associated with that movement. A number of Grove Press publications were displayed as part of the exhibit.

ROSSET: I didn't even go to that show. The whole thing of the Beats has gotten so nebulous and open-ended—so many various writers and artists put under that same heading—that it's become meaningless to me. Jackson Pollock was in that show. I mean, if you asked Pollock about the Beats, he wouldn't have known what the hell you were talking about. The abstract painters were working with space and the relationship of color to color, how to make it move back and forth. They weren't writing about sex.

INTERVIEWER: But weren't they at least influenced by each other—they traveled in similar circles.

ROSSET: They may have been in the same room at the same time, but they wouldn't have known it. Pollock didn't read the Beats. Pollock didn't read anything. Neither did de Kooning. They were artists; they weren't writers. Sure, with Kerouac there was a certain pride in illiteracy. But the painters weren't even *aware* that they were illiterate!

INTERVIEWER: But didn't the Beat writers, when they were younger, look up to Pollock and de Kooning?

ROSSET: I never once heard any of the Beats say anything intelligible about painting. If I'm wrong, show it to me. Clement Greenberg—did he ever talk about the Beat writers? I don't think he would have stooped to that. Or Harold Rosenberg. I used to see Rosenberg all the time, and listen and listen to him. It wasn't something I thought about then, but I don't remember him ever talking about these writers. I used to drive him up to East Hampton with Elaine de Kooning. I don't remember her ever talking about Kerouac. As I say, I don't think they even knew the Beats existed. That doesn't mean that one is more important than the other. But to put them all in one place, to me sort of spoils it. The abstract expressionists were an extremely interesting, exciting group. The same with the Beats. But if you just mush them together, what you've done is lose both.

INTERVIEWER: Certainly the Beats, the pop artists, and the abstract expressionists did complement each other when they were brought together inside *Evergreen Review*.

ROSSET: But that wasn't them. That was us. We saw the connections that they didn't see.

INTERVIEWER: What did the Beat thing mean to you?

ROSSET: To me, it was writing that came out of Henry Miller. Of course, Miller didn't recognize them, either. He refused to. But the writers—Kerouac, especially, and Ginsberg—they had the same free spirit as Miller. They were a way of living, like Miller was. On the road, literally. That spirit. They reflected a feeling of the times that was antagonistic to the academy and the powers that be, as had been Miller. Sure, they were that way for very different reasons, but they were, nevertheless. That brought in a certain amount of gay people, like Ginsberg. You could relate that to Walt Whitman, whom you could relate to Miller. It was pretty much of a line.

INTERVIEWER: How did you first became aware of the Beat writers?

ROSSET: I'm sure it was through Don Allen. Don saw this outpouring of new writing coming from San Francisco. It really was a San Francisco scene. We devoted the second issue of *Evergreen Review* to those writers, like Ginsberg, Snyder, Kerouac—though very few of them were really San Franciscans.

INTERVIEWER: Whose idea was that issue?

ROSSET: Basically Don's. Of course, I knew about the City Lights edition of Ginsberg's *Howl* being banned. We printed *Howl* in the issue, but because the court case was still going on we used an expurgated version. We also already knew Kenneth Rexroth, who was a Henry Miller fanatic, so he was in it. Grove got a lot of writers out of that issue. We became, in a way, the official publishers of the Beat generation.

INTERVIEWER: The second issue of *Evergreen Review,* in 1957, was the first national publication of the Beats as a group.

ROSSET: We were hardly a major national publication. We printed maybe five thousand copies, then went back to press and printed maybe another five thousand. At a loss. We sold the magazine for a dollar, and it was very expensively done. There was a beautiful section of black and white photographs of the poets sewn into the binding.

INTERVIEWER: Was it ever your intent to publish a little literary magazine, in the tradition of the small literary quarterlies that supported the work of the previous generation of modernist writers, like Pound and Joyce?

ROSSET: That may have been Don Allen's concept. But if you look at the first issue, it never really came to be. We did Sartre and Beckett—okay, that might fit. But Baby Dodds, jazz drummer? Don was quite academic. He made people like Frank O'Hara and Kerouac and Ferlinghetti academic. I mean he made it possible for the academy to accept them. When you look in his anthology, *The New American Poetry*, which we published, you can see his influence. That book became the standard, the landmark book, and it sold and sold. It taught poetry to a whole generation of young kids. He established schools of poets with that book, you can see it in the table of contents. He wanted to create a new academy.

INTERVIEWER: If you were to say, "This is the essence of the Beat generation," what would it be?

ROSSET: Well, to me, it was two writers. Kerouac and Ginsberg.

INTERVIEWER: Not Burroughs?

ROSSET: Well, no. Burroughs was so special by himself, very special in a literary sense. The heart and soul of the Beats were Ginsberg and Kerouac: Kerouac, the heart, and Allen, the brain. Allen was the organizer, the conceptual person who guided it. He took care of everybody. He was the shepherd of the flock, in a sense, and some of the sheep were, you know, Burroughs, Kerouac, McClure. It wasn't easy to keep those people in the same line, believe me. You had to be a sheepdog to go around and find Corso or whomever. Allen molded things, like Burroughs. I mean, he brought Burroughs's manuscript of *Naked Lunch* in the door one day.

INTERVIEWER: What do you mean, he brought it in the door?

ROSSET: It was a big manuscript. We were committed to doing *Naked Lunch*, but we kept stalling because it was insane to go into the face of the wind with that book when we hadn't yet won on *Tropic of Cancer*. Burroughs would have been much harder to defend than Miller. You could make a case that Henry Miller was an established twentieth-century writer—especially after the *Lady Chatterley* case. But Burroughs was much wilder, and nobody had ever heard of him. Lawrence had set the stage for Miller, in a sense, and Miller set the stage for Burroughs. But at the time we signed the contract for *Naked Lunch*, we still hadn't won anything. We were right in the middle of *Chatterley*. Had we just gone ahead and published Burroughs it would have been a mess because we already had so many lawsuits.

INTERVIEWER: What was it that attracted you to the manuscript of *Naked Lunch*?

ROSSET: I think it's a work of genius, especially the part about the Dr. Benway character. Now, when you read it, it sounds almost coherent. But back then, well . . . it was like looking at an abstract painting. No one had ever seen anything like it before. Reading that book was *something*. It was the way that he turned the language and concepts around, using a good figure, a doctor, to send up the whole society. Of course Burroughs had strong concepts about all kinds of drugs, you know, whether they were good or bad, and also how to break your habit. That was very special to him. I can't imagine Kerouac being too involved in that particular kind of thing.

INTERVIEWER: Do you remember first meeting Burroughs?

ROSSET: I remember being around him in the sixties, in Paris and in New York. He was very quiet, sort of strange. Severe.

INTERVIEWER: Severe?

ROSSET: I remember a party that Ted Morgan gave for him, about fifteen of us there. Burroughs didn't say a word. And then suddenly, apropos of nothing, he stood up and put his finger to his head like a pistol. He said, "I don't see how people can shoot themselves in the head. All that blood." Obviously I never saw him with a real gun, shooting apples off heads or whatever . . . ! He had a very midwestern posture, almost T. S. Eliot–like. I did not think of him as in any way related to somebody like Kerouac. Kerouac was relaxed—as a person more like the painters. Burroughs was very stiff. Ginsberg was always quite calm, more and more expert at his métier. If you saw him in the beginning, he was just learning. But he kept on the same track, and he didn't go against what he did. In other words, he never said, "Oh, I was a young kid then," and drop it. He developed through the years in a natural way. Kerouac didn't last too long at being good. There were not too many years at the top. Some of the things he wrote later were really, I think, quite inferior. The last years of his life he sort of fell to pieces, and he became very angry at his book publishers, who we *weren't* by then. Thank God. I think Farrar, Straus took him on. He also had become violently anti-Semitic. He used to call me at my home in East Hampton and tell me how he hated the Jews. He'd complain about Roger Straus, or about his other publishers. To him they were all Jews . . . the Jews were after him.

INTERVIEWER: And he called *you*?

ROSSET: All the time. I'd listen to this and I'd say, "Yeah, right, yes," just hoping that he'd stay at the phone and not come and see me! Listen, I'm sure it didn't bother Allen Ginsberg, and it didn't bother me. His anti-Semitism wasn't personal. I just couldn't get him off the phone. I could be totally wrong, but he seemed to me to have a lot of violence in him, just beneath the surface. Just a little. I don't know if that was true, but it was the way he looked. I was a little afraid of him. He'd been involved in some sort of a murder scandal at Columbia University, which I was very aware of. He had a football smashed face. He looked tough. I did have one marvelous day with him. Claude Gallimard came to New York—they were publishing Kerouac—and like all French tourists they wanted to see the American beatnik. So Gallimard and two or three other people from his publishing company came to our house on Eleventh Street to meet Jack—and his mother. With his mother around, Jack behaved like a little prince. She played the piano and sang songs in French—God knows what Gallimard thought about that! Jack drank lemonade. It went off beautifully. I remember walking out the door with him—I wanted to get him out of there before something happened—and he said to me, "Hey, I carried that off pretty well, didn't I?" "Yeah, you did, thanks." And I meant it—*thank you!*—I was scared.

INTERVIEWER: Would it be possible today to start an *Evergreen Review*?

ROSSET: I don't know. There was a disaffection in the society in the fifties, as there is today. But people like the Beats, though they were disaffected, were charged with energy about it. Even Beckett was, in his own way, as was Ionesco. Now there's a malaise, but there doesn't seem to be anything creative happening in response to it.

INTERVIEWER: In 1964, *Evergreen* changed format from a trade paperback to a regular, glossy magazine. Why did you decide to go to the larger size?

ROSSET: We wanted more attention. More distribution, more readers, more advertising. But the first issue we did like that was confiscated by the district attorney in Nassau County. That was a kind of discouraging first step. I don't know how many copies got out of Nassau County alive.

INTERVIEWER: Why was it confiscated?

ROSSET: It was seized because of photographs I had brought back from Paris, pictures of nudes by Emil Cadoo that we printed in the issue. We also used one for the cover. They're beautiful photos, and now they would be given a PG rating. They're very cloudy, and you'd have to have a fair amount of imagination and ingenuity to see anything happening in them. But the district attorney apparently did. He came from a place appropriately named Hicksville, Long Island. The issue was printed there, and it was all ready to be bound, but a woman who worked there had a husband who was a detective for the vice squad. She went home to him and reported this terrible stuff that we were publishing, and it all ended up in the district attorney's office. They took all the copies to the police station, unbound. It was a mess. That issue was never bound properly. So Cy Rembar, who was one of our lawyers, started a lawsuit using a rarely used law from 1898 against the district attorney, personally, for arresting us. And it worked. He finally said, "Leave me alone and I'll leave you alone."

INTERVIEWER: That issue of *Evergreen*, number 32, has fiction by Norman Mailer, Jean Genet, Burroughs, Ionesco, and Robert Musil, poems by Günter Grass, Michael McClure, and Lenore Kandel, and a play by Rolf Hochhuth. Pretty impressive lineup.

ROSSET: The change in format did not change the tenor of the magazine—except that we added the photographs, in color. I felt that there ought to be a larger audience for what we were doing. We'd reached a plateau in circulation in the small size, about 20,000 an issue, and nothing we did managed to break through that ceiling. I felt that the small size was a format that limits you to a particular audience. The trade-paperback format worked in the begin-

Controversial covers of Evergreen Review.

ning, because we were able to confuse bookstores as to what we were. We were treated as both a book and a magazine—we got the best of both worlds. But it kept us within a certain circle. With the large format, circulation eventually grew to over 150,000. Then with the next issue, number 33, we had another problem with a printer. We published a poem by Julian Beck that ended with the line, "Fuck the USA." They wanted us to take the line out. We said, would it be all right if it read "Fuck the Soviet Union"? They said sure—a very good example of what we were up against at the time. Probably if the poem said, "I don't like the United States," that would have been all right. "Fuck the Soviet Union" was all right. But to put the two together . . . ! We lost that printer. We kept losing printers, one after another.

INTERVIEWER: Aside from the Julian Beck poem, that issue has fiction by John Fowles and Kerouac, excerpts from Jakov Lind's *Soul of Wood* and Brautigan's *Trout Fishing in America*, a piece by Michael O'Donohue, Jan Kott's essay "King Lear or Endgame," and an essay on writing for the theater by Harold Pinter. You also included some of the Cadoo photos from the previous issue with a paragraph about the confiscation of the magazine by the Nassau County DA. After having problems with one printer, you went to another printer and published the same photographs!

ROSSET: That is *very* funny! We thought we'd try it again! We used the occasion to say this is what we did last time and what got them upset. The new printer was willing to print the photos, but not the poem! We published it anyway.

INTERVIEWER: Though Grove started out primarily as a literary publisher, over time the company did more books of an overtly political nature, like Frantz Fanon's *The Wretched of the Earth* and *The Autobiography of Malcolm X*.

ROSSET: Fanon was published by a very left-wing, radical French publisher, who we bought it from. It was a more important book for Africa, Algeria in particular, more than here. I mean, people here had a lot of terrible problems and poverty, but nothing like in Africa.

INTERVIEWER: The black nationalists sure took it up.

ROSSET: Far more than Martin Luther King. The Black Panthers, definitely. It was a revolutionary book. Malcolm X, though, I don't know. He wasn't political in that socialist way. Malcolm X was very revolutionary when it came to the treatment of black people in this country, and so on, but I don't think he had Fanon's kind of insight about political organizing and economic analysis. I wonder if Malcolm X ever heard of Fanon. I doubt it. No, his movement got translated into Muslim practice. That never impressed me as being brilliant politically. It still doesn't.

INTERVIEWER: Didn't Grove acquire *The Autobiography of Malcolm X* after he had been assassinated?

ROSSET: The book was already in galleys when we got it. Doubleday was the original publisher, but they gave it up. In the paper, Nelson Doubleday said, "I don't want my secretaries to be killed because of this book." We paid twenty thousand dollars not to Doubleday, but to Alex Haley. I don't think Haley would have let any money slip away from him.

INTERVIEWER: What was it about Malcolm X's book that attracted you to it?

ROSSET: Malcolm X got assassinated, that's number one. He was a renegade who had something very interesting to say—powerful social comments to make about poverty and our government. The book is brilliant. Of course, he was much less of an establishment figure than he is now. In those days he was really a fringe person. Now he is a saint. He was a very exciting figure, very articulate. At the time he made that one terrible statement, though now in retrospect it doesn't seem so off base. When Kennedy was assassinated he said, "The chickens have come home to roost." Then it sounded awful—nasty and violent. But it was true. All the enemies that Kennedy created came back to haunt him. And it happened to Malcolm X, too. He was almost assassinated at least once before. His house was burned down. He was living in constant danger.

INTERVIEWER: Aside from publishing black nationalists like Fanon and Malcolm X, Grove was also doing books by Che Guevara and Fidel Castro.

ROSSET: Fanon didn't write anything for us. He'd written a little masterpiece, but we got a book that was already done. With Che and Castro it wasn't so easy. I mean, there you had to be inventive.

INTERVIEWER: Inventive in what way?

ROSSET: Well, Fred Jordan and I flew to the mountains of Bolivia in search of Che's diaries after he was assassinated. Everyone was trying to get that diary, including the CIA. We got a tip from the Cuban delegate to the UN. Eventually we found some pages in Cochabamba and published them in *Evergreen* in a whole issue dedicated to the spirit of Che. Paul Davis did a painting of Che for the cover; we made a poster of it and put it all over New York, in the subway and at bus stops. It was everywhere. That aggravated the anti-Castro Cubans and, I think, led directly to the bombing of Grove.

INTERVIEWER: The bombing of Grove?

ROSSET: One night in 1968 there was a series of bombings, ten or eleven, by a group who identified themselves as anti-Castro Cubans. They blew up Japan Air Lines, the Canadian Consulate, and they thought they'd blown up the apartment of the UN delegate from Cuba—except they got the wrong apartment. We were one of the targets. I met a guy who lived across the street from Grove and actually saw it happen. In the middle of the night some people drove past the office in a pickup truck and launched a rocket through the second floor window. Pow! Better than the Bay of Pigs! They caught the guys who did it, and it turned out that they were all reserve officers in the American Air Force who had also been working for the CIA at one time or another. So at the trial the judge announced, "These are good people, they never did anything before." He let them go.

INTERVIEWER: When did you hear about the bombing?

ROSSET: Shortly after it happened. Early in the morning I got a phone call from my secretary. She was the first one to go to the office. The police were the only ones in the building before her. She noticed a stab wound in the Paul Davis Che poster on the first floor. The police did that, not the Cubans. The Cubans just drove by; they didn't stop.

INTERVIEWER: What was it about Che and Castro that you thought was worth the risk?

ROSSET: I liked what they were doing. They were anticolonialists at a very high level; they were romantic figures. . . . As if Kerouac had been political, let's say. Later Fidel double-crossed me with his puritanism . . . when he went into the homophobe thing. That was terrible. And Che left, you know. It's one thing when you're on the outside fighting for the revolution, it's another thing entirely when you've won. After they took power, Che had to leave Cuba; there was no place for him. He left and went up into Bolivia, into *Bolivian* you might say. That's a pun. Even so, I think what Castro did, with all the ups and downs, was quite marvelous. And it still is. The insanity of this country not to be able to surmount a few fanatics in Miami. It is tragic.

INTERVIEWER: In the sixties, Grove also did many New Left and counterculture books, like how to dodge the draft, books about drugs. Mass-market paperbacks.

ROSSET: We found ourselves immersed in an audience, right? It was suddenly more saleable, or commercial. It was a part of the times. The flood was on our side for a moment. I keep thinking of that wonderful photo of Burroughs, Allen, and our editor Dick Seaver at the Chicago convention in 1968, amongst all those goddamn cops! The people I had at Grove were hardly against me. We were pretty much on the same course.

INTERVIEWER: As the sixties progressed, Grove published quite a lot of writing and art that was influenced by psychedelics.

ROSSET: To me that was a sideline phenomenon. It didn't intrigue me quite as much as it did others in the company. Certainly, it was of very great importance to Burroughs and Ginsberg, so that was of interest. I did not like Timothy Leary. He made psychedelics into a religious thing. I admired Leary for escaping from jail in California. That was his high moment to me! I would have helped him do that. Nothing else. I was outside of it. But not outside of *taking* drugs, if somebody gave them to me. I took LSD, which I didn't like.

INTERVIEWER: When was that?

ROSSET: The very early sixties. Allen Ginsberg and Timothy Leary gave LSD to me and a woman friend of mine. I'd never met Leary before, or really even heard of him. They came to my place on Eleventh Street—Leary, Allen, and his friend Peter Orlovsky. Leary gave us this big handful of pills. Well, I suppose we didn't have to take them . . . but he was from Harvard. He seemed kind of respectable. At that time acid wasn't that well known. I'd heard of it, but I didn't know anything about it. But it had an *effect*, I'll tell you. My apartment had two floors, and the three of them went upstairs and turned on African music and danced while my friend and I became paranoid. We backed into the corner of the room we were in. We couldn't figure out what was happening. Joan's paintings kept coming out of the wall, and I'd go and push them back into the wall! But my friend was in a state of terror. Then Allen came to us, and he told us something that night I have never forgotten: he taught me how to throw up. It was fantastic. I had an absolute phobia about throwing up, and ever since that night I can throw up on command. It doesn't bother me at all. He taught me how to relax, that throwing up is not a bad thing. He coaxed and coaxed, to get rid of some of the LSD. And it worked.

The next day I went to Grove Press, and when I came back to the apartment my friend was lying unconscious in a big pool of blood in the living room. She had tried to commit suicide—slit her wrists with a razor. Thank God she was still breathing. So I picked her up, got her upstairs. The building had four floors. Fred Praeger, the publisher, was my tenant—he had the other two floors. Praeger was an acknowledged CIA agent. He was coming down the stairs with this guy in a black suit and a white handkerchief in his pocket. I said, "Can I borrow that?" I made a tourniquet from his handkerchief. St. Vincent's Hospital was one block away, thank God, and I got her there. It took them three hours to sew her up.

INTERVIEWER: What an insane experience.

ROSSET: Afterwards Leary said it was my fault because I hadn't guarded her for seventy-two hours or something. So he takes her to Massachusetts—and he tried to get married to her! She would call me and say, "I don't know if I should marry Leary." I'd say, "Don't do it!" He convinced her that her bad experience was my fault, that I didn't nurture her properly and create the right environment for her. Then I got a letter from him with all these questions about the LSD. It had questions like, after you took the LSD did you feel (a) 10 percent better, or (b) 20 percent better, and so on. How did this affect your religious feelings? Did you have more of a feeling of God? I was so infuriated that I gave it to somebody I knew from Harvard Medical School, a psychiatrist. He said, after reading it, "I am ashamed to be associated with Harvard!" Shortly after that they threw Leary out.

INTERVIEWER: How did Grove get involved with Abbie Hoffman and *Steal This Book*?

ROSSET: Jerry Rubin's girlfriend, Nancy Kurshan, used to work for us at *Evergreen*. Abbie at that point had done a couple of pieces for *Evergreen Review*, and so had Jerry, I think. I never really liked ei-

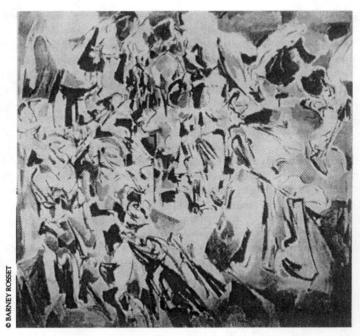

*The Mitchell painting out of which came the shapes that terrified
Rosset when he took LSD with Leary.*

ther of them. Coming from an orthodox political standpoint, I dis-
trusted the Yippie idea. I felt they were making use of the moment
to a very strong degree. To me, Allen Ginsberg was real, as were
Kerouac and others. But I always thought that Abbie and Jerry
were somehow using the political climate to suit themselves,
though certainly with a great deal of dash, talent, fervor, and madness. They were the cream, the froth at the top of the wave, but I
really never trusted them.

INTERVIEWER: Then why did you publish them?

ROSSET: Abbie brought us *Steal This Book* because, though Random
House had been publishing him and were happy to have him as
an author, they wouldn't publish *Steal This Book*. I made a point to
never look at that book. I never opened it. To me, if Random
House wouldn't publish it, that was enough: we would do it. We
arranged with him that he'd publish it himself and we would dis-

tribute it. There was a moral imperative for us to do something because here was a guy fighting for the things that we believed in,
and he was being censored by his publisher.

INTERVIEWER: Did you have problems getting the book into bookstores?

ROSSET: Well, at that time Grove Press was actually being distributed by Random House. Abbie called his publishing company Pi-
rate Editions—the spine of his book was a picture of Random
House being blown apart. So obviously we couldn't distribute it
that way. We had to make deals with other distributors and give
them an extra 10 percent discount. Because people *did* steal the
book. It wasn't exactly popular with the conservative elements of
our society. Also, it had instructions about how to make Molotov
cocktails.

INTERVIEWER: In 1976, Vice President Nelson Rockefeller headed
up a government commission to investigate covert domestic operations by the CIA against perceived enemies of the U.S. government. When the report was issued, Grove Press was cited as one of
the principal targets. Wasn't Grove one of the only commercial
businesses targeted by the COINTELPRO program?

ROSSET: Yes. So we tried to get our files under the Freedom of Information Act. Ultimately we got something like ten thousand
pages of documents. In the process we discovered that they had
found another Fred Jordan, in Illinois or somewhere. It was a case
of mistaken identity. They had the two mixed up. Then they found
another Rosset, who was also in the Communist Party during
World War II, if you can believe that. Whatever I did was bad
enough, but they also added to it what this other guy did.

INTERVIEWER: When did the FBI begin keeping files on you?

ROSSET: At college. I was one of those "Jewish radicals" at UCLA,
which is where I went after I left Swarthmore. They had my files
from my grade school in Chicago, Frances Parker. Once I was
asked the question who is the most important person in the
world? I was twelve years old. I said Benito Mussolini. I had read
a book called *Sawdust Caesar*, which was very anti-Mussolini. I
wrote to the author, George Seldes, a few years ago and told him:
Do you know all the trouble you caused me? They carried that

statement in my files for fifty years. They were trying to say I was pro-fascist. Then, during the war, I had trouble getting into officers' training school because they thought I was a communist. They also thought I was a Japanese spy. They couldn't decide!

INTERVIEWER: Why did they think you were a spy for Japan?

ROSSET: Because I knew two girls from my high school who were half Japanese—both married to people in the American armed forces, I might add. The FBI said that I consorted with "Japanese whores."

INTERVIEWER: You got in the army nonetheless and while there you studied film, and after the war you produced a feature film, *Strange Victory*. So there was a natural connection between your early interests and when Grove began to distribute films.

ROSSET: We had a collection of important, avant-garde films that nobody else had, which started when I bought Cinema 16 in the early sixties. Maya Daren, Stan Brackhage—we had all his stuff. Some Kenneth Anger. We had Jack Smith's *Flaming Creatures*. And a film by Genet, the only film I know of that he made, and it's marvelous. Actually, that film lost before the Supreme Court. It is still theoretically illegal to this day. Many, many films. We had a couple of Lenny Bruce's movies, Godard's *Weekend*, some great Czech films.

INTERVIEWER: But the biggest success was definitely *I Am Curious (yellow)*. How did you come across it?

ROSSET: During the Frankfurt book fair, I read an article in the Manchester *Guardian* about this Swedish film, *I Am Curious (yellow)*. I thought, That's for us, how do we get it? So Christine, my wife, and I got on a plane from Frankfurt. I bought it right there on the spot for a hundred thousand dollars. That was a lot in those days.

INTERVIEWER: Knowing full well that this film was going to have trouble when it got to the U.S.

ROSSET: Right. But it was serious—about class struggle in Sweden, and about women's rights. Supposedly it had a lot of sex in it. Male frontal nudity. It's about a young girl whose father was in the civil war in Spain—the only thing he ever did in his life. She's doing a study of classism in Sweden, and she decides that the upper class in Sweden are as bad as they've ever been—terrible. Her boyfriend exploits her, and she practically kills him. She's running her own sad little world. That's what it's about. And it's not very happy—there is some sex in it, but I mean . . . very little.

INTERVIEWER: But that's what got everyone's attention.

ROSSET: I suppose! It was another one of those things. People showing it ended up arrested all over the country. We had to go from state to state, again. When our case came up before the Supreme Court, Justice Douglas, whom we once published in *Evergreen*, excused himself. The decision was four to four, which meant that the old decision, which we lost, stood. To this day it's against the law to show *I Am Curious (yellow)*. But by that time the question was moot, because we'd already shown the movie in every major city in the country.

INTERVIEWER: You must have made a lot of cash from that film.

ROSSET: *I Am Curious (yellow)* was a big success. But it was a disaster for us in many ways. Because we made a lot of money, I went and bought a lot of foreign films—which were no longer commercially viable because all the art theaters had closed down, overnight, in 1970. They had started showing X-rated porno films. There had been a big market for foreign films in this country, and suddenly it was gone. After *I Am Curious (yellow)* played, that was the end. We killed our own market.

INTERVIEWER: And Grove had put a lot of money in European films?

ROSSET: Hundreds of thousands. How did I know there wouldn't be a market there the next day? We had destroyed it! And there was no VCR. No cassettes. And no theaters. But we had all the fucking films.

INTERVIEWER: Between the mid-fifties and the late sixties, Grove had grown quite large.

ROSSET: Well, when Fred Jordan came Grove was four people, including the accountant. Fred started doing business and sales, but

I couldn't constrain him to that. He leaped over to editorial, sort of imperceptively. When I hired Dick Seaver to be an editor in 1959, there still weren't many people. Dick was also very important to the company. But by this time we had about three hundred people. We had a book club, a warehouse, a film department. We moved into this huge building on Mercer Street. We had a special executive elevator.

INTERVIEWER: Pretty exclusive.

ROSSET: We lost touch with the masses. I'm only half joking. The whole thing was not for real. It was an unreal time.

INTERVIEWER: That feeling of unreality must have grown throughout the sixties, as the underground became more popular and drugs became so much a part of the scene.

ROSSET: Yes, it did. We had our book club in a place on Varick Street. When you walked in you knew that half of the people working there were turned on. Over on Hudson Street, in the warehouse, we had people stealing more books than we were shipping. Even the union allowed us to hire detectives! It didn't help. They were taking them out in truckloads. We finally had to give the warehouse up. Not long after that we had to let almost everybody go.

INTERVIEWER: Surely, considering the content of both the books and films you must have had problems with the feminist movement?

ROSSET: One morning I was with Fred in Copenhagen. I got on the phone with my secretary. I said, "How are things?" "I'm not in your office today. I'm one floor down." "Oh, why?" "Well, your office is occupied by all these women." It was the height of Women's Lib. They demanded that we build a child-care center and that we pay a royalty from our erotic "Anonymous" titles to the prostitutes of New York City!

INTERVIEWER: Did they do any physical damage?

ROSSET: Well, they broke up the furniture, but who cares? In fact, in court they claimed they did more damage than they actually did! They *wanted* to go to jail. In order to get them off we had to say they didn't do anything. This was Cy Rembar's finest hour.

He fought to get them off, though we were supposed to be the prosecution. First, we arrested them, then told the cops to let them go—cops don't like that.

INTERVIEWER: Many people like to think of publishing as a gentleman's profession. Obviously you saw Grove differently. It was much more confrontational and took risks, financial and otherwise, that other publishers wouldn't take. You never thought of Grove as a publishing company in the way that people thought of Knopf or Random House?

ROSSET: No. And neither did they. Neither did the Knopfs or Random Houses think of us that way.

INTERVIEWER: How did they think of Grove?

ROSSET: Bennett Cerf, of Random House, was extremely cordial and friendly. But Alfred Knopf was hostile. He thought we weren't in the same class with him. When I say class, I mean what's thought of as class in society. He came from what he considered a great aristocracy of wealth and tradition and so on, and we hardly fit in. When he did *Lady Chatterley's Lover*, he expurgated it. Over my dead body would I have done that. And Knopf didn't appreciate that, you know. Robert Bernstein, then president of Random House, I think, said of Grove . . . well, he was speaking of me. He said I was a maverick. Not in the mainstream. He was right.

—KEN JORDAN
1997

Lawrence Ferlinghetti

"Only the dead are disengaged," says Lawrence Ferlinghetti of his commitment to art. A teacher of French language and English literature; a book reviewer for the *San Francisco Chronicle;* a painter, businessman, and poet; Ferlinghetti is perhaps best known for promoting dissident literature. Born in 1919 in Yonkers, New York, he spent his childhood shuttling between an aunt, an orphanage, and family friends. His father died before he was born and his mother, like Ginsberg's, was institutionalized. Without guidance, Ferlinghetti joined a street gang and was sent to reform school before finally enrolling in Columbia College. There he studied with Mark Van Doren and Lionel Trilling. After briefly serving in World War II, he received his M.A. from Columbia in 1948 and his Ph.D. from the Sorbonne in 1951.

In 1953, he moved to San Francisco, where he opened City Lights Bookshop, the first all-paperback bookstore in the country. The store became a hotbed of Beat activity, hosting readings, events, and meetings for Beat writers. In 1955, Ferlinghetti founded the City Lights Books Press, which published Beat literature throughout the fifties and sixties, most notably Allen Ginsberg's *Howl* and Ferlinghetti's own collection of poetry, *A Coney Island of the Mind* (1958).

The publication of *Howl* in 1956 gained City Lights international renown. For his role as publisher of the indecorous poem, Ferlinghetti was tried on charges of obscenity. In what became a landmark victory for freedom of speech advocates, he was ultimately acquitted. The incident drew attention not only to Ferlinghetti and Ginsberg—the book rapidly sold over ten thousand copies—but to the insurgent ideologies of the Beat writers at large.

Other poetry collections include *Open Eye, Open Heart* (1973), *Landscape of Living and Dying* (1979), *Love in the Days of Rage* (1993), and *A Far Rockaway of the Heart* (1997).

© ABRAHAM ARONOW, COURTESY OF CITY LIGHTS BOOKS

*W*ashington Square lies at the center of San Francisco's North Beach district. A well-manicured plot of dark green grass, the arbored square is lined with benches and rests in the shadows of the white-washed towers of Sts. Peter and Paul church. From one corner of the square, at the intersection of Union and Stockton Streets, a lightless alleyway ends abruptly at the foot of a squat, gray building. The alley is called Via Ferlinghetti, named after Lawrence Ferlinghetti in honor of his legendary bookstore, City Lights. With its unswept wooden floors and sagging shelves, its chaotic stacks and handwritten signs, the store provides a popular haven for the bookish. It is a San Francisco landmark.

Though he is now seventy-eight years old, Ferlinghetti still participates in the operations of City Lights Bookshop and its publishing efforts. This interview took place in the offices above the bookstore, which Ferlinghetti has occupied for the last forty-five years. He wears blue jeans and a pale blue Oxford shirt, not dissimilar to the color of his eyes. The *crown of his head is smooth; the silver hair of his temples and beard is closely cropped. In his right ear, he wears a shiny hoop which he spins between his thumb and forefinger in moments of reflection. A small staff circulates around us as we speak. Behind Ferlinghetti's desk rests a glass-encased bookshelf housing a collection of first edition City Lights printings. Large windows look out onto Columbus Avenue. Rush hour is nearing and we compete with the din of passing traffic. Adding to the commotion, it is just before a Columbus Day weekend and the navy's squad of precision jet pilots, the Blue Angels, are practicing overhead for an upcoming performance. They pass frequently at low altitude, causing windowpanes to quiver. After a particularly deafening pass we begin.*

．．．

INTERVIEWER: I'd like to start by getting some of your reminiscences about the Beat writers and the Beat movement.

FERLINGHETTI: As if it were all over? It's really a continuing tradition in American writing, going back to Walt Whitman and Poe and Jack London, beyond the Beats, who were only one phase of this literature, continuing today in new outsiders.

INTERVIEWER: Still, you are one of the few left. What was it like when you came to San Francisco in 1950? Is that where you first became involved with the Beats?

FERLINGHETTI: Well, I *really* wasn't one of the them. It was only when we opened up City Lights bookstore in San Francisco in 1953 that I started meeting the new American poets. Poets naturally congregate in bookstores. Then we started publishing. Allen Ginsberg's *Howl* was the fourth book we published and that was in 1956.

INTERVIEWER: When you first came to San Francisco, what was your intention? Did you want to open a bookstore?

FERLINGHETTI: No, I didn't. I was an unpublished writer and my intention was to be a published writer, not primarily a poet. I had written a novel in Paris and it didn't get anywhere in New York. I was teaching. Because I had this doctorate from the Sorbonne, I thought I had to be a professor. I tried it and realized I definitely wasn't cut out for it. For a while I taught at the University of San

A City Lights gathering, 1965. Front row: *Robert LaVigne, Shig Murao, Larry Fagin, Leland Meyezove (lying down), Lew Welch, Peter Orlovsky (looking up).* Middle row: *David Meltzer, Michael McClure, Allen Ginsberg, Steve (friend of Ginsberg), Gary Goodrow.* Back row: *Stella Levy, Lawrence Ferlinghetti (with umbrella), Daniel Langton, Richard Brautigan, Nemi Frost.*

Francisco, which was strictly a Jesuit university. I thought it would be like Fordham in New York. But it wasn't. One day I was teaching an upper-division course in Shakespeare to a group of nuns. A book on homosexual interpretations of Shakespeare's sonnets had just come out while I was reviewing books for the *San Francisco Chronicle.* So I brought this book to class and while I was holding it up to discuss it, the head of the department walked in. He was a Jesuit with an M.A. . . . . He just stood there shaking his head and then walked out. One wasn't even supposed to mention the word "homosexual" in the fifties in Catholic classes. So that was the end of my brilliant teaching career. I wasn't cut out to be a teacher anyway. I was too selfish and too interested in doing my own writing.

It gave me a headache to think about getting up in front of a class every morning. It still does. I'd rather be dreaming, walking the waterfront, hanging out in cafés, painting deathless nudes.

INTERVIEWER: You weren't interested in talking to students about your craft, about poetry?

FERLINGHETTI: Of course not. The fashionable obsession with "craft" in poetry and with "process" in painting these days is really a way to be a poet or a painter without having much to say. As if "craft" or "process" could replace imagination and genius vision. Could you imagine Shelley discussing "craft"?

People like Allen Ginsberg, who was a great teacher, loved teaching. He ended up teaching at Brooklyn College for the last decade of his life. Because I first published the Beats, I was grouped with them as a poet and my poetics were assumed to be the same as theirs, whereas actually my poetics are totally opposed to Allen's.

Since Allen Ginsberg died, the press really has been looking for a spokesman for the Beat generation. I was supposed to go to Prague last spring and I was scheduled to go just about the time Allen died. When he died, I canceled the trip. And they said, "Well, that's too bad. There were going to be thousands at the train station to meet you!" As if I were Allen—I am not eager to meet thousands at train stations. Allen loved it. He got his energy from the crowd. Thus he could perform no matter how sick he was offstage.

INTERVIEWER: In what ways are your poetics different from Ginsberg's?

FERLINGHETTI: Allen's school of poetry, which is a definite school in this country, is in the Naropa Institute in Boulder, Colorado, where he and Anne Waldman founded the Jack Kerouac School of Disembodied Poetics. I would call it the "graph of consciousness" school of poetry because the poetry, as conceived and as defined in this manner, is exactly what goes through your consciousness at any particular moment. The poem becomes a literal transcription—with as little interference and censorship as possible—of the mind's action. The surrealists would have called this automatic writing. But Allen was a Buddhist—his poetry was influenced by "first thought, best thought," a Buddhist concept. Ginsberg had a crazy, creative mind, really a genius consciousness, a sort of a rat-pack mind that siphoned everything from all directions: whatever he wrote down on the page was always interesting. If the mind is comely, everything that mind produces is comely. I'm paraphrasing Allen. But when you have many students taking classes using the graph of consciousness technique, you get many whose minds really aren't all that interesting. They're not genius conceivers and their poems may be quite boring. A poem about what went through your mind while brushing your teeth must have more in it than water and toothpaste. A "sawmill haiku" must saw off more than wood.

INTERVIEWER: What did you think of Burroughs's cut-up technique?

FERLINGHETTI: Those guys were real cut-ups. Burroughs got the idea from Brian Gysin and Harold Norse. Norse claims to have given the idea to Brian Gysin at the Beat hotel in Paris, but it was obviously an outgrowth of dadaist and surrealist methods. It was nothing new to world literature; it was new to America. I've tried cut-up when just fooling around. But I don't want to ruin my poem by cutting it up. I'm not going to take a statue, a lovely, perfect statue, throw it on the ground, pick up the pieces at random, and paste them on the wall, or leave them strewn around on postmodern gallery floors with an inscrutable title.

INTERVIEWER: You have said that you find Gregory Corso more original than Ginsberg.

FERLINGHETTI: When did I say that? But, yes—that's true, I think. And Allen would have agreed. Corso's poems are so thoroughly original that they never imitate or echo great classic lines. When we published *Gasoline* in 1958, it was the second most important Beat book we published after *Howl*. Introduction by Allen Ginsberg: "Mad mouthfuls of language . . . He's got the angelic power of making autonomous poems like God making brooks." Jack Kerouac felt similarly about Corso. Kerouac once wrote that he was "a tough young kid from the Lower East Side who rose like an angel over the rooftops and sang Italian songs as sweet as Caruso and Sinatra, but in words." Corso is certainly the most important Beat poet after Ginsberg. Shelley is his first love, but he's the most American of poets—great original pure American lingo! The late proletarian poet Jack Micheline is close to him in language. Corso is a great tragic poet, often a tragic-comic poet, and so was Micheline, who has been much ignored as one of the important original Beats.

INTERVIEWER: Kerouac said in his interview with *The Paris Review* that he didn't believe in any Beat community. He said you and Ginsberg were interested in that sense of community and wanted to create what he called a "frenetic kibbutz."

FERLINGHETTI: Allen certainly did. Jack didn't want to have anything to do in groups. When he became famous overnight after the publication of *On the Road*, he immediately started cutting out. He didn't want to be around. He couldn't handle the fame. The way he handled it was to drink more and more.

But the Beats were a community, driven by three main motors. One of them was Allen Ginsberg himself and what some people called "Allen Ginsberg Industries." He kept a New York office with other poets employed full time, disseminating his messages and supporting many poets. Even while Ginsberg was dying, he was still calling up all his old friends around the country to ask, "Do you need any money?"

The second motor, chronologically, was City Lights Bookshop as a literary meeting place and as a publisher. We were a center where the press could come and find out what was happening and that's still the way it is today. The third motor is the Naropa Institute's Kerouac School of Disembodied Poetics.

INTERVIEWER: On the eve of publishing Ginsberg's *Howl*, had you anticipated the reaction?

FERLINGHETTI: Yes indeed! We submitted it to the San Francisco chapter of the American Civil Liberties Union before it went to the printer to see if they would defend us if we were busted for it. They committed themselves ahead of time. And thank God for the ACLU because we would have been totally out of business without them. We were just a little one-room bookstore. The forces of censorship in the fifties, like McCarthy's Un-American Activities Committee, knew very well they could drive a small, dissident organization out of existence just by indicting us. They knew we wouldn't have any resources. Luckily, we won the trial. It put Allen Ginsberg on the map and put us on the same map as a small dissident publisher.

INTERVIEWER: Did that create a lot of momentum afterwards?

Allen Ginsberg, Anne Waldman, and Gregory Corso at the Naropa Institute, 1975.

FERLINGHETTI: Of course. Successful publishing houses often have an early coup that is quite often scandalous. With Random House, it was *Ulysses*.

INTERVIEWER: Was there anyone in particular who influenced your poetry when you first started out?

FERLINGHETTI: My French aunt, Emily. She was quite crazy, a 1920s flapper. She wore cloche hats and considered herself a writer, but she was so crazy that she never managed to write anything down. She just lived it. My first writing was to her, in French and in English. We lived in France when I was very small and French was my first language. She took me back to New York when I was about five or six. She got a job as a French governess in Bronxville in a branch of the Lawrence family that had founded Sarah Lawrence College. Then she became increasingly afflicted with paranoid fantasies, disappeared, and later was committed to a mental hospital for many years. I would write to her. It seemed to be the only thing I could do well and that is how I became a writer. It's a little like Anaïs Nin writing to her absent father.

INTERVIEWER: At some point, you joined the navy?

The "Howl" trial.

FERLINGHETTI: Yes. During the Second World War. The year before the 1944 invasion, I was executive officer of a submarine chaser. It was a small vessel for which we trained a Norwegian crew. We were in port near Glasgow in 1943, training young Norwegians who had escaped from occupied Norway in open boats. We trained them to run the ship—the full complement was thirty-three men and three officers. Then we turned the ship over to them and they sailed off over the horizon towards the Shetland Islands and we never saw them again. We were working with the Norwegian underground and that ship was used in many successful underground raids on the coast of Norway. It became famous in Norway.

Just a couple of years ago a translator, Jón Jónsson—a Norwegian living in Paris who had been translating my poetry—read in my biography that I had been working with the Norwegian underground on a subchaser. He tracked it down and found that there was a monument to the men and the ship in a Norwegian city. The ship had become a real symbol of resistance to the Nazis.

In an early "Autobiography"—a long poem full of parodies— I wrote: *I have seen the educated armies on the beach at Dover/ I landed in Normandy in a rowboat that turned over.* Actually, we did row ashore to the port of Honfleur about two weeks after the invasion

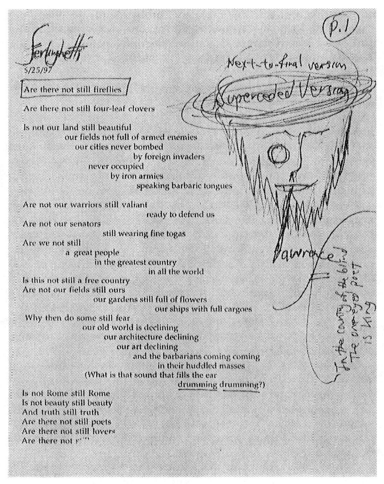

Ferlinghetti
5/25/97

Next-to-final version
Superceded Version

Are there not still fireflies

Are there not still four-leaf clovers

Is not our land still beautiful
          our fields not full of armed enemies
               our cities never bombed
                         by foreign invaders
                    never occupied
                    by iron armies
                         speaking barbaric tongues

Are not our warriors still valiant
                         ready to defend us
Are not our senators
                    still wearing fine togas
Are we not still
          a great people
               in the greatest country
                    in all the world
Is this not still a free country
Are not our fields still ours
               our gardens still full of flowers
                         our ships with full cargoes
Why then do some still fear
               our old world is declining
                    our architecture declining
                    our art declining
                    and the barbarians coming coming
                         in their huddled masses
          (What is that sound that fills the ear
                         drumming drumming?)
Is not Rome still Rome
Is not beauty still beauty
And truth still truth
Are there not still poets
Are there not still lovers
Are there not r‴"

Lawrence

In the country of the blind
The one-eyed poet
is King

A Lawrence Ferlinghetti manuscript page.

had started but we quickly retreated when German snipers—
trapped on the roofs of houses by the harbor—started firing at us.

INTERVIEWER: You saw Nagasaki, didn't you?

FERLINGHETTI: About six weeks after the bomb was dropped. A
square mile of mulch, that's what it was. Unbelievable. We didn't
even know what atomic radiation was in those days. We just went

in there like tourists. My ship came into port and we went over there on the train and we just walked around. We didn't have any protective gear. Nobody knew it was harmful. We didn't know that a whole culture had been destroyed in the blink of Satan's eye.

INTERVIEWER: Did your military experience contribute to your pacifist philosophy?

FERLINGHETTI: Not really. I was a good soldier. I had a lovely war, never killed anything, never got shot, even though we were in the Normandy Invasion the very first morning. Some claim it was the last "good war." I was politically illiterate until I came out to San Francisco and started listening to KPFA Pacifica radio, which in those days was really the voice of the Left. It was founded by conscientious objectors like Lewis Hill and various anarchists like Kenneth Rexroth. Rexroth had a program on there—he didn't cover just poetry. He reviewed every field: astronomy, philosophy, geology, art. I really got my political education listening to him. He came from near Chicago—a working-class poet, but much more than that . . . He is said to have arrived in San Francisco the day George Sterling died in 1928. There was a group of early programmers at KPFA who were really important—Alan Watts, Phil Elwood, Elsa Knight Thompson, and William Mandel, the Soviet affairs expert who had been on there all these years and was recently forced out. Evidently, KPFA is trying now to become more like NPR. I am involved in a group called Take Back KPFA. Last year it seemed as if the station's original concept and aims were being completely decimated. The intellectual content of the programming had deteriorated, and the station seemed to be contributing to the dumbing down of America. But now there seem to be some great signs of regeneration.

Next to the University of California, the station was probably the most important intellectual influence in the Bay Area in the late forties and all during the fifties—even in the sixties. Some of the founders had been in conscientious objectors camps in places like Waldport, Oregon. For instance, William Everson, who later became Brother Antoninus, had a printing shop in the camp. He printed Kenneth Patchen's poetry among others. Some of them came to San Francisco to make contact with Kenneth Rexroth. When the Beat poets arrived in the fifties, Rexroth was a kind of paterfamilias, the father figure for us all. He had soirées every Friday night at his house. I didn't say a thing for about the first year; I was too much in awe. He was a great polymath, a great essayist and critic with an anarchist point of view, and a great poet—the outstanding characteristic of Rexroth's poetry was its *sublimity*. It could be said that Gary Snyder's poetry is an echo of his.

INTERVIEWER: So how did you finally develop your political awareness?

FERLINGHETTI: Rexroth picked me out of nowhere. I was completely unknown except for a little self-published book of poetry here at City Lights called *Pictures of the Gone World*. In 1958, just when *Coney Island of the Mind* was coming out, he asked me to perform with him at the Cellar Jazz Club here in North Beach. Fantasy Records recorded the show on two LPs: one was called *Jazz and Poetry in the Cellar*. Rexroth was on one side and I was on the other reading poems from *Coney Island of the Mind*. On Rexroth's side was a poem called "Thou Shall Not Kill: An Elegy on the Death of Dylan Thomas"—a much fiercer castigation of American consumer society than "Howl." A vicious indictment of consumer society: "You killed him, you son of a bitch in your Brooks Brother suit." Of course, Dylan Thomas killed himself with liquor, but symbolically Rexroth nailed the inhuman forces and greed in American society.

INTERVIEWER: Did you feel as if City Lights was in competition with New Directions?

FERLINGHETTI: Hardly. They were my early role model, but we certainly weren't competitors back then. New Directions was the most important avant-garde publisher in this country from 1939 to the time that Grove Press started publishing in the fifties. When I started reading American poetry, I was reading the early New Directions books. They were the first to publish Dylan Thomas, Ezra Pound's *Cantos*, William Carlos Williams, early Tennessee Williams, Muriel Rukeyser. . . . If it was avant-garde, New Directions published it. James Laughlin, the publisher, was the last of the great patrician editors.

I remember the old New Directions offices were at 333 Sixth Avenue in the Village, in a small, pie-shaped building. Laughlin's office was on the top floor in the corner. When I was living in the Village, I used to look up there and, boy, it was like the tower of ivory. I never thought I would be published by them. It was really Rexroth who got Laughlin to publish the new poets. Laughlin was in Asia putting out an annual literary anthology, *Perspectives USA*.

He was out of the country quite a bit of the time, just when the Beats were first being discovered. Rexroth was one of his authors: he kept writing letters to Laughlin exhorting him to wake up and get with it, telling him what was happening out here. So it was due to him that New Directions gradually started picking up on Beat writers. It was well into the sixties before Laughlin caught up with Gary Snyder, Robert Duncan, Charles Olson, and Gregory Corso. He never did publish Ginsberg. We could have kept these authors to ourselves at City Lights but I always felt the function of the little press was discovery. After that, they should be free to sign on with whomever they please. Let the greedy have at them! Thus we eventually let Harper and Row take Ginsberg away from us. (Allen wanted it.)

INTERVIEWER: Why do you think Laughlin never published Ginsberg?

FERLINGHETTI: Laughlin never seemed interested in him. Ginsberg had sent him manuscripts that did not excite him. When *Howl* was published, Laughlin wrote me and said, "Allen suddenly got good."

INTERVIEWER: As his editor, did you have a good working relationship with Ginsberg?

FERLINGHETTI: We had enormous political solidarity—as did all the Beats. During the thirty years that I was his editor, we never had a falling-out over an editorial matter. In fact, without too much ado, I persuaded him to leave out a whole section of "Howl," one whole, single-spaced page with a roman numeral at the top. I don't know what happened to that page. It didn't show up in *The Annotated Howl*—a huge volume that Allen edited. There's no trace of that page anywhere . . . the first twenty years or so, I did *all* of Allen's editing—as well as proofreading and book design. In the last ten years of his time with City Lights, a good deal of the nuts and bolts of editing Allen was done by City Lights's present managing director, Nancy J. Peters—who is, by the way, I believe, one of the top literary editors in the U.S.

INTERVIEWER: Why didn't you like that section of "Howl"—the part you persuaded him to leave out?

FERLINGHETTI: Well, it didn't fit in with the rest of the poem. It was like a fifth leg. So now it just has four parts. I also persuaded him

to change the title from "Howl for Carl Solomon" to just "Howl."
Carl Solomon ended up on the dedication page. This way, "Howl"
became less of a private missive than a universal message.

INTERVIEWER: The Beat movement has always had its critics. Some
have called it on the one hand pointless—

FERLINGHETTI: That's a pointless criticism.

INTERVIEWER: —and on the other hand pernicious. How have you
answered those criticisms over the years?

FERLINGHETTI: What do they mean by pernicious?

INTERVIEWER: Amoral, irresponsible.

FERLINGHETTI: Oh, good! That's excellent. That's a really high
compliment! Pernicious. The Beat generation is pernicious. Nothing
wrong with that! I mean, wanting to destroy materialism takes a
little perniciousness. Positively amoral! Worse than that—the
Beats are home-wreckers, perverts, child seducers, anarchists,
subversives, saints! Would you want your daughter to marry one
of them?

INTERVIEWER: Were the Beats anti-American?

FERLINGHETTI: No, sir, Senator McCarthy!

INTERVIEWER: Antigovernment?

FERLINGHETTI: Seriously—one can't really generalize. Kerouac
certainly wasn't antigovernment or anti-American. When I came
back from Cuba in 1959, I asked him if he would like to join the
Fair Play for Cuba committee of which I was a member. Without
batting an eye, he said, "I've got my own revolution out here. The
American revolution." As he got older, he became more reactionary. Ginsberg was born into the old communist labor movement and the old radical intellectual Jewish traditions of this
country. But I wouldn't say he was anti-American either. His book
The Fall of America is not an anti-American book.
    Burroughs was another story. He was above the battle. He
was above nations. He had a worldview of which America was
only one part. He was probably the most sardonic writer that

America ever had. He could be devastating. His last writing was published in *The New Yorker* after he died. One page from his journals. He had so many phrases in there—he could just lay out a whole scene or a group of people in one sentence. He was a misanthrope. He really had no use for mankind. So you can see how very different these writers were. The thing that held them together was that they were all dissidents or outsiders in one way or another.

INTERVIEWER: What about Gary Snyder?

FERLINGHETTI: Snyder was or is an ecological dissident. An ecological consciousness. Of course, today you would hardly call that dissident. But back then, most of the tenets of the counterculture of the sixties were first annunciated by the Beat writers: the first stirrings of ecological consciousness, the first movement towards Far Eastern philosophy, Buddhism, pacifism, the first use of psychedelics to expand consciousness since Poe and Fitzhugh Ludlow. Before the Beats, the drug of choice for American writers was alcohol.

INTERVIEWER: What are your impressions of American intellectual life today as opposed to during the height of the Beat period in the fifties?

FERLINGHETTI: I don't know where intellectual life is these days. It seems to be disappearing into a picture tube. The new cold war is the war against the computer—the human against the unhuman. At City Lights, we published a book called *Resisting the Virtual Life*, followed by another book which is also a deep critique of the computer: *Close to the Machine: Technophilia and Its Discontents* by Ellen Ullman. It's on the cutting edge.

There's a technological revolution going on now which is just in its primitive stages. The world is rushing together at a fantastic speed, converging in an electronic black hole. Things are changing so rapidly that it's impossible for a writer or a poet or an artist to synthesize it fast enough to make anything meaningful of it. You can write a novel overnight and the next day it is outdated. If James Joyce were around today, what would he do? Or if Ezra Pound was faced with writing a final canto, what would he do?

The natural thing is to turn inward, to find your own paradise within; there is no more "escape." When Gauguin wanted to get away he went to Tahiti; that was easy. But if you go to Tahiti today there's the Hilton. Still, there must be an island further out, a truly remote section of unadulterated beauty. But if you go there, you'll find Club Med. American corporate monoculture is homogenizing the world. Travel becomes narrowing rather than broadening. But even this view will be a cliché by the time it is printed.

INTERVIEWER: So where does all this leave the artist and the poet?

FERLINGHETTI: Out there on the Last World Border, before nations disappear completely. Before the end of the twenty-first century, nations, per se, will probably no longer exist. They are already unable to maintain their borders and their entities. Technology doesn't respect national boundaries, nor does pollution, nor do the internet and fax, nor do the multinational corporations. . . . But the poet and artist will still be here trying to fathom man's fate . . . dancing on the rim of the world.

—ANDREW P. MADDEN
1998

Notes on Contributors

JEFFREY BAILEY (Paul Bowles interview) won the *Atlantic Monthly* short-story contest in 1967. Among the authors he interviewed are Christopher Isherwood, Gore Vidal, Gavin Lambert, and Anaïs Nin. His work appeared in *The California Quarterly, The Advocate,* and the *New Orleans Review.*

TED BERRIGAN (Jack Kerouac interview) was a forerunner of the New York School of poetry in the late sixties and early seventies. With Ron Padgett, he wrote *Bean Spasms* in 1967. Other books include *Train Ride* (1971), *Red Wagon* (1976), and *The Sonnets* (Grove Press). In 1991, eight years after his death, *Nice to See You; Homage to Ted Berrigan* was published—a volume of essays, poems, and reminiscences.

THOMAS CLARK (Allen Ginsberg interview) was poetry editor of *The Paris Review* from 1964 to 1973. His most recent collection of poems, *White Thought,* was published in 1998. He teaches writing at New College in California.

ROBERT FAGGEN (Ken Kesey interview) is associate professor of literature at Claremont McKenna College, adjunct associate professor at Claremont Graduate School, and a contributing editor of *The Paris Review.* His most recent book is *Robert Frost and the Challenge of Darwin* (University of Michigan Press).

KEN JORDAN (Barney Rosset interview) is the director of new media development for an advertising company in New York.

CONRAD KNICKERBOCKER (William Burroughs interview) was born in Berlin in 1929 and educated at Harvard. A contributor to *Esquire, Life,* and *The New York Times,* he died in April 1966.

LEWIS MACADAMS, JR. (Robert Creeley interview) was an editor of *Mother* records. His books of poetry include *City Money* and *The Poetry Room.*

ANDREW P. MADDEN (Lawrence Ferlinghetti interview) is a freelance writer and features editor of *The Red Herring.* He lives in San Francisco.

GERARD MALANGA (Charles Olson interview) is a photographer and poet. His most recent book of poetry is *Mythologies of the Heart* (Black Sparrow Press, 1996). Two books of his photography are forthcoming: *Resistance to Memory, Portraits from the Seventies* (Arena Editions) and *Screen Tests-Portraits-Nudes: 1964–1996* (Steidl Verlag). He lives and works in New York.

ELISSA SCHAPPELL (A Semester with Ginsberg) is a contributing editor at *The Paris Review* and *Vanity Fair*. Her first collection of short stories will be published by William Morrow in 1999.

LINDA WAGNER-MARTIN (Robert Creeley interview) is Hanes Professor of English and Comparative Literature at the University of North Carolina, Chapel Hill. Her most recent books are *"Favored Strangers": Gertrude Stein and Her Family, Telling Women's Lives,* and *The Mid-Century American.* Forthcoming books include *Sylvia Plath, A Literary Life* and *Ernest Hemingway: Seven Decades.*

ELIOT WEINBERGER (Gary Snyder interview) is the editor of *American Poetry Since 1950: Innovators and Outsiders.* His books of essays include *Works on Paper, Outside Stories, 19 Ways of Looking at Wang Wei,* and *Written Reaction.*

A NOTE ON THE TYPE

The principal text of this Modern Library edition was composed in a digitized version of Palatino, a contemporary typeface created by Hermann Zapf, who was inspired by the sixteenth-century calligrapher Giambattista Palatino, a writing master of Renaissance Italy. Palatino was the first of Zapf's typefaces to be introduced in America.

LaVergne, TN USA
22 November 2009
164931LV00001B/127/A